# SNAPSHOTS 3

*Sonya
A Pleasure —
Best Wishes
Frank Holloway*

Love
& kisses
& best wishes
Grandmother

# SNAPSHOTS 3

## Unveiling the Classroom of Life

### FRANK MARAJ

The Journey Begins Anew

Order this book online at www.trafford.com
or email orders@trafford.com

Most Trafford titles are also available at major online book retailers.

© Copyright 2014 Frank Maraj.
All rights reserved. No part of this publication may be reproduced, stored in a retrieval system, or transmitted, in any form or by any means, electronic, mechanical, photocopying, recording, or otherwise, without the written prior permission of the author.

## Editor and Co-author: Diana Maraj
**Cover design: Ron Hines**

Printed in the United States of America.

ISBN: 978-1-4907-4699-9 (sc)
ISBN: 978-1-4907-4698-2 (hc)
ISBN: 978-1-4907-4697-5 (e)

Library of Congress Control Number: 2014916649

Because of the dynamic nature of the Internet, any web addresses or links contained in this book may have changed since publication and may no longer be valid. The views expressed in this work are solely those of the author and do not necessarily reflect the views of the publisher, and the publisher hereby disclaims any responsibility for them.

Any people depicted in stock imagery provided by Thinkstock are models, and such images are being used for illustrative purposes only.
Certain stock imagery © Thinkstock.

Trafford rev.   10/07/2014

   www.trafford.com

North America & international
toll-free: 1 888 232 4444 (USA & Canada)
fax: 812 355 4082

# Contents

**Part One: Re-adjusting to Canada .................................................. 1**

| | | |
|---|---|---|
| Chapter 1: | Ms. Jillian H. ............................................... | 3 |
| Chapter 2: | Voices from the Past ..................................... | 12 |
| Chapter 3: | The Melting of Decades ................................ | 15 |
| Chapter 4: | At Miami ..................................................... | 18 |
| Chapter 5: | The Evening Stranger at the Bay ................... | 21 |
| Chapter 6: | Striking Resemblance ................................... | 23 |
| Chapter 7: | A Journey with Pa ........................................ | 25 |
| Chapter 8: | Mr. Lazee ..................................................... | 28 |
| Chapter 9: | A Journey of Discovery ................................ | 35 |
| Chapter 10: | Trinidad Bound ............................................ | 45 |
| Chapter 11: | I Will Not Hire You… ................................... | 47 |
| Chapter 12: | Renewal ....................................................... | 49 |
| Chapter 13: | A Promising Phone Call ................................ | 54 |
| Chapter 14: | Rental… It's Doable ..................................... | 55 |
| Chapter 15: | Failure Looms .............................................. | 57 |
| Chapter 16: | Not another Car Transaction! ...................... | 62 |
| Chapter 17: | The Family Grows ........................................ | 64 |
| Chapter 18: | Go Home: Go Back Home… ......................... | 67 |
| Chapter 19: | You Did Not Get the Job… ........................... | 72 |
| Chapter 20: | A Routine Visit Or? ...................................... | 75 |
| Chapter 21: | The Tide Begins to Turn ............................... | 76 |
| Chapter 22: | Habbie Jassram: His Moment… .................... | 78 |
| Chapter 23: | At Last… Stability ........................................ | 82 |

Part Two: Finding A Path ..................................................................... 83
   Chapter 24:   A Much Needed Resolution ................................... 85
   Chapter 25:   Smoking Dangerously .............................................. 89
   Chapter 26:   Troubles in the Kitchen… ........................................ 92
   Chapter 27:   Expulsion from "My" Own ..................................... 99
   Chapter 28:   The Rambler Ford Exchange .................................. 102
   Chapter 29:   An Accounting Challenge ....................................... 105
   Chapter 30:   Hunting for a Home ................................................ 109
   Chapter 31:   Half-Day ................................................................... 114
   Chapter 32:   Sudden Sadness ........................................................ 118
   Chapter 33:   Classroom Antics ..................................................... 119
   Chapter 34:   Searching .................................................................. 122
   Chapter 35:   A Calculated Move .................................................. 125
   Chapter 36:   High Hopes ............................................................... 129
   Chapter 37:   A Sense of Optimism ............................................... 135
   Chapter 38:   The Calm before the Storm .................................... 138
   Chapter 39:   A Swelling Tide ........................................................ 142
   Chapter 40:   A Door begins to Close ........................................... 146
   Chapter 41:   As One Door Closes… ............................................ 151
   Chapter 42:   Saying Farewell ........................................................ 153
   Chapter 43:   Reflections 1974-1975 ............................................ 154

**Part Three: Entering the Elementary System** ............................................. **155**
    Chapter 44:    Half Day's Pay ............................................................. 157
    Chapter 45:    Respect… ..................................................................... 161
    Chapter 46:    The Unthinkable .......................................................... 162
    Chapter 47:    Truth Directive ........................................................... 166
    Chapter 48:    Emerging Insight ......................................................... 169
    Chapter 49:    Two Misguided Friends ............................................... 173
    Chapter 50:    An Unselfish Request ................................................... 177
    Chapter 51:    Precedent Setting ......................................................... 179
    Chapter 52:    I Become the Student .................................................. 183
    Chapter 53:    Soccer on Ice! .............................................................. 186
    Chapter 54:    Putting my Dream on Ice ............................................ 188
    Chapter 55:    Modest Gains .............................................................. 190
    Chapter 56:    Life's Interconnectedness ............................................. 191
    Chapter 57:    The Good Neighbour .................................................. 194
    Chapter 58:    Settling In ................................................................... 196
    Chapter 59:    A Class Trip? ............................................................... 197
    Chapter 60:    The Lesson .................................................................. 199
    Chapter 61:    An Afterthought: Falling Short .................................... 201
    Chapter 62:    More Adjustments ...................................................... 204
    Chapter 63:    Baby Steps .................................................................. 206
    Chapter 64:    Disarmed .................................................................... 208
    Chapter 65:    Spike ........................................................................... 210
    Chapter 66:    Operation Citizenship ................................................. 213
    Chapter 67:    New York Beckons ...................................................... 215
    Chapter 68:    No Discussion…You Listen ......................................... 217
    Chapter 69:    My Turn ..................................................................... 219
    Chapter 70:    Presumptuous ............................................................. 225
    Chapter 71:    Good News—All Around ............................................ 228
    Chapter 72:    Magical Memories ...................................................... 230
    Chapter 73:    A Sobering Reality ...................................................... 232
    Chapter 74:    I Want to be Wrong! ................................................... 234

**Part Four: Returning to the Secondary System ............ 237**

- Chapter 75: Another First ................................................. 239
- Chapter 76: Colossal Error! .............................................. 241
- Chapter 77: A Bad Seed? .................................................. 245
- Chapter 78: Standoff ......................................................... 248
- Chapter 79: Adjustments ...................................................253
- Chapter 80: The Evaluation .............................................. 260
- Chapter 81: Voices… ......................................................... 265
- Chapter 82: Just an Illusion? ............................................ 269
- Chapter 83: Nothing Ventured… ..................................... 272
- Chapter 84: Teachers are Students too… ........................274
- Chapter 85: Humour in the Classroom .......................... 277
- Chapter 86: Marking Woes ............................................... 281
- Chapter 87: Judgement .................................................... 285
- Chapter 88: A "Quick" Dimension ................................. 287
- Chapter 89: Fears Dispelled ............................................. 289
- Chapter 90: Life's Lessons ................................................ 292
- Chapter 91: Claimed .......................................................... 294
- Chapter 92: Who Is Teaching Whom? ............................ 298
- Chapter 93: One Student's Conviction .......................... 300
- Chapter 94: And Mr. Bright Takes Over ........................ 304
- Chapter 95: More Change ................................................ 308
- Chapter 96: The Race ........................................................312
- Chapter 97: Temper, Tempered… ...................................316
- Chapter 98: Final Moments ............................................. 319

**Part Five: Retirement and Identity: Philosophical Musings..........323**

    Chapter 99:   Change................................................................. 325
    Chapter 100: A Realization..................................................... 328
    Chapter 101: Reuniting With…............................................. 330
    Chapter 102: The Past Is…...................................................... 337
    Chapter 103: Affirmations....................................................... 342
    Chapter 104: Fallout................................................................. 345
    Chapter 105: Currents.............................................................. 347
    Chapter 106: New Memories................................................. 350
    Chapter 107: Swept Away........................................................353
    Chapter 108: A Lost Soul.........................................................357
    Chapter 109: Two Different Dispositions...........................361
    Chapter 110: Multi-Generational......................................... 363
    Chapter 111: More Pressure.................................................. 366
    Chapter 112: Becoming........................................................... 368
    Chapter 113: Developing Roots............................................ 370
    Chapter 114: Without You......................................................374
    Chapter 115: Gandhi… Ever Present.................................. 376
    Chapter 116: On Ma................................................................. 381
    Chapter 117: On Mr. Mandela...............................................391
    Chapter 118: Pa's Gift............................................................... 394
    Chapter 119: Witnessing......................................................... 399
    Chapter 120: Jailed................................................................... 407
    Chapter 121: Reflections on Identity....................................413

# *Dedication*

*Once again,
with love,
I dedicate this book to my three children,
Trevor, Lee-Anne, and Dee-Dee,
to my grandchildren, Jayden and Jasmine,
and to the memories of Ma and Pa.
Undoubtedly, you are my inspiration.*

# Acknowledgements

*To all my students and former students both here in Canada and in Trinidad, thank you for your continued inspiration.*

*For transcribing my difficult handwriting into printed text, so graciously, I deeply thank you:*

*Christina Campagna    Susan De Gagné*
*Chloe Hudson    Kalon De Gagné*
*Kim McKinnon*

*Thanks to my colleagues and coworkers,* **from every corner of the school,** *who have accommodated and rescued me without protest, thank you ever so kindly.*

*To that group of friends, and you know who you are, who have insisted that these final chapters be completed. Thank you ever so much for embracing this work. A very special thank you is extended to the very young ninety-seven year old Sybil Johnson for her valued insights.*

*Tracy Rob, how do I thank you? You have been a pillar of strength throughout this work. Diana and I are forever indebted to you and your willing spirit.*

*To my daughter, Dee-Dee, for her words of wisdom and guidance across the miles.*

*To my daughter, Lee-Anne, who reminded me that her mother is amazing; but she's not Wonder Woman. Well, I am now grounded in that*

*Frank Maraj*

*thought and am now aware that I need to be more mindful. Yet, thank you for your astute observations, and critical insights.*

*Ron Hines, your design and creativity regarding the cover of Snapshots 3, is truly remarkable. My sincere thanks, Ron.*

*To my family - Ma and Pa, Clive, Dolly, Boysie, Paula, Pinky, Kay, Basdaye, Kalie and Suresh - thank you for continuing to enrich my life.*

# With Gratitude

*Diana,*

*Where would I be today without you?*
*Your steadfast dedication and commitment to me*
*and Snapshots 3 has not been easy.*
*Your countless hours and personal sacrifices have not gone by unnoticed.*
*Without your touch Snapshots 3 would simply not be the same.*
*Indeed, you have transformed my life's work.*

*In all of these,*
*you have been the bedrock of my life.*

*Love always,*
*Frank*

# Preface

Perhaps one of the things for which I am most grateful that came as a result of these most recent writings, is the expression of true appreciation from our daughter, Lee-Anne. I'll let these words that she wrote to her father speak for themselves.

Thank you, Lee-Anne,
Mom

Dad,

Thank you for writing these books. Thank you for the transparency you show – your thoughts, though painful to read at times, are refreshingly honest. And I enjoyed the stories so much! I am grateful to have had this opportunity to get to know you through your writing - to learn about the joys and struggles of your childhood. Thank you for introducing me to Pa, the grandfather I never knew; you made him come alive through your writing. Thank you for your reminiscences about Ma, the grandmother I didn't know well; how she loved us all! Thank you for the transparency you have shown. Thank you for wanting your children and grandchildren to know you enough that you dedicated yourself to these projects. Through reading your novels, I have come to understand myself more. I am grateful to you and Mom for this, and I am inspired.

Lee-Anne

# Author's Note

*I acknowledge that this work required tact and sensitivity. A great deal is in the here and now...*

*It also requires a sense of integrity and courage to share these stories.*

*Therefore, if at any time throughout this project I have appeared unduly critical or personal, then once more, I ask for your understanding. It is not my intention to offend anyone.*

*Did everything in this work occur exactly as recorded? I have once again attempted to capture life as it happened. I may have taken certain liberties and at times I might have unwittingly dramatized certain incidents to make the story interesting.*

*Although the stories are not necessarily in chronological order, I have attempted to give some logical order to the time of the occurrences. In some instances, fictitious names have been used.*

*Above all, I hope this work keeps the stories alive...*

*P.S.*

*Is there any hint of "that colour" in any of the stories narrated in Snapshots 3?*

*Perhaps.*

# Also by Frank Maraj

**SNAPSHOTS: A LIFE REVISITED**

*Published by: Trafford (2008)*
*ISBN: 9781426903861*

*A reflection on a young Trinidiadian's life – full of heartache, regret, and hope. By chronicling Snapshots of his life, Maraj allows readers to gain some understanding of a very different culture – growing up poor in Trinidad. He struggles with balancing his responsibilities to the family after his father's premature death, with his compelling desire to go abroad to study.*

**SNAPSHOTS II: NAVIGATING THE UNIVERSITY YEARS**

*Published by: Trafford (2011)*
*ISBN: 9781426953224*

*Frank shares stories of his early days in Canada that are both entertaining and thought-provoking, providing an uplifting story of determination. He captures the humour and the horror of his first encounters with the foreign concepts of cooking, snow, and driving. Snapshots II: Navigating the University Years chronicles the very real difficulties Frank faces whil adjusting to cultural and social differences and contradictions. The dream to remain true to his homeland remains staunch to the fore of Frank's every move. He wants nothing more than to return to Trinidad. Despite the fact that financial difficulties continually plague his life, nothing proves insurmountable – until he seeks to realize one of his biggest childhood dreams, returning to Trinidad to teach. Frank leaves his wife and young son in Canada, and ventures home with high hopes of assuming a position that he thinks was designed especially for him. But then, disaster strikes…*

# PART ONE

Re-adjusting
to
Canada

# 1

# Ms. Jillian H.

The door to Mr. Abraham's office was closed. My eagerness to see the man may have been responsible for the knock which was perhaps a bit too enthusiastic.

When the door was opened, it was not the face of a Mr. Abraham which met mine. It was not the face of any man which met mine.

It was the face of a woman; moreover, it was the face of a woman decidedly displeased.

Nothing was said as she opened the door. Aside from obvious displeasure, I could read nothing else from her expression.

As she continued to look me over, my discomfort became palatable. Old insecurities wormed their way back into my brain and I wondered if there was something wrong with me. Had I come at the wrong time? Had I come to the wrong place?

I checked my memory bank; I was correct. This was the right place and the right time. My appointment was with Mr. Abraham, the man in charge of Government Housing and Accommodation. It was he I was expecting to see when the door was opened. Perhaps some expression of surprise translated to my face, but I felt that there was nothing more that could be responsible for the cool reception from the other side of the door.

"Do you think I am deaf?" she queried. Her haughty tone did nothing to put me at ease.

"Sorry."

"Well, don't just stand there; come in."

I followed her lead but stood somewhat awkwardly inside the spacious room.

"Well, sit down!" she commanded as she resumed her position behind one of the huge oak desks.

Grabbing the nearest chair, I sat awaiting the next set of orders.

After a long fifteen seconds, during which time nothing was said by either one of us, I ventured in a respectful but timid voice, "Mr. Abraham's not here?"

"Well, that's obvious, is it not? He is not here, and he won't be here. I am handling you. Now, you are applying for housing?"

"Yes, ma'am."

As she stared, I could feel both her voice and her eyes accusing me in tandem. I wondered what I had done to warrant such curtness and officiousness.

"Well, here is the application. Fill it out and return it… at your convenience."

Those last words *at your convenience* would seem to suggest some effort on her part to manage a small degree of civility but the manner in which those words were spoken could not be mistaken for anything other than dismissive in nature. Even though I sensed that she wanted nothing more than to be done with me, I persevered in asking, "Yes, ma'am… but ma'am, should I not fill it out right away and…"

As if to confirm my impression of her, she stood and reiterated, "Yes, you will fill it out and return the completed form… but you won't fill it out here."

Still somewhat dumbfounded, I stood and walked toward the door continuing to wonder why I was being ushered out so quickly. I could readily see that there was more than enough room to accommodate me at one of the other empty stations. In my mind, the most pragmatic course of action would be to invite me to sit and complete the forms right there in the office where I would have had easy access to clarification should I require it. I was almost certain that Mr. Abraham would not have treated me with such discourtesy. During our previous telephone conversation, I had been given the opportunity to explain fully my circumstances to him. Mr. Abraham understood that I needed to secure accommodations here in Thunder Bay almost immediately before I could start working at any job. His voice conveyed a measure of both graciousness and compassion and I looked forward to meeting the man to whom I was entrusting so much. I must have taken a bit too long in contemplation for once again *her* haughty and dismissive voice ordered, "Well, off you go… Now!"

Her contempt was obvious; her stare was unmistakable; she was the complete antithesis of Mr. Abraham. I left that office feeling that I had just been tossed out like some unwanted stray.

*\*\*\**

Once in the hallway just outside the office door, I began to shake. My emotions were raging up inside me. I was seized by the temptation to reenter the office, rip the application form to shreds, and defile her desk with the dregs. The mere thought of such rebellion brought a smile to my face. I indulged in the luxury of fully playing out the scenario in my mind. I would enter the room without uttering a word. I knew that she would have many words to use against me. Still silent, once the deed was accomplished, I would take my exit. My heart would feel the triumph of my rebellion and I would be vindicated.

But… once again rational thought prevailed. Once again I knew that I had more than just myself to consider. I had a family now and I had to do what was best for them. Thus, I forced myself to banish these selfish contemplations and focused on completing the task at hand—namely the application form.

Once again I returned to the office still unable to shake the vestiges of uncertainty and nervousness. Outside the door I hesitated. Do I knock before entering or do I just enter? My nerves got the better of me and I did both. I knocked, and without waiting for an invitation to enter, I walked in.

Wrong.

No sooner had I opened the door when I heard her bark, "How dare you come into this office without my permission! Get back outside and knock, and wait for instructions!"

I felt as if once again I was a small child being reprimanded by my teacher and I was tempted to be compliant and say, *Yes, Teacher*, but I did not. Instead, I made a brazen move by continuing to walk toward her desk and I handed her the application. To her credit, she received the form and quickly began to scan it for details.

After finding the first error, she wasted no time recalling her most contemptuous voice and began her reprimand, "You did not fill out the address section – you *do* have an address, don't you?"

The contempt was not restricted to just her voice, it translated into her look too.

I tried to explain, "Please let me explain, ma'am."

Miss Jillian just went berserk, "Don't call me ma'am. I am nobody's ma'am. My name is Ms. Jillian H. You understand that? Ms.! Ms.!"

"Yes, ma'am. Oops... sorry ma'am... yes, Ms. Jillian H."

I had not meant to be funny. And, Ms. Jillian H. was most certainly not amused. I had to tread very carefully. Ms. Jillian was indeed most serious. I'm not certain which act of negligence she considered more grievous an offence... the omissions on the application or me referring to her as ma'am.

I took the application from her, filled in Diana's Rainy River address and phone number, and handed it back. She completed the cursory review of the form. Unable to find fault with anything else, she rose from her chair and once again dismissed me from her presence.

"That's all. You will be contacted sometime!"

At that point, I should have turned and walked away, but I needed more. I had to ask, "When, when?"

She seemed offended that I was still questioning her and was most pointed in her response, "When we have reviewed your application, that's when."

And then she added with a hint of what could only be described as delight, "You have to wait your turn just like everyone else."

Some internal force propelled her to go on with her reprimand, "You do not think that you can just march in here and have your way. That will never happen!"

"Ms. Jillian, allow me to explain. I would appreciate..."

"Explain what, precisely?"

"Ms. Jillian, I have two job prospects; one is as a substitute teacher, and the other is as a part time cab driver. Mr. Abraham indicated that I might qualify and that he might be able to speed things up. Could you assist me...?"

Before I could finish my explanation, she cut me off by declaring with the utmost authority, "You have to take your turn like anyone else. Just who do you think you are... some kind of prince? Well, you are no prince here. And you see how truly foolish you are! You came here without your wife – why? That is so typical of your type."

Why was her attitude so combative? What did she mean by *your type*?

I had to remind myself not be uncivil. I was the one in need. I was the one who required her assistance. Once again I tried to explain myself.

"Ms. Jillian, there is a reason why…"

It was useless. Her mind was closed; she was beyond reason. Indeed, it seemed that reason had surrendered to irrationality. Her voice assumed a heightened quality of screech amplified by an assumed air of righteous indignation.

"Oh, yes, you meant to leave your wife – and your child – somewhere. You came here alone by design. You choose to assert your manly authority. You want to be the man – just like all *Asian* men."

"But that is not true Ms. Please may I…"

"It is true! You cannot deny it. You and all men like you like to wield your authority over your wives; the women in your lives have no choice; they have no say. What's more, they must be subservient. You *men* have all the say. Right?"

With the utterance of each successive phrase, she inched her way closer to me until our faces were but inches apart, at which time she thundered, "You have a need to feel superior. You think men must be in charge of everything, all the time. Well, I am here to inform you that we women will no longer tolerate it. We have moved out of the dark ages. This is the Seventies. You hear me? The Seventies!"

How could I do anything *but* hear her? She was virtually on top of me.

What I did not understand was her belligerence toward me. What had I done to cause such a reaction?

Once again I attempted to reason with her hoping to quell her anger.

"Ms. you are making a mistake. Please, let me…"

"No! I am not mistaken about you and your kind… not one iota!"

There it was again; the words, *your kind*.

"Your kind?" I repeated the words back to her, essentially hoping for a retraction or at the very least some further clarification of the phrase.

The hoped for retraction never materialized but a forceful clarification was imminent. Clarification came clothed in further insults. These she wasted no time in barking at me. "I do not approve of you. Truth be told, I despise you; I despise you and your kind. Now, go!"

I thought she was done with me and I wanted nothing more than to escape. But, she had one more set of gems to reveal. She seemed to revel in the utterance of each syllable, "You will be contacted later on…

after *I* have reviewed your application. And know that I am in no rush to review your file. You see, I am on to you and people like you. You get your pleasure from power and control over the women in your life. Well, you won't get a chance to pull any of that with me. I, thank God, I am a woman born of liberation…"

I was done. Former thoughts of escape evaporated, for now, I too, had something to say; the words simply exploded from my mouth, "Then, *woman*, take your liberated view and liberate me from my confusion. So far I do not understand the root of your attitude toward me. Miss Jillian, yes, I will still extend to you the simple courtesy that you refuse to show me and I will call you Miss, but you must be plainly told that you have been nothing but rude and condescending both in your words and in your attitude since I walked through that door…"

I had more to say but she refused to hear me out, "How dare you – you Asian reprobate, how dare you attempt to lecture me! I will not have it! Leave, now!"

I, however, was just getting started. Nothing, save death, would prevent me from having my say, "Woman, I don't know how you attained the position you currently hold, but from what I have witnessed thus far, you are totally underserving of it. You possess neither the graciousness nor the simple civility that such a position requires. You lack even the most fundamental elements of good manners and common sense. Your new found liberation has left you blind to anything but your own self-interest. Your liberated view is so narrow in scope that it threatens to alienate you from, at the very least, half of society."

Then I stopped. Slowly the realization dawned that I had destroyed what small chance I had of being approved for any form of housing. I had to accept it.

I turned to leave.

I looked up.

For a brief moment our eyes met but I could not read her expression; I averted my eyes. It was then that a picture on the mantle claimed my attention; it was a family portrait. I recognized Ms. Jillian immediately. She was surrounded by three young children—two boys and a girl. There was something about one of the boys that reminded me of my own son, Trevor; they shared some common features and their complexions were somewhat reminiscent of one another. I noted too, that there was no father figure in the portrait. I was overcome by sadness. Something changed in me and once again, prompted to speak, I found myself saying, "Ms. Jillian, I am sad. I take it that you are the mother of those three lovely children."

"That picture does not concern you," she barked. "I will thank you to mind your own..."

I ignored her and continued, "How relieved I am that your children are not present to witness your vitriol. Know this; your mind is dangerously warped and your thoughts are toxic. Don't worry about me and my family. We will be fine with or without your assistance. I suspect it will be without. My worry is for you and for your children. I feel that you are completely unaware that you may very well infect your children with your venomous thoughts. I hope that does not happen. I wish you well."

I turned to the door and let myself out.

The door had barely shut behind me when I heard her call, "Mr. Maraj, Mr. Maraj. Please... a moment."

I looked back. The door was open and Ms. Jillian stood tentatively at the entrance. She seemed somehow *different*; her head was slightly bent; her face was flushed; her voice was softer, more plaintive, and, dare I say, faintly apologetic, "Mr. Maraj, please come on back. I am so sorry. I am ashamed of my conduct."

In complete shock, I followed her back to the office. She motioned for me to sit. She was pensive; no trace of her former self remained; she seemed transformed.

"Mr. Maraj, I come from a large city and I have met people like you... Indians... Asian Indians."

She paused. I sensed that she needed time to ponder her next words. She struggled to continue, "It is my experience that the people I have met, people like you – tend to be highly manipulative in manner and grossly superior in attitude. I have been involved..."

She stopped. It was apparent that my presence had resurrected some deep sadness in her life. Painful recollections were reflected in her voice, "Clearly, I lumped you in the same category as the other Asians I have met. It *was* personal; I did act incorrectly. Worse still was the fact that I also was without courtesy. I really was rude. Would you please forgive me, Mr. Maraj?"

I sensed the sadness deep within her and wondered about the circumstances that had conspired against her to cause her to denounce

Asians at large. My mind then went to the world in general and I began to wonder how many of us could be guilty of making a similar mistake. Indeed, how many of us have already made such a mistake. Ms. Jillian was truly contrite and broken. I did not know what to do following such a confession. I managed a simple, "Ms. Jillian, thank you."

"No more with this Ms. Jillian. Mr. Maraj, I am Jillian and I am so pleased to meet you."

"And I am Frank. Thank you, Jillian."

"Shall we start over, Frank?"

"Yes, let's."

"Frank, there is something that is puzzling me."

"Puzzling you?"

"Yes. You have made me wonder about something. Do you understand what the Women's Liberation Movement is about?"

"No, not really."

"Where have you been?"

"In a fog of my own."

"What is your opinion of this movement based on your understanding?"

"I am not sure I understand it. Perhaps you can help me with something that has had me troubled for quite some time."

"Tell me how I can help."

"Well, some time ago, when I was at university, I offered my seat on a crowded bus to a young lady. To my shock, she responded in a most sarcastic manner by saying, 'Do I look helpless? Save that for your mother.' And ever since then I have been confused about my role in this new society. I still am confused."

"Oh dear, I am sorry. Frank, all I can say is that sometimes we get carried away with our need for independence. You have given me some reason to do some more thinking on the subject. But, let's leave that discussion for now; it's time to attend to you and your family. Shall we?"

"Yes, let's."

By the time that meeting ended, I felt that I had my life back; everything was back in order. I had the promise of an apartment that would be available almost immediately; I was ecstatic over the dramatic turn of events.

Just outside the office, I encountered a man about to enter. When he saw me he paused and queried, "You are Mr. Maraj?"

I recognized the voice instantly. "Yes," I responded, "and you must be Mr. Abraham?"

As we shook hands he expressed his regrets for having been unable to tend to me in person and added, "I trust that all went well with you and your meeting with Jillian?"

I smiled and answered a happy, "Absolutely!"

# 2

# Voices from the Past

That event occurred in 1973 only days after I returned from Trinidad. Still suffering the emotional scars from my unsuccessful efforts to gain a teaching position at the university in Trinidad, I realized that I needed to get past that disappointment and put all my efforts into establishing myself in Canada. That last trip to Trinidad had so injured my spirit that it would be years before I could venture to even think about returning.

Since then, the decades have flown by and I am hard pressed to believe that it was now September, 2011. It was late in the evening and once again I was absorbed by a television documentary chronicling the events of the sixties and seventies. In particular, it focused attention on the Women's Liberation movement and was attempting to assess the pros and cons of the movement. Immediately my mind rocketed back to the incident recounted in the previous chapter. My head was swimming in a wave of nostalgia when the sudden ring of the telephone jolted me back to the present.

"Hello?"

"Mr. Boodram?"

I hesitated; I had not been referred to by that name for a very long time, not since I was a teacher in Trinidad at St. Charles High School in the 1960's.

"Yes, speaking."

The voice continued, "Well, Mr. Boodram, I am Nankee, a former student of yours from St. Charles. Do you remember me?"

An awkwardness came over me. It had been a good fifty years since my days at St. Charles. So many students had come into my life in the interim. So many memories fluttered in and out of my mind; it was a most difficult challenge to keep everything sorted. Just days ago I had been surprised by yet another call from a former student from Trinidad… Ingrid. She too, I struggled to place. I did not want to appear to be insulting to my students yet, my mind did not have total clarity. Over the years, having been consumed with other life challenges, I failed to maintain a connection with either the staff or the students from St. Charles. I searched my memory for an answer.

"Please forgive me, but at the moment I do not recall that name; give me time and…" "Well, Mr. Boodram, she assured me, don't worry that you do not remember the names of your students at St. Charles. You do remember St. Charles Girls' High School…"

"How could I forget St. Charles?" I interrupted. "I remember St. Charles as if it were yesterday."

"Oh, Mr. Boodram, I am so pleased that you said that. Your students are going to be so happy to learn that you remember us. This is good news. And I have some other good news. We are having a class reunion in March. Your students wish to see you. Mother Dorothy is most anxious to see…"

My voice betrayed the excitement I felt upon hearing the name of my former teacher and principal; I was incredulous, "Sister Dorothy will be there?" *(I still thought of her as Sister Dorothy even though she became Mother Dorothy during my later years at the school.)* "She is not abroad?"

"Sister is not abroad; she is here and will most definitely be present. Can you come?"

A quiet excitement exploded in my mind. I was filled with sweet nostalgia. Faces of the many students surfaced; specific names, however, remained buried. Then I recalled clearly the face of Sister Dorothy.

"Mr. Boodram, will you come, please?"

"Oh dear, Nankee, unfortunately I will not be able to attend…" "No?" "I am so sad. My youngest daughter, Dee-Dee, is getting married right around the time of the reunion. There would not be time enough to do both so sadly, I will have to say no to the reunion. I am so very sorry…"

"I understand. And your students will understand. But I just wanted you to know that they were so hoping that you could be here."

"I just wish…" "Well, Mr. Boodram, I understand. Let me give you the number of Mother Dorothy. She would love to hear from you."

That phone call from Nankee had come late in the evening in February, 2011. Truth be told there is scarcely a day that goes by when I do not think of my time at St. Charles School. This was especially true each year in Canada when the new school year began. I found myself talking to my new students about the daily school traditions that I had grown accustomed to in Trinidad. I told them that each day began with a morning greeting. This tradition was so ingrained in me that I had to find a way to incorporate it into my Canadian teaching experiences. This was neither a strategy nor a ploy; it was not a clever technique or a design tactic; it was my reality. Over the years, the greeting has metamorphosed into a friendly game in Canada. What began as a somewhat novel (albeit, awkward) experience for the students, has developed into an expectation of me even now as a substitute teacher.

Indeed, I did miss St. Charles School; and now, at this stage of my life, suddenly to be in contact with a former student, rekindled a desire to return to Trinidad and reconnect with my St. Charles family. This reunion was long past due.

With Sister Dorothy's phone number clenched firmly in my hand, I resolved to make contacting her a top priority.

# 3

# The Melting of Decades

"Hello?"

"Sister Dorothy?"

"Yes, speaking."

"This is Frankie Boodram."

"Oh, my – at long last. It is you, Frankie!"

"Yes, Sister, it is."

"Frankie, can you come to the reunion? Everybody is excited. We miss you."

"Sister, I am sorry I will not be able to attend."

"And why not, Frankie Boodram; your students are looking forward to seeing you. And I would like you to come."

"Sister, my daughter's wedding is scheduled for that very week."

"I know, but you do have a couple of days in between the two events. You could still come?"

"But Sister, where I live in Canada, it will…"

"Frankie, you are phoning me from Canada?"

"Yes, Sister."

"Oh dear, I thought you were in Trinidad… I understand."

After a brief moment of silence, Sister resumed, "Frankie, can you come sometime later this year then? It might even be better – we would have a dozen or so of your former colleagues and students and would have a chance to really catch up. Would you come later then?"

"Absolutely!"

"I should let you go. Keep us posted. Can't wait to see you. Bye, Frankie."

Sister called me "Frankie," just as she had when I was but a student in her French class. What delightful memories began to stream into my consciousness; within moments my mind was flooded. One memory takes precedence over all others. It was 1959; with half of the semester still to finish, our French teacher had to leave his position quite suddenly. Being without a teacher was particularly serious because we were due to face the dreaded Cambridge Exam at the end of the term. Sister Dorothy, angel that she was, came to our rescue; she invited our class of boys to join her class of girls for French classes in the girls' school. It was the very first time I had experienced a mixture of boys and girls together in one classroom. This novel combination led to some very interesting antics while both the boys and girls vied for attention. None of this seemed to bother Sister in the least. She managed to navigate her way amongst us with ease, never once losing her winning smile or her poise. Through it all she wielded her own special brand of authority. It was in Sister Dorothy's person that I first bore witness to a gentle soul's love for teaching.

During that time I did everything to avoid attracting attention. I was buried in problems just trying to survive each day. Sister, sensing my reticence to engage with the others in class, one day asked,

"Frankie, it seems to me you are troubled. How can I help you, Frankie?"

The phrase, *How can I help you, Frankie?* created in me a whirlpool of emotion. I remained quiet, fighting hard to contain the feelings that threatened to overwhelm me. In my life, such an invitation did not come my way. I felt like a person; I felt considered. Nevertheless, I could not tell Sister my problems even though I wanted to.

"Frankie, what is troubling you? Is it about family? Relationships? Money? School? Or is it something else?"

In truth I had been preoccupied with each facet of life that she mentioned, but above all else, I knew that I would divulge none of this to her. It was not that I did not *want* to share my thoughts with her; it was that I *could not* share my thoughts with anyone. I had always been very protective and guarded when it came to addressing my own private thoughts.

Sister, much to her credit, understood that I was exceedingly shy. I do not remember what assurances she uttered next or what words she used, but I began to speak to her from my heart, "Sister, I am having troubles understanding my world in religion. I am born a Hindu and educated a

Catholic. Sometimes I feel at home in one, then at other times I feel for the other. Religion is not easy."

I spoke at great length about my uncertainties. Sister never once interrupted; she just listened. I surprised myself with all that I revealed. Sister made no attempt to sway me in the direction of her faith, and for that I was grateful; even as a student, she allowed me my dignity and did not attempt to strip from me my personal beliefs.

For a brief moment, Sister took her leave. When she returned, she carried with her a book which she placed in my hands saying, "Frankie, I wish I could take your troubles away. I cannot. Yet, I would like you to read this book. I hope it helps."

I read the book and treasured it not only because of its content, but also because of the person who gave it to me.

For many years now the memory of this book has lain dormant. Because of this recent conversation with Sister Dorothy, old memories began to surface: memories of a special teacher extending compassion and lightening the load of a troubled spirit.

After several more telephone conversations with Nankee, I made arrangements to travel to Trinidad in late October, 2011. I looked forward to whatever form this mini-reunion would take. I could not wait!

# 4

# At Miami

It was in late October when I boarded a small plane in International Falls, Minnesota. At Minneapolis, I would then switch planes and catch a connecting flight to Miami, Florida, where I intended to spend the night. I was excited as I caught my first real glimpses of Miami from the shuttle bus which was transporting us to the motel. Everywhere were reminders of Trinidad. Both the warm weather and the swaying palm trees resurrected memories of Trinidad; the presence of shorts and sandals confirmed the vision. Yes, I was now on tropical grounds.

I had but a few short hours to take in the sights before retiring for the night. People from the motel had told me that if there was but one place I had time to visit it should be to a place simply referred to as The Bay. It was purported to be a most beautiful place in Miami. I was directed to go to a type of bus terminal where I could secure a ride to The Bay. It was some distance away... too far to walk. Several vans were waiting at the terminal for passengers. I climbed aboard one and told the driver that I wanted to go to The Bay. I paid the required fare up front and took my seat. Before too much time had passed, the driver stopped to pick up a group of people who were walking along the side of the road. They too, paid a fee to the driver and took their seats. Soon we were well on our way down the busy highway through dense traffic. There was no denying it; Miami was huge. I could hardly wait to see the beautiful sights that The Bay had to offer.

Suddenly, the driver veered off the main thoroughfare, and entered a secondary roadway. The district seemed unusually congested and singularly unattractive. I was left to wonder if the motel staff was having a laugh at my expense. This was not at all what I had been led to expect.

Many restaurants and businesses lined the busy streets. We ventured farther and farther from the business end of the district. Soon we came to a neighbourhood that was decidedly residential and most definitely unattractive. The area appeared exceedingly run-down. It reminded me somewhat of the seedier side of New York in the seventies.

With this latest turn, I became quite uneasy. I looked around me; no one else seemed to be sharing my discomfort at our surrounding. The other passengers seemed unperturbed by the scenery.

My unease turned into alarm when I saw the skeletal remains of several burned out cars; orphaned tires and stray car parts completed the look of abandonment.

I began to think that the driver had forgotten about me. He seemed to be completely absorbed in conversation with his other passengers. When I tried to hint that I feared that I had been forgotten, he calmly assured, "Oh, yes, I have you in mind. Do not worry. I know this neighbourhood. I have lived here. Everybody knows me..."

But, I *was* worried. Burned-out cars, derelict housing, forsaken souls wandering purposelessly amidst the debris... informed a scene that signaled nothing but danger.

Shortly, we stopped; every single passenger, with the exception of me, disembarked. Only slightly ashamed to admit it, I was relieved to see them go. The van picked up speed as we headed out of the neighbourhood. The driver turned his head toward me and asked, "Were you uncomfortable?"

"Yes."

"Sorry. I know those passengers. No one wanted to bring them here. They were desperate. I had to help them. I hope you understand."

"Driver, why is it that no other driver wanted to bring them here?"

"You got a good look at that neighbourhood. Did you?"

"Yes, I did."

"And how did you feel? Like you in another world?"

"Yes, it was different."

"Well, I thought you would not mind if I helped them out. This area of Miami is their world. They cannot afford to live elsewhere. You see this is probably the worst area in Miami. There is massive unemployment, and..."

He stopped.

I urged, "And... you were saying..."

"Frequent killings!"

I was quieted. He continued, "I believe that you just witnessed the real shady side of Miami…Now off we go to The Bay. You will like this section of Miami. It is really something. You are in for a treat."

I was heartened by his words and when we finally arrived at The Bay, I found myself offering the driver a tip. He smiled and remarked, "Thanks. Is this for taking you into the shadier side of Miami or getting you out of it?"

Without waiting for an answer, he was gone.

# 5

# The Evening Stranger at the Bay

An extravaganza of lights emanating from the cluster of shops and restaurants illuminated the entire bay district; a duplicate image reflected in the gentle undulations of the ocean currents lent a softer and more subtle beauty to the entire scene. I fairly floated along the path, mesmerized by the varied images embedded in the cool waters.

Before too long, one restaurant claimed my patronage. I do not know whether it was the promise of patio-style dining or the tempting menu (featuring black-eyed peas and plantain) which made the ultimate decision, but, decidedly, it was the right decision.

Quietly satiated after my meal, I resumed my walk. Within minutes I was immersed in the sounds of the Latin American beat. I made myself part of the small group of onlookers appreciatively gathered around, simply breathing in the familiar melodies of decades past. The music was a perfect blend of guitars, pan flutes and voices. I moved in closer, steadying myself near a post. The stage was set for quiet, nostalgic reflection.

My peripheral vision caught sight of the solitary figure of another male "islander" standing but a few short yards from me. He appeared to be in his mid-fifties. There was nothing about him that should have claimed my attention; nothing aside from the fact that he appeared to be staring directly at me. I hastened to look away and allowed the music to envelop my mind and spirit. When the magic of the music ended, I turned to move on.

There he was again—closer than before. He was a stranger, yet, there was something about him that seemed oddly familiar. He was simply dressed: white t-shirt, khaki pants and open sandals. His pants were folded up several times, stopping just below the knee. His unshaven face and disheveled hair were bold accents to his piercing eyes.

Then it hit me—I was staring at the very likeness of Pa! Everything about him, from the hair to the folded pant legs, reminded me of Pa!

My mind assured me that it was not Pa; it knew that Pa had passed on decades ago. Shaken and troubled, my heart had its doubts. I forced my feet to move toward an exit. When I looked back, I saw no sign of the stranger. I told myself that I must have imagined the whole thing.

It had seemed so real—everything was so reminiscent of Pa—but, wait. There he was again, ahead of me on the side of the path—staring at me with the same sort of look Pa had borne just before he died.

I hastened my pace and headed out of The Bay and toward the main road. I moved past the stranger without looking directly at him.

When I reached the road, I turned; he was still there—watching me. About his mouth played the slightest hint of a smile; his hand was raised as if in silent greeting.

Within seconds the shadow of an oncoming shuttle bus broke our connection. I boarded the bus. All evidence pointing to his existence vanished by the time I took my seat. I returned to my motel in quiet confusion.

# 6

# Striking Resemblance

With the *stranger's* image still burning in my mind, I was unable to lay claim to anything that remotely resembled sleep that night.

Had I still lived in Trinidad, seeing someone who so closely resembled Pa may not have carried so great an impact. But, I had been living abroad for over forty years, and for forty years thoughts of Pa had been tucked away in my subconscious. When I was last living in Trinidad, it was quite common to engage in conversations about the mystery surrounding death and the possibility that those who have passed through this life can sometimes find a way to communicate with those who have been left behind.

That has not been a common experience in Canada.

I found my mind shifting gears and moving back to the Trinidad of my youth replete with all the superstition and strongly held beliefs of the time.

As much as I tried to dismiss the appearance of the stranger as a mere coincidence that had no real bearing on my life, I couldn't.

My sleeplessness belied this truth. I succumbed to the traditions of my roots. This stranger had come into my life for a reason. Was it merely to take me back all those years to the time when Pa had passed or was there a message to be read from the slight smile and gently raised hand?

For years I have wondered in silence about the last look from my pa. It had been so perplexing. I often wondered if he knew that he had very little time left in this world. *Was I now to embrace the smile of the stranger as somehow being a silent message from Pa?*

As a boy, I had been told that the dead did return to this life in some form to watch over us. Was this presence therefore a visitation from my father? Was I being gently returned to my roots? In any event, the mere existence of this stranger took my mind on a journey into my past—deep into my past in search of Pa.

Willingly, I yielded.

# 7

# A Journey with Pa

A huge hand tugged at my shoulders. I opened my eyes. It was Pa.
"Frankie, wake up son. It's time. Go wash up."
"Yes, Pa."

Obediently, I rose from my *bed*. My bed, a product borne of Ma's creative energy, was but a simple mattress. Nothing went to waste back when we had very little. Everything found a secondary purpose. Empty sugar bags were dutifully washed and hung to dry. When enough bags had been thus saved, they were sewn together to form a covering; this covering was subsequently filled with loose straw and leaves from the coconut tree; this became my mattress. In a similar fashion, Ma magically transformed empty flour bags into a blanket.

I woke up happy; I had a bed all to myself and I slept luxuriously.

I stumbled sleepily over to the wall. Looking back, I realize that the wall itself bore silent testimony to our poverty (even though at that time in my life I did not know that we were poor for we had a roof over our heads and usually had food to eat) This wall was constructed from wood of non-uniform length and width procured from the bargain section of the local saw mill. On the left side of this wooden wall was a large nail; on that nail was anchored the sum total of my possessions; I quickly grabbed a T-shirt and a pair of short pants, and headed out—out to Pa.

"Frankie, I have a bucket of water for yo shower. Don't forget to brush yo teeth."

I felt like a prince for I did not have to go down the street to the public tap to bathe. Pa had brought a bucket of water for me. How grand. All that remained was for me to brush my teeth. I took the bucket of water from Pa and approached the wooden shower stall situated in the back yard. This stall, made from older wood, afforded one a modicum of bathing privacy. No sooner did I enter the stall when I discovered that I was without a toothbrush. I remembered that I had discarded it only last evening. There was nothing to do but replace it. Off I traipsed to the back yard; in the back yard, close to the railroad tracks was a bank of shrubbery rich with twigs. With my home-made knife, I quickly cut off a small twig. I whittled away at this small twig until I transformed it into something that looked like an unsharpened pencil. This pencil-like apparatus I then put into my mouth and began chewing; the chewing continued until the various strands in the twig separated into sinewy *brushes*. I returned to the shower stall and completed my preparations quickly knowing that Pa was waiting. In a very short time I was at Pa's side.

"Ready, Frankie?" There was a hint of something different in Pa's voice. It was something that I rarely detected. He spoke in an almost teasing manner.

"Yeh, Pa. Ah ready. Way we going, Pa?"

"I have a surprise for you."

"Surprise, Pa?"

"Yeh."

Now his tone made sense to me. Immediately visions of candy and ice cream raced through my mind.

But the surprise Pa had in mind was a surprise of a different nature.

Pa walked to the mule at the front of the yard; as he untied the mule from the lime tree he announced, "We going to the blacksmith. Yo can hold the rein and lead the mule. Yo big now."

All visions of candy and ice-cream disappeared but I was not disappointed. Pa said that I was big now. Joy burst out and I uttered a heartfelt, "Thank you, Pa."

My heart swelled with pride upon hearing those words from Pa. To be deemed big enough to walk ahead of the mule, leading it rather than following behind, was a supreme compliment for me.

My enthusiasm would not be contained; immediately, I rushed forward and, grabbing the reins, ordered a decidedly grown up command, "*Come on!*"

Much to my delight, the mule responded; there was no denying it now, I felt all grown up.

Along the way to the blacksmith shop, we encountered some of the boys from the neighbourhood. Looks of genuine surprise spread across their faces when they saw me leading the mule; I was in heaven.

Suddenly, the mule started to limp; soon all forward progress stopped. Somewhat bewildered, I asked, "Pa, ah did something wrong?"

"No, no Frankie. The mule has to have new shoes. Ah will take over from here."

I did not understand the concept of *new shoes* for the mule.

*I* did not have *new shoes*. Actually, I did not have *any* shoes. How is it then, that this mule, – a mere animal – needed shoes?

My child mind could not fathom the concept.

Pa bent to inspect the mule's hooves. I could hear his voice uttering gentle and soothing assurances to the animal. This behaviour was so uncharacteristic of the Pa I knew. Usually, Pa and the mule were battling; Pa always managed to find something about the animal with which to be displeased. Today was different. Today, Pa was different. Perhaps that is why this memory is now so firmly anchored in my mind. It is a memory that I find myself embracing when too many negative images flood my mind. I need to know that there was another side to my pa, that, although rarely seen, did nonetheless, exist.

Pa continued to coax the mule along the path.

At long last, we arrived at the blacksmith shop.

# 8

# Mr. Lazee

"Budricks, ah happy to see you. So you brought the mule."
"Yes, Lazee – just as I told yo."
"And who is the little one? He so small – my he is small."
"This is Frankie. He is the fourth child. Yes, he tiny. Skinny fo' sure."

As Lazee approached, he gave me a good looking over. He mumbled something under his breath. I did not hear what he had said but the child in me wondered if he found me to be a somewhat likeable child.

Mr. Lazee then led us all, the mule included, into his workplace – a makeshift room put together with odd pieces of wood and posts; this room was protected from above by a galvanized roofing material. Thousands of ancient pieces of steel were hanging on every available wooden surface.

On the far side of the room an iron anvil was secured to a log. Beside the log was a deep pit filled with burning coals; at the center of the pit was a piece of steel. Not only did the steel feel hot, it also looked hot.

Mr. Lazee then pulled a single bucket out from a huge stack of buckets; this he turned upside down and resting it on the floor; he then picked me up and placed me on top of the bucket.

Next, he brought the mule nearer to the anvil. Many things puzzled me about what was going on. *Why were hot coals burning and nothing was cooking?* Why did Mr. Lazee have the mule so close to the burning coals? And, perhaps, most perplexing of all, why did Pa insist on calling this man *lazy*? To me, he appeared to be anything but lazy.

After securely tying the rope from the mule to a post, Mr. Lazee lifted the mule's right hind leg. The mule reacted somewhat nervously to the close inspection.

"Budricks," Mr. Lazee began, "that foot is in bad shape. But... I can fix it... I think."

"Lazee," Pa explained, "ah know ah waited too long. Do what you have to...Yo know ah depend on this mule to make a living. It not easy to get work these days. We have a big, big, problem..."

Pa's voice took on an odd character; it and Pa became noticeably quiet and sad.

I was accustomed to seeing Pa as a man very much in command, barking out orders and taking the lead. This Pa was a new Pa. This sadness was new and I was both surprised and silenced by it. It had me wondering if Pa was alright.

When Mr. Lazee next spoke I could hear deep concern resonating in his every word.

"Budricks, you have always faced problems. I know it is not easy; you have a big family, many mouths to feed. So, tell me what this problem is..."

"Lazee, my friend, this problem is about *trucks,* big trucks."

Then Pa became silent; Mr. Lazee urged Pa to explain the problem more fully. Pa continued, "Lazee, we in trouble for sure. Big trucks are taking over the transport business. The truck owners get the best jobs; they get the meat, we with the mule and cart get the scraps. We get the leftovers that the truck owners don't want. Ah having a hard time making it my friend."

I sensed Pa's pain. Inside I too hurt for him. Then Mr. Lazee spoke, "Budricks, you are a Hindu. I am a Catholic. Yes, so we have different religions, but we have one God. And this same God looks out for all of us. I will pray for you my friend, just have faith. Okay?"

A barely audible *yes* came from Pa's lips, but under his breath I heard him whisper, "Ah need help now, and Bhagawan have no time for me. Maybe He don't know me..."

I did not hear the rest of Pa's words. I wish I had. While I did not comprehend fully Pa's words, I was, however, able to intuit Pa's sentiments. I understood even if I did not comprehend.

All the while they were talking, Mr. Lazee continued to work.

I was still confused as to the exact nature of his work. His eyes searched his surroundings, then he headed to the back wall. From there, he pulled out a string of horse shoes of varying sizes. He measured several different ones against the heel of the mule to determine which one would secure the closest fit. Settling on one, he then approached the pit where the coals were burning and placed the selected shoe inside the coals. Soon the steel shoe was a blazing hot red from the intense heat of the coals. I was awe-struck by the entire process.

Mr. Lazee then grabbed some tongs and transferred the burning steel to the anvil and began hammering on the steel. Inside that dark room the sparks that came while he was hammering took on a radiance like nothing I had ever before seen. The sparks seemed to magically transform into tiny red butterflies and were suddenly flying in all directions.

Once again, Mr. Lazee placed the hot steel back into the burning coals. Pa and Lazee exchanged glances. All was well.

Soon the bent steel turned white. Once again the now white hot shoe was placed on the anvil and Mr. Lazee hammered intently with the solid concentration of one who knew what he was doing. He continued to mold and fashion that piece of steel until the end product closely resembled the model he had selected.

I understood that Mr. Lazee was making a shoe for the mule; what I did not understand was how this shoe was going to be secured to the mule. I was soon to find out.

Mr. Lazee, at one point, took the burning piece of steel and placed it against the bottom of the mule's hoof. Immediately upon making contact, with the hoof, smoke erupted. I was horrified and yelled,

"No, no. Stop! That too hot! Yo hurting the mule."

Quick to understand my mind, Pa assured, "Frankie, no, no! He is not hurting the mule. He is helping the mule. Yo will see, okay?"

"Okay, Pa."

Then Mr. Lazee returned the hot shoe to the anvil and continued to refine his creation. Again he measured the shoe against the heel. Suddenly, he immersed the hot shoe into a barrel of water. Immediately the air was filled with the hissing of hot steam. He took the shoe to the mule and smiled at Pa saying, "Well, Budricks, this is a good shoe. It will work."

Pa seemed relieved.

In Mr. Lazee, I saw a hardworking tradesman who was not just a blacksmith but rather an artist. But, the job was not yet done. Mr. Lazee continued on with his task. As he worked, he sat on a small stool. Raising the mule's hoof, he placed it on his apron and held the hoof securely between his legs.

Pa was at the other end of the animal stroking his head.

Mr. Lazee smiled and talked quietly to himself as he continued his work. (I noticed that Mr. Lazee did an awful lot of talking to himself.) Once again he held the shoe against the mule's heel. I watched in amazement but I still did not understand how he was going to attach the steel to the foot.

In disbelief, I saw Mr. Lazee hold up a spike and a hammer. No, it could not be. He would not think of driving a nail into the foot of a live animal. But I was wrong. Mr. Lazee was about to do that very thing.

He did not look drunk so I determined that he must be crazy. I looked at Pa. He did not look as if he was going to do anything to stop the madness. The responsibility fell to me; I had to do something. I ran to Mr. Lazee and begged,

"Mr. Lazee please don't hurt the mule… don't drive the nail…"

I reached for the nail. Before I could lay claim to the offensive weapon, Pa grabbed me by the arm and took me the where he had been standing at the head of the mule. He encouraged, "Frankie, rub the mule. Stroke the head. It ok – ah promise."

In spite of my feeling to the contrary, I listened to my pa. My heart pounded, wracking my chest in an almost audible protest. I heard the harsh shrill sound of the hammer. I thought that I was going to be sick. I expected the mule to react violently to this assault. Again I was proven wrong. At most, the animal seemed to be mildly inconvenienced. The deed, now accomplished led me to ask, "Pa – why the mule not in pain? Look, Pa – so many spikes hammered into the raw flesh… How come he not in pain?"

"Frankie – that's how God made the mule. Just watch Mr. Lazee – look what he doing now?"

I looked. Mr. Lazee was cutting the edges of the heel – peeling the heel like one would peel a potato.

Then Mr. Lazee, seeing my anguish, began to explain, "See Frankie – no pain."

"How come?"

"That is the way. That is just God's way."

"It seems that God gave the better way to mules than to we humans…"

For a moment Mr. Lazee seemed perplexed. Then he looked first at me and then at Pa and said, "Budricks, my friend you have a thinker, a fine thinker. He may be skinny like a pin but he have a mind. He is going to go some place. Yes, he is."

I did not quite understand this grown up talk. There was so much about life that I did not understand. But, I was learning. Until today I had no idea that hammering nails into the hoof of a mule did not cause pain. The nails would have hurt my feet, so I reasoned that our conditions were much the same. That thinking was simply another aspect to the innocence of childhood.

Pa held out the reins to me and signaled me to take over. What a day! Again I was to lead the mule. I could hardly believe it.

But first, the mule and I needed to have a talk.

"Mr. Mule, I am taking you home. Yo okay with that?"

The mule snorted his understanding. No longer in pain, he was steady and ready. His body, infused with eagerness, seemed to signal his approval.

I looked to Pa, impatient to be on my way— impatient to prove myself in this world of grown-ups.

Pa motioned for me to wait. He walked over to Mr. Lazee, reached into his pocket, pulled out a sum of money and offered it apologetically, "Lazee, my friend, yo did a good job. I owe you more than…"

"No, Budricks, that amount is fair. I remember what you did for me. I still have some of the rice you gave me… you don't owe me one single cent more."

Pa smiled and the two men shook hands. In that exchange I witnessed something truly magnificent. I did not have the words to express it at that moment but I did understand the depth of the honour of the moment. Neither man sought to take advantage. Each one acknowledged his indebtedness to the other. This was civility in one of its purest forms.

My mind now moved to my own situation.

Now, surely, it was time to go; I could not wait to take my place at the head of the mule.

Just as Pa joined me by the mule, Mr. Lazee intoned, almost as an afterthought,

"Budricks hold on. I have something. You must have one."

Instinctively, I recoiled.

I knew what was going to happen next. It was the same thing that always happened when men got together. They were going to drink. Drink rum.

I did not like it when Pa drank. When he was under the influence, he was predictably volatile and disruptive.

But, I was merely the child. I had no control. I had no say.

Nervously, I waited as Mr. Lazee began the familiar ceremony.

It started with the production of two banged up tin cups whose best days were decidedly long past. He then brought out a huge bottle filled with a very dark liquid. From this bottle, Mr. Lazee poured a substantial helping. It was considerably more than the amount I was accustomed to seeing Pa have at one serving, and I was appreciably horrified.

The fact that it was still early on in the day only served to increase my fear. From past experience I knew that one drink was seldom enough for my father and his friends; invariably, one drink would be quickly followed by another and then another. This behaviour could easily have explosive consequences. I braced myself for a long day when I saw Pa down his drink in one motion.

"Lazee, this powerful. Man this drink is strong..."

"And, Budricks, it very sweet. I like it. This is a special batch of Mauby. Nelly really went to town on this batch... I will tell her how much you enjoyed it. She will be pleased."

I relaxed; Mauby was not like rum. It was non-alcoholic and an absolute favourite beverage among all age groups on the island.

I felt a bit ashamed that I had immediately assumed the worst about Pa and Mr. Lazee. My shame became even more acute when Mr. Lazee produced a full bottle of sweet drink just for me. In one hand he held the sweet drink and in the other a small cup. He filled the cup to the brim and offered me both the bottle and the cup.

"Go ahead," he urged. "This is all for you. Enjoy."

I hesitated. A whole bottle of sweet drink all for me seemed somehow sinful. I was unaccustomed to such excess.

Pa urged, "Frankie, go ahead, have it. All for yo, Son. Enjoy."

Pa's smile was genuine. Inside, I too was smiling. I was comforted knowing that Pa was looking out for me. I felt that I was in a special world with my Pa.

In years to come I would wonder when and why this special world ceased to exist. When and why did my relationship with Pa change?

Pa raised his cup; Mr. Lazee did likewise. Smiling, they both turned to me; mirroring their actions, I too raised my cup. In the simple decency of that moment, came a taste of heaven.

Soon, we were headed back home. It did not matter anymore whether or not I led the mule. My mind was elsewhere.

I had had a glimpse of the adult world. Something that Mr. Lazee had said to Pa early on in the day stayed with me. He had intimated that while there were different religions, there was only one God. This thought played in my mind frequently over the years as I contemplated the various aspects of religion and the nature of God.

That day I witnessed something else too... something that would remain firmly rooted in my mind as a very precious memory. In all the time that Pa and I had spent with Mr. Lazee, never once did either of these fathers swear or make comments that were in any way indecent. The idea that another type of existence lay beyond my narrow world of experience was being seeded in my consciousness.

And I was at peace.

# 9

# A Journey of Discovery

**M**ore memories of my father come to mind as I find myself absorbed in recalling the distant past…

Again Pa had promised to take me with him on a trip. To be sure, I was excited. The morning of the adventure finally arrived.

"Yo ready, Frankie, for the trip?"

"Yes, Pa."

"Then way we go."

Like a curious puppy, I followed eagerly in my father's footsteps.

Shortly after leaving Back Street, we turned right. Our progress was halted at the railroad tracks as a train was crossing. The train was long and the wait seemed endless. Pa became impatient, even irritable. He complained, "The bloody train again!"

I looked closely to see where the blood was on the train. Seeing no blood, I asked, "Pa, where is the blood?"

"Frankie, don't be stupid!"

"Pa, ah stupid?"

"Frankie, stop yo talking!"

"Yes, Pa."

I remained quiet, yet I wondered whether I was in fact, stupid. I tried hard not to think I was stupid. That notion was unleashed so frequently in my world at school that I desperately fought to prevent any trace of this plague from invading my world at home.

Something else was puzzling me. Why did Pa call the train bloody? I saw no blood. Was my father going blind?

The train slowed, then stopped. Normally when a train stops at this crossing, it clears the crossing. Today this did not happen. Today we had to wait and Pa, clearly agitated, shouted, "Yo stupid, stupid train. Ah could kick the daylights out of you!"

I was about to ask Pa why he called the train *stupid*. The train was not stupid. What was happening to Pa?

Pa began to pace.

A mix of grunts and grating complaints accompanied the pacing. Assuredly, choice words and colourful language followed the complaints.

I thought that the word *stupid* was reserved for describing human and animal conduct. In my child's mind it did not make sense for Pa to call the train stupid. But, nevertheless it put me to ponder, *does the train have a mind; can the train hear Pa?*

This was the way I saw things—very literally.

This tendency to take things literally also occurred at school. Only a few days ago, my teacher was making polite conversation with one of her favourite students. She asked, "Stuart what are you having for lunch today?"

"Teacher, I am so excited. I am having a hot dog!"

I shrieked in silence at the image of some poor dog now becoming Stuart's lunch. My brain froze on this image. I was transfixed.

*How could you?* I wondered. And, more fundamentally, *Why would you?*

Thoughts immediately went out to Rover, our dog. All I could think about was Rover becoming someone's lunch. My stomach recoiled at the thought. This visual is so strong in me even today. I struggle against the imagery every time I hear talk of hot dogs. It should therefore not be any surprise to learn that I have never eaten a hot dog to this very day.

At last the train cleared the tracks and we continued onto the dirt road, the Macoya Road, that stretched endlessly before us.

Back then, fields richly laden with sugar cane or corn bordered the road on either side. Cucumber, pineapple and potato fields also claimed many acres. This stretch of the Macoya Road and its fertile fields is where we, as children, played hour after hour.

It was here that we flew our kites.

Kite flying began as a simple innocent game. Soon the game became transformed with the addition of one small accessory—a razor blade.

With the advent of the razor, the game metamorphosed from an innocent childhood pursuit to out and out warfare.

The original game had very simple well defined goals: keep your kite up in the air higher and longer than anyone else.

Nothing was simple about the modified game. It became highly competitive and even vicious. Few rules were attached to this new game. One rule, however, was taken as a given and understood by all participants never to be broken. The razor blade attached to the kite had to be of the *used* variety—one that had been discarded by its owner after multiple uses.

The object of the game was simple—launch your kite with the sole purpose of annihilating every other kite in the sky. Along with great excitement, this game generated great rivalry!

After several miserable defeats, I sought a way to give myself an edge over my competition. Here I have to make a confession and own up to my deceit. In my desire to do better at the game, I think that I convinced myself that I was breaking no rules. I managed to tell myself that I was merely being clever.

One day, while walking home after another miserable defeat, I searched the neighbourhood for a discarded razor blade. Eventually, my effort was rewarded and I found one. The deceit did not manifest itself into my thoughts until I returned home to the sight of Pa shaving in the back yard. Nearing the end of his routine, Pa nicked himself and became furious. I assumed that the razor blade was at fault; I decided that I would remove the offending blade and replace it with the one that I had found. I told myself that my blade was much shinier than Pa's blade and as such it was much better suited to Pa's needs.

Carefully I made the exchange. That is how my next kite became equipped with a *not so used* used blade.

The very next day I joined the group of flyers and quickly guided my kite high up into the air. It immediately inflicted irreparable damage on the competition; with each encounter, all opposition was destroyed.

That day, I was victorious.

Victory, however, did not flow long or deep.

To the others it seemed incredulous that one so inept as I had proven to be over the past few days, could suddenly be so improved.

Immediately they launched an investigation. (Frankiegate lol)

Before long, Jobee, a neighbourhood friend, but now rival, made this assertion,

"Frankie cheat. He hav a bran' new blade. He not fair! He need a lesson…"

I tried to protest.

I tried to tell them that my blade had indeed been used.

They would have none of it.

I received the customary beating for such a transgression.

But, that was not the end of my punishment. While my body was yet recovering from that discipline, the boys decided upon an additional judgement. This boys' court decreed that I was to be suspended from any further participation in kite flying until further notice. Furthermore, it was concluded that there would be no appeal. This decision was unanimous.

There were additional ramifications on another front… with my father.

When I returned home later that day, I was met in the yard by a decidedly unhappy Pa. His scarred and bleeding face bore the evidence of my deceit.

Somehow he, too, knew of my subterfuge.

He came straight to the point, "Frankie, yo switch the razor blade?"

"Pa, please let me explain. I was just trying…"

"Frankie, just answer me. Yo did it?"

In his hand I could see the broad leather belt. My body recoiled; my mind steeled to the inevitable. Had I not been there a thousand times before?

"Yes, Pa. I did it."

Again my body paid the price for my deception.

The tears I cried then were not so much as a result of Pa's strapping, but rather because I had been effectively ostracized from my friends.

Not knowing the true source of my tears, Pa attempted an explanation, "Frankie, what ah do, ah do for the best."

Then he left.

That was as close to an apology from my father that I ever remember getting. I cherish that moment to this very day.

(Now, I should return to the story at hand.)

We had come to the end of Macoya Road and were about to cross the next major two lane highway. Having been built by Americans who were highly regarded for their engineering skills, it is appropriately called the The American Highway.

Pa ordered, "Frankie, turn left."

"Left, Pa?"

"Yes."

My little heart became excited. It was very aware of the fact that in this direction one would soon come upon various tents where vendors sold their wares. Most notably, in addition to the regular fruits and vegetables, many also offered various treats for sale. Among those treats were usually an assortment of fudges and coconut sugar cakes. I counted them among my favourites. But, above all this, I craved ice cream; I began to wonder if ice cream might be available at one of the vendors; soon wonder gave way to open anticipation and I was almost certain that an ice cream treat would soon be in the offing.

This rationale did not come out of nowhere. Because of the nature of the directions that Pa was giving, I reasoned that he was headed to the sugar cane factory. It was relatively close. Happy was I in the knowledge that Pa was going to buy me a treat. I could not wait.

Soon we came to the Vanlow River. Almost everyone from the neighbourhood came there to bathe. For a moment I wondered whether we would stop there for a quick swim as it was quite hot. We passed the Vanlow River without stopping and then came to the aforementioned vendors. First my eyes and then my feet were drawn to a lady churning at a tub; I knew that she was making ice cream; I veered automatically towards her.

From somewhere behind me I heard Pa's voice command, "Frankie, keep walking!" "Pa, ah need to rest..."

"Frankie, keep walking straight."

"Yes, Pa."

Gone was any hope of an ice cream treat.

We continued our endless trek under the blistering sun. Exhaustion crept into every muscle. Nothing seemed quite familiar. I wondered where were going. Pa had simply said a trip, and a trip usually implied some kind of a treat. Thus far, there was no end in sight, worse there was no treat in sight.

"Pa, where we going? I am tired now. We need rest."

Pa gave no indication of a response. Perhaps he had not heard me. Once more I asked. Still no verbal response... only that stare of his that I had come to know so well.

He muttered something under his breath. I made a wise decision and said nothing more.

Eventually, his irritation with me won out and again he blustered, "Frankie, yo walking too slow. Yo have to walk faster."

"Faster Pa, but why, Pa?"

"Yo always asking questions. Well, ah have to go meet a man."

"But, why, Pa?"

"Yo bothersome, Frankie. Keep quiet."

After disclosing this bit of information, Pa seemed even more agitated.

I tried as best I could to understand the source of his anxiety. It was beyond my comprehension. All I could do to help was to attempt to pick up my pace. The hot concrete gave no reprieve to my burning feet. Despite a parched throat and blistered feet, I trudged on.

We walked in silence for some time again. My memory could find no time in my life when I had ever walked this far. Still hoping that somehow now Pa would recognize my plight and agree to a short stop, I slowed my pace a little.

Still Pa ordered, "Frankie, come on, yo must keep up. Don't be lazy."

Stinging from that last comment, but too tired to protest, I continued.

Finally, we arrived at Arima. Pa said that this was where the man lived. My mind could barely fathom the distance we had walked, for Arima was a good eight miles from Tunapuna. Is it any wonder then that I felt fatigued?

Still we walked on, for now we had to find our way to the man's home.

But, Pa knew the way and within minutes we were standing in the man's yard. It was a place very much like our home back in Tunapuna. Relieved to have finally reached our destination we made our way to the side of the house. There, under the shade of a mango tree was a wooden drum brimming with a most welcome sight... water. We saw several calabash cups resting on a bench near the drum. Immediately Pa picked up one of these cups, filled it with water, and handed it to me. Without a second's hesitation, I downed the welcome liquid. It mattered little that the water was slightly warm; it was wet. Still not fully satiated, we went back for more.

Having somewhat quenched our thirst, Pa began to look around for signs of life in the home; seeing no one, a new form of agitation set in.

I waited.

Pa paced… miserably.

Then, we both waited.

Eventually, Pa could take the waiting no more and yelled, "Frankie, le' we go nuh! That blasted crook is…"

I did not take in any more of his colourful dissertation regarding our missing host…

Pa left the property. I was reluctant to follow. I had not yet recovered enough to begin another long trek home.

But, Pa had made his move, and it was my duty to follow.

I felt a huge let down and wondered why we had come here in the first place. I wanted to ask the question but Pa was already too far ahead to hear. At the intersection, Pa waited for me to catch up. I hurried when I saw him waiting. As I drew closer I heard him mutter, "If ah see that man, ah fix him good."

"And I wondered what was wrong with this man that Pa had to *fix* him."

"We were about to turn off the road when someone in a very old jitney yelled, "Budricks, wait, wait! It's me, Roopy!"

Pa stopped.

I stopped.

Roopy parked the truck and got out.

Pa, clearly vexed, exclaimed, "Roopy, yo said yo will be home waiting for me. Way the h*** yo been? Yo can't be trust to keep a simple promise!"

Roopy met Pa's anger with calm, "Budricks, Ah happy to see you. And yo have your son with you. That is nice."

Perhaps sensing that angry words would not get him any satisfaction, Pa came directly to the point and asked, "Yo have it?"

Pa had still not explained why we had come all this way to see this man so my mind was still actively wondering about this *it* that they were both talking about.

"Yes, ah have it. And yo going to like it. Come, get into the truck."

We boarded the old, struggling truck. Soon we were back in Roopy's driveway.

Soon, my curiosity about this –*it*- would be satisfied.

Roopy disappeared to the back of the yard. The time he was away proved to be too much for Pa. Pa paced irritably for some minutes.

Roopy reappeared.

When Pa saw him he gasped, "Tell me it is not that thing!"

At first, I did not see what Pa had seen.

Then *it* came into full view.

There, before us, was what appeared to be the skeletal remains of a cow. It looked so emaciated that I was surprised to see it standing at all.

So this was the *it* that Pa had travelled so far to find.

In an instant I knew what it would mean for me and for the rest at home: more work.

Pa, still furious at Roopy, escalated his tone, "Roopy, yo is a scamp. This is no cow. Way is the cow I agree to buy? Way me cow?"

Sheepishly, Roopy countered with, "Budricks, ah swear on me mother grave…"

Pa interrupted, "So yo now go swear on yo mother grave, Roopy? Yo no-good crook. Yo mother a saint. But yo… yo got no shame. All o' we had a deal. We had a price. I know yo break yo promise. I know yo sold that cow yo promise me. And now yo want me to believe that this is the same cow. Yo going straight to hell, Roopy."

I was afraid for Roopy.

Pa walked up to Roopy, all the while shaking his fist.

"No, Pa! Don't."

Momentarily distracted, Pa wheeled around.

Roopy shrieked, "Don't hit me! I am no crook, Budricks."

"Yo a liar, Roopy! Worse yo is a snake."

The air became thick with their yelling and cussing.

I went to the bench and sat, my head bent.

Distressed at their insanity, I did not know what to do or where to turn. I could stand it no longer.

They seemed oblivious to me. Rising from the bench, I headed toward the street. Where I was going, and what I was doing, I had no idea. All I knew was that I had to get away.

Before I could reach the street, Roopy found me.

"Frankie, Son, we sorry. We not fighting. Yo Pa and me… we have a… a disagreement. It will be okay. Y'understand?"

"Yes, Uncle Roopy." (Even though Roopy was not my real uncle, it was a common sign of respect to attach this kind of title to elders in our lives.)

"There's a good boy. And Budricks, we have to settle our affairs peacefully. Ah tell you what. I give you a real deal. How about I knock off a quarter of the price…"

"Roopy, for that scrawny animal? No way. Frankie, le' we go. We wasting time here. Roopy, ah coulda buy two cow for that price – two."

Pa pulled on my arm and made a motion to leave.

Roopy ran ahead and pleaded, "Ah give you the cow for half price. Yo know that's a deal. What yo think now?"

"I will need a stiff one for the road!"

This *stiff one for the* road turned out to have something to do with a bottle of rum, for in no time at all, Roopy was inviting Pa to take a seat on the bench with him while he poured each of them some dark liquid from the bottle. I took special note of the glasses that he used. They were real glasses. I was impressed.

When the glasses were almost emptied, Roopy teased, "Budricks – ah treated you like a prince. Now give me the cash."

Obligingly, Pa reached into his pocket and pulled out a bundle of folded notes. He then placed the cash into Roopy's hand. I had never seen so much money at one time. *Pa must be rich,* I mused to myself. When I saw Pa down the rest of the drink in one motion, I started to worry. I had seen Pa drink like that many times and that was when things usually started to go wrong.

"Roopy," Pa began, "that was a stiff one."

Then he looked over at me and said, "Frankie, yo see that black cow?"

"Yes, Pa."

"Grab the rope, and let's go."

"Go where, Pa?"

"Home."

"But, Pa I can't get the cow on the truck by myself. I need help."

"We don't need no help. We not using the truck. We walking home with the cow."

"Pa, all the way back home… walking?"

"Frankie, yo not listening. I *said* we walking."

I could not fathom the thought of having to walk all those miles again, and this time with a nearly dead cow, when Roopy had a truck.

Even more confusing than that was the behaviour of Uncle Roopy and Pa. One minute they were at each other's throats, and the next minute all their differences were settled.

At this moment, both Uncle Roopy and Pa were most agreeable.

As Pa and I began our trek home I was set to ponder, *Indeed, who was the clever one in this transaction? Who outsmarted whom?*

Pa was talking to himself, "Ah is no dummy..."

I could hear him whistle faintly. Pa was happy.

*Would Pa's recently acquired happiness result in my happiness too? Might Pa now be predisposed to offering me a treat along the way?*

# 10

# Trinidad Bound

Remembering Pa that way was good for my soul.

The morning brought me face to face with the reality of the final leg of my journey home.

This visit would be unlike any other visit home. This visit was primarily structured around a mini reunion... reunion with a few former teachers and students. More importantly, it held the promise of a reunion with Sister Dorothy.

The emotional pull that meeting with Sister Dorothy had on me exceeded that of going to any large scale reunion. I was rather looking forward to our small, intimate group.

A thousand curiosities took flight to my past as I boarded the plane bound for Trinidad. I clearly recalled the faces of both the staff and the students of St. Charles. I especially recalled the face of Sister Dorothy. These remembrances had been aided somewhat by pictures that I had reviewed as recently as last week when I was preparing for my journey home. Then I remembered that those pictures were available to me at that very moment for I had actually placed them in an envelope in my carry-on luggage.

The urge to review those pictures once again proved irresistible and I reached up to retrieve the brown envelope into which I had placed the cherished photos.

Those images reflected who we all were in 1960's. This was now October of 2011. Nearly five decades had passed since I last beheld those faces. I could not begin to imagine what those faces looked like today. I, myself have transitioned through so many phases since those early years.

Then I wondered briefly how I would look to them. I tried to imagine some of their questions.

*Mr. Boodram, what has happened to you all these years?*
*Where have you been? What happened after all this time?*

Even questions regarding my decision to not return to Trinidad to teach plagued my mind.

I feared that they would think that I did not like Trinidad anymore… that I had somehow lost my affection for my native land.

Those thoughts made me melancholic. I remembered with sadness the face of Mr. Winchester, the man who effectively changed the course of my life in 1973. How could I tell them of the events spanning the time between that fateful day in 1973, to the present?

It is that period of time that I will endeavour to breach through the course of this narrative.

# 11

# I Will Not Hire You...

The day may have been bleak in the fall of '73 when I appeared in the office of Carl Roach, the owner of Roach's Taxi, but upon seeing Carl, my spirits were anything but bleak.

His enthusiastic greeting made me feel very welcome indeed, "Frank Maraj... so pleased to see you. In fact, I was thinking of you lately. How are you? I hope you are here looking for a job..."

Nothing he could have said would have made me any happier; a job is the very thing that I needed; his offer came at exactly the right moment.

"Carl yes, yes, I want to work and I can start immediately."

"Great, I have a position for you."

"Thank you, thank you, Carl."

"Oh, and Frank, you'll be happy to know, Carl added, that this is no part-time position; I'm offering you full-time work with good solid hours. When can you start?"

Carl, expecting immediate enthusiasm to his generous offer, was somewhat confused by my unexpected silence.

"Why the glum face? Did I say something wrong?"

I was searching for the appropriate words, "No Carl, you did not say anything wrong. It is just that I was hoping for part time work only. I cannot accept a full-time job..."

"You cannot accept a full-time position! Carl was incredulous. Well, I must say, things have certainly changed. You're not the Frank we know. Frank..."

"Carl, please let me explain my situation."

"Go ahead!"

Clearly, Carl was irritated by my response. I struggled to explain, "Carl, as you know, I am now a qualified teacher but I am a qualified teacher without a teaching position."

"All the more reason why you might want to accept a full-time job," he interjected. His voice had just a hint of an edge to it. Then, softening a little, he added, "And it's yours for the taking… I think."

"Carl, please hear me out. Here is my situation. I want to teach but there is simply no job out there for me right now. I have a family to support and I must find work. I am asking you to hire me on part time, please. I am…"

"Why only part time then, Frank? Why not full-time?"

"I have signed up at the Board of Education as a substitute teacher. I am hoping that if I can get enough work that way, that when a job opening becomes available, I may be considered for the position. I must keep myself available for any teaching opportunity during regular school hours. Carl, now do you see, that is the reason why I cannot accept your offer of full-time work?"

"And when it suits you, you will then work for me. So Frank Maraj, you now think of me and the rest of us as second class…"

"Carl, I hope you know that that is simply not true…"

"Frank, check out your own words; you want me to work around your agenda. Let me tell you this…"

Clearly agitated, Carl now added a measure of disappointment to his voice when he pointed out, "Frank Maraj, teachers are a dime a dozen. Every single day graduates with degrees are knocking on my door looking for work. I could have my pick of any number of them… and here you stand, turning me down."

"Carl."

"Say no more. I will not hire you, Frank Maraj. It's that simple."

Turning his back on me, Carl walked away.

Taking with him, my hope.

# 12

# Renewal

Restlessness plagued my mind and invaded my sleepless night.

Early the next morning, I went back to Carl's office.

Margaret, Carl's ever reliable dispatcher, was on duty.

"Margaret, I would like to see Carl."

"Say, you look awfully… tanned. Have you been back to the Caribbean…?"

The ringing of the telephone interrupted her inquiry. I knew she was busy. I really should not be bothering her.

She made an effort to reconnect, but was again distracted when one of the drivers approached her with a problem of his own. Completely unflappable, she resolved the situation with ease… as usual.

Turning to me, she asked, "Sorry, Frank, how can I help you?"

Encouraged by her willing spirit, I continued, "Margaret, it is so good to see you. Here is what I need. I would like to take Carl out for coffee."

"You want to take him out?"

"Yes."

"Well, Frank, that's impossible. He has a million and one things on his mind. He couldn't possibly go… But, then again, it is precisely what he needs… a break from everything."

While she thought further about the request, I remained silent.

I knew that she had decided to humour me when she abruptly wheeled her chair to Carl's office door. Stopping at the door, she knocked rather forcefully and announced, "Carl Roach, you need to be out of this office. For you own good, leave."

"Listen here, Margaret. I am your…"

"Never mind the speech. Give it to me later. Frank Maraj is here; you need a coffee break. I have work to do and you are no help. Please, go."

Only mildly surprised by Margaret's intrusion into his life, Carl grabbed his jacket and motioned to me, complaining, "Frank, let's go. I believe that I have just been thrown out of my own office."

"Seems to me Carl, you need a strong cup of coffee. What say we go take care of that right now?"

We walked across the street to the nearest coffee shop. I ordered for both of us. Carl added nothing to the dark brew. He took it straight and black. I, however, added two or three cubes of sugar and a significant number of creamers.

The way Carl approached his coffee was the same way he approached me… straight and without embellishment.

"Frank, why are we here? Are you trying to talk me into hiring you? You already know my answer…"

"Carl, I accept that you will not hire me. I can handle that. Something else is on my mind. I need to…"

"You have something else on your mind? Frank you may as well take your turn speaking up. Seems the whole world wants a piece of me. Now let's hear your complaint."

"There is no complaint, Carl. None."

"No complaint, Frank? Then what do you want?"

"Carl, yesterday you stated that I was treating you second class. That's bothering me. That you did not hire me part-time is not a problem; it is your accusation that saddens me."

"Accusation? What accusation?"

"You said that I treated you as second class."

"And that is what has caused you all this grief? I don't understand why that thought even stayed with you."

"Carl, you have always been protective of me and generous towards me. That comment seemed so out of character. It was as if you had forgotten who I was… Is there something else bothering you? Is something wrong, of a more personal nature, Carl?"

"Wrong, wrong? It seems the whole world is against me right now! And I cannot talk about it."

Clearly he was troubled. He looked away, and then wiped his forehead.

Eventually, he spoke; this time he was much softer, "Frank, I have much on my mind. And I am aware that I have been very difficult lately. I wish…"

"Carl?"

"Frank?"

"May I ask if someone close to you is gravely ill?"

"Heavens no! It's nothing like that."

I breathed a sigh of relief.

"Frank, is that what you were thinking that someone close to me is…"

"Yes. I am so relieved that that is not the case. Are you facing financial distress Carl?"

My question was bold; perhaps, even out of place. Carl's raised brows indicated his momentary surprise, "Frank it is, and it is not. Let's talk about you. Tell me why you were so affected by my accusation. Help me understand."

I found myself rambling, "Carl, I come from a background where all my life it would seem that I was climbing out of the abyss of poverty. No matter how high we attempted to climb, we never once felt superior… to anyone. In all my life I would never have thought that I could ever be accused of coming close to even the suggestion of superiority. And, Carl, for you to think that I considered you or anyone else to be second class… all I can say to that is that you are wrong, dead wrong."

"I think that I already knew that, Frank. Sorry. Of course it is not true. You know, Frank, I could learn something from you my young friend. Here you are not upset, not yelling, not cussing. You have a right to do so. Yet, in your own way, you tried to be thoughtful to me even after I turned you away. You have a good heart, my friend."

"I am trying, Carl."

"Is that the reason you came to me?"

I said nothing.

He continued, "You are very sensitive, Frank. Perhaps too sensitive for your own good… But I am happy to see you. I thought you were in Ottawa. Gone for good. Why are you back here in Thunder Bay?"

This was not the time to tell anyone about my crushing encounter in Trinidad. I stated my situation as simply as I could, "Carl, I have returned to start life here anew."

"Frank, you are starting fresh?"

"Yes, Carl. Starting fresh… from scratch."

My mind wandered. I so wished that things had worked out in Trinidad. An acute sadness swelled within me.

Carl noted the change in my demeanour, "Frank, you seem sad. How can I help you my young friend?"

Carl and I were making a connection. I wondered why Mr. Winchester and I could establish no connection. But, I had to stay focused. Carl was reaching out to me. But… I felt my mind slipping… wandering…wondering. I had to shake myself out of the past. My present was here in front of me right now. I had Dianne and Trevor… and another one on the way. I took to silently reprimanding myself, *Frank Maraj, stop wallowing. Get a grip on yourself.*

I looked Carl directly in the eye, "Carl, thank you ever so much. There is a way you can help me. Let me drive for you once more… part-time."

Carl bristled slightly upon hearing the word *part-time* again, "Part-time?" he repeated.

"Yes, Carl, part-time. If you agree, you must know that you would be doing me a huge favour."

For a moment, Carl was silent. He had another sip of coffee. I did likewise.

"So, Frank, you are really serious about this teaching thing?"

"Yes, Carl, as a substitute teacher I have to be available to accept a position each day…"

"And if you don't get called, you want me to call you…"

"Exactly, Carl… or, I could call you each day that I do not get a call from the board. I would have to keep myself available until around eight-thirty each morning… This is how you can help me to become a teacher."

"All right Frank, I get it. So you want to be a teacher…"

"More than anything Carl… and yet if I am to drive a taxi

I want to drive for you, Carl, only you… no one else… Roach's Taxi, that's all."

"Then Frank, welcome aboard once more."

"Carl, thank you."

Carl's words, *welcome aboard*, meant the world to me.

"Do you have an address and phone number here in the city yet, Frank? I'll be needing a number to call you… especially on week-ends."

"Not yet, Carl. I still need to find a place to live."

"You don't have accommodations Frank? I know of a program that can help people in your situation get assisted housing. Are you familiar with that government program? It bases your rent payments on your income. Have you heard of it?"

"No."

"Then come with me to the office. I have information for you. It's on file."

# 13

# A Promising Phone Call

Carl and I returned to his office in a much better mood than when we had left. Turning to Margret, he greeted her playfully, "Hello, Margaret. Why are you looking so serious?"

She stared at him, looked at me, and, deciding to ignore both of us, continued on with her work.

Carl retrieved the phone number from somewhere in his office. Handing it to me, he urged me to make the call right away. Left alone in his office, I made the call.

A Mr. Abraham answered my call and invited me to come and see him later that same day at 4 o'clock. His final words led me to believe that I might be accommodated, "Mr. Maraj, have faith. I understand your situation and I am sure we can help you out."

When I came out of the office, I noted that Carl was just quietly sitting… waiting.

"Well, Frank, what's the good word?"

"Good news. I have an appointment with Mr. Abraham this afternoon. He thinks he can help. How about that?"

"Make sure you know where you are going. You are a cabbie you know. Just keep in touch."

Upon returning to his office Carl turned up his radio – perhaps a bit too much for Margaret's liking. She chided, "Frank, what did you put in that coffee you gave to Carl? Look at him. I can hardly believe the change in him. Lately he has been so glum and gloomy – even depressing."

"I can't believe that I had anything to do with that, Margaret. All I know for sure is that I am very happy. You will be seeing me soon. I'll be back here driving a Roach's cab. Is cab number seven still up and running?"

# 14

# Rental... It's Doable

When we left Ottawa, we did so as minimalists. Everything we owned, including our young son, Trevor, was packed into that small, red, four-cylinder Plymouth Cricket.

Now, thanks to Ms. Jillian, we had our own apartment which was equipped with two essentials: a fridge and a stove. Other than that, we had no other amenities—no table and chairs for the kitchen, no furniture for the living room, no crib for the baby, no bed for us. This, thanks to Carl, was about to change.

In addition to hiring me, Carl had performed one more act of kindness and generosity. He seemed to be able to intuit that my financial situation was indeed dire and before I left his office to attend to my appointment with Mr. Abraham, he pressed an envelope into my hands, "Frank, I know that things are pretty tough for you right now. I want you to have this to get you started."

I began to protest, "Carl, you have done more than enough already. You are willing to take me on. And I am certain that between that and some supply work, we will be okay."

"Frank, you now have a family. And you are starting fresh. I know that you came here with very little. Please, let me help."

I remembered saying no to two of my much beloved professors when they had reached out to help. I wanted to say no again... but I realized that that was just my pride talking. I had to think beyond myself to my family.

With great humility I accepted the envelope. With its contents, we were able to scour the want ads and furnish our apartment with the necessities of life.

I am ever so grateful to Carl for this generosity.

*** 

When Diana first saw the apartment, she was impressed with its spaciousness. She was also worried; she was worried about paying the rent as I had not yet begun to work when we moved in, "Frank, how are we ever going to afford the rent for this place?"

I happily shared with her the fact that we did not have to pay rent just yet.

She did not understand.

I explained, "We are staying in a government sponsored housing program. These apartments are called low rental units."

"Low rental?"

"Yes. We pay a portion of what we earn. The rent is geared to our income."

She seemed relieved (as was I when I first learned about it).

I had much to be thankful for; I had Diana and Trevor and a most comfortable apartment. And… Trevor's playmate will be due in a few short months from now. (It was already October and the baby was due in early January.) Already I had some shifts driving taxi.

I eagerly awaited my first assignment as a substitute teacher. I was qualified to teach in either elementary or secondary schools. Perhaps too, I was feeling somewhat optimistic about the fact that I had several years of experience in Trinidad at both the boys' and the girls' schools. I was hopeful that that would give me confidence to tackle teaching in Canada.

I was both excited and nervous as I anticipated my very first teaching assignment as a qualified teacher. I had reason to be optimistic for the occasions during which I did my practice teaching were received quite favourably.

I recalled with some satisfaction my very first experience in a Canadian classroom when I was an undergrad student. I had been invited to be a guest speaker in a Grade 5 class at a Catholic school. That singular experience, however, may have set me up for some unrealistic expectations.

# 15

# Failure Looms

I do not recall whether the story I am to recount is my very first experience as a substitute teacher. It certainly claimed my earliest attention. The dispatcher on the phone directed me to an elementary school. I was both nervous and excited.

After checking in at the office I was given the details of the assignment. I was substituting in a grade seven class located on the second floor. While I was scanning my assignment one of the secretaries asked, "Mr. Maraj, are you acquainted with the concept of the open classroom?"

My blank stare gave her her answer.

Her next comment, "Good luck," was said without so much as the slightest hint of a smile and aroused in me a certain measure of foreboding.

Rising from behind her desk she then offered, "Mr. Maraj, I will show you the way."

The school had two levels. The secretary walked me to the stairs leading to the upper floor. There she stopped, gave final directions to the classroom and once again said, good luck. People said good luck all the time when one is embarking on a new venture. These words were usually spoken with a smile and with the unspoken assurance that everything would be fine. Again, there was no smile and no hint of assurance in her words. I had the feeling that these words were not being spoken out of politeness; I felt, that she felt that I would indeed need a considerable measure of luck in order to survive my day. My sense of unease increased considerably.

My heart beat faster; my legs became heavy. The simple act of climbing became an Olympic event, an event for which I felt that I had not had sufficient training.

The closer I came to the classroom, the greater my apprehension. Students of all shapes and sizes were fluttering up and down the stairway, flinging both words and the occasional school supply, at one another. They were completely oblivious to my presence. My identity as an adult in the building was inconsequential to any of their actions.

I walked into my assigned room; I could not believe what I saw.

First, I noted that there were no walls separating what appeared to be three distinct classes. My room was in the centre of the three areas. There appeared to be an adult in each of the other two sections. I assumed that they were the teachers. The students in my area were carrying on loud conversations with students from both the right and the left sides. Paper kites and notebooks alike found their wings in that open space.

*How on earth does one begin to command the attention amid such lawlessness?* I wondered in silence. *But,* I reasoned, *classes had not officially started; the bell had not yet rung. Perhaps this was the way students released their excess energy. Once the bell rang, and the opening exercises commenced, certainly the students would settle.*

The bell rang.

Nothing changed.

The students, en mass, totally ignored the bell.

A new fleet of planes buzzed overhead.

The misguided antics not only continued after the bell but accelerated in some quarters.

The teacher on my left was handing out seat work in spite of the fact that few were in their seats. The teacher on my right attempted, unsuccessfully, to get the attention of her students.

My confidence all but disappeared.

I had to do something. "Class, excuse me, please… I began rather hesitantly."

Then a paper airplane came flying in my direction.

I ducked.

The students laughed.

This gentle approach was not working.

Raising my voice slightly, I spoke with a little more authority, "Class, may I have your attention?"

One student hollered out the word, *Sure* as he threw a piece of chalk toward me.

Nothing had prepared me for this type of behaviour. Nothing in my background and certainly nothing in the teachers' college classroom management course had prepared me for this.

To be fair to the students, however, I must be clear that no one was engaged in any behaviours that would be considered dangerous. Their conduct was simply chaotic – a free for all.

Then, seemingly from out of nowhere, a new presence emerged. Before I could clarify in my own mind what was happening, the woman positioned herself in front of the class and boomed in a manner closely resembling the air of a sergeant-major, the command *SHUT UP!*

Following her command, an air of change blew across the room, silencing the entire floor. I, too, was silenced. As this sergeant-major edged towards me she directed, "Now, take control."

Then she promptly disappeared.

Once more I reached out to the students.

"Students, my name is…"

Before I could finish, one student yelled, "He has a name. Hey, guys, this teacher has a name!"

Laughter filled the room. Awkward embarrassment consumed me. It was an embarrassment not unlike that which had befallen me in Trinidad on my very first day as a teacher. I recalled that even then I had to momentarily ignore the behaviour while I fought to find a way to gain their attention.

I knew I had to change my approach. But, I could not do it in this climate of freedom.

I don't know what thoughts entered the minds of those students as I excused myself from the room. Did they think that they had won? Did they think that they had scared me off?

I don't think that I gave them much time to ponder the question, for within moments I had returned, armed with a plan and a new resolve. Emboldened in spirit, I re-entered the classroom. The students, once again, were flying free with their perceived victory. There was no point in using my voice. I marched to the back of the class and picked up the books of one of the students. I then signaled for him to come to the front of the room with me. I did the same thing with another student, this time a female student. Slightly dazed, these two complied. I led these two students from the classroom out into the hall. The class quieted momentarily. Still not using any words, I motioned for the rest of the class to follow suit. Initially, only a few filed out into the hall, but within minutes all of the rest, eventually followed suit, reluctant, but curious.

I marched them to an empty classroom. (When I had first left the class, it was to determine if there was an alternate place that I might be able to take my students. As fortune would have it, one class was away of a field trip for the entire day and I was given permission to use the space.) I entered the empty room first, directing the students to their respective seats.

Some students were still quietly chatting. Most were curious and silent. I was encouraged.

I had most of their attention; my next move had to garner *all* of their attention.

*What was it to be? What did I know about more than they knew?* The answer became obvious. The answer of course, was Trinidad.

I went to the blackboard and drew a large scale but very coarse likeness of Trinidad. Of course, no one knew what it was at the time.

My creation gained their attention and prompted their comments.

"What's that? It's weird!"

"You are right, young man, absolutely right."

"Right about what?"

"Right about my creation, right about my artistry."

"You are an artist?"

"In a way I am an artist."

"But, that drawing is really no art."

"Students, that drawing is supposed to be a map of Trinidad."

As they stared, I continued, "I believe I am the only human being that could misrepresent Trinidad that badly…"

"Trinidad?" echoed one student.

Then I explained to the students that I was from Trinidad and that Trinidad was my home. "We have some traditions in Trinidad; traditions that you might find a little different. I will share one with you today."

I stood in front the students, and respectfully said, "I am Mr. Maraj. Good morning, students."

They were quiet; I went to the board and wrote my name: Mr. Maraj.

Once more, I said, "Students, good morning."

Pointing to my name and then motioning encouragingly to them, some of them got it.

A barely audible *Good morning, Mr. Maraj,* was returned to me.

What the effort lacked in volume was more than compensated for by the total quiet in the room. I felt that I had made a breakthrough. I felt that at that very moment, my life as a teacher, had taken root.

I thanked them for their courtesy in making this transplanted foreigner feel welcome in a Canadian school.

Next, I told them that their teacher had left them an assignment. They did not wish to start the assignment; they wanted to know more about Trinidad, and they wanted to know more about me.

I wanted nothing more than to give in to their request, but my first duty was to their teacher. I proposed a compromise, "Students, I would love to talk about Trinidad. First, you must do your work for a while. Your teacher would be pleased, you would be pleased and I would be acting responsibly. Now let's get started."

And, these students, who, only moments ago, seemed uncivil and unreachable, worked with diligence and respect. I was pleased.

The rest of the day continued without incident.

Even after all these years, I remember these students and the unique initiation into my teaching career here in Canada.

# 16

# Not another Car Transaction!

I was the not so proud owner of a red four-cylinder Cricket. It had served us well in our move from Ottawa to Thunder Bay, but I could no longer afford the payments. I was making plans to sell our faithful possession.

One day while visiting with our beloved friend, Professor Cornell d'Echert, conversation shifted from the philosophical to the pragmatic. I explained that I was about to sell my car. He wanted to know more details about the car. As I recounted the salient facts, he immediately became excited and exclaimed, "My boy, do I have a home for your car!"

"What home, Professor?"

"My home, of course."

"You want to buy my car?"

"Of course. It is a lovely car. It is exactly what we need. I like everything about it."

"But, Professor, you are so… tall, and my car is so small."

"Nonsense, Frank. It will do just fine."

"Professor, you have to try out the car, first. You must see if it is a good fit for you."

"Really Frank, you worry too much, it will be just fine."

"I insist."

"Alright, just to please you."

He opened the front passenger side door, grabbed the bar underneath the seat and moved the seat all the way back to its furthest extreme and climbed in.

I could not believe that his *seven foot* figure would fit inside this *tiny* car. The name of the car itself, Cricket, implied *tiny* and his wanting it for himself, completely defied any logic... I could not believe that he was remotely considering the possibility of buying the car from us. He not only sat, he nestled. To put me at ease he said, "There! This is most comfortable. See, I was right. Consider this car sold. Now, are you ready to accept my car on trade?"

For a moment I was startled.

Professor owned a grey Rambler. I had not yet recovered from my last Rambler experience. Never would I have thought of even considering another Rambler... But this was *Professor... my* professor.

I summoned up my bravest face and announced, "Professor, you have just solved my problem. Not only have I sold my car, but I also now have a car to replace it."

"Frank believe me, this car has been very faithful. She will do just fine. I am sure of it."

"Thanks, Professor."

"Now my boy, we have to arrive at a price for your car. How much do I owe you?"

I did not know what to think or say. This was my former teacher and now friend. How does one talk about money with a dear friend? Before I could come up with an amount, Professor made an offer. The offer was more than fair. It was generous... too generous. I did not feel right in accepting such an offer. I protested, "Professor, this is more than fair. It's too much!"

Professor would have none of my protestations. "Stop acting as though I did you a favour," he countered.

"Yes, Professor."

I made no further protests. But, in my heart, I knew that this was Professor's way of looking out for us.

I should have been completely satisfied. I had a car – free and clear.

But my mind was still uneasy about this particular car – my new, old Rambler?

Was it an oldie but goodie as Professor had suggested?

Or was it just an oldie?

Time would soon be the revealer.

# 17

# The Family Grows

That fall of 1973 brought a measure of good luck. I was re-establishing myself in Thunder Bay, we had a decent place to live, and I was finding work both as a substitute teacher and cab driver.

The year 1974 started began with another form of luck.

It was early morning, January 3rd. Before I was ready to be roused from sleep, Diana gently nudged me and announced, "Frank, it's time. We have to go to the hospital now."

I stared at her through the eyes of drugged sleep. "Are you sure? Can't I sleep just a little longer?"

She urged, "Frank, it is real. At my last visit, the doctor said not to waste any time getting there. You have to take me… Hurry."

While Diana awakened Trevor, I hurriedly dressed and headed out to the Rambler. It was minus thirty degrees Fahrenheit. The coldest day we had had this winter.

Trusting that nothing would go wrong on such an important day, I inserted the key, pumped up the gas and pressed down on the accelerator. Upon turning the key, I was met with a distinct protest. The more I coaxed, the more the car groaned.

Diana and Trevor were dressed and ready to get into the car. Unfortunately the car would not accommodate us that day. I called our friends who had agreed to look after Trevor while Diana was in the hospital, explaining our plight, and hoping that the husband would be able to pick us up. This was not to be. Elaine explained that Von had already left for work. But she was up and ready to receive Trevor; she urged me to bring Trevor as soon as I could.

I rushed into the parking lot hoping to prevail on someone, *anyone*.

It was only 6:30 in the morning. Very few people were on the road. Precious minutes passed. I flagged down the only car I saw as it was pulling out of the parking lot. It was a Mini-Austin, a quarter of the size of a regular car. I flagged down the driver and pleaded, "Please can you help? My wife is in labour and my car won't start. Please, can you take us to the Port Arthur General Hospital?"

The driver was a student on his way to class at Confederation College. He commented that he would be late if he were to drive all the way over to the Port Arthur side and then back to Con College.

Not wanting to inconvenience him, I urged, "You hurry to class. Thank you anyway."

I turned away and scouted the parking lot for another prospect. There was none.

The young man in the Mini-Austin pulled up beside me, "Buddy, hurry. I will take you."

Trevor and I climbed into the back of the car. Diana sat in the front and held on. It took twenty minutes to get to the hospital. Diana absorbed every bump in the road without complaint. I could see her stiffen in silence with each contraction. When we reached the hospital, our good Samaritan declined any reimbursement; not even so much as the cost of a simple cup of coffee. As he left us he simply said, "Man, good luck."

He asked one final question before he left, "What are you hoping for?"

"A healthy baby girl," was my gleeful response.

"Good luck to both you and your family. I wish you all the best."

After settling Diana in the labour room, I determined, based on our twenty-seven hour marathon labour with Trevor, that I had several hours before I would be required to be back at the hospital. I had to get Trevor to the babysitter and I had to get my Rambler looked at. I do not know how any one of these things was accomplished as everything is a hazy memory. I know that I made it back to our apartment during which time I received a call to supply teach for that day. This, I had to decline. But, they understood the situation.

It was mid-morning when I finally managed to return to the hospital. I went straight to the maternity ward to see Diana. When I found her, I prepared myself mentally for the long day ahead. I asked Diana how she was doing. She answered my question with a question of her own, "Frank, are you ready to see your daughter?"

I did not comprehend what she was saying. It made no sense. How could she know the baby was a girl? That could not be determined until after the baby was born.

I repeated the words in my head... *Until after the baby was born.*

"Are you saying that you've already had the baby? How could that be? Trevor took so long..."

"Are you ready?" she repeated.

I was more than ready.

Thus did our Lee-Anne make a quick entry into our world. Fortune smiled on us that day.

Ever since that day, I was never once without work as a teacher. The only day that I was not called to teach was the day we attended the wedding of a very good friend of ours, Friday, May 10th, 1974.

That good fortune was soon to be tested.

# 18

# Go Home: Go Back Home...

Thunder Bay was treating me well. Every morning I received a call from either the elementary or the secondary school to teach. The calls from the elementary schools invariably came ten minutes before any call from the secondary panel. I always accepted the first call even though it came at a substantial financial cost. Back in the seventies, a supply teacher was paid twenty-seven dollars and fifty cents per day at the elementary level and thirty-seven dollars and fifty cents at the secondary level. While slightly saddened by this discrepancy in pay, nevertheless, I was most grateful to be working as a teacher. On the weekends, I drove taxi for Carl. Between the two sets of work, we survived.

One Saturday evening, while driving taxi, I was dispatched to the airport. I was to pick up a Mr. Vinchenski. Upon arriving at the airport I stepped from the car and perused the crowd for my fare. People came and went. No one approached my cab. I decided to go inside the airport for a closer look. First, I donned my taxi hat and ensured that my badge was obvious. There could be no mistake: I was a Roach's cab driver. Within seconds, a voice hailed, "Hey, you!"

The voice was decidedly unfriendly but it caused me to turn in its direction. The voice belonged to a man of Napoleonic stature. This forty-year old, five foot nothing of a man further blustered, "Yeh, you. I'm talking to you. Grab my bags."

"Sorry, Sir, but I am already booked."

"You're booked? Well, I booked a taxi."

"I am looking for a Mr. Vinchenski."

"That's me! Grab my bags! Everybody knows me. Where are all the regular drivers?"

I hesitated, but only briefly; his gruff tone worried me and his message implied that because I was not recognizable as one of the regulars that I was somehow substandard. I tried to convince myself that I was simply overreacting. Giving him the benefit of the doubt, I responded with a polite but decidedly cool, "Certainly, Sir."

He headed outside toward the cab leaving me to tackle his cumbersome luggage alone. They were exceedingly heavy and I wondered what could be in them. As I reached the car and just as I was about to hoist them into the trunk, the man cautioned, "Be very careful with those bags. They are valuable."

My mouth spoke before my brain had time to think, "What are you transporting, gold?"

My innocent, if not playful, comment was met with a surly retort, "None of your business, Cabbie. Now drive."

If I did not know my place before, I certainly knew it now, "Yes, Sir."

I climbed into the driver's seat. He was already perched in the back. I awaited his instruction. None came. I proceeded out of the airport. As we approached the first set of lights, I was forced to ask, "Where to, Sir?"

Still, he did not respond. I made my own decision. I turned to go to the Port Arthur side of town. While doing this, I glanced at him in the rear view mirror to gauge his reaction to my decision. He did not take kindly to me looking at him in the mirror and wasted no time in telling me so.

"What are you looking at, Cabbie?"

When I did not respond, he followed up with a completely different question. "Cabbie, where are you from?"

"Port Arthur."

"Don't be smart with me. I know that. What *country* did you come from?"

I had been asked that question many times before, but never quite like this. This question was usually asked by people genuinely wanting to know me. His question, however, had a sinister quality about it that made me not want to answer.

"Hey Cabbie, I asked you a question? Do you not understand English?"

Whether I responded or not, I felt that this man was trouble.

I continued to drive, choosing to remain focused on the traffic ahead. After considering my options for a moment, and not wanting to appear to have an attitude, I decided to satisfy his curiosity, if indeed that is what it was. But, before I could get the words out, he attacked with more commands, "Cabbie, answer my bloody question right now!"

Ordinarily, this would have pushed me further into stubborn quietness, but, perhaps because I was already thinking of answering, I blurted out the singular word, "Trinidad!"

"Trinidad? Where the hell is Trinidad? In Africa?"

Not knowing how to respond, again I remained quiet.

He proceeded to answer his own question, "No! No! You are not from Africa. Apes come from Africa. You come from that Turban Clan. Yes, your people wear turbans. Then as if he was really seeing me for just the first time, he asked, Cabbie, where is your turban?"

How does one respond to such rudeness? With rudeness? With sarcasm? With silence?

The manner in which the question was framed was both insensitive and offensive. Had it been couched in a tone and language that bespoke genuine inquiry, it would have invited a response.

If I were to set him straight by stating that I did not belong to that particular sect might be viewed as a slight against that group of people. To begin to answer that question one would need time and energy. Not only that, one would also need a receptive and open mind at the other end of the transaction.

This man possessed neither of those qualities.

I therefore again chose to say nothing.

My silence engendered in him open hostility.

"Cabbie, I really don't care where you come from. I have news for you. We don't want you and your people... you know... your turban clan, here in our country!"

I was frozen in time. The twin arrows of alienation and rejection hit hard. My soul's demolition was imminent. I had not yet recovered from my rupture from Trinidad. Was Canada renouncing me as well?

"Go home," he commanded. "Go back home!"

*Go home?* I asked myself. *Just where was home? Trinidad does not want me... And now it seems that Canada, too, was rejecting me.*

I was *countryless*.

Perhaps I had heard incorrectly. I turned my head and asked for clarification, "Mister, what did you just say?"

"Look where you're going! Don't be looking back. I don't want to see your *BLACK* face. You people infest our cities with your taxis. You take away our jobs. We don't need your kind – especially here in Thunder

Bay. We don't have *blackies* as cabbies. Now go pack and go back home to whatever country you came from. We are sick of you and your kind!"

Every ounce of strength I possessed was straining against the temptation to lift his short excuse of a man from the vehicle and toss him head first onto the hard pavement.

Surely science will one day find a way to rearrange our brain cells and remove the prejudice and bigotry that inhabits our world. My hands, however, wanted to perform that task right that minute.

I found it hard not to hate.

The harsh reality of his open hatred toward me forged its way into my soul. I was tempted to give in to the black abyss of despair. I was sinking dangerously low. A sane thought boosted my resolve. I would not allow this bully to dictate my actions. My soul belonged to me and I would not let his warped and leprous bigotry jaundice my principles.

Thus, I began my subterfuge.

Pretending to hear an unusual sound coming from the engine, I calmly slowed down the car and pulled ever so gently off to the shoulder all the while muttering, "Not again!"

Opening the hood, I began to examine the engine. (Anyone who knows me would immediately laugh at this because I can barely distinguish the battery from the engine.) I was playing for time; time to cool down; time to combat my natural inclination to react physically to this severely deformed excuse for a man.

Bending over the engine, I was still struggling to find a way to right the situation.

Before I knew it, Mr. Vinchenski was standing at my side mocking me, "What is this stunt? What are you playing at? Let's go, Cabbie, you're going to make me late!"

I closed the hood, walked to the rear of the car and held the back door open. As he climbed in, he could still be heard to be muttering to himself about stunts and lateness.

I paid him no mind as I returned to the wheel. I forced myself to concentrate. Not wanting to hear another single complaint spew from his mouth, I turned the radio on. Immediately, the cab was inundated with the blast of a raucous guitar.

From the back seat, Mr. Vinchenski thundered, "Turn that blasted noise off! What's wrong with you? Don't you have an appreciation for real music – that noise is fit for monkeys – not humans. So, monkey, you like monkey music…"

I was tempted to retaliate verbally, "Sir, I prefer apes, and you Sir, are the perfect specimen of an ape!"

I refrained from uttering those words. I did so not from any misplaced affection for the fare in my cab, but rather because I did not wish to insult the ape population by putting him in their category.

I pulled the car off to the shoulder of the road once more and cautioned, "Sir, please take care not to distract me any further. In a few moments, I will have you safely at your destination. Thank you."

Then I took a deep breath and cautioned myself, *Frankie – try to steady yourself. Take no heed of this man's vileness. Drive carefully.*

He continued to unleash his arsenal of bigotry; I turned up the volume on the radio. Finally, he was silenced.

We reached the hotel. He preceded me out of the cab. As he made his way toward the lobby, I followed, struggling with his bulging luggage. A book threatened to burst from one of the suitcases. I pushed it back in, but not before I glimpsed the title.

Once inside the lobby, Vinchenski asked the cost of the fare.

After I told him, he reached into his pocket and produced the required amount down to the exact penny, all the while complaining, "Highway robbery. Bloody highway robbery!"

Reluctantly, he parted with the money.

But, before he could disappear, I called him back by name, "Mr. Vinchenski…"

He turned.

"I have something for you."

He approached.

I extended my hand and returned all of his money to him and said, "Your debt has already been paid."

"What do you mean? Who paid the fare?"

"A cabbie."

"A cabbie?" He glanced around to see if another cab driver had suddenly appeared. "Which cabbie?"

"Me."

I left him, dumbstruck.

As I walked away I saw again in my mind the name of the book that fell from his bag. The title read: *The New Testament*.

And I wondered, *To what was he a testament?*

# 19

# You Did Not Get the Job…

Sadness seized me, and at the moment I could not understand the fullness of my sadness. I was perplexed. A feeling closely akin to despair and anguish took hold of my soul. Then, ever so slowly, I came to realize that my agony was not the result of this singular interaction with Mr. Vinchenski. He, himself, could very well have been the brother of a certain Mr. Soulless.

Mr. Soulless was the principal of a high school in a small town – Black River of Northern Ontario. Some miles away from Black River was an elementary school, a wonderful country school, where I had had the pleasure of being a substitute teacher for a couple of weeks. Imagine if you would, that a student of the senior grade, on my very first day, asked, "Mr. Maraj, how do you like your coffee?"

I was in heaven now; I had been met at the entrance of the school and escorted to the staff room by two students. One student explained, "Our teacher told us to take care of you. He says you really enjoy coffee. Do you Mr. Maraj?"

"Oh, yes, I do."

"Then tell me, how do you take your coffee?"

"With milk and a generous helping of sugar."

"So be it, Mr. Maraj. Welcome to our school."

That scene became a daily ritual. How responsive and attentive were all the students, not just the senior class. What a treasure it was to be part of this school.

I did not mind the travel from Black River to this school. Diana, Trevor and Lee-Anne were all comfortable at the residence we secured in Black River. Together we would stroll and explore the town. It was modestly equipped with its own hospital, a couple of stores and modest supermarkets. It had everything we would need for everyday living. Diana particularly favoured the park! I had my eyes set on a house – quite a large home – that was for sale. The asking price was almost $13,000. I reasoned that the price was almost double the annual salary of a beginning teacher. All I needed was a job in Black River. I began dreaming of that house, and the job I did not have… then opportunity knocked.

The head of the English Department was about to advertise for an English teacher. He had spoken to a close friend of his, whom I had met previously while attending university. He had been, coincidentally, one of my associate teachers at one of the high schools in Thunder Bay. Cameron spoke of me to his friend Levi. It did not take very long for Levi to seek me out. After our initial conversation Levi asked, "How would you feel, Frank, about teaching here at our high school in Black River? It's just a small town, and you may not…"

"I love Black River. And I would absolutely love to teach here."

"You do?"

"Yes, definitely," I enthused. "This town is ideal for my family."

"I understand you have two young children."

"Yes! And it is because of that that I welcome a chance to start my career here at Black River. It has all the everyday amenities, hospital, supermarkets, and other small shops. Yes, I would very much like to settle here."

"Frank, I cannot wait to introduce you to my principal. I will be in touch."

Of course Levi arranged for the interview. Thus a panel of three interviewed me for the position. I left the interview with a good feeling. All three members of the panel shook my hand and assured me that I would soon be hearing from them.

Once outside the interview room, one of the interviewers commented in private, "Frank, you were so good. You are my choice. I can't wait for you to be part of our school."

Encouraged by this, I dared to hope.

As we walked away from the school, talk drifted to the topic of soccer. One of the men suggested that I could be instrumental in advancing the school's soccer program. All this positive energy further raised my hopes.

That evening the two men paid me a visit at home. I opened the door with a smile when I saw who it was. After an awkward moment of silence when neither of them said anything, my smile faded. They looked fragile and sad.

I knew the news could not be good but I had to hear it for myself. Looking dejectedly at Diana and me, they broke the news, "Frank you did not get the job."

They both looked so sad. I was shocked by the announcement. I had but one question, "Can you tell me the reason I did not succeed at the interview?"

They looked at me and shook their heads; they looked somewhat ashamed.

"You know gentlemen, I am disappointed that I did not get the job. But please help me to understand where my weakness is so I can prepare…"

"Frank, it has nothing to do with you having a weakness or fault. It has everything to do with our principal having preconceived notions about you based on the colour of your skin and your cultural heritage."

"You can fight this, Frank. This is outright prejudice."

This incident came on the heel of my encounter with Mr. Vinchenski. Both Mr. Vinchenski and Mr. Soulless (the name I gave to the principal) could very well be connected to Trinidad's Mr. Winchester.

*How was I to survive this tidal wave of rejection? I needed a plan; I vowed to rise above all this…*

## 20

# A Routine Visit Or?

Now, more than ever, my focus was on securing work as a teacher. To further that end, I determined to once again visit the Board of Education in Thunder Bay. The Superintendent kindly consented to see me for a few minutes. After inquiring about job availability in the city, the Superintendent informed me that prospects were virtually nil for any full-time positions. He did, however, hold out hope for supply work on a temporary basis if I were to remain in the area during the upcoming school year.

Somewhat disappointed, I left the office. I knew that Carl would do all he could to keep me employed throughout the summer driving taxi. Somehow, I knew that we would manage. We always did.

As I stepped outside, I heard someone call me by name. As I turned, I saw the familiar frame of Professor Cornell d'Echert.

After reminding me of our upcoming dinner engagement, he took his leave. But, not before indicating that he had a special couple that he wanted me to meet and who had also been invited to dinner that same evening.

I simply had no idea how fate was once again poised to intervene in my life at Professor's!

# 21

# The Tide Begins to Turn

The following Saturday, at Professor's home, Diana and I were introduced to Professor's old friends, Vincent and Barb. There was an instant connection. Vincent seemed somehow familiar. I could not quite place him in my memory.

Madame announced that Vincent had news of interest to me.

Somewhat quizzical, I turned to look at Vincent.

Vincent revealed that he was the principal of a small elementary school in White River and had just posted a job vacancy at the Board office. He then asked me if I would be interested in working at his school.

"Interested? I would be delighted."

"We can take care of the formalities in due course. I just want to know that you accept the job. You can forward your resume and application later. Of course the Board will have to convene and approve… but that is a mere formality. Congratulations, Frank and welcome aboard."

We all raised our glasses and made a toast to commemorate the event.

Some time later, Vincent asked if I remembered him from a class that we shared a number of years ago. I told him that he did indeed look familiar but I had trouble placing him.

He then reminded me that we had both taken a class with Mr. Westover during our final year of our Bachelor of Education degree.

He said that he remembered a question that I had posed of a fellow student after an amazing presentation by that student. In his mind, the memory was unforgettable. He then asked if I knew what had become of the friend since graduation.

I told him that the last I heard, he had planned on returning to Trinidad.

We rejoined the others.

***

Vincent revived a memory about my old friend, Habbie, that I am now prompted to share.

## 22

# Habbie Jassram: His Moment...

Habbie Jassram stood at the podium poised to speak. His cough signaled his readiness to begin.

Immediately our class quieted.

Dr. Westover, himself, had expressed a keen interest in Habbie's chosen topic: *Concerning Trinidad: A Close Examination.*

The class, too, showed a heightened interest in the topic. Habbie commenced, "Dr. Westover, fellow classmates. I wish to introduce to you, Trinidad. In particular, I direct your attention to the current educational system and the attending difficulties that such a system of education foster."

All eyes were glued on Habbie. Habbie proceeded to describe the British system of education that had been instituted, and has prevailed in Trinidad for decades. Of particular interest was his passionate and reasoned argument that the current British standard of English should no longer be the preferred medium for examinations. Habbie hammered home his point with the power of personal conviction. "These examinations are written by the British, for Trinidad. At first glance, one would not question this practice. It has existed this way for all of our lives and it seems so normal. But," Habbie asserted, "this practice is not normal; and, furthermore, it is not right. It presents and represents a marked injustice to all Trinidadians."

He paused. All eyes were glued on Habbie. Clearly inspired, he continued with utmost confidence. "The children in Trinidad do not speak standard British English. Their conversational language is an adaptation of English—a Trinidadian patois; this patois is the common language of Trinidad; it is the language that unites us and reaffirms our sense of community. I am standing here before you to argue and assert that it is this Trinidadian patois that should be recognized and acclaimed as normal for both the spoken and written language of Trinidad. The imposition of the British standard of written and spoken English inflicts undue hardship on our children. Requiring them to learn a way of speaking that is foreign to their normal discourse, is not only senseless but also useless for the majority of Trinidadians. Do you take my point?"

He paused once more and took a sip of water. I looked around. Everyone was nodding in agreement. Habbie then exposed further problems that he deemed threatened the educational and emotional welfare of children from a poor county like Trinidad.

Finally, Habbie moved away from the podium and positioned himself at the very center of the classroom. From there he made his final passionate appeal. "It is nearly impossible for the student in the classroom to contend with a foreign language that is imposed by a foreign administration. It is my contention that if such a system is allowed to continue in Trinidad, that system will forever be regressive, rather than progressive."

He continued, "I do not reject the British, summarily. Let the British continue to set examinations for the British employing British Standard English. It is time for Trinidad take a step forward and institute Trinidadian Patois as its indigenous language. It is not just the **right** thing to do; more so it is the *just* thing to do."

Before Habbie could utter his final *thank you*, he was inundated with thunderous applause from the entire class. Dr. Westover was delighted with the presentation and Habbie's reception by the class.

I, too, was in awe of my fellow countryman and friend. Furthermore, I was in awe of his ability to stand before a class of English speaking Canadians and make such an impassioned speech. I loved that he was being received so well by our classmates. Indeed, Habbie enjoyed his moment.

When the room quieted and the applause faded, Dr. Westover invited the class to ask questions of Mr. Jassram and his stated position.

The class was still in the throes of excitement. Habbie's passionate plea seemed to have won over the entire class. No one was poised to argue against Habbie's premise. No one ventured to volunteer to step forward.

Once more Dr. Westover encouraged, "Surely, someone might have a question for our Man of the Moment."

Still, no one volunteered. Dr. Westover then scanned the class searching for a volunteer. When his eyes reached me, he stopped.

My mind recoiled at the thought of being singled out.

*Please,* I silently begged, *Not me, Sir. Please do not make me...*

Dr. Westover turned his head a little; it was his signature move. It meant that I had been chosen to advance a question to Habbie. It was obligatory. There was no way around it.

A moment ago I witnessed a maestro perform in front his audience. He was rewarded with a resounding applause. Who was I now to raise a question, and not just any question, but a question of depth and substance? I knew that that was the expectation.

All eyes were on me now. Dr. Westover was energized and encouraged, "Mr. Maraj, you have a question for Mr. Jassram. Please stand so we may all hear your question."

I honestly did not have a question. I was still under the spell of Habbie's ardent presentation. *That's it; his very presentation is the key...*I had the germ of an idea; now I just had to figure out a way to frame the question.

I rose. "Mr. Jassram," I began, "thank you for an extremely engaging presentation."

Another great round of applause was freely offered.

I waited.

Somewhat reluctantly, I began. I started off by apologizing for what I was about to do. But there was no other way to make my point. "Oh, I wish I did not have to do this but here goes..."

My voice trailed a little as I searched for just the right words. I spoke directly and pointedly to Habbie. "Habbie, had you been schooled in the very dialect you so convincingly advocated, might you have received this wonderful affirmation that you deservedly warranted from this very audience? In short, Mr. Jassram, would anyone here, other than myself, have been able to understand an argument conducted solely in the colloquial language of Trinidad? The very fact that you used the Queen's English to argue against the Queen's English would be seen by some to be a contradiction."

An excited Dr. Westover paced the floor with glee; the class was buzzing. Renewed energy spurred the class further; students were engaged. Dr. Westover spoke, "Ladies and gentlemen, I realize you have more to discuss. That being so, let us allow Mr. Jassram to respond to his own colleague and fellow countryman."

The class was attentive and expectant. Professor encouraged Habbie, "Mr. Jassram, I do believe you would wish to respond to Mr. Maraj's question. The floor is still yours."

Habbie did not appear disconcerted. In fact he charmed the class with this retort, "Well, Dr. Weston, Frank is my friend… or, shall I say…" He paused, then continued, "Frank Maraj **was** my friend."

The class exploded with laughter and a light banter ensued. This was followed by a hearty applause much to the delight of all.

Of course, when class was dismissed, Habbie chided me for upstaging him. Yet, truth be told, he did receive a very favourable mark on his presentation. When I saw the mark that he received, I presumed to ask, "Habbie, did I help you receive such an excellent mark?"

Habbie, always searching for the edge, responded with a glint in his eye, "Frank, my so called friend, I might have received an even higher grade had you not raised your insidious question."

His huge grin confirmed that we were still friends and that he was still the star in our class.

***

In retrospect, I now understood more completely Vincent's complete fascination with Habbie.

But here we were, still at the professor's home. It was time for Diana and me to leave.

As we travelled the short distance to our apartment, we were in awe of the night's events and truly we felt blessed.

# 23

# At Last... Stability

When Vincent invited me to visit White River in the late spring of 1975, I was most happy to oblige.

The town itself was very small, situated between two modestly populated towns, Marathon to the west and Wawa to the southeast. I was attracted both to the area and to the school.

Vincent seemed pleased that I responded favourably to the new surroundings. We conducted the business end of our venture very quickly and easily. After putting my signature to various documents, Vincent assured me that essentially, I was hired. All that remained was for the Board to give its final assent; this, Vincent assured, was but a formality.

"Frank, consider that you are hired. Welcome aboard!"

Life held great promise and I was looking forward to our next adventure in White River.

I did not know it then, but on my next venture into White River I would be on a mission to undo all that had just transpired.

# PART TWO

## Finding A Path

# 24

# A Much Needed Resolution

My mind was at peace; for the immediate future at least, our lives were secure.

One single long distance telephone call from the Fort Frances Board of Education changed all that.

Miraculously, I was offered a *second* teaching opportunity; this time it was for a Grade 7 class in Devlin, Ontario. Recognizing immediately that Devlin was less than an hour away from Rainy River, my heart leapt.

So many thoughts rushed through my mind all at once; I was speechless.

How was I to deal with this situation? I wanted to accept the offer on the spot. It made more sense from a practical point of view than the assignment in White River. I knew that Diana would want to be nearer to her parents. Our year in Ottawa, so far away from any family, had been extremely rough on her.

But… I had given my word to Vincent.

Something more than a mere technicality stood between me and this second offer—my word.

I had given my word.

My word meant everything.

The voice on the other end of the phone was still awaiting a response. "Mr. Maraj, did you hear me? We would like to offer you the position."

"I would love to be able to accept…" I began.

"Great!" was the response at the other end of the phone.

"But I find that at the moment I am not completely free to accept, as I have given my verbal assent to another principal in another board."

"A verbal agreement is binding and you have to be prepared to honour it."

"I understand. Can you give me some time to resolve the situation before giving you my final answer?

After agreeing to my terms, we concluded our conversation.

I was leaving within the next two days to go to Toronto for six weeks of summer school. I had planned on stopping in White River en route to finalize my plans there with the board.

My focus had now shifted and I was now hoping to be released from my promise.

I worried about initiating the process. My mind swirled with various possibilities.

I arrived at Vincent's office in White River late in the afternoon. Vincent received me with great enthusiasm.

I was unable to return the same spirit to him.

Sensing that something was amiss, he asked if all was well at home with Diana and the children. After assuring him that they were well I began the painful process of explaining the content of my most recent conversation with the Fort Frances Board.

Vincent remained silent throughout the telling.

I felt guilty asking to be released from my promise.

I apologized.

"Frank, you say that you are sorry, yet you want to be released. I am most disappointed. Disappointed in the situation and disappointed in you. I was so looking forward to having you become part of our staff."

"I am truly sorry."

"Frank, you gave me *your word*!"

Then… silence.

His words reverberated in my ears. Yes, I had given my word. Had I not lived by my word? Was not my word the one thing that I could count on? How many times have I asserted, and with great conviction, that my word is my bond? Was I really now considering breaking my own vow?

A clarity of mind befell me and I knew at once what I had to do. I knew what was right and I had been wrong to seek to change it.

"Vincent, I too am ashamed of my conduct. May I ask that you set aside that which I have told you regarding the offer at Fort Frances? That was wrong. I never should have even considered the offer."

Vincent was still angry; he had every right to be so.

Summoning what remaining dignity I had, I donned my most optimistic countenance and once more addressed him, "Vincent, I am happy and grateful for the chance to have a life here. I do look forward to a future here. My family would grow to love it here. Diana's parents would still come to visit. Is the job still available?"

My question was met with silence. Vincent was still immersed in deep thought. His initial anger seemed to have given way to a more pensive frame of mind.

"Is that what is at the root of all this, Frank? Family?"

The transformation in Vincent's spirit was every bit as tangible as the one which had taken place in me. I recognized the impossible position that I had left him in and I sought hard to make amends. Vincent, on the other hand, was undergoing a change that I was as yet unaware. Anger had given way to an illumination I did not fully fathom, as yet. He continued,

"Frank, tell me why you want to teach for the Fort Frances Board?"

"Vincent, I do not have any of my own family living close by me. Some live in New York, and the rest are still in Trinidad. Diana's parents still live in Rainy River. Fort Frances is but an hour away from them. And White River..." my voice trailed.

Vincent completed my thought, "And White River is so very far away from Diana's parents?"

"Yes."

"And Diana wishes to live close to her family?"

"Yes."

"And you Frank? Do you wish to live near your in-laws?"

"That is what I was thinking. But that is a mistake. I am no longer thinking like that. My place is here at this school. This is right."

Vincent interjected, "There is something else that is right!"

"And what is that?"

"Frank, you do want to live close to your wife's family. You have two children and you want them to know their grandparents. Family means so much to you and your own family is so far away... Frank, I have had time to rethink my initial response and I now see that the only reason you wanted to be excused from our contract is because you feel the need to be close to family. Right?"

I nodded.

"That is a good thing."

Then he paused, once more buried in thought. I was thinking how fortunate I was to have this job. I convinced myself that my family and I could make this work, and I found myself able to smile. Vincent's next words caught me completely off guard.

"Mr. Maraj, I release you from your contract." He continued, "Yes, Frank, you heard me correctly. I am releasing you from your contract, subject of course to the Board's approval, which, I can assure you will not be a problem. We'll call an emergency meeting and deal with the issue immediately."

Still, I could not believe what I was hearing.

Vincent smiled and offered this final assurance, "Frank, you are free to accept the offer. You are doing the right thing; you have a duty to your family. God rejoices when we seek to honour families. Perhaps I was being more expedient than thoughtful regarding your situation initially. When I realized that I was the one making the mistake in my thinking I knew that I had to make it right by you. I apologize for making you feel guilty about your request."

"Vincent, please, you honour me with your apology."

"Then, in honour you go. I am pleased that I met you. I wish you well."

"Vincent, I am indebted to you."

As we said our goodbyes, I marvelled at the understanding of this young principal.

Since that day, our paths have never again crossed, but my mind does often reflect on his consideration.

With the lightest of hearts, I resumed my journey to Toronto.

***

Reflection

And now, one of the great ironies of my life seems to be that despite all my formal planning and applications for various teaching positions, jobs for which I had not officially applied were being offered to me.

I am left to wonder if indeed there is a great Force that intervenes on our behalf when our lives seem to be moving out of our control.

# 25

# Smoking Dangerously

About two hundred miles outside of White River, I noticed a grey haze seeping ominously from under the hood of my Rambler.

I tried to assure myself that it was nothing, but, as the minutes progressed, the seeping became a billowing and I knew that I needed help.

I pulled into the first gas station that I happened upon and was informed that I was dangerously low on oil. The problem was easily addressed by the simple addition of several quarts of oil.

I resumed my journey.

I had not been driving too long when I noticed passing motorists waving at me. I waved back. Canadians are so friendly.

Soon, however, the waving turned into pointing and a whole host of drivers began honking their horns.

I looked behind me. I was being followed by a trail of smoke.

Minutes later, a second gas station attendant was selling me yet more quarts of oil. Along with the oil came this chastisement, "Man, you hardly have any oil. That is not just careless, it is downright stupid. I bet your engine is almost smoked! Man, drive any farther and you are asking for it."

In my mind, I felt that I had no choice but to continue on; I had to risk it. So, once again, I added more oil. After refueling, I again took to the highway.

I grew accustomed to the honking… and to the need to constantly add oil. Then, a police cruiser signaled for me to pull over.

After checking both my driver's licence and my insurance, the officer inquired, "Do you know why I pulled you over?"

"Yes, officer, I think I do; my car is smoking excessively and it is probably dangerous."

"That smoke is downright dangerous. Now, you don't strike me as crazy, are you just stupid or what?"

I went silent.

He continued, "I asked you if you were stupid. Answer me."

"I don't blame you, officer. Sorry!"

He pressed the point further. "Well, I'll have to write you up for dangerous driving. Come to think of it, you are pulling a stupid stunt. You could not be that stupid, could you?"

Hearing that word stupid used again and again by this officer challenged everything within me. *How can I reach this man? How do I get him to see that he must not use those words with me? I have fought too hard and too long to crawl out of that dark hole; to be suddenly kicked back into it would be far too damaging a process.*

"Officer?"

"Yes, and what now, Stupid?"

"Call me any names you want. Charge me all you want. Don't call me stupid. Anything but stupid."

The officer looked at me with a great deal of incredulity. Poised behind my wheel, I had no idea just what I would do if he had once again called me stupid. Fortunately, neither one of us had to find out.

After checking his cruiser once more, he again approached me in my car.

"So," he began, "you are coming all the way from Thunder Bay?"

"Yes, officer."

"Where are you headed?"

After explaining to him where I was going and for what purpose, he asked, "Do you know what is wrong with your car?"

"No, not really. All I know is that it needs a lot of oil; no, let me rephrase that; it drinks oil. I seem to need to stop at every gas station and buy more oil. And, the car still smokes. But, never mind my rambling… I am in your hands at the moment. Do what you must."

Then, the officer asked me to open the hood while he examined the engine; he then instructed me to start the car. I did not understand what he was doing, when he asked, "Hey, how come you are driving a Rambler? Don't you know that these cars are pure junk?"

I noted that he did not call me stupid for owning this piece of junk. I answered, "Officer, it is a long story about me and my relationship to Rambler cars. Just know that this car came into my possession out of an act of kindness by a very dear friend. I am grateful to have it. Please do not call it…"

"A piece of junk?" he finished. "Okay," he continued, "let me just say that this car is toast. Buddy, this car is history."

I noticed with no small measure of satisfaction that he was not referring to me as *Stupid* any more. I had been upgraded to *Buddy*.

"What am I to do?" I asked the officer.

"Well, I may have a thought or two on the subject. I will lead you to a garage not too far from here. The owner there will be able to look after you. He'll know what to do. Ready?"

Happy was I to follow.

The owner of the garage inspected the engine and conferred with the officer. From their dialogue I discerned that this particular car required a *specialty* oil… a very *costly* specialty oil. But, I reasoned, if it would help me to reach Toronto safely, it would be worth the price.

I paid the bill.

When I was ready to leave, I sought out the officer, first, to thank him for his direction, and second, to determine what my situation was with him.

When I asked the question, the officer looked confused, "Situation," he queried, "what situation?"

"You know, officer. What are the charges?"

"Charges, my friend? Today, none."

"Well, then, may I buy you a cup of coffee?"

"I'd have to charge you for attempting to bribe a police officer. Now, go on. Safe trip."

Something was still bothering me. I had to ask, "Officer, you seem to have had a change of heart. Why?"

"Does it matter, really?"

"It matters to me."

"You are a stranger passing through a strange land. You have had your share of troubles. You just needed a helping hand. For a moment I had forgotten that. That's all."

That was more than enough.

As he accepted my outstretched hand, I was reassured; civility still existed.

# 26

# Troubles in the Kitchen…

My course was going fairly well at the university but I needed a diversion from my studies and I decided to explore downtown Toronto. During my travels I discovered an East Indian restaurant. The restaurant's menu was displayed prominently in the window bordering the main street. The prices, together with the descriptors of the menu items, proved to be irresistible. With a heightened sense of anticipation, I entered the restaurant and seated myself near the back.

Soon the waitress appeared and took my order for stewed chicken. While I was waiting to be served, I relaxed and luxuriated in the moment. For a few brief minutes I allowed myself to absorb the nostalgia brought on by my new surroundings. I delighted in the familiar sights and smells of my culture. I was so very happy. No small part of my happiness derived from the high degree of anticipation that accompanied the knowledge that soon, very soon, I would have the supreme pleasure of tasting some East Indian cuisine. The coveted stew chicken could not be served too soon. Moments later, my reverie was soon rewarded; a platter of stew chicken soaked in a rich sauce was placed before me; a variety of vegetables and a generous serving of white rice were the perfect accompaniment which completed the picture. My eyes were the first to delight in the richness displayed before me. My olfactory sense wasted no time in catching up. The aroma was intoxicating. My taste buds were begging to be satisfied. I bowed to their dictates and placed a small serving of the sauce in my mouth.

Immediately my taste buds became energized. The taste was different from the Caribbean stew to which I had been accustomed; the taste, while unfamiliar, was most palatable and all my senses rejoiced at the invasion of these new and exotic spices.

I continued my foray into the rice and vegetable mix, and made a conscious decision to postpone the final adventure with the chicken. I loved my chicken and wanted to savour each morsel preferring not to interrupt my culinary experience with further rounds of vegetables and rice. I had consumed the greater portion of the rice and vegetable mix when my craving for the chicken proved irresistible. I could wait no longer. I had to have some of the chicken.

I picked up my knife, centered it over the chicken and made my first cut. Well, I attempted to make my first cut. The chicken would not yield to my advances. At first, I blamed myself for being a klutz with the utensils. Surely the fault lay within me. Perhaps I was not holding the knife at the right angle. But, wait, not only would the knife not cut the meat, but the fork would not pierce the skin. I exerted significantly more pressure but was unable to achieve any significant difference in the result. The chicken was impenetrable.

I feared that the strategy which I next sought to employ would be regarded as unconventional given the surroundings. But, such was my desire to taste the chicken that I resorted to a strategy that was as practical and basic as it was inelegant and pedestrian. I used my hands.

Yes, I succumbed to my basest instincts to win the coveted prize: a taste of the savoury chicken.

I was, however, denied.

To my great astonishment, I discovered that the meat was frozen!

I was in a quandary; I could not think clearly about what my next move should be. For the moment, I sat and waited, immobilized by indecision.

Eventually the waitress returned to my table and asked how I was enjoying my meal.

Not wanting to appear overly critical, I began with the positive. "The taste is outstanding," I began, "but, if I may say, I do have one slight problem."

"And what's that, Sir?"

"The chicken is still frozen."

"Oh, so sorry. I will take care of it right away." The server did not seem at all surprised by my revelation. It crossed my mind that perhaps this was not so unusual an occurrence.

Barely had she left when again she reappeared, steaming plate in hand.

"There you go, Sir, do enjoy your meal."

Once again I approached the chicken with great anticipation. Once again, I was disappointed; the chicken was only partially thawed; the centre was still frozen. I poked hesitantly at the lump on my plate.

My server found a moment to again make an inquiry regarding the state of my meal.

Not wishing to appear to be problematic and negative, I was tentative with my response. "It's a little better, but it still seems somewhat cold."

I was prepared to continue without any further fuss when the server offered, "Well, let me try once more. I do want you to have the full enjoyment of your meal."

As she picked up my plate a second time, the manager approached. My initial reaction upon seeing him was one of delight. We appeared to share the same heritage and I wanted to congratulate him for capturing the authentic taste in his dishes. As he approached, I noticed a distinct lack of sociability; the closer he came to me, the more apparent it became that he was annoyed. His first utterance confirmed my suspicions.

"You order chicken and you eat and now you complain. That trick won't work. You have to pay. Here is bill. Pay, and leave restaurant."

Not for one single moment had I thought of not paying the bill. The insulting words and manner of the manager made me reconsider my options. Not wanting to draw any further attention to myself, I made the decision to pay. Before I could reach for my wallet, this ignorant man once again opened his mouth and dished out a further serving of insults.

"You people full of scams. Your scam is to order and eat. Then you complain food is no good. This is good restaurant for decent people. Your scam will not work. You order, you pay! Now!"

I was not the only patron shocked and stunned by this latest outburst. It was a most awkward moment. I was both embarrassed and insulted by his accusations.

"You pay bill now – the whole bill – the full price. Then you leave!"

I had not said one word up until this point. The whole situation was most uncomfortable to say the least. I felt that I was being pushed to the limits of my own civility.

Without uttering a word, I rose, grabbed the bill and headed toward the cashier. My server tried to intervene. She suggested that perhaps I could pay half the bill since I did not have the full meal.

Upon hearing this, the manager again pounced, "Mind your own business. You have other tables. Go, clean tables. Leave him to me. I will deal with him." Then he pointed at me. "He… he wants free meal."

The whole situation now seemed beyond ridiculous. Things had escalated to such a degree and I just wanted the whole thing settled. But, I would not be bullied. The recommendation from my server that I pay half the bill seemed most reasonable.

I faced my accuser, "Sir, I will pay half the bill, is that acceptable?"

He did not even try to hide his exasperation. He yelled, "You pay full price you scammer! And you pay now!"

Obviously disgusted by the embarrassing display of the manager, some newly arrived patrons turned around and left.

The man would not be dissuaded from his position.

I contemplated my circumstance. And I thought to myself, *Frank, just pay the bill in full and be done with it. And leave. Chalk it up to a life experience.*

While I was thus engaged in thought, the manager stepped closer and threatened, "You pay bill or I phone the cops."

That did it.

I spun around from the register. My blood was boiling. I had been insulted for the last time. He wanted to involve the police. Bring it on. This was not the moment for me to give in to my own anger, however. He displayed quite enough for both of us. Thus, I restrained myself and, drawing on all my rational reserves, I calmly voiced this challenge, "Go ahead. Call the police."

I believe that my calm challenge served only to infuriate him further. Fuming, he made his way to the telephone located at the front of the restaurant in the coffee bar.

I decided to take up temporary residence on one of the stools in the coffee bar. Mistaking my movement for an attempt at flight, he ran toward me, arms flailing, and blustered, "You not leave. Cops on the way."

I pulled out a stool and sat quietly pondering. I tried to resist any thoughts that would lead me to give in to the bully.

Within minutes, a police car parked in front of the restaurant. As soon as the officer stepped inside restaurant, Mr. Manager became reenergized and redoubled his volume of complaint.

"There is the thief. He is sitting there. He ordered meal. He will not pay. He is a scammer. Arrest him."

The officer immediately advised, "Hold on Sir. Calm down. You have made some accusations against this man. I wish to understand what happened. I need you to go elsewhere while I take his statement. Then I will hear from you.

This strategy did not seem to sit well at all with the manager. The accusations continued, "But he is a scammer. His people are liars; and they…"

The officer then spoke more directly to my accuser; there was no hint of sympathy in his voice, "Sir, stop yelling, and come with me."

The two men moved off to one side at which time the officer attempted to tame my defamer.

When he returned to me he introduced himself as Officer Taylor. I then gave a full accounting of what transpired from my perspective. As Officer Taylor listened, he jotted down a few notes. When he left me, he sought out my server. After a brief conversation with her he rejoined the manager who, once again, required calming.

Leaving the manager, the officer approached me and advised, "It is clear that your meal was not fully cooked. It has been my experience that under such circumstances most establishments would not only *not* require you to pay for the meal, but would also be offering you a voucher for a discount on your next purchase. The server said that you have offered to pay half the bill. Is that so?"

"Absolutely."

"Are you sure you…"

"Officer, I consider it to be the right thing to do."

"That seems to be more than reasonable."

Officer Taylor recalled the manager. In the presence of the officer, I reasserted my offer to pay half the bill.

In the midst of the manager's vehement protestations, the officer stepped in and warned, "This customer owes you nothing. Not one penny. I have already told him this. I am now going to advise him to leave and not pay one single cent." He then turned to me and began, "Sir, you may leave any time…"

Before the officer could finish his sentence, the manager reconsidered, "Okay. Okay. I accept half."

With our business thus concluded, Officer Taylor struck up a more relaxed conversation and made general inquiries regarding my origins in Trinidad and my new life in Thunder Bay.

"Toronto seems to be filled with so much misunderstanding and volatility. You must find it so different from life in Thunder Bay. I wish you well for the rest of your stay here in our city."

I so appreciated his well wishes. As we walked towards the door my server came up to me and thanked me for the tip that I left her and apologized for all the trouble.

This must have caused Mr. Manager no end of annoyance, for he soon had her corralled and once again began to reprimand her publicly.

The officer left.

I was frozen in my tracks. As I stood by the cash register, I felt compelled to do or say something to counteract the manager's demeaning attitude.

The manager mistakenly assumed that I wished further assistance and approached me.

"What can I get you?"

"Not a thing. I wish to thank you for such a fine tasting meal… my compliments to your staff."

He must have thought that I was finished for he kept repeating *thank you, thank you.*

I continued, "I want to thank you also for having such a considerate server. She is so good at what she does. I saw how badly you treated her. She does not deserve to be treated so dismissively. But, then, that habit seems to come to you so naturally. It is very obvious that you consider yourself to be superior."

I am certain that he was not expecting such a comment, especially from one such as me.

His countenance turned grave.

But I was not yet finished; Pandora's Box had been opened and there was no way to stem the flow of my indignation.

"See how you have insulted me and denigrated my race. While it might be true that my kind might have misunderstandings with you, is that sufficient reason for you to treat *me* so badly? Did you not realize that I was willing to pay the full bill? But then, that was not the point.

You had to treat me as second class since I was not of *your* kind; I was not sprung from the mother country; no, I am a product of one of the bastard islands; I am counterfeit. To you I am nothing but garbage. Well, I have first class news for you, I am *not* second class."

I went on, "I'd like you to understand that both of us now live in Canada. It is a big country. It has room for us all. Bigotry has no place here; it needs to be checked at the border. Perhaps then, you can become a credit to *your* own kind."

I don't really know why I reacted so strongly. The fact that I needed to respond at all saddened me.

But, this was not the first time that I had had this type of encounter. At University I had a certain professor…

# 27

# Expulsion from "My" Own

Dr. R, my psychology professor at the Faculty of Education, was East Indian. I was excited to think that he and I were linked through our ancestry. I held a secret hope that he could be somewhat of a mentor, for we were loosely bonded through a historical context.

This hope was shattered in our first week of class when he declared, "The soul has no reality; it does not exist." He asserted further that the soul was a figment of the imagination—*a self-induced delusion.*

He concluded his dissertation with these final assertions, "For the purposes of this course, there is no soul; God does not exist. See me only if you can prove me wrong. Otherwise, do not seek to approach me on this matter."

The class sat in stunned silence. I do not think that any one of us had ever borne witness to such unapologetic anti-theist vocalizations.

As he delivered his statements I felt his eyes on me, challenging *my* very soul. This served to increase my discomfort and advance me further down the road into the heart of darkness. He must have known the powerful effect of his words.

My body shuddered at the boldness of his statements. I cannot describe what happened to my spirit when not a single one of us openly challenged his assertions.

As students, we discussed his view, but agreed that since his remarks had precluded any meaningful class discussion regarding *the soul* and *God*, it would be wise to respect his edict.

Over the following days and nights I obsessed over his words. In particular, I wondered why he felt it necessary to crush, from the outset, any view that was counter to his ideology.

I could not reconcile his conviction that there was no soul with the truth that I knew within me. But, I kept my beliefs to myself, never daring to challenge my professor openly. All the while, my heart cried out in silent protest, *Dr. R, I have a soul. It is mine. And I believe in an Eternal Presence. That Presence and I are connected. I do not know how. I do not know why. It is just… I believe.* These thoughts remained unvoiced.

There came a day, not too far into the semester when I needed to see Dr. R for clarification about one of his assignments. Upon arriving at his office, I noted that a line had begun to form. I was not alone in my quest. Quietly, I took my place in line behind the other students. As I waited, still others lined up behind me. The line moved along quite well and soon it was my turn. The professor came to the door and ushered the previous student out. I expected him to motion for me to come inside. He stunned me by directing two students standing together in line behind me to go ahead of me. I noted that both of these students were attractive young ladies. Without a word of explanation, he looked at me and commanded, "You… wait." I could see the contempt raging from his eyes. His voice confirmed what my heart had intuited all along. This man regarded me as an inferior being.

When next it was again my turn, I was ushered into the office without even the most minimal cordiality. Immediately, Dr. R launched a searing lecture. I was very uncomfortable; his words led me to believe that he might have thought that I was seeking, in some way, to be in his good graces. I had to ask myself, *Did Dr. R think that I had come to see him with the explicit intention of currying favour in order to be given a better grade?* That was never my intent; he had to be mistaken.

Next he taunted me by mocking what he assumed were my beliefs regarding God and the soul. He was only fifty percent correct but I did not stay long enough to communicate that to him. His utter disregard for me and others of "my kind" was palpable. His attitude was decidedly dismissive; I concluded that he was clearly unreachable and made the decision to leave his office.

Finally, when I was allowed to speak, I merely stated, "Sorry to have bothered you, Doctor," and left.

The next day, I had a chance encounter with one of the young ladies whom Dr. R had asked to take a place in line ahead of me. I casually asked her how her visit went with Dr. R. She had nothing but words of praise for this professor. Her comments left me wondering how we could have two so very different experiences. It made me wonder also why I had been singled out for a scolding.

That most uncomfortable encounter with Dr. R left me guarded in his presence. In class, I did my best to remain inconspicuous. I always completed assignments but never volunteered answers or queried instructions. The remainder of the semester passed without incident.

We all submitted our final assignments to Dr. R and anxiously awaited our results. All, save me, had their assignments marked and returned. To the best of my knowledge, all but me received a grade. My paper was never returned.

Some voice within me advised against making any inquiries regarding my missing assignment. I let the incident pass.

I wrote the final exam for the course. Once again every student but me received a grade. This time I made an appointment to discuss the matter with Dr. R. When I went to his office at the appointed time, Dr. R. was noticeably absent. I never did manage to speak with him. I had no idea as to my academic standing in his class. My final grade came to me by mail. I passed… just barely.

I began to wonder then, if somehow Dr. R regarded me as an *untouchable*? Did he ever really even *touch* my papers?

# 28

# The Rambler Ford Exchange

With my summer course in Toronto nearing completion, I began my search for a car.

I went to many dealerships and initiated many transactions. Without exception, every deal fell apart the moment I sought to include my Rambler as part of the trade. The moment I mentioned the make of my vehicle, the eyes of the salesmen would glaze over I was quickly shown to the exit.

Although I was fully aware that the Rambler was no bargaining chip, I was not ready to admit defeat; I determined to stay the course. My Rambler, poor excuse for a car as it was, was all I had.

One Ford dealership in Toronto seemed especially promising. Armed with the answers to a few questions, the salesman knew what type of vehicle I needed: a family sedan priced on the "affordable" side.

The salesman took me to a space well behind the main building.

Proudly and with great enthusiasm, the salesman raised his arm and announced with great certainty, "Here it is; the perfect family sedan; priced just right for the family just starting out in life."

Well, I do not know through what kind of lens he was looking, but that is not what I saw. What I saw was a cream coloured full-sized four door albatross. Advanced in years and its body bearing the early stages of rust, it appeared to be anything but perfect.

But, according to the salesman, the price was right; it was the "final" clearing out price.

When asked what I thought of the deal, I agreed that it was a reasonable price. When I inquired further about a payment plan, the salesman showed a willingness to accommodate the idea.

I knew it was time to bring my Rambler into the equation.

I announced, "I have a slight problem."

"Problem? What kind of problem? We can fix anything," the salesman assured.

From my past experiences, I knew enough not to skirt the issue. "I have a Rambler. I need it to be part of the deal."

Clearly, the salesman had not been expecting this. He fumbled for words.

"Would you accept it on trade?" I queried.

"I wish that I had known that before. Let's take a look at your car."

I handed him the keys to my car. When he turned it on, it started right away; the car was on its best behaviour. There was no sign of engine trouble.

"Any problems with this car?" he asked.

I chose to be perfectly blunt and stated, "Yes, it is drinking oil."

"Drinking oil?"

For a moment, he said nothing. Then, he responded, "Ok, we can handle that problem. We have a place for such cars. We can bury it; I mean... fix it. Your Rambler still looks good. But, it is a Rambler, right?"

"What's your final price – the exact figure?"

He pulled out his calculator. He punched in numbers, put his head to one side, nodded, asked himself a few inaudible questions, then sighed and finally announced his "steal of a deal".

Unfortunately for me this deal was still beyond my means.

Sadly, I announced, "Thank you. Sorry, I cannot afford it."

I turned and began to walk away.

Footsteps scurried after me. "What *can* you afford?"

"Truth be told, I do not think that I can afford *any* car right now. I do not wish to embarrass myself or insult you with any other offer. Thank you for your time, goodbye."

Once again I turned to walk away. Already I was preparing myself for the possibility that I might have to make other arrangements to return home.

The salesman rushed ahead of me, "Hold on a minute. Name your price. What can you afford?"

I wrote the price on a piece of paper that included my car on trade. He took the paper from me, motioned for me to wait, and then left.

Within minutes he reappeared; he was accompanied by an older gentleman.

After introducing me to his manager, the manager took the lead and explained, "Frank, my salesman is practically giving away this car. The price you offered is simply not enough. Now, if you could…"

"Thank you. I realize that I am not in a position to purchase a car at this point in time. Sorry, and thank you once again."

I had accepted my fate; I was not meant to have a car.

Before I could reach the exit, once again I heard someone call me back.

"Frank, wait up, please."

The manager urged me to return to the office. I did not see any point in any further talk; somehow he prevailed, and two hours later I held the keys to my "new" sedan.

# 29

# An Accounting Challenge

For the next few weeks, this sedan operated like a dream. It transported me back home to my wife and children without incident. It functioned beautifully during our move to our new accommodations in Emo. And, perhaps most importantly, it delivered me faithfully to and from work each day—a round trip distance approaching 24 miles.

Then, the nightmares began. I began experiencing difficulties with the car. I was saddened. I knew nothing about repairing cars. I knew next to nothing about diagnosing car problems. In Trinidad I counted on my family and friends to steer me in the right direction when it came to cars. Here, in the small village of Emo, I had not yet formed the strong bonds to guide me in this walk of life.

I took the car in to the local garage that I passed each day on my way to work. The manager, Raoul, a most agreeable and conscientious man, had been regularly servicing my car. He was able to diagnose the problem immediately: the car needed transmission repairs. He estimated the cost to be around two hundred dollars. This was close to one third of my monthly take home pay!

My mind raced back to the Ford dealership in Toronto... I had to wonder if the manager and the salesman knowingly sold me a defective vehicle. It hurt to think that I might have been deceived. Then again, I reasoned, these things did happen to vehicles and the men could be absolutely innocent. I dismissed the matter; dwelling on it served no purpose other than to drain me of my energy.

Not knowing if it was wise to invest the money in the repairs, I sought Raoul's advice. Already, I had run up a bill with him of about $200.00 for other repairs.

Raoul acknowledged that while the body of the car seemed to be failing, it was still a very good car. Everything else appeared to me in good shape. I bowed to his advice and agreed to the two hundred dollars repair bill. Now my bill totaled $400.00.

I worried about my mounting bill and expressed this concern to Raoul. His light-hearted banter immediately set me at ease. He teased, "I'm not worried Frank. I know where you live. And, I know where you work."

Raoul did an excellent job on the car and in no time at all I had full confidence in its mechanical abilities. Within the month I returned to the garage to make a payment on my account. As I handed him $200.00 to put on my account, I thanked him again not only for his superior workmanship but also for his much appreciated advice.

As Raoul took the cash from me he made an interesting although somewhat disturbing comment, "Just as I thought Mr. Maraj. You are a gentleman, even for a school teacher. You are a man of your word."

I was curious about his choice of words "even for a school teacher". I sensed that he had just taken a shot at the teaching profession in general and I wondered what had transpired in his life to cause him to make a comment like that.

Some weeks later I returned to the garage to make another deposit. This time I had $100.00 to advance on my debt. The bill was originally $400.00. I had already paid $200.00. The balance owing should be $200.00. Before paying the hundred dollars, I asked Raoul to check on my balance. Raoul pulled my account from his files. His brow immediately furrowed and his tone became serious, "Frank you need to make a sizeable payment. You have an outstanding balance of $600.00."

I was incredulous. Six hundred dollars? That was almost a month's salary! How could that be? Where had I miscalculated?

While I did not wish to dispute his calculation, I knew that something was not quite right with his figures. I therefore asked, in what I hoped was a most polite and non-accusatory tone, to see the file.

Raoul seemed surprised by my request, and, more than a little incensed. "You think I am wrong? Are you thinking I am cheating you?"

I hastened to assure him that that was never a concern, "No, no, Raoul! You would never do that. I am the one who likely is at fault. It is just that I am not remembering the account correctly. Will you help me...?

He showed me my file. The numbers were correct. *But, why was the bill showing a $600.00 balance? It I should be $200.00.* I could not understand the discrepancy in calculations.

Still registering confusion on my face, I handed the file back to Raoul.

"Satisfied, Frank?"

"Thanks, Raoul."

As I was about to hand over another $100.00 in payment a flash of discernment came to me and I asked to see the file once again. This time Raoul readily obliged.

As I scanned the account, I recognized the error immediately.

"Look. Right here, Raoul; here is the mistake. When I gave you the initial $200.00 payment, it was entered on the debit side rather than the credit side. This made the bill total $600.00. That is the error."

After checking the file himself, Raoul agreed, "You are right Frank. Sorry. Let me fix it right now."

He then reduced the $600.00 to $400.00, all the while apologizing to me, "So sorry, Frank. You are right. There, all is well. You just owe me $400.00."

"No, Raoul, I owe you only $200.00."

"What? Frank, how could that be? I just reduced your debt by $200.00. The bill is now $400.00."

It was Raoul who was now confused. He was unable to see the error in his logic.

I was determined to see this through, "Do me a favour. Will you?"

"What do you need?"

"Place in my hand $200.00."

"What?"

"Just humour me, please."

He placed the $200.00 in my hand.

"Would you agree that this is the same amount of money I advanced you a few weeks ago?"

"Yes."

"And how much did I owe at that time?"

"$400.00… Oops, you really only owed $200.00 after that payment was made. I see my error. What a mistake. Frank, I want to make it up to you. What can I do?"

Raoul was really down on himself for making such an error. I had to help him. I suggested that we invite our wives and go out for dinner the following weekend. Raoul loved the idea and insisted that we be his guests. Thus the matter was resolved easily. When the bill came, I must admit that I felt slightly guilty; after all, I had not lost a single penny.

The relationship that was forged between Raoul and me, as a result of all that confusion, endured for many years.

# 30

# Hunting for a Home

Having settled our car troubles, at least for the time being, hunting for a home became our top priority.

Cornerbrook School was just a mile or two off the main highway that passed through the little hamlet of Devlin. We looked at a few homes in Devlin and Fort Frances but could find nothing that was suitable for our growing family and within our limited financial means. About ten minutes west of Devlin was the small town of Emo. The main street businesses that serviced the vibrant population of eight hundred residents, bordered the river. The river afforded a rather unique expression for the town. We were smitten at once with the beauty and charm of this small community.

The people of Emo wasted no time in extending well wishes and friendship even though we were unknown to them. Drivers raised their hands in acknowledgement as they passed one another on the streets; this traditional courtesy was also bestowed upon us from the moment we arrived. This was one of the unforgettable attractions that drew our hearts to the community.

The first person to extend her services to us was the local celebrity named Ella. We always thought that her raspy voice and her weathered and humble look made her the perfect female counterpart for CBC TV personality, Howie Meeker. Having been a single parent before it became the norm, Ella knew how to get through the hard times. Talk about multi-tasking… it can be argued that Ella invented the concept. My wife remembers seeing Ella drive down one of the streets in Emo when she encountered her teen-aged son who was still living at home at the time. Ella was on her way to a home-care patient but she had bread/

buns baking in the oven and more waiting to go in. She hailed her son, and sent him back home to transfer the baked goods from the oven to the counter and put the next set in to be baked. Ella was a teacher, a nursemaid, a baker, a realtor, a pizza parlour operator, a community organizer, a mother and a friend. She was our Emo angel. It was Ella that you could count on during any emergency; if she could not fix the problem herself she could arrange for the appropriate assistance. If Ella knew that we were having company from out of town she would drop off a dozen of her famous "air buns" along with a baked dessert loaf. Every town should have its own "Ella".

But, I digress.

At the time, there were few places for rent or sale in Emo. Ella was our realtor contact. She showed us three homes. One lovely home with spacious and well cared for gardens, had an asking price of $26,000. While it was indeed beautiful, it was well beyond our price range. The second place she showed us was a rental property. The rent was around $220 a month. Since I was looking at a salary of around $650 per month, renting did not make much sense as we would be unable to put any money away for a down payment on a home. Furthermore, considering all the other expenses that come with having a family, we certainly would be challenged to just make ends meet at the end of every month. This financial reality would place us in an exacting position; we would have no room for emergencies, and we would certainly be hard pressed to save a dime. The prospect of owning a home would be out of the question.

The third house that she showed us was a modest three bedroom home not far from the downtown area. Ella knew the owners. (Ella knew everyone.) She also knew that the owners were very motivated to sell. The owner had thirteen children; none of whom lived in the community. We were delighted with both the inside and the outside of this quaint L-shaped house. It was just our size. We hastened to pursue ownership. Ella arranged a meeting with the owner.

After assuring her that we loved her home and were interested in buying it, we addressed the financial element.

The price she quoted seemed reasonable but I had yet to begin work and I had nothing in the way of collateral. I needed to speak with a banker. To this end, the owner agreed to allow me a couple of days to secure some financing.

I went to the bank the very next day to apply for a loan. I was informed that it would take a while for the loan to be processed and approved. I believe that the price of the house was more than twice that of my annual salary. The banker noted that it would be unwise to attempt to purchase a home that exceeded my gross annual income by two and half times. This house seemed to fall within those parameters. Then the officer pointed out further that I would need a down payment to purchase the house. I had no money to put toward the down payment.

I had few options.

I went back to the bank to ask for a personal loan.

"Frank, a personal loan? You have to show cause?"

"Cause, Mr. James? What does that mean?"

"You have to show that there is a good reason for such a loan."

"Oh, it is just that I will need certain things… basic things… to start life."

"Basic things, Frank?"

"Yes."

"You mean like furniture, beds, appliances, and the like?"

"Yes, that is correct."

"And how much would you need?"

"Two thousand dollars?"

"Well, Frank, you would have to have collateral; or you would have to have someone sign on your behalf."

"I have neither."

"Oh, then I am sorry; I'll have to decline the loan."

"Could you advance perhaps a thousand dollars?"

"No, not without collateral."

Hopes of acquiring our little home were fading quickly.

But, I had one last question for the banker. What, Sir, is the maximum you can advance without collateral?

"Nine hundred dollars."

"Then nine hundred dollars it is. Let's sign the papers."

When I walked out of the bank with the nine hundred dollars, I went directly to the Emo Municipal Office where I engaged the employee there to write up an offer to purchase agreement. I explained the terms of the agreement and had them outlined clearly in the document.

I hoped to have my home owner's loan approved within a three month period. Until that was accomplished I outlined how I would offer to pay three hundred dollars a month in rent for the first three months. If for some reason, the loan were not to be approved that total of nine hundred dollars would remain with the current home owner. If, however, the loan were to be approved, the nine hundred dollars would be credited toward the asking price of the home. The normal rent for a property such as the one I wished to purchase, would be around one hundred and fifty dollars. By offering the owner double that amount, I hoped to be seen as a credible and viable risk.

Now, all I had to do was present this extraordinary scenario to the owner and have it accepted by her.

We met the very next day.

"You have an offer for me Frank?"

"Yes, I do. But first let me start off by explaining that I am not in a position to make you the offer that both you and the house deserve; the bank would not approve."

"Frank, what is your offer?"

I wrote the amount on a piece of paper and showed it to her all the while explaining, "I know that it is lower than you were expecting. If you do not accept, I will understand."

"Frank, you can't add a little more…"

"I am sorry. I only wish I could. I do not wish you to feel insulted. Diana, let's go."

As we rose to leave, Mrs. H advised, "Don't leave."

We returned to our seats.

She continued, "Well, it is below what I had hoped for. But, here you are – a young family just starting off – and Diana, you do love it here…"

"Oh, yes, I love Emo. I grew up not far from here. Emo feels like home to me."

She seemed genuinely pleased with Diana's response, "Well, well, how about that. Tell you what; let's make *my* home *your* home."

We were so excited. But there was one more hurdle to cross. How was I to broach this next disappointment? This lady had been so accommodating. What would she think of my next proposal? Would this be the straw that broke the camel's back? Would she throw us out of her home?

I began, "Mrs. H, it will take about three months for the bank to approve my loan application."

She looked disappointed. I knew that she was ready to leave Emo within the week and that she had hoped that it would be much sooner.

"However, it isn't all bad news. I think that I have come up with a way that could be of benefit to both of us."

"What might that be?"

I pulled out an envelope containing the nine hundred dollars and explained, "Here, I am offering you $900.00 in advance to rent your home for three months. If I do not purchase the house in three months, I forfeit the entire $900.00. It is yours. Here I have all the conditions written up in a legal document from the municipal office."

I showed her the document. While scanning it, she commented, "You went through the trouble to get this document. You are very fair."

"Mrs. H, I hope you will still think I am a reasonable person when…"

"What do you mean Frank?"

"Mrs. H, I must ask you to help me once more. If the loan is approved and I do indeed purchase the house – and I am fully confident that that is what will happen– will you allow the $900.00, I am advancing you now as rent to be used as a down payment toward the agreed price?"

For a few minutes after I spoke she was quiet. I knew that she had every right and more than enough reason to turn me down.

"Frank, granted the offer is not what I expected. Yet, no one else has made a single offer and this house would just be sitting here empty anyway with me moving to Atikokan. It will be good to have someone, no, not just someone, you and Diana and your children, here. I accept your terms."

What a remarkable moment. This Mrs. H was giving us a chance to own our very own home. We were all so very pleased and excited.

As if to honour the faith that Mrs. H showed in us, the loan approval from the bank came through within a few short weeks. How pleased was Mrs. H. How grateful were we. We had purchased our first home in this wonderful community of Emo and through this purchase I was once again reminded that the bonds we share in this common humanity are never that far apart.

Mrs. H and our angel, Ella, were proof enough of that.

Finally, I could look toward the future and to my very first day as a fully employed, contract teacher in Canada.

# 31

# Half-Day

Excitement and trepidation were equal partners in my emotions the day I set out for my first day of school in Devlin. There was very little to distract me from my thoughts as I drove the short distance from Emo to Cornerbrook School. I had much on my mind that day, not the least of which was meeting my Canadian students for the very first time.

The small school seemed even smaller as my eyes took in the open acreage surrounding the school. My mind made a hasty comparison between this school and my first high school in Trinidad. There was a natural peace that engulfed one upon entering these country surroundings. In Trinidad, the flow of traffic was dense both with people and with cars. Adults and children alike shouted their greetings to one another; their voices underscored by the ever constant drone of vehicular traffic and the intermittent honking of horns. For just one moment I became nostalgic for the familiar bustle surrounding St. Charles School, and its staff and students; I could see them all so clearly, so fresh and vibrant were the images. For just a moment I wished that I were in Trinidad! Hurtful memories of my last venture to my island replaced the nostalgia, and I knew without question that this was my new reality. The Trinidad dream had been rudely erased.

One question, however, remained unanswered: *How prepared was I to deal with this new reality?*

The excitement that I felt as I entered the school was completely eclipsed by nervousness. When I entered my classroom, the Grade 7 classroom, a few curious but eager faces awaited. My *hello* was returned with a distant but nonetheless respectful echo. The bell rang, signaling the commencement of classes. Once the opening exercises were accomplished, I remained standing in front of the class *expecting* the students to come to some form of order. Such was not the case. They were totally engulfed in their own world of chatter. I did not seem to exist. I made a vain attempt to claim their attention, "Excuse me, students." This resulted in only a momentary lull in their conversation; immediately they withdrew their attention from me and continued their former pursuits.

I had honestly expected the students to heed my presence. When they didn't, I was caught for a moment in the twilight of indecision; my Trinidadian background in education, rich in tradition and respect, failed me. The moment was indeed an awkward one and I knew that I had to employ another strategy if I were to reclaim a measure of dignity for myself.

Thus I found myself standing before the class, raising my voice only slightly above the din of their conversations, and commanded, "Everyone, stand!"

Needless to say, there was no compliance. There was, however, a shared look of stunned surprise. When I realized that my command must have *sounded* as out of place and foreign as I must have *looked* to them, I revised my strategy. My next utterance contained a few more words and I was particularly careful to ensure that the word "please" held a prominent position in my request.

"Students, I have asked you to stand. Please stand up, everyone."

They quieted… then they stared.

All the while I stood there silent and expectant.

The students, while not compliant, were not defiant.

A most awkward few moments ensued while they processed the request. Then they began to stand—at first, just a few.

Still, I said nothing.

One student motioned for other nearby students to stand. Eventually all the students were on their feet… reluctant but acquiescent.

While it was far from the obedience that I had grown accustomed to in Trinidad, nevertheless, it *was* compliance, and I realized that I had achieved some measure of success.

Wanting to build on that moment I continued, "Thank you students. When we do this again, I will ask that you do so promptly and respectfully."

An unmistakable look of rebellion registered on the faces of some of the students and I felt the first cool wind of dissatisfaction blow through the classroom.

I continued, "My name is Mr. Maraj. I am your grade seven teacher. Thank you for obliging me. Please take you seats."

Immediately upon sitting they began chatting again; this time, the chatter was less exuberant but still far from contained. I had a sense that these students were not going to be reeled in easily! Therefore I decided to suspend further directions and set aside any expectations that I might have had.

I headed straight for the blackboard. I proceeded to draw a rough map of Trinidad. While I was thus engaged, I sensed that the students were taking advantage of my turned back to embark upon some adventurous behavior. I'm sure more than one piece of paper was tossed, but only one paper airplane landed near me. Picking it up, I walked around the classroom. My silence caught them off guard, and they too became silent.

"I have no idea how an airplane is able to stay up in the air. It is a human brain that conceived the idea that a plane could fly… not only fly but stay up in the air for hours at a time. Today, we take that for granted. Can you imagine what the human brain is capable of accomplishing? And who knows who among you, history will remember for your achievement?"

Encouraged by their quiet and reflective manner, I continued, "I am from Trinidad…"

"Hey, teacher, isn't that a place like Africa? They practise Voodoo there, right?"

"I believe that a few do."

"Do *you*?"

I did not respond.

It was at this moment that Kenny, a young lad with a confident air and a curious grin, chose to break a pencil.

When I looked at him, he was clever enough to appear apologetic, "Sorry, Sir – just a bad habit."

He fooled no one with his little drama but he stirred up the desired response: the class laughed.

It was obvious that Kenny was a familiar favourite in the class. I, on the other hand, was nothing more than the odd foreigner with strange ideas and foreign requests.

I knew that he could only assume power if I gave mine away. I would not be drawn into a standoff. I would surely lose the whole class. As it stood right now, he had the majority of the class on his side. In contrast, I stood lonely and alone.

For the moment I chose to ignore the taunting of this student in the hopes that I could capture the class in some small way. I went to the chalkboard and wrote the word Trinidad. I remained quiet. That generated some interest as some of the students began asking questions. The questions were diverse in nature and revealed a profound curiosity and intelligence. It was supposed to be an English class; it seemed that history and geography, and English were all occurring at the same time. For a moment, I felt like a teacher... stirring the minds of the youth. Their curiosities about Trinidad, its geography, its history, its everyday life – all these were part of the exchange of active minds at work. Trinidad became a much talked about subject. I was enjoying the moment, that is, until Kenny spoke, "Not interested in your stories about Trinidad."

His rude interruption generated nervous laughter from the rest of the class. Kenny's agenda was clear: he intended to disrupt and challenge me at every juncture; his final goal being that of my ultimate and utter humiliation.

The one thought that was uppermost in my mind was this, *Do not get drawn in! Do not react.*

I ignored Kenny and quietly directed the students to the day's reading assignment. I knew better than to issue a *no talking* edict. To do that would have been to invite open confrontation.

I recognized that some of the students were out to play me. Kenny was one of them; and he had amassed a stronghold of cohorts within the classroom.

This troubled me; I had a class of students unwilling to accept me as their teacher. Adding to this distress was the fact that this was my very first day as a full-time teacher in Canada. That realization was a difficult blow to my psyche.

That reality, however, would have to be dealt with tomorrow; I had a funeral to attend this afternoon.

# 32

# Sudden Sadness

A member of Diana's immediate family had passed away suddenly and unexpectedly. The funeral was scheduled for the day after Labour Day on September 4, 1974. This date was significant for two reasons. It marked the first day of my teaching career in Canada and was, coincidently, Diana's and my third wedding anniversary (the Canadian one).

I did not know anything about unions and contracts and never thought to ask how to handle the situation regarding the family funeral. I simply approached my principal and explained the extraordinary circumstances. He told me that I could have the afternoon off but he cautioned me to be sure to have lessons ready for the supply teacher.

I left the school mourning the loss of my class. I had to clear my head of those emotions so that I could properly attend to the funeral nearly an hour's drive away in Rainy River.

After dropping our two children off at a baby sitter's, Diana and I joined her family at the family home. From there, we made our way to the church.

I do not remember much about the actual funeral. I do remember the feelings of sadness and loss for the young widow and her three little children. The funeral gave me pause to reflect on the passing of my own father and grandmother.

Because I had to plan for the next day of classes, we could not stay long with the family.

After getting our children settled in bed for the night, I sat up late into the evening reflecting on the day's events. Diana thought that my pensiveness was due to the events surrounding the circumstances of the funeral. Only I knew the true source of my sadness: my first day at school had not met with success.

I *had* to find a way to win over my class.

# 33

# Classroom Antics

The next few days were difficult ones for me in that Grade 7 classroom.

I set out certain parameters that were important for my physical and psychological health in the school. To this end I asked the students to be mindful of three things: keep the classroom tidy, organize books and materials neatly, and ensure that the floor remain free of outside sand and mud.

While all the students listened to my words, some resisted active engagement. Not all acted in accordance with my expectations; in fact, a core group banded together in quiet resistance: a resistance choreographed by Kenny.

Before class one day, I observed Kenny deep in conversation with his fans. Immediately I was on my guard. As soon as the opening exercises were over, I began my customary instructions to the students reminding them of their classroom responsibilities regarding organization and cleanliness.

One of the girls spoke up effectively challenging all that I held dear. "Mr. Maraj, we are not city people. We have our own ways. It is natural to bring in dirt and sand into the classroom from the outside. That is our way. That is the way it is here. We are country folks and we like it this way."

Her comments, while neither rude nor rebellious, nevertheless put me in my place. I was the foreigner; I was the stranger; in this part of the country, I was the intruder. I knew that many of the students shared her point of view.

I searched for a way to respond that would allow both of us to maintain our dignity.

*Frank Maraj*

"Celine, thank you. You do present a valid point of view. I will think on it."

"You will, Mr. Maraj? You are not upset?"

"Of course not, Celine. You have expressed an honest opinion. Your views are worth consideration."

"Mr. Maraj, thanks."

"You are welcome, Celine."

Every eye and every ear was focused on our conversation, and for a few brief moments, the entire class was silent. I took advantage of the quiet to direct the students to the questions on the blackboard. Immediately they got down to work. I was encouraged by this small victory and felt the dawning of quiet optimism. Maybe I had made some small inroad.

My optimism was short lived; Kenny saw to that most dramatically.

Kenny *dropped* his pencil; it rolled across the aisle just far enough out of reach where he could not easily retrieve it. This would have been far too simple and not nearly enough fun.

Any other student would have simply stood up, taken the two steps to the pencil, bent over, and picked it up. That would have been the civilized and mature thing to do; but, Kenny was neither civilized nor mature.

Master Kenny and his desk were inextricably conjoined. When Kenny moved, the desk moved. Where Kenny went, the desk went. And right now, Kenny wanted to move to where the pencil was. The metal feet of the desk screeched as they rebelled against being dragged along the floor with Kenny as he attempted to retrieve the pen. Kenny was now the centre of attention. The students began to laugh openly at his antics encouraging further buffoonery. While attempting the retrieval, Kenny manufactured the classic fall. No, Kenny did not fall *out* of the desk. No, that would have been too tame and mundane. No, it took a real mastermind to create the next catastrophe. Both Kenny and the desk toppled over. The class was in stitches. Once again, Kenny ruled the ring.

I couldn't let this action go without acknowledgement. Over the din of the laughter I attempted to address him, "Kenny…"

Kenny's voice was appropriately contrite and oh, so innocent, "Yes, Mr. Maraj, is there a problem? I am so sorry. I was just trying to get my pencil. I did not mean to upset you. Are you upset, Mr. Maraj?"

Before I could answer, Kenny took the lead and cautioned the class, "Guys, you better get back to your work. We don't wish to upset Mr. Maraj. And I know you don't want me to get into trouble."

Then he turned his attention to me, "So sorry, Sir. I did not mean to interrupt your class. Am I in trouble, Sir? Did I do something wrong?" His words dripped with the sarcasm of the self-assured. I shivered at the arrogance of this young man: so practised at feigned politeness and so adept at the art of deception.

His grin suggested that he felt the victory belonged to him.

I approached him and reached out to help him right his desk addressing him quietly, "Kenny, you are not in trouble."

And to the class, I directed. "Shall we all resume our work?"

I moved around the classroom glancing at each student's work. Overall, they demonstrated that they were on task. When I came back to check on the state of Kenny's progress, it was apparent that he had done nothing. Before I could react in any way, Kenny took the lead affirming, "Mr. Maraj, I am trying hard. I don't want to disappoint you. I want to do a good job. You see my point, right, Mr. Maraj?"

Deliberately unresponsive, I chose to walk away from Kenny. He had set his trap and I was not going to be an unwitting victim.

It occurred to me that there were times when a student's attitude could be poisonous and it could threaten to infect the rest of the class. My experience told me that this was one of those times. A teacher had to find the right antidote before the infection could spread. There was no time to lose; I needed to find a solution quickly.

The bell signaled the end of class. The weekend was at hand.

I had to find a solution to contain, if not cure, the growing contamination.

# 34

# Searching

It was time to take a breath.

The last few weeks had been a whirlwind of activity. The tragedy and confusion surrounding the death of a family member, interwoven with the planning and anticipation of preparing for my first days of teaching, wrapped up with the never ending tasks associated with setting up a home, left us exhausted at the close of every day.

The day I was scheduled to meet the transport from Thunder Bay carrying all of our belongings, was the very day Diana received news of the family tragedy.

Diana was alone with our two children at the family home in Rainy River when she received the news. Knowing that family would be returning in the next day or two necessitated an upgrade in our move out of the Rainy River dwelling and into our Emo residence.

Our phone service in Emo was not due to be connected for a few more days so Diana enlisted the services of the local police to get the news to me from Rainy River.

I welcomed the weekend.

It was time to regroup and refresh.

Most of the immediate demands of setting up the home had been accomplished. Diana was absorbed with the care of the children. I decided to devote Saturday night to school matters; my physical need for sleep completely eclipsed any mental desire to devote to school endeavours; exhaustion claimed me and before I knew it, it was already Sunday morning.

Quietly I left the house taking care not to awaken Diana and the children. The sun was just beginning to come up and I took advantage of the morning stillness to attempt to quiet my spirit and clear my mind. Aimlessly I walked, down the main street of town beyond the hospital and across the tracks at the far end of the town. Not wanting to walk along the highway, I turned around and retraced my steps back to town. It was at that moment that I became fully appreciative of the true physical beauty of Emo. As I walked, the spectacular beauty of the gentle bend of the river delicately framing the southern border of the town, dictated that my eyes look up and out rather than down. The view was riveting. The waters were still and the mists of early morning were just beginning their lazy assent to the heavens, as if they too were reluctant to leave this earth.

I sat motionless on the bank of the river, a silent observer to a sacred moment in time. The trees were just beginning to make the transition from the brilliant green of summer to the rustic hues of fall. I was no stranger to such beauty. Witnessing Trinidad's early morning mists rising high above the tree line along the Northern Range often provided a welcome respite for my soul.

The memory filled me with longing and I was unable to resist the wave of melancholy that rushed to the shores of my aching soul… a soul struggling to reconcile the "what should have been" with the "what is".

It was but a few short months ago that I felt destined to be a lecturer of English and Philosophy at the University of the West Indies in my Trinidadian homeland. Now I am struggling to hold on to this Grade 7 class in the Canadian north. Why am I doing this? I want to be back home. The strength of that desire trumped any indignity that I may have suffered there… and therein lies my dilemma and the source of all my melancholy.

I am my own prisoner.

I am filled with self-pity.

I am broken!

Trinidad, you have spoiled me; you did not prepare me for this present reality.

Once again my eyes swept across this *foreign* landscape. My heart cried out, *There is beauty here too.* In that moment everything seemed so alive and magical. The beauty of the moment completely captivated me. The mist of sadness and confusion gave way to a rising peace.

As I reached into the past for an answer, a new clarity of mind dawned.

*Did I not encounter resistance in my very first class on my very first day at St. Charles Boys' School? Did I not employ a strategy to deal with it effectively? I took command.*

My path was now clear. I had clarity of purpose: I knew that I must rise from the well of self-pity into which I had allowed myself to fall; my focus had to be to strive toward the mountain of resolve. In short, I had to take command of my class. It was imperative that I have that sense of command at the core of my teaching.

I moved on from the park and headed home. People were beginning their Sunday routines and I had the whole day ahead of me to consolidate my resolve.

A train whistled through town as I drew close to home. The tracks were just behind the row of houses on the north side of our street. The train somehow seemed familiar and comforting; so too, its whistle.

I saw our little burgundy and white house with fresh eyes; it had never looked more inviting; this was our *home*. I knew then that I just needed to give us all the gift of time…

With time, all things are possible…

# 35

# A Calculated Move

It was Monday morning; I headed out for school before seven o'clock. I needed some quiet time to myself before the students arrived.

I greeted the students as they entered the classroom and immediately following the opening exercises, I dictated my list of expectations to the class. These were the non-negotiables; the most important one was the necessity for each student to work independently for a prescribed period of time. During this time, no one was allowed to speak unless permitted by the teacher.

I knew that to make such an expectation public meant that it had to be strictly enforced to ensure both compliance and consistency. After apologizing to the class for not giving the expectations earlier, I explained that I had hoped to discover the particular nuances of the class before announcing any plans. The time for announcing was now.

On the whole, the class listened quietly to my dictates without so much as a hint of protest. Then, one of the boys looked back at Kenny. Kenny was seated at the back of the class. Kenny seemed poised to launch a volley of facial contortions to break the mood of solemnity. Before he could draw too much attention to himself, I surprised everyone with this forceful and very direct reprimand, "Young man, when I am addressing you please pay attention. That is a courtesy that should be afforded to you, to your classmates, and to your teacher."

Kenny was disarmed by my unexpected reprimand. He resorted to rolling his eyes, the last bastion of dissent for the rebellious. Yes, Kenny was cornered and he was not happy.

From my desk I announced that the next assignment was to be completed individually. I waited with bated breath to see if Kenny and his cohorts would comply with my request.

Five minutes passed without incident. The class seemed intent on their work. Into the sixth minute, Kenny accidentally *fell off* his desk while trying to retrieve his "fallen" pen. As tiresome as these antics had become, they had to be dealt with immediately.

I stopped what I was doing. The class stopped their work. Everyone looked at Kenny. No one was laughing.

My voice was pointed as I commanded, "Kenny, come here to my desk, now! Everyone, back to your work... please."

I watched as everyone appeared to go back to their respective tasks.

To the class, I extended this courtesy, "Thank you, class."

I waited for Kenny's compliance. He had to leave his desk and come to me. I would not go to him. He appeared hesitant. I waited. I busied myself with *work* at my desk.

Finally, he began his approach... to be sure, it was a slow and careless effort, but, nonetheless, he was moving. It may have lacked the urgency and immediacy to which I had become accustomed in Trinidad, but *he* was coming *to me*.

When he was but two feet from my desk he stopped. I continued to appear to be absorbed in my marking. This must have made him uncomfortable. It must have appeared as though I was ignoring him. There was a hint of contempt bordering on disrespect in his voice when he announced, "I am here!"

"Sorry, Kenny."

I continued to mark.

Confusion marked his next comment, "Did you want to see me?"

"No, Kenny, I do not wish to see you. Go home! Bring your parents when next you come to my class! Go."

"But... but... why? What have I done?"

"Kenny, I have a name."

"Okay, Mr. Maraj, why must I go home? What have I done?"

"Kenny, it is not what you have done, it is what you have *not* done!"

Now he seemed truly perplexed and repeated, "Not done?"

"Yes! You have never been polite. You have never been civil. You have never been considerate. You are not ready to learn. Now go home... and bring your parents."

Even though I had spoken quietly, I believe that every single student in that class heard my voice.

Kenny's reprimand, while private, was nevertheless public. I did not yell for all to hear, yet all did hear.

Kenny was quiet – very quiet.

His once confident air gave way to confusion.

"Mr. Maraj, you are not sending me to the principal – you want me to go home."

"Yes, Kenny."

Kenny was speechless. He did not know which way to turn. Then he headed back to his desk. Before reaching it, he turned and walked back to my desk where he stood uncomfortably before me for several moments. Sensing that I was not about to acknowledge his presence, he pleaded, "Mr. Maraj, could you give me another chance?"

I barely looked up at him before returning to my own task.

I did not enjoy what I was doing to this student but it had to be done for all our sakes.

Kenny begged, "Mr. Maraj, I am asking you not to send me home. The last thing I need is to bring my parents here. I already …"

His voice trailed.

I rested my pen and paper and looked fully into Kenny's face saying, "Kenny I sense that you are in some kind of trouble. Yes?"

"Yes!"

"And, if I were to send you home you would be in even more trouble. Yes?"

"Yes."

"Then I won't send you home, Kenny. I will try to help you out of this situation."

"Thank you, Sir."

"You are welcome, Kenny. Now, may I ask you for your help."

"My help?"

"Yes, your help. You can definitely help me."

"How so, Mr. Maraj"

"Kenny, get rid of the stupid antics. You don't need it. I think you are smart…"

"What? Nobody thinks I am smart!"

"I think you are. Give me a chance to help you. I can."

"You can, Mr. Maraj?"

"I believe I can. And I want to believe in you. Would you give me a chance, Kenny?

"You got it, Mr. Maraj."

Then Kenny did something that I will never forget.

He reached out his hand to me.

I received his hand and as we shook, I detected the beginning of tears forming in his eyes. I wished now to rescue *him* so I asked, "Do you need to leave the room?"

He nodded. A look of appreciation now accompanied the tears.

As Kenny left the room, I turned my gaze to the class.

They looked at me, perhaps for the first time.

# 36

# High Hopes

That last encounter with Kenny seemed to have resulted in the establishment of a good measure of understanding and good will. The sounds of confusion and the echoes of disruption were silenced.

I was able to focus most of my attention on the lessons that needed to be covered.

History, in particular the first voyage of Columbus, was a lesson that I was most interested in exploring with the students. We had already read and discussed his first voyage. We had gleaned from our studies that despite mounting financial pressures and allegations that questioned his sanity, Columbus never wavered in in beliefs. Despite all efforts to discredit him personally, Columbus strove to prove that the long held belief that the earth was flat was incorrect. He struggled against great odds to assemble a crew that was willing to follow him into the unknown. At long last he was given a chance to chart his course in search of his dreams.

The class was now ready to begin a new activity segment based on the various readings we had just completed. Before introducing the activity I asked the students if they had any questions regarding Christopher Columbus.

Sarah raised her hand.

I nodded for her to speak.

"Mr. Maraj, earlier you asked us to come up with our own conclusions about Christopher Columbus. You wanted to know what we thought of Columbus and why."

"That's correct."

Then someone teased, "Go for it Sarah…"

And the class smiled when Sarah spoke. Sarah was admired; she was their voice.

"Students, let Sarah finish."

She continued, "Mr. Maraj, you did not tell us what you think. Why didn't you?"

The class picked up on this theme and began a gentle chant. The phrase, "We want to know," filled the room.

Above the chanting I admitted, "Sarah you are absolutely right. Students you are correct. I did not give you my personal opinion."

The chanting ceased.

Sarah pushed for an answer and innocently asked, "Mr. Maraj, do you have an opinion?"

The class found this question to be quite humourous and broke into a mild banter.

Sarah, feeling somewhat responsible for the distraction, apologized. Then she pressed, "Are you, Mr. Maraj, going to give us your opinion?"

And before I could respond, Kenny interjected. "See guys – just as I said – Sarah is going to be a lawyer. She's smart."

Sarah's red face revealed the depth of her embarrassment at the remarks but she sat down without making a fuss for she knew that the comment came from a place of pride. That is something that I will credit Kenny for: he was always ready to acknowledge the greatness in his peers.

To break the awkwardness of the moment I began to answer Sarah's question, "Class I am interested in *your* opinion – *your* thoughts. And, furthermore, I wish to know why you think that way. The *why* part of the answer is crucial. You must be able to defend your opinions about Columbus. In that way you are like lawyers. Once you have done that, then I will share my thoughts. Okay, everybody?"

Now that they felt assured that I was going to be as vested in the process as they were, there was consensus.

We moved on to part two of the assignment – the activity segment.

The students moved into groups of four; they were then instructed to pick one of the topics from the board and present it before the class. This created a distinct buzz of activity. Those who chose a topic first had exclusive rights to that topic. There would be one presenter only per topic. The pressure was on to choose quickly.

I noticed that Kenny and his group seemed to be disengaged and distracted. I approached them and asked if there was a particular problem with the assignment. A member of the group answered for Kenny, "Mr. Maraj, we are going to fail anyway, so why should we try. We always fail in these kinds of projects."

"What do you mean?"

Kenny took over the lead, "We are like the class losers. We know who we are – we are not the bright kids…"

Those words reverberated in my brain. The thoughts were all too familiar to my psyche. I had a sense of their pain and frustration. Had I not been there a thousand times myself? I ached for them. But, this was not the time to reveal my personal academic sores. There will be a time for such an acknowledgement; this was not the time. Right now these boys needed a new strategy. They needed a task that they could do and do well. From my earliest encounter with these boys I knew that they were very theatrical, especially Kenny. I therefore asked them if they would be willing to stage a scene.

Kenny asked, "What do you mean? Like act out a scene?"

"Yes. That is precisely what I mean."

"Well, what do we have to do?"

"Is there something… any idea… that you yourselves can come up with that deals with the voyage of Columbus?"

"Can we make it up and act it out for our presentation?"

"Absolutely."

The day for the presentations arrived and I was encouraged by the level of ability exhibited by all the students. But, there was no denying that it was Kenny and his mates who *stole the show*. While their presentation may not have been the best in terms of *academic* merit, it was nevertheless the most vibrant and engaging of all the presentations.

The scene that the group had chosen to reenact involved the very physical act of rowing against the waves. The presentation was rich in skill and energy. The boys rowed fiercely; in one moment, one of the crew members fell from the raft. All assisted with the regaining of control. Their props, while handmade, indicated a very high level of commitment to the cause. When the crew finally made it to shore, they fell exhausted to the ground.

The applause that greeted them at the conclusion of their presentation was thunderous. Their faces underwent a quiet transformation as the genuine and most generous applause continued. The whole class appeared to have been moved emotionally by the performance of these four young men.

When the clapping subsided it was my turn to address the class. They were very pleased with my observations regarding their substantial efforts and thrilled at the marks that their efforts produced.

I put forth one final challenge and asked each student to take a few minutes to write down what their various impressions were regarding Columbus. I wanted them to capture their thoughts in a paragraph.

They were about to begin that task when Sarah asked, "Mr. Maraj, would you let us give you the answers orally?"

The entire class implored me to agree.

I reflected for a moment then declared, "Deal."

Their responses were thoughtful and passionate; it was clear that they had given serious thought to the character of Columbus. The most startling response came from Kenny. His comment was both candid and revealing, "I really don't know if I admire Columbus. I think he was kinda nuts."

That ignited a host of fiery opposition. The objections to his comments were so fierce that I felt Kenny needed me to intervene on his behalf. "Class, we have to allow Kenny his point of view. We must let him finish making his argument."

Someone added, "Kenny, you better make sense!"

Kenny took the floor, "Columbus had smarts. He had beliefs; he had this dream to sail around the world. I get it. Why didn't he stay home, get married, and raise a family?"

Immediately the situation got hot. Kenny's question exploded a bomb. Emotions were flaring and Kenny was alone trying to put out the flames. Everyone was united against him.

Sarah's voice rose above the din and she directed her question to me. "Mr. Maraj, is Kenny right?"

At first, I was silent. I didn't want to speak until the class was composed. The class seemed to understand my silence and immediately quieted.

"I do not see Kenny as right…," I began.

The class became enlivened once again.

One voice boomed, "See Kenny, even Mr. Maraj thinks you are wrong…"

"Class. Let me finish. I wanted to say that Kenny is neither right nor wrong."

The class seemed stunned as they repeated the word, "*What?*" to one another.

I continued, "Kenny has a valid point of view."

"But Mr. Maraj, where would we be without Columbus? And…"

Then another student interjected a further challenging thought when he challenged, "Maybe we might have been better off without Columbus."

This thought had never before been raised in class. For a moment the class sat in quiet reflection. I was stunned by the comment. I had never ever considered the question. This student's declaration was not made with any sarcastic overtone. He was truly applying his critical thinking skills.

As I thanked the students for their insightful feedback, I wondered about that last comment. The students were really engaged in the topic. They had even managed to move me to ask some new questions.

"Students, I am so proud of you. Your views are fresh and valid. You posed some very interesting and original views. You made me think too. One of you raised a question about Columbus that I had never before heard expressed. I would like each of you to answer that question for yourselves."

Immediately the class became reflective. Kenny asked, "Are you going to make us write out our answers?"

I let my smile be my answer. I did not want to spoil the moment. I still had one more comment to make, "Students, you should be proud of yourselves and each other. What a class!"

I started to clap.

Then the students started to clap. They were applauding one other.

In that moment, the class bonded; that day they demonstrated that they were rooted together. I began to look forward to its continued growth and development.

I began to look forward to my future with these students.

Later on during recess while the rest of the students were outside, one of my students came by to see me. She confided, "Mr. Maraj, you are a funny teacher. But you are so serious all the time."

I did not quite know what to say.

I did not have to say anything, for she continued, "I didn't know whether I liked you when I first met you. You always looked too serious and too professional. But you are okay." As she moved away from the desk she left me with this one command, "Smile."

How could I do anything but?

Mission accomplished.

***

That last encounter reminded me of a conversation that my former principal at the girls' school in Trinidad had with me early on in my teaching career.

Our brief conversation took place privately in her office. After exchanging greetings, she came right to the point. "Mr. Boodram, the students have a complaint about you."

Her directness combined with her serious disposition filled my heart with trepidation. To bring further intensity to the moment, Sister rose from her desk and placed both hands in her front pockets. That stance spelled *serious*.

I could not help but wonder what I had done now?

She continued, "The students think you are far too serious. You don't smile."

"Sorry, Sister …"

"Mr. Boodram, don't be sorry. I approve. You are a dedicated and committed teacher. It is apparent to me that you enjoy your work. You really love teaching; it shows."

"Thank you, Sister."

"Yes, Mr. Boodram, don't change. Be serious for now. There will be time enough later for lightheartedness. Thank you again for your dedication to these students."

I have to admit that I was comfortable in my role being serious and dedicated. But, to attempt to be humorous and funny… I wouldn't know where to start. But, then, this young lady in Devlin thought that I was *funny*.

Maybe there is hope for me yet.

# 37

# A Sense of Optimism

Late in the day, a light snow fell; it was just enough to allow the tiny Devlin church to assume a distinct coziness and glisten under the hazy glow emanating from the light on the corner of the street. The close knit families from Devlin and the neighbouring communities all gathered there; the church was filled – even crowded; all were anxious to see their children perform.

It was the night of our school Christmas concert... my first in Canada.

Everone had been practising for weeks. Getting to this point had not been an easy journey for any of us; the students were not hesitant about vocalizing their reluctance to sing or recite poetry. They had had enough of that sort of thing for the past six or seven years. They wanted something different.

I took all of this into consideration before I announced that they would be performing a play.

"A play? What play?" they chorused.

"Your very own play."

"But we don't have a play."

"You will. You will write it and then you will perform it. Let's get started."

They had to determine the theme for the play. The class brainstormed various ideas. Agreeing on one theme was a major challenge, but soon that hurdle was overcome. One main stipulation was that each and every student had to be featured on stage in some way. Eventually, the skeleton play evolved into its final full draft. The students wrote dialogue, created scenes, crafted costumes and practised, practised, practised.

Since this was my first effort in Canada with such a production, I did not know how to relax about their performance; I am afraid that I was highly demanding and critical.

The primary and junior classes presented first. As usual, their performances were captivating and very entertaining. I hoped that our class would do equally well.

As the evening wore on, it was apparent that some of the students were becoming increasingly anxious. This anxiety manifested itself in various ways. For some it translated into pacing and rapid talking; for others it meant sitting quietly away from the core group; while for others, it found its expression in somewhat rowdy behaviours. Soon, it was our turn to perform.

Their various degrees of nervousness resulted, in my mind at least, to a somewhat compromised beginning to the play. At times, their voices were barely audible. But, as the scenes progressed and the students could feel the audience support, they gained confidence; overall, I was pleased with the performance. At the end of the production, the audience thundered their appreciation.

The applause, however, failed to make its impact on me, for a couple of the students took that moment to act up and engaged in a bout of shoving and jostling. I was so dismayed by this behavior that I lost complete sight of the tremendous effort that they had put into the play. I thoroughly chastised the whole group. I even took that inopportune moment to address all the mistakes that I had witnessed during the course of the production. The shiny glow of excitement quickly faded from their faces and one by one their spirits fell. My spirits too, were crushed. I hated what I had just done, but I felt that it was the right thing to do at the time. What should have been a wonderful night of celebration ended up a crushing disappointment.

Arriving home that night, Diana could not understand my mood. I shared with her what had gone on behind the scenes.

She could not believe that I had chastised the students on the night of their performance. Moreover, she could not believe that I chose to chastise them at all.

"Frank," she began, "don't you know how wonderful and marvelous your students were? I had tears in my eyes during their performance; I was very moved by their sensitivity. I wish you could have seen them as we, in the audience, saw them."

I looked at her. After hearing her speak those words I knew then that I had missed an opportunity to heighten my appreciation for my class and to elevate them in the school.

Thus, when I returned to the classroom the next day, I was energized. "Students, last night, Mrs. Maraj and I had a talk, and I learned a lesson from her. She could not believe that I found any fault with your performance at the concert. In fact, she said…"

One student yelled, "What? What did Mrs. Maraj say?"

"Mrs. Maraj said that you all were simply wonderful and marvelous."

I began applauding. And I teased, "Don't think this applause is for you from me; it's from Mrs. Maraj."

Kenny quipped, "Yeah, right."

"And, students, I wish you and your families a Merry Christmas."

I smiled; their dignity had been restored.

And, now, if I may, in honour of that very first performance in the small community hall in Devlin, Ontario, say from my heart, *"Students – Bravo you are the best!"*

# 38

# The Calm before the Storm

After finding a way to relate positively and meaningfully with my students, I had been riding the wave of optimism. Blind was I to a latent gathering storm. That storm had been conceived in the fall; I, however, was blind and failed to recognize it in its earliest stages. The storm of which I speak took the form of my principal Mr. Bane.

This part of the narrative is particularly challenging to document for it is not my intention to cast aspersions on any one particular individual. I share this story to be true to the narrative of my life story. (It is at this point in time that I am about to capture the challenges I encountered. I do it to be true to the narrative. Yet I do not wish to cast any negative criticism on anyone.) Therefore, I ask for understanding as I embark on this next journey in time.

Early in the fall while on outside supervision, I saw two students engaged in a fight in the far corner of the field. Previous to this encounter, it appeared that the students had been good friends. As I made my way toward them, I could clearly see what was going on. Clearly Dylan had the upper hand; I broke up the fight and sent Dylan to the principal's office immediately.

Dylan was furious and strongly protested against being sent to the office. "Mr. Maraj," he pleaded, "Jeremy started it. I was just finishing what he started."

"Dylan, tell Mr. Bane your side of the story. He will hear you. Now go! Please. I must attend to Jeremy."

Even though he protested vehemently, Dylan did just as I had asked.

I turned my attention to Jeremy; there were no visible signs of bleeding, and all his teeth were intact. Relieved that there were no injuries, I suggested that he go into the boys' washroom to clean up before reporting himself to the principal's office. I did, however, caution him to wait outside the office until Dylan was finished giving his report to the principal.

The bell signaling a return to class had just sounded. As I hurried to my class I spotted Mr. Bane; I gave him a quick heads up about the Dylan/Jeremy affair and indicated that the students would be waiting to speak with him regarding their actions.

I headed to class; Mr. Bane headed for his office.

Later on in the afternoon, I had yet another encounter with Mr. Bane. He actually complimented me on the action I had taken when I sent them to his office where he could deal with the situation. Pleased and encouraged by this unexpected compliment, I carried on with my day.

Within minutes Dylan came to me full of gratitude for what I had done for him.

When I questioned him further about what exactly he thought that I had done for him, he replied, "Because of you and what you said, I am not in BIG trouble with the principal."

Requiring further explanation still, I queried, "Dylan, exactly what is it that you think I did for you?"

"You spoke to Mr. Bane. He said you did. And he also said that you were not sure about what happened outside between Jeremy and me. That is why I didn't get strapped. That is why Mr. Bane didn't phone my parents. That's the one time..." and then he stopped.

I encouraged Dylan to finish his thought. "Mr. Maraj, that was the one time I got justice."

"And, Dylan, what is your punishment for being involved in a fight?"

"I have a couple of detentions. No biggie. Mr. Maraj, thanks for giving me a chance."

Dylan's words, *thanks for giving me a chance*, resonated with me. I took great comfort knowing that I had had the good fortune of being positively acknowledged by both my principal and a student.

I rode that wave of emotion for the next two days until another situation arose involving both the principal and another student.

This next incident made me uncomfortable and would prove to have far-reaching consequences.

Mr. Bane asked that I accompany him to his office. I dutifully followed his lead and soon discovered that there was a student waiting in the office. One look at the student, who was fighting to hold back tears, confirmed that he was troubled and anxious.

Without a word of explanation to me, Mr. Bane reached into the top drawer of his desk and pulled out the strap that he kept there. He ordered the student, Travis, to put out his hand. Travis did not comply. Mr. Bane then turned to me and advised, "Mr. Maraj, I would like you to witness that Travis is being both obstinate and uncooperative…"

Travis pleaded his defense, "Mr. Maraj, Mr. Bane wants to punish me for something that I didn't do. That is why I am refusing to take his strap. I didn't do it."

His pleading words struck a chord in my soul. I knew what it was to be falsely accused and punished. How was I to honour both the student and my principal? I prayed for some form of divine intervention to help me navigate the swelling waters of divided loyalties. Clearly, there was history between these two. Something was amiss.

Not knowing what was appropriate, I chose to rely on my instinct for fair play and offered this statement, "Mr. Bane, I will testify that Tavis indeed is refusing to accept the strap. In that sense, he is uncooperative. I must add, however, that Travis insists he is innocent of the charge."

Mr. Bane, shocked by my response, managed a very cold and decidedly restrained, "Thank you, Mr. Maraj. That would be all."

That was the end of our communication for that day. With a nod of his head in the direction of my classroom, Mr. Bane dismissed me. His coolness troubled me and I wondered if I had offended him. Since he chose not to speak of the situation further, I never truly knew his thoughts. Nor did he ask me to expand on my rationale.

Thereafter, whenever Mr. Bane and I were in the same vicinity, I felt a chilling wind dart from the icy depths of his eyes. I was left to wonder if this treatment resulted because I did not exactly confirm Mr. Bane's expressed contention that Travis was obstinate and uncooperative. Yet, as troubling and confusing as this first year was, the gentle wind of acceptance blew my way in the form of an occasional encouraging word or compliment from a fellow staff member or a parent when I was out in the community. I welcomed the tiniest shred of support.

Mr. Bane's reticence toward me became even more pronounced as the weeks progressed. I felt myself to be constantly on guard.

I tried to overcome these feelings with rational thinking. Perhaps I was simply just too sensitive. If indeed there was a problem worth noting,

Mr. Bane would have informed me promptly so that we could work together towards finding a resolution.

This thinking served to resolve the issue in my mind and once again I was free to concentrate on teaching.

The storm clouds, however, were gathering and I knew not yet the full impact of the destructive force of their winds.

## 39

# A Swelling Tide

May, 1975.

The period of time between January and May had transpired without any major incident. I began to think that perhaps I had indeed misjudged Mr. Bane. I began to relax my guard. Little did I know that this was just the prophetic 'calm before the storm.'

Early one Monday morning I walked into my classroom unaware that a tidal wave of mammoth proportions threatened to end my professional career as a teacher in Canada.

The threat came in the form of a man who introduced himself as Mr. Bartley, the Superintendent of Education. Without a word of explanation as to why he was there, he sat down at the back of the class. It is there that he stayed for the entire day. At first I thought nothing untoward about his presence in my classroom. I reasoned that perhaps this is how all new teachers were treated in the Canadian system of education. As the day progressed and still he remained a silent observer at the back of the classroom, I began to wonder about the meaning of his presence.

On Tuesday, he returned. Again he walked to the back, taking up his former position. I was now very conscious of his presence. Occasionally he would walk up and down the aisles stopping at various students' desks to chat. Today he was making notes. At the end of the day, once again, he departed quietly without a word of explanation. His expression was completely neutral, never critical or questioning; he was simply a presence.

Wednesday came; so too, Mr. Bartley. His presence no longer felt innocent or innocuous. The strain of not knowing was wearing on me. I felt it physically in my body. Sleep was elusive; my voice became sharp and stilted; my wit failed me. Everything about the situation screamed that something was gravely wrong. What was the problem? Why had Mr. Bartley been in my classroom for three days straight?

That night I slept not a wink. I was so distressed and physically exhausted that I seriously considered phoning in sick. It would have been so easy to do; moreover, it was a way to take me out of my misery, at least temporarily. It was with those thoughts that I reached out for the phone early that Thursday morning. The phone was in my hands and I was about to dial. I looked forward to a moment's respite. Before I could accomplish the task my inner voice railed against this action. *Frank Maraj, you are not a coward. If there is a problem at school, take responsibility and solve it!*

For better or for worse, I was compelled to listen to that inner voice; that voice had been my guide on so many other occasions; I dared not turn away now.

With some hesitancy and a great deal of trepidation, I headed out to school. The drive did nothing to dispel my anxiety; when I arrived at the school, I still had no idea what I was going to do. All I knew for certain was that I was going to do something to put an end to all the uncertainty. Today, I would be heard.

Part of me held on to the faint hope that Mr. Bartley might not even be there today. When I failed to see him in any area of the school, as I walked toward my classroom, I admit that I felt a wave of relief. And, if I remember correctly, I believe that I was smiling as I entered my room. Then I saw Mr. Bartley. My smile faded as all the anxiety of the past three days took up residence in my body once again. Mr. Bartley greeted me with a smile. I, however, was beyond such simple courtesy and the questions that had plagued me for the past three days spilled from my mouth.

"Mr. Bartley, why are you here in my class day after day?"

He seemed surprised – genuinely surprised.

"You mean you don't know, Mr. Maraj?"

"No! Why are you here?"

"Frankly, I thought you knew."

"Knew what, Mr. Bartley?"

"Your principal, Mr. Bane, requested that I visit your class…"

"Visit my class? Why?"

"He wished me to observe you."

"Observe me? For three whole days… and counting? Why?"

"He charged that he was not satisfied with your performance as a teacher. He even intimated that you might be incompetent."

So shocked was I upon hearing the word *incompetent*, that I was rendered speechless. As a new teacher, I knew that I still had much to learn about the profession, but to hang the descriptor *incompetent* on me was something that I never would have envisioned.

My head began to spin; my legs grew weak under me; I feared that I would have toppled over had I not had the foresight to be leaning against one of the desks.

All energy left my body; completely traumatized, my spirit languished; my soul, now shrouded in the veil of failure, silenced me.

Mr. Bartley, sensing some of the mental aguish his words induced, hastened to offer, "Mr. Maraj, I have witnessed no incompetence on your part. In fact, I believe that you are doing a fine job with these students."

Buoyed somewhat by these remarks I regained enough of my wits to offer him a simple thank you. A new energy flooded me and I boldly added, "And I would now assume Mr. Bartley that you have no further need to spend any more time here in my class?"

"You are quite right, Mr. Maraj! I am off."

Once Mr. Bartley was no longer a presence in my class, I found myself reflecting on his final remarks, 'You are doing a fine job with these students.' I knew from previous conversations with other teachers that Mr. Bartley did not use flattery when engaged in discussions. For him to direct such encouraging words toward me was most heartening.

I felt a small measure of vindication. School was about to begin and I needed to regain perspective and refocus myself. Knowing what my principal thought of me and my teaching still left me a little off balance. I took some small comfort from the fact that the Superintendent did not seem to share his views. Lost in this world of confusion, I was unaware that one of my grade seven students, Allyson, had been trying to attract my attention. When I was able to focus my attention on her, she asked, "Are you dreaming? You looked like you were in another world."

"Sorry, Allyson."

"Mr. Maraj, who was that man who was in our classroom for so many days?"

"He is Mr. Bartley, the Superintended of Education."

"Big title! Why was he here?"

I answered simply, "He was here to observe and help me."

"How is he going to help you? He did not do anything. Can he teach?"

"Yes! Mr. Bartley once was a teacher. Now with all his years of experience he can help us with his expertise."

"Did he help you? I don't see how."

I smiled at her insight.

# 40

# A Door begins to Close

Now that I knew something about what was at the root of Mr. Bane's actions, I had a decision to make. Do I burden Diana with this new information or do I keep it to myself? We shared so much but there were some things I felt that I needed to keep to myself. This situation, however, was not one of those things. Since this knowledge had the potential to change my whole attitude, Diana had the right to know.

Upon returning home that evening, Diana read the troubled look in my eyes. I made no effort to keep it from her.

My next words surprised her, "Diana, do not be shocked if you see me come home any day at any time."

"Frank?"

The raging storm of doubt struck the shores of my soul with its full intensity. The declaration that my principal deemed me incompetent, railed against my very core. A wave of despair engulfed me and ushered me toward the stony shore of despair. Diana was my buffer.

And so, I told her everything, from the initial encounter with Mr. Bane to subsequent intense scrutiny from Mr. Bartley. Through it all, she listened; I could sense her emotion for me; her eyes filled with tears. Then she told me something that she had observed from our very first meeting with Mr. Bane. She said that she could tell that we were on a collision course from the beginning. She had observed that our philosophies were diametrically opposed. Mr. Bane came from a background in psychology; my background was philosophy. Diana said that she observed how differently we viewed the world from our earliest conversations over dinner. She had hoped that she would be proven wrong over time.

Through her tears she voiced her support, "Frank, know this: you are a fine teacher. I know it even if you don't. Never doubt it."

Diana had always been my strongest support. I never allowed myself to believe her words before, but today I desperately needed to be buoyed by some other strength.

As Diana freely allowed her tears to fall, I wanted to do likewise. But, in that moment, a sobering reality struck fiercely. Life was no longer just about me, nor was it just about Diana and me. We had a family; Trevor and Lee-Anne needed us both. We had to be strong for them. We both directed our attention to them and for a single moment the world was again a good place to be and I allowed myself to put the whole Bane/Bartley affair behind me. For a brief moment I was at peace.

Diana's strong words of support strengthened my spirit. Her words brought to mind a sentiment that one of my colleagues at school had just recently shared with me. She surprised me when out of the blue she stated, "Frank, boy I wish I could do what you do in the classroom. You certainly have those students in the palm of your hand. We admire you."

I believe that I thanked my colleague for her kind words. But, because of all the turmoil and resulting uncertainty in my life at the time, I do not recall receiving her comment with any degree of enthusiasm. Self-doubt and second guessing my every move had woven a web of discouragement in my soul and I was unable to receive and fully appreciate such words of support.

I had often wondered what this particular teacher thought of me. I was envious, in the nicest way, of her free and energetic manner with the students. She was so spirited.

The day following Mr. Bartley's exit from the school, I awaited word from Mr. Bane.

I waited in vain.

There was no communication.

For the next few days, I waited.

Still, nothing.

Over time, my class revealed their true promise. Together we were making strides.

I wanted so badly to be part of the staff: to be a part of everything at that school. I dared not dream. I lived in the twilight of uncertainty: never truly able to relax my guard or enter into a full relationship with the staff.

It was more than two weeks later that Mr. Bane accosted me outside while I was on morning supervision.

His words were curt and emotionally restrained, "Mr. Maraj, a word with you."

"Yes, Mr. Bane."

"Are you planning to return here to Cornerbrook next year?"

His question completely baffled me. *What did he mean? What other option did I have?* I never considered going elsewhere. I had come to love this small community of students.

My mind was whirling. I so wanted to make things right between us. But, judging from the coldness in his voice, this would not be accomplished easily.

I knew that an answer in the affirmative would not be well received. Oh, how I wanted to be wrong about what I had been sensing. Not wanting to pursue that negative train of thought, I searched my mind for ways to initiate a conversation that would allow us both to come to some understanding and reinstate a degree of mutual respect.

I knew that from his perspective I had made mistakes—perhaps some serious mistakes. But, what was missing from the equation was effective communication. I needed to know from him what I had done wrong. This was my opportunity to unearth the answers to the questions that had been plaguing me. This was an opportunity. I decided to seize the moment.

"Mr. Bane, I am planning to return. Yes, and I am hoping…"

I did not get to finish my thought, however, for Mr. Bane interrupted me. He physically pulled himself up to assume the greatest height possible and with all the authority accorded to his position as principal, he declared, "Mr. Maraj, then know this. If you intend to return to this school next year, I will expect a formal lesson plan for every single lesson you teach for every single day until further notice. And, furthermore, I expect said lessons to be on my desk by 8:00 each morning! Do you understand?"

War had been declared; the powerful principal had the lowly teacher on his knees. Victory was imminent.

But, wait. I needed to take a moment to reset my mind. I knew that I could not compete with his power; I had no power to match his; all I had was my sense of fair play. His action somehow did not seem fair. I needed a moment to think. First, I cautioned myself not to react. I had to find a way to stand up to this man without disrespecting either him or his position.

He awaited my response. I truly believe that he thought that he had effectively cornered me and taken away all my options. For a brief moment, so had I.

Then, from somewhere deep within came a response. It bore the earmarks of all to which I aspired, and I countered his remarks with measured civility.

"Mr. Bane," I said simply, "your demands will be met."

He looked surprised. But, I was not yet finished. I continued, "And, Mr. Bane, please let me inform you that I will be forwarding a letter to the superintendent."

Saying nothing, he simply stared.

"And, in that letter, Mr. Bane, I will be requesting that Mr. Bartley grant me a substitute teacher to cover my classes for a few days."

Mr. Bane, was taken completely off guard by my announcement and blustered, "Whatever for? I do not approve..."

"It is beyond your approval, Mr. Bane. I require that time so that I can observe you, the master teacher, at work. After all, Mr. Bane, as the master teacher, you possess the best techniques and the highest ability; I am but a lowly teacher, whose abilities are suspect, and whose competence is in question."

He was indeed quiet.

I continued, "And Mr. Bane, you can expect a copy of *that* letter on your desk almost immediately."

His face changed colour assuming a discernible purplish hue. Now, visibly agitated, he declared, "You think you are smart, don't you Mr. Maraj? Well, well, we will just see about that."

Clearly he was determined to end my teaching career.

I really do not think that I was trying to be smart. I was merely struggling against all odds to defend myself. I did not know what else I should have said or could have said to change the swelling tide of his obvious dislike. Strangely enough, I felt no anger... only pain and sadness: sadness because our relationship had devolved to this base level. I had hoped that the two of us could have resolved our differences face to face like mature, educated, rational beings. I had assumed that the qualities of civility and decency and the desire for fairness could elevate the educated mind above the pettiness of self. In this, I was sorely mistaken. This reality saddened me greatly and I wondered what value there was to an education that gives us empirical knowledge that stretches our minds, while neglecting the more subtle spiritual values of generosity and civility.

Walking away, I could not help but wish that we had been able to find a common ground for discussion. I truly wondered what my fault had been in all of this.

I had no idea what was to become of me.

# 41

# As One Door Closes…

Encouraged by one of the more senior teachers from Donald Young School in Emo, it had been my custom to make the occasional visit to the school to borrow various materials that could be of use at Cornerbrook School.

I felt the need for such a visit after this most recent unpleasant discussion. While in the library, my friend met me and took me to see his principal. Following a brief introduction, the principal, Mr. Burton, surprised me with a most encouraging sentiment.

"Mr. Maraj, we have been hearing some good things about you and what a fine teacher you are."

To say that I was surprised, is an understatement; I was shocked. But, it was a good shock; just what my spirit needed to hear.

He continued to make small talk.

"Well, Frank, you are a long way from your roots. Whatever brought you here to this neck of the woods?"

After responding to his question, we moved on to various other topics with a special emphasis on education. Time got away from us and I had to bring our conversation to an end for I needed to find the research materials I needed for my next unit. My closing remarks prompted this from Mr. Burton, "Well, Frank, I will come right to the point; I need a grade seven teacher. Would you be interested in the position? We would love to have you on staff. Interested?"

Struck dumb by surprise at the unexpectedness of his announcement, I fear I merely mumbled.

Confused by my response or lack of one, Mr. Burton asked, "Mr. Maraj, I am not understanding you. What is your answer?"

Gathering both my composure and my voice I responded, "Mr. Burton, thank you. Thank you! I am very attached to the students at Cornerbrook. Would you give me a little time please?"

"Yes, yes. Of course. I understand. Yet, don't take too long to get back to me."

As I left the school, I do not recall walking out of the building. My feet, along with my soul, fairly flew home. As I reviewed the situation in my mind, I realized that Mr. Burton was not just having a "chat" with me. No, not at all; this clever principal had been interviewing me all along. Well, the "interview" must have gone quite well for there to have been a job offer at the end of it.

His closing remarks, "We would love to have you on staff," became a pillar that I would cling to for the next few days as I contemplated my decision. Those words infused new life into my languishing soul and I smiled gratefully.

Within that same timeframe, the principal of another neighbouring school contacted me; he wanted me to come to see him at my earliest convenience. I obliged him the very next day. My curiosity was satisfied almost immediately after entering his office when he, too, told me about a job vacancy at his school and offered me a job.

I was on top of the world. I now had two job offers and both were very compelling. Common sense ruled in favour of Donald Young School for I lived in its backyard, practically. It was a mere five minute walk from our home.

I could not get over the shock of having been offered two jobs: jobs that I did not know even existed; this time the shock was refreshing.

# 42

# Saying Farewell

Once I made the decision to leave Cornerbrook, I did so quietly. My heart was both relieved and saddened. People understood my decision to accept a job in the same community in which I lived. No one, save the main actors in the most recent drama, knew the real reasons directing my departure.

Outside of the school I had come to know many families, and over time we had forged a mutual friendship. Several of these families openly expressed their heartfelt disappointment regarding my decision to leave. They could not possibly understand what was at the core of my decision.

One of the mothers of one of my Grade 7 students paid me a visit at school to express her concerns. It was an emotional encounter. While she understood the pull to be nearer to my young family it was with some reluctance that she was saying good-bye. She voiced her sentiments in this manner, "Mr. Maraj, you belong to our Cornerbrook School. For now it's okay to leave us. I consider that you are merely on loan to the other school. Remember to return to our community. Will you?"

I cannot forget those Devlin families. I will never forget Devlin. I was truly sorry to leave.

Saying goodbye, 'tis never easy…

# 43

# Reflections 1974-1975

Desperately I had sought to find a way of life in Canada that I could embrace; I wanted to feel at home in Canada. My resolve had been sorely tested during my very first year. And yet, through it all, my difficulties were not because of the students. On the contrary, my students propelled me onward; they forced me to stretch beyond my conventional structure to embrace a new Canadian-based reality. That truth is undeniable.

While Emo was a most delightful and welcoming community, at times, however, it felt very small. My roots were planted in a densely populated island; life was filled with constant activity and engagement; there was always a cinema or a restaurant just waiting to be visited. At times it was a challenge adjusting to the quiet life in Emo.

Diana faced no such challenges; she loved Emo; she was finding her place in the community and was beginning to forge friendships; above all, Emo was an ideal place for us to raise our children.

Still estranged from my island, I was determined to forge anew in Canada. I held on to the conviction that this was the right decision for my family.

# PART THREE

## Entering the Elementary System

# 44

# Half Day's Pay

August, 1979.

Some years had passed since my departure from Devlin. The Donald Young staff was a tightly knit group of dedicated, hard-working individuals. Collectively, their spirit was one of congeniality and inclusiveness. I formed a strong working relationship with many of the senior teachers and a deep appreciation for the level of commitment from the teachers of the primary grades. I especially marveled at the abilities of the kindergarten teacher and her endless patience with the multitude of physical and emotional demands placed upon her during the course of a single day.

We had established many strong ties with our Emo community of friends. Several families opened their homes to include us in their lives. Their friendship and willingness to welcome us meant the world to us. We have never taken for granted their many kindnesses.

I was especially grateful for my job. While thousands of graduates with impressive teaching qualifications were still without employment in Ontario, I counted myself to be among the truly blessed. Not only did I have a job that I truly loved, I was within walking distance of the job site. Everything seemed to have worked out in my favour.

Not only that, but Diana and I were anxiously awaiting the arrival of our third child. The new school year was about to begin; Diana had already been in the hospital for two days; still there was no baby and a staff meeting was scheduled at school for the next day. It was called a Professional Development Day and all staff members were expected to be present: no exceptions. At that time, our Federation had not yet negotiated parental leave for men and I looked to my principal for a sense of understanding and compassion.

It was with no small measure of trepidation that I sought out the counsel of my principal. After explaining the situation to him I asked to be released from the mandatory attendance at the staff meeting. At first, Mr. Burton was reluctant to agree; he recounted that several serious issues were due to be presented to the staff during the meeting and it was imperative that all be in attendance. Upon further reflection, he gave his reluctant consent but advised that the Board may see fit to dock my wages for the time I was to be away.

Having decided that I did not wish to make life any more difficult than it had to be and not wishing to give my principal any reason to question his own compassion for my plight, I took precautions to ensure that I would be fully informed regarding the details of the meeting. Will Jenkins, another staff member that I had come to know quite well, consented to update me on the more salient details of the meeting. Thus I ventured to the hospital feeling reasonably assured that I was not neglecting my duty as a teacher.

I arrived at the hospital expecting that Diana would be close to delivery. Such was not the case.

Two days ago Diana had been admitted to the hospital; already two weeks overdue, the decision was made to induce her labour. This process continued for two days without result.

We had become quite close with one of the families in Emo and the young mom had generously offered to have our other two children, Trevor and Lee-Anne, stayed with them while I was at the hospital with Diana. Their three girls were lovely children and got along very well with ours. It was an incredible relief to have them in such a caring setting. I spent the entire afternoon at the hospital but there were no new developments; Diana seemed no closer to delivery than she had been for the past two days. At ten o'clock on the third evening, I prepared myself mentally to once again return home to begin the process all over again the next day.

My process was very different from Diana's. Each night as I went to pick up Trevor and Lee-Anne from the home of our friends, I had to find a way to ask them to once again care for our children for a next day. My mind and my spirit recoiled at each new imposition; our friends, however, never once made me feel the burden of my requests.

But, this third night, something was different at the hospital; this time the labour continued past ten o'clock. It, in fact, intensified. Minutes later, the nurse decided that it was time to summon the doctor. The doctor, however, never made it to the hospital in time for the delivery. The nurse, accompanied unintentionally by this most unprepared and unwitting father, welcomed our noisy Dee-Anne into the world. Never had I intended to be a part of the delivery process; never had I been raised to expect that of myself. Diana had resigned herself to that reality. Yet, there I was, actually present at the birth of our youngest child. That was the first time that this youngest child forced me to re-evaluate my long held perceptions about myself, and, truth be told, it would not be the last.

As I looked at my newborn child, I beheld the face of my Ma; I cannot explain it. I did not speak of it; I merely wondered at the discovery.

It was very late when I finally made it home. I had much on my mind, not the least of which was the fact that tomorrow I would encounter a whole new group of students for their first day of school. After much tossing, I fell into a restless slumber.

Early the next day I reported to my principal, Mr. Burton. He explained that the Board might have to deduct my pay for my absence the day before.

Without uttering a word, I reached into my pocket and produced a paper (thanks to Will, a co-worker) listing the items discussed at yesterday's staff meeting and detailing the various points made by the staff. After allowing Mr. Burton sufficient time to peruse the list, I stated, "Mr. Burton you must do what you must do. I needed to know what transpired at that meeting and I found out. Thank you for your time."

That afternoon, as I prepared to leave for the hospital, Mr. Burton called me over to announce that he was recommending that the Board not deduct any wages from my pay. I thanked him for that recommendation and immediately left for the hospital.

A number of years ago, I missed half a day of school to attend a family funeral on the first day of class; this year, once again I missed a half day of school. The circumstances surrounding the two occasions were very different, for today, I was the proud father of our third child.

My mind flittered for a moment to the young mother whose loss of a husband was the reason for the first absence and who thereafter bore the burden of raising three children on her own.

Then, inexplicably my mind drifted to my own mother and I wondered about her life. She who had born nine children... never once knowing the security of a hospital surrounded by a team of competent doctors and nurses. I thought of my mother who relied on only herself and the charity and compassion of good neighbours and family.

Then I thought of myself, and my new responsibilities.

Diana and I alone are charged with the awesome responsibility of looking after our family. I was not sure how we would manage this task so far removed from where I thought we would be at this stage of our lives. I had expected that we would be living in Trinidad. I had expected that I would have been a working professional. I had expected also, that Diana would have been working. Together, in Trinidad we would have had easy access to both child care and home care. There were many caring women in Trinidad who would have willingly accepted employment in a home such as ours. I confess that even after these several years, I sometimes find myself in the throes of this old mindset, and mourning the absence of its reality.

Such a mindset, however, served no useful purpose now. It, in fact, was a distraction and I resolved to divest myself of it. I had to focus on the here and now of the reality of life in Canada. And the sooner, the better.

# 45

# Respect…

While the staff at Donald Young School was receptive and warm, the same could not be said of the students.

My first day was a challenge; no red carpet for this teacher. With few exceptions, over the next several days, the students made no real overtures to extend a welcome to this "foreign" teacher. This is not to suggest that the students were impolite or indifferent; they simply regarded me as a curious intruder in their midst.

My insistence on neatness and organization in both their academics and in their care of the classroom itself was observed but definitely not embraced.

I felt them withdraw in a blanket of distant politeness. It was as though they had posted this message: *Mr. Maraj, you want our respect? Earn it!*

# 46

# The Unthinkable

From the outset I understood the message and I knew it was going to be difficult to win over these students. After some reflection, I accepted their unspoken challenge; I made a conscious decision to work towards earning their respect. This decision was easy to embrace for it mirrored my own personal creed. I knew that respect was the pivotal factor in achieving solid classroom discipline and control. I had understood this from my earliest years as a beginning teacher at St. Charles High School in Trinidad. Indeed this motto of respect had been my constant guide and companion as I attempted to navigate my way through the difficult challenges of the classroom.

In an effort to gain the respect of this class, I set myself the challenge of learning more about who they were as individuals both within the walls of the classroom and out in the general community. I wanted to know about their lives: what they liked and disliked and how life was for them at home. Music played a significant role in many of these young lives; Donald Young School was renowned for its well-established choirs. Most of the students were athletic and participated in baseball, hockey, football, and cross country running. Soccer was a relatively new sport in the district and this is where I saw an opportunity for me to become involved. I knew little about football, baseball or hockey. Determined to become involved, I volunteered to assist in the soccer program.

Many of our students came from a demanding farming background. I had the utmost respect for all their parents who tried to instill their work ethic in their children as many were consumed doing chores after school. It was ever my intention to share my admiration for their devoted family efforts. Sadly, for whatever reason, I failed to do so.

I felt that I failed this class in another way and it is with deep sadness and regret that I now hesitantly recount another event that reveals the flux that education was going through in the seventies. As educators, we were challenged on many fronts.

During the early fall while I was in the middle of a class discussion, Rocky, one of my students, yelled out in agitation; the interruption was sudden and most unexpected; boldly, he directed his remarks to another classmate.

"Benny I am going to plow into you if you don't shut your trap."

Benny must have said something that I did not hear but it had an obvious and immediate effect on Rocky. Before I had a chance to intervene, Rocky thundered back in retaliation, "Benny your mouth is too big...."

Rocky had risen from his seat and was beginning to approach Benny in a threatening manner. I knew that I had to intervene in some fashion.

"Rocky," I shouted. "Stop! Now!"

I raised my voice a few decibels and reissued the command; Rocky stopped. I then ordered him to leave in classroom and await me in the outside hall. Rocky made no move to comply. He was locked in a staring war with Benny who, by this time, had assumed an equally threatening stance.

Positioning myself between the two boys, I ordered, "Benny, sit down and get back to your work. I will see you in a moment."

After Benny complied with my request, I turned all my attention to Rocky, "Come on... to the hallway... please... Now!"

And then the disgusting words spewed from his mouth, "F*** you!"

I reacted.

An uneasy hush fell over the entire class. Every pair of eyes was silently accusatory: including Benny's.

I ordered Rocky to await me in the hall. He complied.

As Rocky left the classroom, I turned my attention to the class. Clearly they were deeply resentful towards me.

"Students," I began.

Some raised their heads; others did not.

I could not speak. I had to sit down. No one said anything. A quiet seized the class. Now I had to contain my own feelings and address the need at hand.

"Class, please excuse me. I have to attend to Rocky. You have your assignment. Please begin your work."

I then asked Benny to come with me into the hall where Rocky awaited.

Immediately, Rocky declared, "I did not mean to cuss. I did not mean to cuss you, Mr. Maraj. What I said, I said to Benny."

The realization that the words had not been directed at me, was like a balm to my soul.

Then Benny added, "Are we in trouble Mr. Maraj?"

*Was I hearing these boys correctly?* An aura of calm enveloped the three of us and it was with great gratitude I embraced it.

"Rocky, are you okay?"

"I'm fine. What's going to happen to me and Benny?"

Benny, too, was anxious and tearfully asked, "Mr. Maraj, are you going to report us to the principal and to our parents?"

"Benny, we will work this out. Both of you will have to write out in your own words what you were upset about. Benny, you go back to class. I will see you later."

I checked in on the students as Benny opened the door to the classroom. All was quiet.

I then turned my attention to Rocky. "Rocky, I have to report this incident to the principal and to your parents. It is…"

"Oh God, no! Mr. Maraj, please don't call my parents. My father will bury me!" Then, he broke down; he did not even try to stem the stream of tears.

Clearly, Rocky was not concerned about my reaction in the classroom.

"Rocky, I'm sorry…"

"Mr. Maraj, you don't need to apologize to me. I am the one that cussed in class. I never should have said the 'f' word. I disrespected you, and you are a decent teacher. I am the one who should be saying sorry. I really am so very sorry, Mr. Maraj."

He stopped. I was without words. How this student has honoured me with his apology… Can I do less?

Before I could respond, Rocky continued, "Mr. Maraj, punish me all you want. Give me lines; give me extra work; give me a detention. Just don't report me to the principal. I am already in deep trouble with him. I did not really mean to cuss. It's just…"

He paused, "It's just that I hear it all the time."

His words penetrated my soul. In that instant I felt an inexplicable bond with this fragile youth. He, who had presented as rude and wayward, transformed before my very eyes. He was simply, Rocky, a twelve year old boy in need of understanding and compassion. The tragic look on his face took hold of me in a way that I cannot explain.

Rocky seemed driven to supply further assurances. "Mr. Maraj, Benny and I will work thing out. We will be friends again. Don't worry. You have my word."

I felt the sincerity of his words.

"Okay, Rocky. Just hand in your report. You and Benny will both sign it. I also will write up a report as a matter of record."

Rocky cut in, "You won't show it to…"

"No, but I will have to produce it if ever this were to…"

"Mr. Maraj, you won't ever have to. I promise nothing like this will ever happen again. Thank you, Sir. Thank you for being so understanding."

*The issue never resurfaced. The students of that Grade 7 class came on side with me. Without words they seemed to have understood the deep challenge that I faced as their teacher. Thank you, students.*

Afterthought

For the remainder of that day, I expected at any time that the principal or a parent would venture to visit me. I had been bracing myself all day for that eventuality. I searched for an explanation that would account for my behaviour. It was no easy matter to do so. Yet deep in the inner recess of my memory bank, traces of a way of life that laboured to hold on to any last vestiges of decency were deposited into the core of my spirit; cussing was always that vile menace that threatened to dislodge the delicate balance of civility.

# 47

# Truth Directive

After the passage of a few months, I settled in quite comfortably at the school. No longer did I feel that I was a stranger; the students were gradually becoming more welcoming and I felt encouraged. I had no idea that trouble of another sort was brewing.

At our next staff meeting, Mr. Burton declared that we were bound by professional duty to "communicate to parents, accurate information regarding their children's academic status." We were strongly advised to tell the truth plainly and politely. He concluded his remarks by noting that "parents were owed the simple truth."

The entire staff embraced the directive and a few days later we were afforded an opportunity to meet the parents at an informal "meet and greet" in the school.

One couple in particular expressed interest in meeting on a more formal basis to discuss their son's progress. We arranged the meeting for the following day after school.

The mother came right to the point and asked how her son was doing.

Her direct question deserved a direct answer.

I informed her that her son was working to the best of his ability and was reading at a *grade three level.*

This news shocked her.

She began to pace the floor; processing the information was difficult. I could see frustration yield to anger. When she spoke, it was the anger that commanded her tone, "I won't stand for this! I demand to see the principal. Something has to be done. This is not right!"

Before I could offer any suggestions, she left and I wondered what trouble had I just unleashed!

While I was not privy to any knowledge of what actually transpired during the meeting between the principal and the mother, I sensed the gravity of the situation when the principal remarked, "Mr. Maraj, you have one mighty angry parent on your hands. Be careful," it suggested to me that I was to blame in some way. Yet, I did not know what I had done wrong.

My fears were compounded a few days later when my principal advised, "Frank, please be available at lunch time. We have visitors coming to see you. It will be okay." I did not have long to wait to find out who exactly my visitors were.

I was not surprised to discover both Mr. and Mrs. Jenkins in the office. I was, however, surprised to find the new Superintendent of Education also in attendance.

I remained quiet.

The superintendent addressed me directly, "Mr. Maraj, you reported to Mrs. Jenkins that her son, Jesse, is reading at a grade three level."

"Yes, Sir."

"She wants an explanation."

"Sir, I regret that he is at that level and Mrs. Jenkins is quite understandably upset. I assure you that I will do everything within my power to help upgrade…"

Mrs. Jenkins interrupted, "Why are you questioning Mr. Maraj? He is the new teacher here. He really cannot account for our son's poor level of achievement."

And then, Mr. Jenkins, who, until now, had been quiet, exploded, "I demand the truth! I want satisfaction! I want answers. Why is it that my son cannot read?"

Clearly, the situation was becoming more intense. I felt that I ought to speak, "Mr. and Mrs. Jenkins," I began, "give me the opportunity to help Jesse. It is true that his academic standing is not where it should be…"

"And whose fault is that?" thundered Mr. Jenkins.

"Mr. Jenkins, I ask you to give me a chance to work with Jesse."

Then Mrs. Jenkins spoke up, "Mr. Maraj, our quarrel is not with you, it is with…"

"No, please, Mrs. Jenkins.... our concern now is to devise strategies to upgrade Jesse. I am going to need your help; you have to be my allies. How about it? Will you join me in helping Jesse?"

By now, some of the anger had dissipated. Mrs. Jenkins, striving valiantly to contain her emotions and restrain her outrage, responded in the affirmative.

I thanked them both for coming and for being willing to partner with me to help their son. I assured them that I would contact them soon when I had devised a course of action.

As he prepared to leave, I could feel Mr. Jenkins' eyes on me; when he held out his hand to me, I grasped it with both of mine; our understanding went beyond words.

Later that day, the superintendent peeked in to my classroom and casually quipped, "Mr. Maraj, good job!"

The torrential downpour seemed to have run its course.

## 48

# Emerging Insight

My experience with Jesse's parents should have taught me a lesson: when divulging "truth" one should be careful to temper it with a sprinkling of common sense. I, however, had yet to learn that lesson as this next episode reveals.

My Grade 7 students and I had settled into a regular routine. Most seemed to have accepted me and my standards; everyone was working; some were working more diligently than others. The one glaring exception was Johnny Rivers. His effort was sporadic at best; more often than not, the majority of his day was spent distracting others from their work. Overall, his performance lacked genuine effort.

One day, as I was marking one of his assignments, it became obvious that the work he had submitted was not his. The content was expressed in a manner far more competent than anything that he had hitherto been capable of producing. It wasn't long before I discerned the real author of the work. It was apparent that he had "borrowed" another student's work (without permission) and tried to pass it off as his own. I returned all the assignments save his. I asked him to come up to my desk where we could have a private word.

I presented his assignment and asked him pointedly, "Johnny, tell me the truth. Is this your own work?"

Johnny bent his head and said nothing. Moments passed without a response and I progressed to the next level of interrogation.

"Tell me whose assignment you borrowed."

His long silence was followed by a sulking blend of indignation and accusation when he charged, "I did the assignment. Stop picking on me."

When I produced the very notebook from which he copied, he stared, seemingly dumbfounded; then he looked away.

"Johnny, it is clear…" I began.

"What is clear," Johnny interrupted, "is that you are picking on me. Now I *know* that you do not like me."

Shocked by Johnny's remarks, I repeated his accusation incredulously, "I do not like you, and I am picking on you? Why would you say such things? They are not true. I do not understand. Johnny, why would I pick on you?"

"Because I am Indian – that's why! You don't like me because I am Indian."

My initial bewilderment gave way to confusion by this latest charge and I challenged, "Johnny, how has your being Indian got anything to do with your performance?"

"Mr. Maraj, you don't like me because I am Indian. That is the truth."

"Johnny, that is not true. What is true is you behave as though you are lazy."

"Oh, my lord, now you are calling me lazy!" He walked away.

I did not pursue the matter. I decided to let the situation rest for now. While I was extremely concerned about his accusations, I felt that he was unreachable while in that particular mindset. That night after reflecting on the matter, I resolved to contact his parents to discuss my concerns.

As things turned out, I did not have to contact the parents; the next day they were already at the school and awaiting my arrival. My principal met me in the hall as I was entering and escorted me to his office. His furrowed brow complemented his serious tone.

"Mr. Maraj, Johnny is here with his parents, Mr. and Mrs. Rivers. They are here to see you regarding Johnny; they feel that you have offended their child."

Mrs. Rivers spoke first. "I cannot tell you how shocked I was, Mr. Maraj, to learn that you called my son a lazy Indian. I find that racist."

"Mrs. Rivers I am so sorry you are offended. However, I did not call Johnny a lazy Indian."

"What exactly are you saying, Mr. Maraj. Are you now calling my son a liar? My son does not lie. That much I do know and I'll swear to it!"

"Mrs. Rivers, is it possible that there has been some misunderstanding here?" I found my most conciliatory tone before I uttered this next statement, "Did Johnny tell you that he had copied someone else's work – word for word?"

The answer was evident in the surprise on both their faces. I took advantage of the ensuing silence to explain what had transpired yesterday.

When I was finished, Mr. Rivers spoke, "So, you did say to Johnny that he was acting lazy?"

"Yes, I did say it. You have to face it. Johnny is not just *acting* lazy, he *is* lazy. And I am so sorry that I had to say that to you."

Annoyed, Mrs. Rivers continued her attack. "Nobody calls my child lazy."

"Then let me temper my words and say that currently, Johnny is not productive."

There was silence.

I took that moment to reach out to Johnny and his parents. I continued, "Mr. and Mrs. Rivers, there is a great deal more at stake here than the question of Johnny's laziness. You think that I have offended your child? Did you ever stop to think that there might be another version of the story? Did you ever think to seek clarification from me, his teacher? Did you ever think that by not doing so you could have offended me? I wanted nothing more than to help your son, Johnny."

Mr. and Mrs. Rivers appeared reflective.

I turned to Johnny. His head was bent. Wanting to reach out to him once again, I said, "Johnny, I meant no harm. I just wish that you could understand…"

Johnny lifted his head slightly and offered, "Mr. Maraj, I am sorry. It is my fault." Once more, he bent his head.

Wanting to restore some measure of dignity to this young man I said, "Johnny, thank you so much for your apology. It helps me. You can help me in another way… I need to know what I may have done that would lead you to call me *racist*."

Before Johnny could respond, Mr. Rivers offered, "Mr. Maraj, we now realize that we have misunderstood you. What our son said to us made it sound like you were racist. You were trying to reach our son."

Mrs. Rivers spoke softly, "I spoke out of turn when I called you *racist*. Mr. Maraj, I am sorry. I did not have all the information. I wish I could explain. It has become a way of life. We feel so threatened all the time but we were wrong about you. I'm glad we could meet and get this sorted out.

We'll be speaking to Johnny further on this matter. There won't be any more misunderstandings."

"Thank you both. But, I need you to know that I will continue to press Johnny to perform. Do I have your support in this?"

Mr. Rivers was quick to respond, "You have our support *and* our respect. Thank you, Mr. Maraj."

After the parents left, Mr. Burton commented, "Mr. Maraj, you handled that situation very well."

I did not think that I had handled anything. All I wanted to do was to help Johnny Rivers succeed.

If anything, I still had so very much to learn.

# 49

# Two Misguided Friends

During those first few years at Donald Young School, I had been tested, both emotionally and intellectually. The everyday reality of having to make instant decisions weighed heavily on my mind for there was always the concern that my judgement in these matters could be misguided. Not having been raised in the Canadian culture, further compounded my difficulty.

One more incident, while not as dramatic as the previous two, is, however, of equal significance.

While leaving the school to go to outdoor supervision, I decided to take the farthest exit on the east side of the school. To get there, I had to walk through a secondary set of doors that set off the gym, library, and kindergarten areas from the rest of the school. I did not normally take that exit and I do not know what force propelled me in that direction. As I walked down the long corridor, I soon found myself in the midst of a fracas. To the left of me, two senior male students were exchanging punches. Clearly, this spot had been chosen precisely because of its isolated nature.

There was, however, no escaping my responsibility; they knew that I had seen them; I knew that they knew that I had seen them; I *had* to act.

"Boys," I directed, "follow me!"

I could sense that my directive caught them a little off guard. I'm almost certain that they would have been expecting me to demand that they stop fighting. I hoped to accomplish that by issuing the command to follow me. They could not both fight and follow.

I began to walk away immediately after I spoke, not entirely sure if they would comply; neither boy was a member of my class.

When I had taken a few steps I turned my head ever so slightly and I could see from my peripheral vision that both boys had begun to follow. Relieved, I decided to increase my pace.

I really did not know what precisely I was going to do with them; the mere fact that they were not continuing to fight, revealed, at a certain level, their respect for authority. Eventually, the boys caught up with me. We all stopped. I looked at each one; I noted that they were almost as tall as I was. Their frames were rugged and they were well on their way to adulthood.

Crete, spoke first, "Mr. Maraj we are here. You told us to follow you."

Nelson added, "You caught us red-handed, Mr. Maraj; I suppose you are going to send us to the principal, like everybody else does."

Just then the warning bell signaled the commencement of the afternoon classes. I needed to buy myself some time. "Boys," I began, "I have to go to class right away. Would you come and see me at recess please."

We went our separate ways.

At recess, the boys came to my classroom. They were both very quiet. I took the initiative. I had been able to make some inquiries regarding the two of them and I had a sense of where they were coming from.

"Were you fighting because of a… girl?"

Somewhat surprised by the directness and accurateness of my question, the two nodded their heads in embarrassed affirmation.

Now that I understood the situation, I had to determine the best way of helping these two misguided friends.

"Boys," I counseled, "I have some more thinking to do; come and see me after the last class. I need some help from the two of you. It would be good if the two of you were to come up with a plan to solve this problem."

As they left, they exchanged puzzled looks. I had no doubt that they would be back at the end of the day. By the time that they returned, I had had time to reflect seriously on their situation. But, before I could speak, Crete took the initiative, "Mr. Maraj, you have no reason trust us. We know what you are thinking. We are always in trouble."

Nelson chimed in, "Mr. Maraj, we know we were wrong to fight. Fighting is against the rules. We lost it. We are really supposed to be best friends."

"Boys, I have to say, given the way you were pounding each other, I never would have guessed that you were best friends. Are you still best friends?"

They exchanged glances. Nelson continued, "Mr. Maraj, you asked us to come up with a plan for you to consider. Well, we think we have... Punish us all you want. Just don't report this to the principal. We are begging you..."

Crete added, "We are already in big trouble with the office; one more complaint and..."

I felt that I understood their concern, "Boys, I have listened to you and I will consider your request. I have written up a report regarding this incident. I will hold onto it. And, I will defer reporting this matter to the principal..." I paused, "provided that this type of behaviour never happens again."

The surprise on their faces was genuine. I could tell that they were pleased to be thus acknowledged. I then inquired, "Regarding your punishment, what advice do you have for me?"

Nelson suggested, "Give us two weeks of lunch detention... twenty minutes a day. Is that too easy?"

"Seems fair. Now, you must show up with a novel."

They agreed.

They thanked me over and over again; they were so appreciative.

And they kept their promise showing up on time, faithfully... *with* their novels. Over the course of the next week I took the time to chat with them each day. At first we talked about the novel; later, as they became more comfortable with me, they shared a little about their lives. Their lives had not been easy. They had suffered many personal tragedies and hard knocks. I was reminded of my own travels down that rocky road.

Then, on the fifth day of detention, I informed the students, "Boys, today is your last day of detention."

Surprised by my announcement, they asked, "Why, Mr. Maraj? We agreed that we deserved the two weeks."

"Yes, what you say is true. But there is more to the situation than punishment. Boys, you made a mistake. You owned up to your mistake and you accepted my guidelines. It seems to me that you have had to *grow up* a little. Your commitment to your detention is deserving of consideration. Based on your dedicated integrity in honouring this pledge, I have taken it upon myself to alter the terms of your detention. You have earned it. Yet, boys, it is my duty to remind both of you that I still have an official report..."

Crete smiled as he said, "Mr. Maraj, you will not have to worry. Thank you."

Nelson was silently pondering this latest twist. "Mr. Maraj, why are you doing this? Why are you giving us a chance?"

I simply smiled and ushered them out.

Left alone, I pondered his question. Why *was* I giving the boys a chance? I really didn't know for sure. What I recognized was this... all my life I had wanted to be a teacher. What lessons are learned if we do not extend the hand of charity to one another especially when it is deserving... and, sometimes, even when it is not?

I cannot say that my actions were right or wrong. All I came to know for certain was that these two young men were respectful and decent in the core of their being. I wanted them to know that they were deserving of trust. I wanted them to know that even though they were bound to make mistakes, mistakes could be forgiven. But, above all else, I wanted to erase any hint from their minds that they were considered mere rejects.

I worried constantly that a child once placed on the road of rejection is more prone to take the path of alienation. Left alone, soon bitterness and hate become his allies. What chance therefore, would such a castaway have in the adult world? These were mere children in need of adult acceptance, compassion, and understanding. Who was I then, to deny them what I, myself, had craved so much as a child?

# 50

# An Unselfish Request

Eventually life at school assumed a smooth predictability. The weeks rolled by in rapid succession and I felt that I was gaining the confidence of the students. One day, Chad, one of the class favourites, came to see me before class; an air of excitement surrounded him… an eagerness and earnestness of purpose engulfed him.

"Good morning, Chad," I greeted him, "what's on your mind?"

"It's about Theo… his birthday is coming soon. I don't think he's ever had a birthday celebration. He can't remember the last one. He comes from …"

He hesitated for a moment searching for just the right words to explain his friend's situation.

"It's like he doesn't really *have* a home… He's been bumped around lots… I don't think that he has any real family."

"Chad I understand. What are you thinking? What do you want to do?"

"Well, Mr. Maraj, I was sort of thinking that if each of us could contribute a quarter we could have a celebration with ice cream and cake. I was wondering if you would speak to the class about the idea."

While I was put to thinking, he continued, the excitement in his voice obviously building with each word. "Mr. Maraj, he will be so surprised. We won't let him know a thing. He will positively flip. And, I know that the class will be happy to do it. How about it, Mr. Maraj? Will you help?"

I loved Chad's energy. He was growing into quite the young man. Supportive, compassionate and visionary: rare qualities in someone his age.

I wanted to honour his commitment to a fellow student. Was this not one way to acknowledge the "Judeao-Christian heritage expounded in the Education Act? But, the idea was Chad's and his alone. I encouraged him to take the next step himself.

"Chad, you take charge. You speak to the class. I will be your support…"

Chad needed no convincing. He readily jumped at the opportunity and began planning out the details.

I was honoured to be both a quiet witness and silent partner in the enterprise.

## 51

# Precedent Setting

I began class with my customary "good morning" greeting.

It had taken extensive coaching, but the students had come to accept this idiosyncrasy of mine as completely normal and had fallen into step with the morning routine. Truly, I had earned their responsive "good morning."

Today, however, the routine was going to be broken. Today they were about to be addressed by one of their own. Theo was absent, so this was the opportune moment for Chad to present his ideas to the class.

After I smoothed the way for Chad to make his pitch, Chad made his way to the front of the class. He began somewhat hesitantly and apologetically, "Well, guys...this is different... kinda strange and weird... me up here talking. Usually I'm back there yapping..."

The class giggled.

"Anyway, you will notice that Theo is not here at the moment. Mr. Maraj made sure of that."

Someone bantered, "Detention again?"

"No! No! And I don't blame you for saying that. Seems Theo is always in trouble. He thinks that nobody likes him. No, Mr. Maraj has just sent him on an errand," Chad explained gently.

The class became quiet as it absorbed the full impact of Chad's words.

Chad was a natural leader and a wonderful spokesperson. The students were drawn to his presence. I, too, was listening attentively.

"Well, class, it's Theo's birthday. I was just thinking that if each one of us could contribute a quarter, we could throw him a party."

It seemed that everyone but me was fully apprised of Theo's particular circumstances so no one questioned the rationale of Chad's proposal.

He was barely finished speaking when an affirming voice called out, "Yes, let's do it."

As it turned out, that voice represented the collective view, and soon Chad was occupied forming committees and delegating the various tasks of collecting money, purchasing supplies, and decorating.

It looked like all the bases were being covered. One area, however, had been overlooked. Bringing the class back to attention, I could not help but address the one glaring omission, "Class, I noticed that you did not include 'clean up' in your list of duties."

Once again, it was Chad who assumed the leadership role, "Mr. Maraj, we don't worry about clean up. We have janitors. That's their job."

"Yeah, they get paid to do that kind of thing," echoed a like-minded individual from the back of the room. A chorus of *yeahs* and *yesses* reverberated on the heels of this pronouncement.

Once again I was forced to examine my expectations to determine what attitudes I possessed that might be at odds with the Canadian experience. I was pretty certain that not many parents of present day Canada would take exception to my views on this. Even so, I tempered my response, and began with a non-threatening comment before initiating an alternative perspective.

"Class, I see where you are coming from. I can also see how that makes sense. I, however, would like you to consider things from another point of view… This is our classroom. We take care of it. This is our party. We take care of it. That means that we clean up our own garbage."

Not everyone accepted my logic and a debate ensued. The discussion became heated and the tone of the class was escalating. I did not like what I was witnessing. The increasingly intuitive Chad seemed in tune with my body language. He approached me to ask a most curious question.

"Mr. Maraj," he began somewhat tentatively, "can you wait in the hallway for a moment? I will come and get you."

I did not have to be escorted; I willingly left. About two minutes elapsed. Chad came out and indicated that everything had been resolved. The class was calm but there was an air of expectancy as I entered. I smiled my approval at the improved tone in the room. While Chad took his seat, another student stood to inquire, "Mr. Maraj, do you have any other concerns?"

The class was beaming; so was I.

Early the next morning, Brenda, one of the girls from the class, came to see me. She seemed sad. While her message may have contained an element of apology, her delivery was distinctly direct, "Mr. Maraj, I am sorry but I will not be contributing to the party. My mom says it's not right what you are doing for one student. She doesn't agree."

To say that I was surprised is an understatement. Honestly, I was not prepared for such a challenge to the class initiative.

The girl then pressed the point home by asking, "Mr. Maraj, would you do this for every student in your class?"

The whole situation caught me quite off guard. I recognized that at its root, the question was fair and was deserving of an answer. After quick reflection, I gave my honest response.

"If I had to, I would – absolutely!"

"I will tell my mother what you have said," parroted the young innocent.

I was taken aback by her question, and I began to doubt myself: was *I* doing something wrong; was it an error in judgement to encourage altruism in my students?

At noon the party was in progress. The balloons, the cake, and the ice-cream created a festive mood. And, Theo… he was absolutely elated. For once, he was the centre of attention… and it was all positive. I glance over at Brenda. There was no hint of negativity in her manner; she seemed as genuinely happy as anyone else in that room. My concern for her lessened as I noted that in every respect, Brenda continued to be an integral part of the class.

Later that day, Chad came to see me. I sensed the gratitude in his heart when he affirmed, "Mr. Maraj, what you did for Theo today was very decent and Christian."

He left so quickly, I had no time to respond.

I wanted to tell him that it was *he* who possessed the decent and generous soul. It was he who had the initial plan. I was merely the vessel through which his Christian ethic had to flow.

That evening my mind returned to Brenda and to her mom. I was ever so saddened to know that my actions were regarded as being somehow "wrong" and inappropriate by Brenda's mom. Far be it from me to assert that what I did for Theo was "right"; but, I do know that it was not "wrong." Not wrong in the sense that it is never wrong to extend a hand of love and compassion to others. Not wrong also from the point of view of a teacher seeking to encourage students to give voice to the most altruistic and selfless parts of themselves.

I truly wished that Brenda's mother would have intuitively understood the gift of spirit that was being extended by one so young as Chad.

The one redemptive quality in this whole ordeal was the indisputable fact that despite her stand on the issue, Brenda's mother allowed her daughter to participate in the event. That day, because of the actions of one single individual, our class became united in spirit. My heart was bursting with pride for Chad, the one student who showed all of us the true principle behind the concept of brotherly love.

## 52

# I Become the Student

Weeks turned into months and the waters calmed; I felt free to embrace new challenges.

One day after school I happened to pass by the gym when I came upon a small group of boys playing what looked like a game of hockey. I looked on with curiosity at their activity. I recognized one boy, Kent, from my class.

He called out, "Mr. Maraj, come and play with us."

Those words, 'come and play with us' were magical. They appealed to the child in me and I could not resist. Moreover, I *wanted* to play.

There was just one problem: I did not know *how* to play.

At this point I should admit that there was perhaps a larger problem: a problem that I myself had created. Its roots date back a number of years while Diana and I were still in university.

Diana and I had been invited out to dinner at the home of friends. After our evening meal, our host asked if we would join them in watching a hockey game.

Back then, I knew nothing about the game, but I did know that our hosts owned a huge twenty-seven inch colour television. This, in and of itself, was enough of an enticement for me to say yes.

Within minutes the television set was on and the game was in progress. This is what I saw: grown men racing around an oval sheet of solid ice carrying wooden weapons. Now, truth be told, I know that what I just referred to as weapons were not really weapons; they were the instruments of the game. However, to me, at least, they seemed to be used more in the employ of attack than as instruments for the game itself. Players wielded the sticks without restriction, inflicting untold harm on the opposition. Blood flowed freely. Occasionally, some would drop all pretense of playing the game, dropping their gloves and attacking their opponents with their bare hands. This behaviour during a *game* left me speechless. I feared for the lives of the men engaged in the sport. Moments later, as if to prove me correct, one player was knocked out and lay motionless on the ice: a pool of blood oozing from his injury. The injured player was carried off the ice.

I did not understand this game; moreover, I did not like this game.

If this was hockey, I was vehemently against it and I made a silent declaration right then and there that, *No child of mine will ever play hockey!*

I have made very few outright vows in my life. Those I have made I have laboured to honour. Now, here I was with a group of young boys asking me to play a game in which I had sworn never to participate. They seemed to love their game. I forced myself to take a closer look; this game was quite different from the one I witnessed some years ago on television.

The participants were not men, but young boys. The instruments were plastic, not wooden. Furthermore, they were playing indoors on a gymnasium floor in their running shoes rather than on a full-sized outdoor ice surface. This game had much to recommend it. They seemed to be playing actually, not battering one another. Further, they were actually having fun. My mind was being turned…

Then Kent handed me a stick and quipped, "Just your size Mr. Maraj, join in."

"But boys, I really don't know how… I have never…"

This admission seemed to please the boys more than anything and they enthused, "Well, Mr. Maraj, we'll just have to be your teachers today. Are you ready?"

All four boys tutored me in the art of floor hockey. I could not believe the surge of power I felt as I attempted to blast the little plastic puck into the net. At one point the boys found it necessary to chastise me regarding my style.

"No, Mr. Maraj! Don't shoot like that."

I did not understand their concerns. One of them explained, "That shot you were about to take is the slap shot and it is not the right choice for indoor hockey."

Then the boys took turns demonstrating the various shots for the game, all the while explaining the distinct purpose for each choice and the clear method in which each was to be executed. With the wrist shot and the snap shot, the sticks were never to come up beyond the knee. Because of this, there was little danger of accidentally striking someone on their upper body.

In time, I became an avid fan of this game of floor hockey and came to embrace the wrist shot and the snapshot as two of my favourite moves. Often I would choose to stay after school to play with the ever growing group of boys. Once the boys realized that they now had *a teacher supervisor*, they organized themselves into more formal groupings that were often very competitive.

I was always there right in the middle of all the activity... very happy to be playing Canada's national sport.

My involvement in school sports was not limited to the indoor variety.

A few students occasionally played soccer outside. It was still just the mid- seventies and soccer was just beginning to make inroads into the district. Delighted to witness one of my favourite sports being played here in Canada, I joined the players.

I was able to share some of my soccer knowledge; with their increased understanding of the game, soon the level of play improved. Other staff members were drawn to our activity. Before long, we had established teams of play for both indoor and outdoor soccer. This development quite naturally gave me a deeper sense of purpose and an increased sense of acceptance and belonging. When the principal himself seemed pleased with my efforts, I felt that in some small way I too was contributing to the welfare of the school.

Then a singular and most curious event occurred.

# 53

# Soccer on Ice!

It was the mid-seventies and it was Saturday night. We received but *one* channel on our modest television in Emo: CBC; and, CBC hosted but *one* program on Saturday night: *Hockey Night in Canada*. At that time, hockey held no appeal for me and Saturday night quickly established itself as *company night*. On this particular Saturday night we were without company.

I was restless. Diana had just put the children to bed and was settling down in front of the television to watch a bit of the hockey game. For some reason she was excited about the game; she begged and pleaded with me to "just give it a chance."

I resisted.

She insisted. Then, she got up, grabbed me by the hand and escorted me to the couch. "Come on, Frank… please, for me… just for a few minutes. It really is getting very exciting. Just take a look."

She held my hand and escorted me to the couch, reiterating, "Please… for me… for a few minutes."

Reluctantly, I gave in to her urgings.

I knew that Canadians loved their hockey. It was really hard to find people to visit with on a Saturday night. But, somehow we managed. This Saturday night was different. Almost everyone we knew was home glued to their television sets. It is only now, in retrospect, that I understand the reason why: the game was Russia versus Canada. (Neither one of us knew it then, but I was being initiated into a sport that was to claim many of my nights as the years progressed.)

A player dressed in red and white with his stick lifted to his chest was about to ram the opposing player dressed in all red, on the boards. At the very last second, the player in red shifted position. The attacking player hit the boards hard and fell to the ice in obvious pain. The red player then skated off with the puck and effortlessly passed it to another teammate, who in turn, passed the puck to a winger; the winger pretended to shoot and then passed the puck back to the player who initiated the whole move. Unguarded, he scored. Caught up in the excitement of the moment, I jumped up from the couch and immediately began to applaud the masterful play. To Diana I enthused, "This is soccer... *on ice*!"

In an instant I saw the sheer grace of the game – the skating, the team work, the passing and the execution. In that one moment, I fell in love with hockey. I did not even attempt to contain my excitement. Then I looked at Diana; she who only moments ago was begging me to watch the game was decidedly not excited. When I calmed down enough to ask her what was wrong, she responded with a small measure of reprimand, "Frank, you are cheering for the wrong team."

# 54

# Putting my Dream on Ice

The enthusiasm for and appreciation of the game of hockey generated by this game, coupled with my own first hand witnessing of school children becoming consummate skaters in just a matter of days, stirred in me a desire to try the sport myself. Diana was all too willing to help make my dream a reality.

The very next time we were in Rainy River visiting her parents, Diana disappeared upstairs to the attic. When she emerged, she was smiling. Her hands proudly produced a pair of men's skates. They were nothing like the sturdy shiny black molded pair that we had just recently purchased for Trevor; these were floppy, brown, and bent, and sported more than a hint of rust on the ever so dull blades. They were, nevertheless, skates. These were dutifully donned; while somewhat snug, they did fit... more or less. (In retrospect, I think that 'less' was a more accurate descriptor.)

These ancient relics from the pioneer days were transported back to Emo where they remained sitting in the back entry of our home until the following weekend when both the weather and my temperament seemed to be in sync. As a family, we ventured to the outdoor rink beside the school. Happy am I to recall that we were the only ones out there early on that Saturday morning.

Trevor and Lee-Anne had already taken to the ice. Trevor glided... and fell; got up... tried again... and fell again. This process he repeated several times. Eventually, he was able to master the ice. Lee-Anne, on the other hand, got on the ice the first time and never fell at all. Mind you, her steps were tentative and short, but she managed to maintain her balance without insult or injury to herself. Surely, I could do the same.

Diana finished lacing up my skates and assisted me to the ice surface. When I stepped onto the sheet of glass, the world slipped out from under me. I crashed spread-eagle onto the cold icy surface. Getting up was no easy task. Diana, however, had prepared for that eventuality. Out from the trunk of our car she pulled one of our kitchen chairs. She brought it to me and with her aid and the assistance of that chair, once again I wobbled to my feet. This time I managed only half a stride before bumping my head on the ice. Where was the grace in that? Diana urged me to hold on to the chair and propel myself around the rink just until I got a better feel for the skates and how they performed on the ice. I gave it perhaps all of thirty seconds thought before I declined. Off came the skates. Off I went from the ice. I had to face it; skating was not for me. No matter how beautiful and easy it looked from my perspective as a spectator, I had to accept the reality that I did not have what it took to become a participant. I vowed to appreciate the art from the stands.

Since I was never able to master the art of skating, I contented myself with being an avid supporter of *soccer on ice*. This, to me, represented the enjoining of two separate worlds. Thanks to the young students at Donald Young School who, in large measure, introduced me to their world of winter sports, I had a chance to embrace a thrilling and important part of Canadian life. Because I was able to successfully weave the love of soccer that I inherited from my Trinidadian roots into this unfamiliar world of hockey, I was able to strengthen the bonds that I shared with both countries.

## 55

# Modest Gains

A theme of cooperation was characteristic of my other relationships with staff members themselves. At first, the scales were unbalanced; I seemed to need all the assistance. Rarely was I called upon to share any *expertise*. All classroom teachers were expected to deliver expert guidance in every single area of the curriculum. Sometimes, I was able to arrange a 'switch' with another teacher and take over one of their weaker or less favoured areas while they leant their proficiencies to enrich my grade seven class.

At other times, when such accommodations were not feasible, I resorted to begging, and borrowing, (but not stealing), ideas and materials from my coworkers. For this assistance, I was most grateful.

School tradition dictated two annual concerts: Christmas and Spring. I thoroughly enjoyed being involved in these events. Our activity spilled out and we quickly became active in the annual Rainy River District Music and Drama Festival. Our students performed very well at these events and on occasion were invited to appear in the time honoured *Festival of Highlights*. Such recognition in and of itself, seemed to invite appreciation from colleagues. Along with this appreciation came requests for assistance in putting on productions from other classes. I cannot adequately express how wonderful was that feeling of acceptance that accompanied these requests.

I was growing and quietly learning as a teacher, and I was grateful for the modest confidence that these requests engendered in me.

This, however, did little to assuage feelings of aloneness that still plagued me here in this new country.

# 56

# Life's Interconnectedness

How do I confess that in the very midst of all this "success" something was missing from my life?

I was blessed with a wonderful family but I suffered from loneliness.

My sense of self eluded me. *I* was missing from the equation. Trinidad was missing from my life. This hurt me more than I realized.

Little did I know when I moved to this beautiful little community of Emo that I would be presented with challenges that I did not know how to surmount.

The very real physical beauty of this small town was not lost on me. Nor, for that matter, was the real beauty of its inhabitants. From the outset, people had reached out to include us in their lives.

Nevertheless, my soul ached for Trinidad.

I missed Trinidad with all its colours and contradictions; I missed its crowds; I even missed its ridiculous traffic and characteristically loud island music. I especially missed its multiple movie houses and its huge variety of restaurants.

Yet, for all its *busyness*, Trinidad had offerings of peace and tranquility for those who would seek out its various mountains, fields, beaches, and isolated hamlets. It was undeniable; Trinidad had stamped an indelible footprint at the ground level of my soul; it was exhausting trying to free myself from her grip.

For me, Christmas in Emo was a most lonesome affair. Diana, on the other hand, was in heaven. Emo was everything to her. Having been born in Fort Frances and raised in Rainy River, moving to Emo was like moving back home for her. It required very little adjustment; Emo was a true haven. Diana cocooned herself in activities surrounding the church, and the school, and minimally expanded her world to develop friendships with other young mothers in the area. For Diana, Emo was the complete package. She, herself, desired so little of the city with all its noise and crowds. But, hitherto unknown to me, these things were imbued in my very lifeblood. I longed to catch a simple breath of the city. A quiet desperation descended, alleviated only temporarily by the occasional escape to Thunder Bay, Winnipeg, or Duluth; I longed for a miracle to cure my malady.

Late one evening as I walked the streets of Emo during the Christmas season, I noticed the presence of cars visiting from other provinces. These cars heightened my sense of loneliness for they represented the gathering together of families.

My heart hurt.

That Christmas we had no family visitors.

I loved family life; I loved family gatherings.

That walk intensified my feeling of separation from Trinidad. My longing for Trinidad was assuming proportions hitherto unknown.

I could not understand myself.

I could not ask for a more loving and embracing life at home. It was Diana, Trevor, Lee-Anne, and later, Dee-Dee, who imbued me with the spirit to survive this wretched plight.

Yet, I needed something more to lift my spirit from despair.

\*\*\*

Later that night, an avalanche of snow descended on our town.

My driveway was a dense sea of white. I despaired at this otherwise lovely sight.

The reality that I was responsible for clearing away this mountain of snow had me feeling somewhat defeated as held up my modest shovel against the mountain of whiteness in my driveway. Nevertheless, I began my labour.

I barely made a dent in the imperial avalanche, when the municipal plough graced our street. With powerful broad blades, it made clear a path in the street; it did this, however, at the expense of my property. The modest inroads I had made in my driveway were completely wiped out by the plough when it transferred the street offerings of white into an additional three feet of elevation.

Defeated, I fell into the newly deposited bank of snow wallowing in self-pity.

It was at that moment that I came face to face with the reality of my isolation. I had no close family to turn to for assistance. In Trinidad, even the most distant family member would only be a couple of hours away. Here, in Canada, I was essentially days away from my family.

I was alone.

I had to face that reality.

The grandmother of all instincts bore the inevitability of my Canadian existence in my brain and announced, "Deal with it."

In short, I had been kick-started. A new energy surged through my body. I grabbed the shovel and began a relentless attack on the white invasion. I kept up this pace for several minutes.

Then I heard a familiar sound… it was the grader returning for a second go round. I scurried out of its way, wondering what more damage it could possibly want to do to my property. The grader came closer and closer. It reversed and entered my driveway. I wondered if the driver had seen me.

Then, in one continuous motion the entire driveway was cleared; I simply stood there, shovel in hand, speechless. The driver poked his head out of the cab. Sporting the biggest grin, he teased, "Well, Mr. Schoolteacher, how do you like our Canadian snow?" Neither expecting nor wanting a response, he left while shouting a final customary farewell, "Have a nice day!"

I was speechless.

I do not recall saying thank you to the driver of the plough that day. I recalled only that mere moments ago I was felt defeated and alone.

Suddenly, I was filled with a new emotion. This one act of kindness was my minor miracle. It was most timely.

That act of kindness on that cold winter day taught me that acts of neighbourliness were alive even here in this isolated community in Canada.

Then I heard the distant whistle of a train. I watched, motionless, as carriage after carriage streamed along the tracks. For a moment, my thoughts transported me back to Trinidad and for a moment I was rooted in my own back yard in Trinidad. And, once again I mused at life's interconnectedness.

# 57

# The Good Neighbour

That kindly act reminded me of an incident that had occurred in the late fall of the year. We purchased our home in late August without seeking professional inspection services. Such a thought never occurred to us. We were, however, given information regarding the name of the local carpenter who had recently worked on the house. In fact, he and his wife, (Len and Dorothy) lived just down the street in a home that bore a striking similarity to the outside of our house. In addition, when considering some initial renovations to the house, I had engaged Len's services. By the time of this event's occurrences, we were well acquainted with one another.

As was my custom upon awakening, I looked forward to my morning shower. It was during that time and in the confines of the steamy warm room, that I put the finishing touches on my plans for the day. I delighted in luxuriating under the gentle but invigorating rush of hot water. The air that morning held a distinct chill; how happy was I to be indoors.

After brushing my teeth, I prepared to turn on the shower. First, the hot, then the cold tap… nothing… I tried again… still nothing.

I called out to Diana, "Something strange is going on. I can't seem to get any water to run out of the taps."

Diana tried the taps herself. When still no water was forthcoming she calmly announced, "Guess the pipes are frozen, Frank. It happens sometimes in houses without basements."

I froze at the mention of frozen pipes. I had no idea what she was talking about but obviously it was nothing about which I had the vaguest clue. I did not have the slightest clue about how to begin to resolve the issue.

Then I remembered Len and his kind offer of assistance if ever I were to require it.

Knowing that both Len and Dorothy were early risers, I rushed down the street to their house. Even though it was just seven thirty, Dorothy greeted me with a smile and welcomed me into the house. Len was still at the kitchen table finishing breakfast. He looked up at me quizzically over the rim of his coffee cup. Without waiting for him to ask I blustered, "Len, I need your help."

An alarmed look crossed his face as he queried, "Are Diana and the kids okay?"

"Yes, yes. Everyone's fine but the water pipes in the house are frozen. We have no water."

Len assured me that he would check out the pipe situation and Dorothy offered to look out for the rest of the family.

I stood on the landing soaking in the assurances. I knew that I should be returning home to inform Diana that Len would be coming over but something was holding me back. Len noticed my hesitation and raised his eyebrow as if to ask, *Is there something else?*

Without thinking, I blurted out, "Shower. I need to shower."

They laughed heartily at my forwardness and Dorothy grabbed a towel from the cupboard and handed it to me. Gratefully, I accepted the towel and disappeared into the bathroom. I don't think that I overstayed my time in the shower, (it was probably half the length of my showers at home) but just as I was finishing up, Dorothy tapped on the door and cheerily advised, "Frank, as soon as you are done there, come back to the kitchen. I have your breakfast all ready for you. It is on the table."

I sat down to this unexpected feast of scrambled eggs, toast and jam, and coffee. Breakfast had never tasted better.

True to his word, Len came to the house and resolved our frozen pipe issue. Never once did he complain about having to venture under the house and crawl amid the dirt. At the end of the day I went back to his house to pay my bill. As I reached into my pocket to retrieve my wallet, Len stopped me with this gentle chastisement, "Frank, what I did was from one neighbour to another. That's all. Welcome, my friend."

And that friendship endured. We have not forgotten you Len and Dorothy. You made Emo home.

# 58

# Settling In

Wandering the streets of downtown Emo became a favourite pastime of mine. Initially it was the beauty of the river that compelled me to the area. As I became more familiar with the downtown merchants, I would enter the various stores under the pretense of browsing. Without really recognizing it, what I was seeking in reality, was some form of social engagement.

The staff in all the various businesses in Emo were highly accommodating in this respect. This served to further tighten the bond between Emo and myself.

The staff at the local hardware store was especially friendly. Their complementary coffee was especially enticing with its "Help yourself" sign displayed prominently in front of the coffee pot. Initially it was the coffee that drew me into the store, but it was the friendly staff and courteous reception that made me return week after week. The sense of small town hospitality was omnipresent and it permeated every corner of the rustic building.

To this frequently homesick Trinidadian, this hardware store became my Saturday morning anchor; how gladly did my feet propel me there.

No longer was I just a mere visitor in Emo. Gradually, I became accepted as a permanent fixture. Perhaps, more importantly, *I* was beginning to accept Emo as home.

While thoughts of Trinidad were always on the horizon, gone was my desperation to retreat there at the slightest whim. My life, both at school and within the community, became clothed in stability.

# 59

# A Class Trip?

Back in my Grade 7 classroom, I overheard students talking excitedly about an upcoming trip. They repeatedly referred to it as a *class* trip. If it is indeed a *class* trip, shouldn't I, the class teacher, know something about this trip? I was completely ignorant about the culture surrounding this event. It was only when the principal inquired as to how the plans were coming along regarding the trip, that I became informed as to my role in this major undertaking.

When he told me that I was *in charge*, I naively asked, "In charge of what?"

"Every single thing. That class trip is your baby. Have you ever planned a class trip, Frank?"

When I shook my head, *no*, he reached into a nearby filing cabinet and pulled out a bulging file folder. Holding the file in his outstretched hand, he offered it to me.

"Frank, it is good to be organized. I keep everything on file. I expect that you will do the same. Here. Take this. It will help keep you on track."

Then he quipped, "Better get started. And Frank, keep me posted… every step of the way."

The more I read the folder, the more my head began to spin. The responsibility was all inclusive from planning the destination to arranging the accommodations, the transportation, the chaperones and the fund-raising.

I returned to the principal to ask but one question. "Do I have a choice as to go or not to go?"

His answer was a perfunctory, "No."

Sensing my state of mind, he offered a few words of sage advice, "Frank, you are in charge, yes, but you need to delegate; you hear me, delegate some of the responsibilities. You'll be okay. You'll see."

Certainly we went on school trips in Trinidad, but they were nothing of this magnitude. Our school trips consisted of one day outings to see a movie or perhaps an excursion to the coast. These trips were not planned by the teachers but by the principal. This does much to explain my perceived reluctance to undertake such a venture. It seemed that teachers in Canada were expected to assume a more active role in taking on added responsibility. I was innocently ignorant of this fact but once it was explained to me, I understood my role more clearly and was ready for the challenge. I was in charge and I was to delegate; these were two areas in which I had confidence. The fog had lifted.

Next, I met with my class and together we defined the parameters of the trip and individual responsibilities of each member of the class.

Our trip to the Winnipeg Zoo was taking shape. I had but one area of concern… fundraising.

Traditionally, the students approached the various businesses in town to ask for donations to help pay for the trip. Personally, I did not see the wisdom in that tactic. Somehow it seemed incongruous with the values of independence and personal responsibility that we were trying to instill in our students. In light of that, I proposed a different solution.

# 60

# The Lesson

When I first proposed that the students seek *to earn* the money they each required for the trip, I was met with a measure of opposition.

"But we always go canvassing; we always ask our families and the local businesses to give us donations."

"Yes, Mr. Maraj, we ask for money and we get it. We don't understand you; why spoil a good thing?"

These two voices represented the general tenor of the class. It was my job to help them look at things from another perspective without alienating them.

"Students what you propose is perfectly acceptable. It is not wrong to seek help. Believe me, I understand your viewpoint. No problem."

I paused to look at my students. They were still listening; I hadn't lost them yet.

I continued, "Asking for help is one way. Helping yourself is another way."

My pronouncement was met with quizzical looks. "What exactly do you mean, Mr. Maraj?" "Class, what I'm trying to say is simply this: let's not go around asking for a handout. Instead, let's approach everyone and volunteer to help them in some way; let's offer to do things for those from whom we expect to ask for funds."

One student caught on immediately, "You want us to work and earn the money."

"Exactly. We will hit Emo and your family with this simple idea… we need money… but, we want to work for it."

The class was now buzzing with ideas. They embraced my proposal completely.

Over time I received many positive and encouraging words from both the families of the students and business community. Parents reported that their child was willing to help out with more chores at home. One business in particular summed up the general tenor of the community when the owner said, "Mr. Maraj, I can't tell you how impressed I am with your students. They were here volunteering to help… they offered to wash cars or anything else that needed cleaning… And, do you want to know what impressed me the most?"

I nodded.

"They said *please* and *thank you* and they meant it. What hand did you have in all of that?"

Quietly pleased with this commentary, I smiled.

Yes, the students were learning.

But, so was I.

So was I.

# 61

# An Afterthought: Falling Short

After consulting with the chaperones, I ensured that our expectations regarding student behaviour on our Winnipeg trip were clear to the student population. My main concern was behaviour; I ensured that the students knew that they were to conduct themselves properly at all times and in all situations. If I would have been asked if this was a realistic expectation, I would have replied that I expected nothing less than complete compliance.

I outlined the guidelines that we put in place regarding student comportment at the hotel. The students had an assigned curfew. Additionally, they were cautioned that they were not to enter the hotel restaurant unaccompanied. Furthermore, they were advised that they were to enter the restaurant as a group and sit at assigned tables. Hotel management had gladly consented to accommodate our students in a designated area to more easily service our needs. To their credit, the students complied with all of these demands without complaint; their excellent comportment earned them considerable admiration voiced by both the chaperones and the hotel staff. When we left Winnipeg, we all were happy.

On the way home, however, I discovered that one group of students had broken the rule regarding the curfew. This indiscretion caused considerable inconvenience to the chaperones. Had I been informed of the situation when it happened, it would have been quickly dealt with on that last evening. Because the situation came to light on our trip home, I had to conduct my investigation of the incident on the bus. I began by speaking to the students involved in the incident. I spoke with each one individually in turn. Not one of the students blamed any other student for his indiscretion. Each assumed full responsibility for his own action. Because of this incident and the resulting "inquisition" the whole tone of the trip changed. The once chatty and light-hearted group quickly dissolved into one of silent discord. No one was happy. One of the chaperones recognized how much the mood had changed and sought to do something about it. He began by working on me. He knew just what to say.

"Mr. Maraj, thank you for inviting me on this trip. What a tremendous group of students; you must be so proud of them."

I was caught completely off guard. His comment gently disturbed me from my negative focus. By complimenting the students he forced me to see the bigger picture. He made me realize that I was too focused on the one small indiscretion. Truly, he made me realize just how insignificant that one act was.

He continued to compliment, "I have been on many trips. I have to hand it to you. You certainly have a way; you do expect perfection, don't you!"

"Do I?" I was dumbfounded by the comment.

"These students respect you. They will do anything for you. Let them know how proud you are of them."

From the vantage of hindsight, I now recognize how difficult it was for me to release myself from my high expectations. To accept nothing less than stellar behaviour from the students immediately within my charge went against every fiber of my being. I did recognize however, that to continue with the *inquisition* in the same manner was futile. Sadly however, the wonderful words of wisdom from the chaperone were only half absorbed by my overly critical spirit and I missed a golden opportunity to tell my students how perfectly wonderful they truly were. It is so obvious to me now in hindsight to recognize just how wonderful they truly were on that trip.

There was something lacking in me as a teacher that I failed to recognize it back then. I wish I could go back in time; I wish that I had had enough confidence in myself to let some of the little things go. As a beginning teacher in a foreign land, I was on guard constantly; I worried about making mistakes, and, consequently was loath to let anyone else make any either. I wish that the garment of *consummate properness* had been stripped from my baggage. (I wish that my need to be clothed constantly in the garment of consummate propriety had been stripped from my baggage.) But, I continued to learn.

And, after all this time, may I now say to my students, "Know this, students...you were simply magnificent."

# 62

# More Adjustments

I spent five years teaching Grade 7. I had learned a great deal from both staff and students alike. As year five ended, my principal paid me a visit.

His initial comments were very encouraging as he commented on how much I had grown as a teacher. He might have even alluded to the fact that I was enjoying some success in that capacity.

When he commented, "It is now time to consider another challenge," my skin prickled and my defences went on high alert.

"From time to time we rotate our teachers," he continued.

The mere idea was unsettling.

"Frank, I am recommending that you accept the position of teaching the Grade 5 class next year."

I was dumbfounded, "Grade 5?" I stammered.

"Yes, Frank. That level is most ideal. The students are so willing at that age."

"But, they are so young," I countered.

My comment must have surprised my principal for he questioned what I meant by "young".

Fearing that I had somehow been offensive or disrespectful with my comment, I hastened to add, "I am just not sure that I can do a good enough job at that level." At the heart of the matter, was just more of my own insecurities coming to the surface. In Trinidad I had taught at the high school level only. Teaching Grade 7 had been a bit of an adjustment… but… Grade 5? I was not sure I had what it took to teach at that level.

"Don't worry about it, Frank. You will do just fine. I know it. In fact, I think that you will really enjoy it."

"Do I have any say in the matter? Do I have a choice?"

"Not really," he grinned.

And, thus, my career as a Grade 5 teacher began.

# 63

# Baby Steps

I approached that first day of my new assignment with great trepidation. I still believed that I was unsuited to this grade level. My initial voyage was one of great discovery.

Determined to remain true to who I was as a teacher, I began the day in my customary way.

I interrupted their excited first day chatter with, "Good morning, Grade Five."

I barely made a dent in their world. Only a handful of students responded.

So caught up in their own excited chatter, they were completely oblivious to me. Amid the chatter of first day excitement, I agonized over my next step. I did not want to raise my voice…not on their first day with me. Besides, they were so young…

I remained motionless and perplexed, unsure of my next move.

I must have posed quite the odd presence in the room for one young girl approached me with a smile to ask, "Mr. Maraj, are you okay?"

"Not really," I replied with only half a smile.

"What's wrong?" she persisted.

"Well, I need the class to come to attention."

Without hesitating for even one second, this same young lady turned to the class and, summoning up her loudest voice, commanded as only a ten year old could, without guile or reprimand, "Guys, Mr. Maraj wants us to be quiet. Now listen up!"

Immediately, the class hushed. All eyes turned expectantly to me. The girl took her seat among her peers.

I cleared my throat and began, "Students, when I stand before you, I expect that you will quiet down immediately and come to attention. The behaviour that I witnessed earlier might be construed as disrespectful. Given the circumstances of our initial official meeting, I am choosing to overlook that indiscretion and deem that…"

Before I could finish, Mandee's hand shot up. This was the same young lady who assisted me earlier. There was a quizzical look on her face and no hint of embarrassment in her voice when she asked, "What is indushion or deemm…is that part of a submarine?"

Several students giggled. And another asked,

"How were we disrespectful? We are good students Mr. Maraj."

Completely disarmed by the unaffected innocence of my new students, I surrendered. I had to rethink my approach to these students and adjust my language to suit their developmental level. Gradually, I would have to begin the process of helping them to understand me and to adjust to my expectations.

I wondered how we would fare on this year long adventure.

# 64

# Disarmed

I firmly believed that once I had explained my expectations regarding classroom conduct and procedures and once I myself made the necessary adjustments regarding my own conduct that I would achieve a considerable measure of success in the area of classroom management. This certainly proved to be true in the early days of our mutual adjustment. I began to relax into optimism.

The semester was well underway. The students and I had achieved a degree of mutual understanding. When instructed to work "independently" the students knew exactly what was expected of them. The two greatest requirements were: working alone, and no talking. Silence was an absolute prerequisite. Thus far, the students had been compliant. A simple look with raised eyebrow in the direction of a transgressor, was all it took to reinstate compliance. Dead silence prevailed…that is, until Mandee's indiscretion.

I had been assiduously working at my desk, trying to get caught up on some marking. Every so often, I would raise my eyes and glance around the room to ensure that all were actively engaged in their work. The glance became a penetrating stare if I discerned the slightest measure of noncompliance.

The room existed as if all in it were under a spell…me included. Once again I became absorbed in my marking. Ever so gradually, I became aware of sound. It was the sound of a tiny voice just elevated sufficiently to be barely audible above the prevailing silence.

When I raised my head to glance around the room, it did not require any effort to find the offending party. She had indeed made herself most conspicuous by turning her body completely around in her desk.

Completely oblivious to her own transgression, Mandee continued to transgress.

Her friend caught my glance and tried to caution Mandee by placing her finger to her lips. Mandee, however, completely oblivious to this overture continued her chatter.

Had Mandee been even the least bit cognizant of her friend's attempt at assistance, I might not have had to undertake any further action.

But, she wasn't, so I had to.

"Mandee," I called, with a hint of sternness, "come to my desk, please."

The phrase, itself, *come to my desk,* should have signaled to Mandee that an offence had been committed. That, coupled with my stern tone, should have set off warning bells that punishment was both imminent and unavoidable. Students requested to come to my desk, came with a degree of contriteness if not apprehension. But not Mandee.

Mandee smiled broadly as she sauntered regally to my desk. When she reached the desk, she propped her elbows on the smooth work surface, and, cupping her chin in her hands, looked up fawningly eyes that sparkled.

She was completely oblivious of her *crime.*

"Yes, Mr. Maraj. You wanted to see me?"

Then, she batted her eyelashes.

She had no idea that she had transgressed in any way.

I was completely disarmed by this child's innocence. I forfeited totally my need to command or even reprimand this innocent.

All I could manage with respect to a rebuke was, "Mandee, return to your seat. Get back to your work."

Without registering so much as a hint of despair, she casually raised herself up from my desk and acknowledged, "Yes, Mr. Maraj."

And then she added, "Anything else?"

Her complete lack of guile was totally disarming.

# 65

# Spike

The years spent teaching at the grade five level were glorious ones. Within the confines of those walls I discovered a new world; a world where children were still children; a world where the twin virtues of respect and affection were allowed to coexist. There was one occasion however that revealed that it was sometimes difficult for some children to embrace such notions.

On that day, one of my students, Christine, ran into the classroom complaining about one of the boys. As she began to speak, she choked up. Her friends, Jan, and Claudette, who were only moments behind her, voiced their support.

"It was Spike, Mr. Maraj…he, he cussed and said nasty things."

"We didn't do anything."

"Mr. Maraj, it's like he's gone crazy."

Collectively, the three of them laid out a convincing case against Spike. They demanded to know just what I was going to do about him. The three victims shared a common mindset: Spike had to be brought to justice and they were more than willing to prosecute.

After calming the waters, I assured them that I would talk to Spike.

Eventually, I found him, distressed and forlorn, slouched against a tree in the far recesses of the school compound. It appeared that he wanted to be forgotten.

"Hello, Spike," I ventured.

He did not answer. Yet, he did look at me. His eyes were tearful; his face was smudged with a mixture of dirt and tears. I could tell that he had been crying.

"Spike, we need to talk. I understand…"

He immediately blurted out, "Yes, Mr. Maraj; I did it. I said bad things... I'm guilty. I'm always guilty. I'm sorry I used the cuss word. It just came out. I am sorry about the cuss word because I know how you feel about anyone using those words. But I'm not sorry for the other things I said."

"I understand. Did the three students do something to provoke you?"

He thought carefully, "No, not today..."

"But, why did you...."

"It's the way they looked at me, Mr. Maraj. Always judging me. Always treating me like a nobody. And they have said things to me in the past. It's just that today I was fed up, and I let them have it... So I am guilty."

These were the words of a broken and hurting soul. The child had been cast aside by many of the students in the school. Forced to console himself with his own company, he had become a loner; dispirited.

I searched for the right words. I struggled to find the balance between teacher and adjudicator.

When I did speak, I was careful not to sound judgemental for clearly Spike had already prosecuted himself.

"Spike, you reacted today and you said some not so good things. You had cause. Yes?"

"I did, Mr. Maraj."

"Spike you were hurting. And you reacted. Perhaps the way you reacted is..."

Mr. Maraj, I know. I reacted badly. And I have to be punished. Right?"

"Yes."

"And you are sending me to the principal."

"No, Spike. What you have to do is worse than 'go to the principal.'"

"Worse, Mr. Maraj? What's worse than that?

"You are going to apologize to the students..."

"No! I can't do that. They hurt me. They always hurt me..."

"Spike—that's not all—you have to apologize in class..."

"Mr. Maraj, I can't do that..."

"Spike what I am asking is hard. I know. I won't *make* you apologize in front of the class. Yet, if you did, you would be helping me, and helping the whole class, every one of us."

He looked at me and bent his head. I was not sure whether he would apologize to the girls in front of the class. Then this bruised soul said these unforgettable words, "Only for you Mr. Maraj; I trust you."

We headed back to class. Spike's words overwhelmed me. Spike would never suspect how much those words meant to me or what they indicated about his character.

Once back in class, I asked for everyone's attention.

I turned my eyes to Spike and began to address them, "Class, something happened today on the playground. It concerns Spike, and three other students."

I stopped and I invited Spike to come before the class.

He rose from his seat at the back of the room and made his way to the front. His eyes filled with tears as he addressed the three whom he had offended, "Girls, I cussed. I said bad things. Mr. Maraj asked me to apologize. I am sorry."

His stubby fingers awkwardly brushed aside the tears streaming from his eyes.

I was proud of him but, the matter did not end there.

I took my turn at addressing the class.

"Students, Spike did a wrong. He came before the class and admitted it. This is our class. We do not hurt each other. Some of you also made mistakes."

I paused.

"There are those of you in this class who, by your actions, have hurt Spike. You may not have said anything directly to him, but he got the message that you did not care for him."

Then I posed the final question, "Is there anyone here who recognizes that they might have done something to make Spike feel bad about himself? Like he was rejected?

Immediately, the three students stood up before the class and apologized to Spike.

That moment stands out for me as among one of the best moments in my initial years in Canada. I marvelled at the sheer goodness of the moment.

As the class returned to the normal work routines, I cast a quick glance in Spike's direction... He caught my look and smiled.

# 66

# Operation Citizenship

At the end of the year my principal issued an edict in which he stated that every classroom teacher was to ensure that all texts in the classroom were to be in good standing. Furthermore, he declared that said books were to be free from unwarranted scribbling.

Considering how I had grown up to value and treasure books, I threw myself into compliance with my whole heart. His directive was a most responsible one and I admired him for taking this action.

Accordingly, the next morning I announced to the students, "Class, today we are conducting a very special activity—Operation Citizenship."

Lisa commented, "Fancy title, Mr. Maraj. What do we have to do?"

I explained, "Students you all know how hard our principal works to make sure that things work well in our school. He is always trying to improve our school..."

I did have a chance to finish as Warren agreed, "Yes, he comes early to school, and floods the rink so we can skate."

There was lively discourse in class, and though some students did not approve of some things the principal did, as a class, they agreed and admitted that Mr. Burton was a hard-working principal who cared for our school a great deal. At that point, I explained, "Mr. Burton would appreciate very much, if we all would be good citizens and look after the books in our class. In short we would undertake to clean and repair all books."

Warren queried, "And that is Operation Citizenship?"

"Yes."

"That's not so hard."

"Class, I have a list here of the various work brigades. There will be five brigades. Each brigade has a designated colour. Each colour is responsible for a particular activity. For example, the Red Brigade is responsible for book repairs. The Green Brigade is responsible for removing all unnecessary pencil marks and so forth. I have also assigned a work area for each brigade. Shall we begin?"

I posted the several lists on the chalkboard. The students were about to start when Lisa exclaimed, "Mr. Maraj, something is dreadfully wrong!"

In an instant, all activity stopped; every eye was trained on Lisa.

"Lisa, what is wrong?"

"But, Mr. Maraj," her voice was now a little more playful, "how can we work happily without our *usual*?"

"Our usual?"

"Yes, Mr. Maraj, without our *ice cream*?"

"Yes, ice cream." echoed the entire class in a singular voice.

It didn't take long for me to respond. "Your ice cream will be here at lunch," I smiled.

Both Lisa and Warren approached me at my desk. Lisa teased, "We know why you are so happy."

"And why do you think I am happy?"

"Because you are enjoying this work. You are always making us take care of our books—right? And you like us, Mr. Maraj, don't you?"

I was taken back a bit by Lisa's directness and I could not respond; I continued my work in silence.

Then Warren had his say, "You are just that way. You even make us clean up the floor—all the time."

These two students had me figured out. They returned to their stations and joined their classmates.

That group of grade five students became a chain gang—each brigade performing at a maximum, dutifully and cheerfully. I was both delighted and proud.

The year was coming to an end and I had managed to stay afloat in this brand new grade five vessel. I began to relax. I had to admit that I was enjoying the adventure.

Nothing about that day hinted at the stormy weather ahead.

# 67

# New York Beckons

The last day of school was a professional activity day. The students were not in class and the teachers spent the day in meetings and tidying up any loose ends in their respective classrooms.

Diana had been preparing for the end of school for the last week. We were planning our annual trip to visit my family in New York City and Diana had been cleaning the house and packing up the suitcases for our next adventure.

At the end of the day, she brought the children to meet me in the parking lot at the school. Everything was in the car, packed and ready for me. This had become our custom over the past few years. I so looked forward to meeting my family in New York. My mother was there along with my sisters and their families. Two brothers were there as well and I wanted to be part of the family mix. Summer was the only time when we could manage the trip.

That particular summer we overstayed our time in New York. As a result, I had to rush the return trip in order to allow myself one last Sunday at home before school reopened.

We arrived in Emo on the Saturday before school began. On Sunday, although I was exhausted, I forced myself to go to the school. I was not panicked for I had done some preparatory work before I had left for summer vacation and I was reasonably assured that I would be ready for classes.

What I was not ready for, however, is the sight that greeted me after I opened the door to my grade five class.

Shock waves surged through my body as I took in the scene: a veritable mountain of books had been piled on the top of my once clean teacher's desk. No fewer than three hundred books occupied every square inch of space on my desk. That mountain of books took on the form of a spacecraft, foreign and threatening. Helplessly, I became at once transformed; I was a frozen block of ice, capable of neither movement nor thought.

As the minutes passed, I thawed. When I was sufficiently able, I turned and my feet propelled me in the direction of home. My classroom was not my classroom; it had been overrun by some distant foreign invader.

Soon I would learn that the invader was neither distant nor foreign.

# 68

# No Discussion...You Listen

Anxiety and unease were my companions as I walked to school the next morning. I tried to convince myself that it had all been just a very bad dream; the mountain did not exist. When I first entered my classroom, I avoided looking at my desk. This tactic proved useful for only a few seconds. I forced myself to glance in the direction of my desk. It had been no dream; the mountain was still there.

I stood in silence before the massive heap of books.

The voice of my principal brought me out of my delirium.

"Mr. Maraj, is there something you want to ask me?"

My initial reticence to speak prompted further urgings from the principal, "Mr. Maraj, you have any questions?"

"Just one."

"And what is your question?"

"Who is responsible for placing these books on my desk?"

"I am!"

After a moment of silent reflection, I responded, "Thank you. You have answered my question."

My principal wanted to pursue the conversation and began to dialogue anew, "But, let me tell you..."

I could not let the discussion continue. My mind was not ready. Besides, the students were due at any moment. I tried to deflect his efforts and stated as calmly as I could, "No, this is not the time. My students will be here momently. Do excuse me. To be sure we will talk, but it must be later."

It was with great reluctance and some small measure of displeasure that he left.

I felt justified with my decision to defer our "talk" until a later time because at that moment the needs of my students took precedence over anything else. I had to regain my focus and prepare to take charge of my class in spite of the towering pillars on my desk.

My desk, or rather the mountain of books on my desk, became the focus for each student as he/she entered the room.

After the opening exercises were completed, I redirected any queries concerning the books. I had no answers to give them. I had more than enough questions of my own.

Once again, during the recess break, my principal tried to approach me to talk. Still, I was not ready.

"Mr. Maraj, I believe you *should* want to talk to me; we have a problem..."

"I agree. Yes, there is a problem, and it needs to be addressed. Could we meet at lunch time, please?"

"We should clear up the problem here and now..."

"Please, not now, could we meet at lunch time at your convenience."

He really wanted to clear the matter up right at that very moment, but I had not yet given ample thought as to why these books were placed on my desk. I was anxious and hurt and not yet ready to have a discussion. My mind was in a state of confusion.

The appointed time of our meeting arrived and so did my principal. Still unwilling to address the issue, I took the lead and tried to defer the discussion until after school.

"Sir, I believe that it would really be better if we met after school. I am not in the right frame of mind to talk about the matter right now. Is that okay with you?"

"No, it is not; I want to end the matter now. It is quite simple really. I gave you instructions and you did not fully comply."

"Sir, you say I did not fully comply. We cannot talk anymore. I am upset."

"And I am upset also. So let me tell you why I am upset with you."

"Sir, I cannot reasonably discuss this matter, nor anything else right now. Please, let's do this after school. Please..."

Finally, he agreed but on one condition. He affirmed, "I speak my mind first. You listen."

I now understood that this was not to be a discussion...

# 69

# My Turn

I had to steel my mind in preparation for my next encounter with Mr. Burton. I knew that it would involve some measure of discomfort for both of us; this fact was unavoidable. I just prayed, however, that I would have the right words to convey my point of view without alienating my principal.

I was particularly grateful for my new set of students in my Grade 5 class. Their generous and gracious attitudes were accompanied by their equally open and willing spirits. They were able to distract my mind somewhat from what I knew I had to face at day's end; the exceedingly good nature of my students made the day manageable.

When the students were dismissed for the day, Mr. Burton entered the classroom; we greeted each other amicably and each of us took a seat.

Mr. Burton took the lead, and, as was his habit, his comments were pointed and direct. "Mr. Maraj, you wanted to know who put that pile of books on your desks. I am responsible. I suppose you want to know why?"

"Yes, I do, Mr. Burton."

"Well," he continued, "let me give it to you straight."

"I expect nothing less."

"Mr. Maraj, I gave specific instructions that you and all members of the staff were to repair all books, and get rid of all unnecessary scribbling on the books. My instructions were clear…"

I was about to respond, but clearly Mr. Burton was not yet finished. As he continued, his voice became more commanding, "Mr. Maraj, were my instructions not clear to you?"

I felt a silent rebellion swelling in my chest. My agitation was palpable.

He prompted, "I am waiting on your answer. Were my instructions clear?"

"Yes, Mr. Burton, they were clear."

"Then, Mr. Maraj, I am left to only one conclusion: by not complying with this request, you, in fact, disobeyed. That is serious. And, furthermore, you made no visible effort to clean up the books that were placed on your desk."

My anger was continuing to build. But, it was not yet my turn to speak. I waited.

He continued. "Is that the kind of example that you wish to set before your students? They are young and impressionable. That was wrong on your part Mr. Maraj. And, to tell the truth, I am most disappointed in your attitude."

My insides were crumbling. I could feel my body trembling, aching to respond to these misplaced accusations.

Again he continued. "Mr. Maraj, everyone on staff has complied—everyone but you. Your action can be construed as insubordinate. I can write you up as insubordinate. That will be on your record. Now, what do you have to say for yourself?"

At that point I felt completely humiliated. I wanted the freedom to respond to his remarks in kind. But, I knew that that would be wrong. I had to search within myself to find that place of rational thought. My comments had to come from a place of respect, not from reaction.

I took a moment to reflect on Mr. Burton's positives. I knew that at heart I both liked and respected this man. I recognized that at heart he was a good principal and he ran his school as a captain would run his ship. In this moment of extreme agitation, I knew that I had to find a way to elevate my mind from the negative emotions that I was nursing in silence. I struggled to hold on to a modicum of self-esteem.

It was at this moment that I remembered the time not too long ago when I was vying for a position as lecturer in the Department of Education, at the University of the West Indies, in Trinidad. I pushed that humiliation from my mind. It was time to face the reality of now. I now have a mountain of books staring out at me from my desk. The man who put them there was accusing me of insubordination. While I had little respect for my accuser in Trinidad, this situation was quite different. It required a different tactic for I had come to know and respect my principal and was prepared to overlook some of his brash mannerisms.

It was most taxing however to try to find a way out of this most difficult moment.

I had to find a way to address my principal and to counter his accusations without anger and in a carefully measured tone. I began tentatively, "Mr. Burton, is it my turn to have the floor?"

"Yes, Mr. Maraj."

"I will answer you. But I need your permission to speak freely."

"To speak freely, Mr. Maraj?"

"Yes, I do have some things to say to you."

"Speak your mind Mr. Maraj, but first answer my question and tell me why you did not clean up and repair the books."

"Mr. Burton, I have a question for you. Do I strike you as the type of teacher who is rebellious and argumentative?"

"No Mr. Maraj, not at all. That is why I was so terribly shocked and disappointed. All you have to do is apologize for your negligence."

"Apologize? Mr. Burton, by temperament I am the one most likely to apologize when I have done a wrong."

"But, you *were* wrong."

"Mr. Burton, we agreed; no interruptions; this is my turn."

He crossed his arms in silent protest.

I resumed, "Mr. Burton, I did not mean to appear insubordinate. You see I did repair and attend to the books that needed attention. I did that before the summer holidays. These books that you placed on my desk were ones that we are not currently using. Some of them are very old and in very bad shape. But, despite this fact, I simply could not throw them out..."

"And why not, Mr. Maraj?"

"Mr. Burton, I carry in my soul a lesson of life from my earliest years. It is a most difficult thing for me to throw a book in the garbage. Books carry in them an element of the sacred. I cannot, in good conscience, throw them away."

Mr. Burton was stilled; he unfolded his arms; I knew I had his attention.

"When I was a young child, there were times when my parents could not afford to buy me so much as a simple pencil. Can you imagine that to own a pencil to take to school could pose a financial hardship for a family? If having a pencil could do that to a family, imagine how much more difficult it would be to own a book under those circumstances.

When I was a child, books were exceedingly hard to come by. I could never hope to own a brand new one. I learned that I could buy discarded and second hand books and survive in school. I would often have to take parts from several discarded books to make up one complete text book. I know the value of a book. I do not take their value lightly. In addition, I knew not the luxury of having my own notebook. I had to resort to using brown wrapping paper to write out my notes and to do my math homework.

"And now, look at our current situation. This is a world where pens, pencils, paper and books are readily available; it is so easy to take these conveniences for granted; if pages are missing or torn, the whole book is so easily tossed… like yesterday's garbage. Why is that? Have we now arrived at a point in time where we can afford to throw away books for which we have no current use? I believe that these same books may be sacred to others elsewhere. Mr. Burton, my very DNA would need to be completely reprogrammed in order for me to remotely consider throwing away a textbook."

He was now listening—really listening. I had more on my mind. I liked my principal and I trusted him. I reasoned that if we were to continue to grow our professional relationship in a healthy manner, then the issue of him placing those books on my desk had to be addressed openly. Thus I continued, "Mr. Burton, allow me to state my thoughts directly regarding the mountain of books that you placed on my desk. You need to know that I consider that decision to be totally inappropriate. In fact, truth be told, I consider that line of thinking not just inappropriate, but immature as well…"

Mr. Burton attempted to defend himself, "But sometimes some of the staff can act like children and…"

"Be that as it may, you, Mr. Burton, can never act childish. You forfeited that luxury the moment you became principal…"

"Frank Maraj, you have no idea how hard a job it is to command respect. You have to always be directly in the frontline…"

"Mr. Burton, you cannot *legislate* respect. You have to *earn* respect. You have, this habit, and I will tell it to you right now, of going around the school and bossing members of the staff. You wish to command and have the staff obey. That attitude is misplaced in our school. We all are professionals; you absolutely have no right to treat your staff as anything less than as professionals."

"But if they want to be treated as professionals..."

"Mr. Burton, your staff *is* professional. You are the one whose behaviour appears unprofessional..."

He began looking a little less comfortable in his seat. Yet, to his credit, he was still listening.

"Mr. Burton, let me tell you exactly how I felt when I walked into my classroom and saw that heap of books on my desk...

"I felt belittled; I even felt like I had been reprimanded. I am a grown man... I am married and have children of my own. I am a professional. I try to keep myself professional in all of my actions and attitudes. Upon seeing those books I felt for a moment that I had been returned to the dark ages where reason and good sense had been buried. In short, Mr. Burton, I felt violated..."

His eyes opened large.

I had to continue. "What I cannot understand is this. At heart you are a good man and a worthy principal. You, by your own example give so much to this school. You are dedicated and committed to the school and to the students who pass through these halls. As a staff, we all recognize that. What I do not understand is this: Why do you feel the need to lord your position over us? Mr. Burton, you lead by example; that is so obvious. Now you must treat us with the respect due us. Please, I beg of you for your own sake, do not demean yourself, or us, by engaging in any more stunts of this kind. Please, no more..."

"Does everyone feel the way you do?"

"I cannot answer for anyone else. I answer for myself only."

"Have you spoken about these things with other staff members?"

"Let me answer your question this way, Mr. Burton. If I have a concern about you, I will choose my time, and I will mark my words. To be sure I will come to you. Know that I have not expressed my opinion or thoughts regarding the books to any member of the staff. That matter concerned you and me. Thank you for giving me a chance to speak my mind openly to you. And Mr. Burton, I am sorry if I caused you distress."

"Frank Maraj, are you finished?"

"I am finished, Mr. Burton."

"You sure criticized me!"

"Sorry."

"In a way, it is okay. You spoke your mind."

I remained quiet while he spoke.

"I like that about you; you squared off with me. I don't agree with everything you had to say. But, you did give me some things to think over."

Then he did a curious thing. He went to my desk and picked up one of the books. Then he shared something about himself, "Mr. Maraj, I too remember being poor."

Lost for a moment in his own world, I was left to wonder if he had just reached out to me in his own way.

A grin graced his face and he teased, "Mr. Maraj, you are not thinking of having me put away this entire pile of books all by myself… are you?"

This lighter good-natured side of my principal was also very true to his personality. There, at that very moment emerged the principal we could all appreciate. I hoped that my response would convey that message, "Mr. Burton, my grade five class is keen and willing. Let us not deny them the opportunity to be civic-minded. Shall we let this wonderful group of students solve *our* problem? After all, books are but passports to their future."

And he grinned as he quipped, "Mr. Maraj, you are not only a teacher, now you are a teacher turned philosopher."

Now, I *knew* that I was in good hands…

# 70

# Presumptuous

*Days turn into weeks, weeks become months, and months advance ever so stealthily into years. In birth, time heralds the individual into this world; in death, time reclaims the individual and sends it on to the next stage. Time, and time alone, reigns supreme.*

What had begun, in my mind at least, as a temporary assignment, was approaching the ten year mark at Donald Young School. I still mused, from time to time, about returning to teach at the secondary school level. But, for now I was content; I had become rooted.

Then, one day, Mr. Burton drew my attention to an advertisement from the local board office announcing that the Board was seeking a Language Arts Consultant. Further, Mr. Burton encouraged me to apply for the position based on my proven history at the school and on my personal credentials.

My personal doubts were rooted in my past misadventures with the interview process but I followed Mr. Burton's advice and applied.

In due course I heard back from the Board and was granted an interview.

In the Board Room, a large panel of interviewers faced off against me. They appeared, to me at least, to be most intimidating, but I tried to mask my nervousness with friendly overtures for I recognized most, if not all, of them.

The interview was intense, but it was fair. The first part of the interview was based on fact and knowledge, allowing candidates to relax their guard and establish their confidence. In the second half of the interview, questions of a deeper and more complex nature surfaced. They demanded a deeper, more probing and philosophical response. (Or so I thought.)

"Mr. Maraj, let us suppose that you were to be the successful candidate for the position—Language Arts Consultant, what would you personally bring to this position that would be of advantage to our students, and to our teachers?"

I was pensive. It was a pointed question and I had anticipated that I might be asked a question along this line. I was focusing my response when I was asked by one of the interviewers,

"Mr. Maraj, did you hear and understand the question. Do you wish..."

Thank you Sir. I do not need the question repeated. I thank you for such a question. Thus I rendered my viewpoint. They listened attentively for the several minutes that I made my address.

The interview came to an end. I was cordially received. I reasoned that the final question gave me a chance to share my vision for our schools and I felt somewhat hopeful.

I returned to school and buried myself into my everyday routine. Soon news arrived; the position was declared redundant as severe cutbacks and budget readjustments nullified that position. That evening after school, I encountered Mr. Burton. "Frank, I am sorry. Another day will come. Are you okay?"

"Mr. Burton, thank goodness I am here at Donald Young. I am at home here..."

"I know what you mean. You are not trying to get out. You just need something more up your sleeve."

I was quiet. He understood. I was indeed appreciative of my principal's support.

***

Several weeks later I was on supervision duty outdoors. One member of panel of interviewers who recently conducted the interview saw me and approached. He came directly to the point.

"Frank, I have to ask you something."

"Yes, please go ahead."

"Regarding the interview, you did a fine job, except in one area."

I listened with quiet intensity.

"At the very end, you were asked a very simple basic question. Man, I don't understand you. He hesitated, then, he asked, "You ready for this?"

"Yes, say what you need to say."

"Frank, you were asked a simple question. You might have done well to give a *page*; you gave us a *novel*. Man you have to be basic. You were supposed to be brief."

"Mr. V, now may I ask you a question?"

"Certainly. Anything."

"My question is this. Why were you selected to be a member of that panel of interviewers?"

"Frank, that question could be considered to be quite impertinent… I am a Principal in case you forgot." After continuing at some length to defend his position, he concluded by asking why I would ask such a question and reminded me that I could be accused of being a bit presumptuous.

I responded with a slightly heightened degree of intensity, "What I find presumptuous is this. There is a panel of distinguished professionals poised to interview me. My credentials are in Language Arts, English and philosophy."

"So what's your point?"

"My position is this. Not one of you gathered at the Board Room possessed English qualifications. Is it possible then, that you did not comprehend my viewpoint completely?"

He was about to reply. He looked truly annoyed. But, before he could frame his response, I took the initiative, "Mr. V, if you were to hire a music teacher, would you not include in your panel someone who is knowledgeable in music, someone qualified in music? Does that not make good sense? To be perfectly candid, one might infer that all of you, collectively, demonstrated some disrespect toward me as a candidate by not having someone qualified in Language Arts and English serving on the panel. Was there any one of you on that panel with those qualifications?"

He was quiet, and it was not like him to remain quiet. I continued, "Mr. V, I am trying very hard to not take it personally. I mean no offence, and I thank you for your suggestions. I have always looked up to you, and respected you. I still do."

He walked away; as he did, he looked back. The faintest hint of a smile played across his lips.

# 71

# Good News—All Around

In the spring of 1985 a position for a teacher of English at Fort Frances High School was posted. I forwarded an application and awaited a response.

Then one day in early June, Mr. Burton entered my classroom smiling, "Well Frank, you are in luck. Finally your wish to be a teacher of English at the high school is granted. I know this means a great deal to you. Congratulations, Frank."

Based on his words alone, I assumed that he had been informed that I was the successful candidate for the job at the high school. I, as yet, had received no official confirmation of the position. His comment catapulted my spirit into another dimension of reverie. Deliriously happy with this sudden change of fortune, I blurted out my appreciation, "Mr. Burton, thank you for your understanding and support. I am very grateful."

"Frank, we have come a long way together. And you deserve this opportunity. You love that poetry and Shakespeare thing. Good for you."

He was on his way out. He turned back with a grin and teased, "We will miss you... I think."

Later, I reflected on his sentiment that we had come a long way together. Yes, we had, and I realized that I owed much to this principal.

Then Dirk walked in, pulled out a chair, and sat down. I waited for him to speak, but he just sat there for the longest time... quietly... with his head bent. I too was quiet. Finally, he broke the silence, "Frank, we go back together many years."

"For sure Dirk; we do."

"Man, that was some experience we had team-teaching together. Frank, congratulations. I am excited for you."

"Dirk, I don't know if I have ever officially thanked you. I am indebted to you for so much…"

"Indebted? Whatever did I do?"

"Dirk, I remember only too well how helpful you were to me from the very beginning—even when I started at Cornerbrook School during my very first year. You provided me with a wealth of materials and resources. You shared both your knowledge and your resources with this pauper, freely. Thank you my friend. And, I owe you for something else."

"And what's that?"

"You are partly the reason I came here to Donald Young. I felt that I could count on you."

"And I know that you had another job offer at a different school. I was relieved and excited when you chose Donald Young School. Are you looking forward to going to the *Big School*?"

"Yes, but I am nervous. Am I ready for high school?"

"Frank you belong there. Go! It's time to move on with your life. It's time to do what you were meant to do. Now, as you move into the Big League, don't forget your friends here; I am glad for you."

As he walked away, I was left wondering, *Had I been away too long? Would I be able to make a successful transition?*

Furthermore, and perhaps even more importantly, **Was I really ready for the high school?**

# 72

# Magical Memories

Dirk had insisted that I belonged to Donald Young School. And, in so many ways, I had. The community had infused in me that sense of true belonging. It was however, school life that anchored me so completely. Fractions of memory flashed before me.

The little faces flushed with anticipation as they waited for me to finish lunch so we could all play soccer on the field outside... The protective voices from inside the staffroom shooing away the students so that I could finish my lunch...

The magic of playing soccer over the lunch hour paid great dividends for both the students and for me. The affection that the students developed for the game spilled over into their interpersonal relationships within the classroom setting and ultimately toward me where a spirit of good will and camaraderie generally prevailed. During this time, I too actively relived a bit of my own childhood as I reconnected with my inner ten-year-old on the field.

I reflected too, on the many moments when our school received district wide recognition for its participation in the annual District Music and Drama Festival. Our teachers seemed especially gifted and talented in bringing to the fore the many talents of our students. One year, even my little group of Grade 5 students, received high praise from the adjudicator for their recitation of a most difficult and lengthy poem called, *The Creation*. The students deserved every ounce of praise lavished on them for they had prepared most assiduously for their roles and were diligent in their attempt to capture each varying nuance of the poem.

I still see those students practising in tiny nooks, crevices, and hallways. Most times, most of the students were on track, and it was not a difficult task to re-focus others who may have strayed temporarily. And, as always, when the students needed some considered attention, they succumbed invariably to the magical combination of *Ice Cream and Kenny Rogers*.

I happened on this magic quite by accident over the course of one lunch hour when I ventured out to the grocery store in Emo. As I stood in line to pay, I noticed a customer holding a one gallon pail of ice cream. Immediately my mind raced to my Grade 5 students. They had been working ever so hard; I felt that they deserved a treat. What better treat could there be than ice cream? I bought the ice cream, some cones and napkins. As the students settled in to their afternoon routines, silently, I served each child an ice cream cone. Not a word passed between us. When each child had been served, I returned to my desk and pretended to be absorbed in some marking. I heard quiet whispering among the students; they smiled at one another and at me. One solitary soul approached and whispered an appreciative *thank you*. I recognized that that student's words represented the statement of gratitude from the whole class.

As the months passed, the music of Kenny Rogers was introduced into the mix. As was my custom, I often had an L.P. album playing on my record machine before class officially began. On this particular day, I was listening to Kenny Rogers. As the students entered the class, I lowered the volume. One student asked if I would turn up the sound so all could hear what music I was listening to. That singular moment became etched in my mind as a pivotal moment in my relationship with that particular group of grade five students. But, one student, on one occasion, threatened to upset the delicate balance. Not long after Kenny Rogers' music had become a bit of a tradition in my class, in walks little Miss Wanda and her vehement protestations, "Oh, no! Not Kenny Rogers *again!*"

Immediately, I felt bad. *I had overdone it with Kenny Rogers and the students were sick of it.* I turned off the record player. The moment was most uncomfortable. Wanda, perhaps sensing my discomfort, and without missing a beat, stood up and demanded, "I want my Kenny Rogers, Mr. Maraj; I was just kidding."

Thus, Kenny Rogers and ice cream became staples in the Grade 5 classroom diet.

# 73

# A Sobering Reality

Later that night as I pondered my present circumstances, I took time to reflect on the years spent at Donald Young School. I felt conflicted; my life, both at the school and in the community continued to prove very fulfilling. I enjoyed a reasonable degree of success with my students and had formed a tangible bond with the parents in the district. *Why then*, I asked myself, *why then am I leaving?*

It struck me then that this was the very question I had posed in 1967 when I was making preparations to leave my post at St. Charles Girls' High School where I had also laid claim to a measure of stability in the community and success in the classroom.

The very forces that propelled me out of a relatively comfortable and secure life in Trinidad to the unknown adventures that awaited in Canada, were the same forces enticing me to embrace a Canadian high school experience. My own personal dreams and aspirations were no less powerful now than they were all those years ago in Trinidad. While the possibility of returning to Trinidad as a teacher had all but ceased to exist as a viable option, the dream of once again becoming a high school teacher was still very much alive. It was this dream that propelled me to venture onward to the next path in my life's journey.

A dark shadow threatened to block the anticipated smooth transition from the elementary to the secondary panel.

It was my principal, Mr. Burton, who bore the burden of breaking the news to me the next day. After calling me into his office, he closed the door and announced, "Frank, I want to be clear. You did not get the job you applied for."

To say that I was stunned would be an understatement. Disappointment, disbelief, dismay… along with an acute sense of anxiety and panic… flooded my core.

I choked out the words, "I did not get the job?"

No, Frank, not the job for which you applied. You did, however, meet with success in another way. Frank, you have been transferred to the high school for one semester."

*One semester? What was going on here?* Something was amiss. I needed answers. Answers that Mr. Burton could not possibly know.

Mr. Burton, himself, seemed confident. "Frank, you're in. You've been given a marvelous opportunity. It's up to you whether you stay in or not."

Over the next few days I was left to wonder why it was that I thought that I had been awarded the *full-time* position. Had I been presumptuous?

*Only one man had the answers to my questions.*

# 74

# I Want to be Wrong!

On the last day of school in June, I made an appointment to see Mr. Landers, the principal of the high school. I had but one concern.

We met in his office; his towering presence, while friendly, was somewhat intimidating. Having had occasion to sit in on committee meetings on which he was the chair, I knew him to be equally authoritative and forthright.

True to form, he wasted no time; he came to the point directly. "Mr. Maraj, you indicated in your phone call that you had a concern you wish to discuss with me?"

Following his lead, I too spoke plainly, "Mr. Landers, first, I wish to thank you for accepting me at the high school for a semester."

He smiled and I continued, "I do have one question regarding the position that was posted for a full-time teacher of English. I applied for that position but received no response regarding it. Why was I not considered at all for that vacancy?"

I think that the question may have caught him off guard. While not completely unwarranted, it was certainly unexpected. He looked at me for a moment in silent reflection. He then rose from his chair and began pacing back and forth in front of his desk. He did this for only a few moments.

Silently, I awaited his response.

He returned to his desk and stood in front of his chair, arms splayed at either side of the desk as he gripped its edges. He looked at me over the rim of his silver glasses and reiterated my question. "Mr. Maraj, you want to know why you were not considered for the full-time position… Do you *really* want to know?"

"I really want to know."

"Do you want the truth?"

"The whole truth, Mr. Landers."

"Then here it is, Mr. Maraj… You are far too soft-spoken, not to mention that you are just too polite…what is even worse, you appear to be too much of a gentle man." As he leaned in, he made this final assertion, "The students at this high school will eat you alive and spit you out! You would not survive the year!"

Delivering that last part of the message seemed to have exhausted his energy. He sat down, removed his glasses and began cleaning them.

While I was silenced upon hearing his explanation, I was not insulted. No, on the contrary, I was flooded with a sense of relief.

Reaching out to shake his hand, I smiled. Mr. Landers seemed somewhat confused by my reaction. "Thank you for your honesty, Mr. Landers. Now I know that I can come to the high school and work for you."

Mr. Landers, looking even more confused, asked, "Mr. Maraj, am I understanding you clearly? Were you thinking that you would *not* report for duty here in August?"

"Mr. Landers, the simple truth is that I do not really know what I would have done had we not had this little chat. I, too, had misgivings."

"And now, Mr. Maraj?"

"And now, Mr. Landers… now I look forward to coming to the high school. I am hopeful that I can prove you wrong."

"Please, Mr. Maraj, do that; do exactly that. I *want* to be wrong!"

# PART FOUR

Returning to the Secondary System

# 75

# Another First

At long last the much anticipated day arrived. As I readied myself to face the day, I noted that more than a decade and a half had passed since I last taught in an actual high school. Even the knowledge that my stay might be for one semester only could not dampen my excitement.

As I approached the school, excitement gave way to nervousness as I questioned how I would fare in this new environment.

I had passed by this school at least twice a day over the last few years on my way to Emo from our home in Fort Frances where we had relocated in 1981. The daily commute to Emo was a welcome time for planning and reflection.

My travel time had now been reduced from thirty minutes to six. I had barely enough time to organize my thoughts before I found myself in the parking lot.

At the time, the school accommodated around twelve hundred students. It seemed cramped for space as it sat a mere block from the heart of downtown Fort Frances. Bordered on all sides by roads, there was no allowance for or evidence of any sports or recreation areas. The school was showing its age... but I loved it. It represented where I wanted to be. I took a deep breath, walked into the building, and headed straight for the office. After introducing me to the office staff, the principal left me to secure some necessary paperwork. After filling the necessary forms, I headed for the staff room. The room was virtually filled to overflowing with the general hum of laughter and friendly banter. The principal proved to be a central character in the mix as he welcomed everyone back from summer vacation. I stood on the fringe soaking in all the drama. Truly this was the heart of the school.

I took a cup of coffee with me to my room on the upper floor and began the task of setting out books for my period one students.

The classroom boasted no special features; long and narrow, it housed about forty individual desks. The teacher's desk was on a platform, slightly elevated from the rest of the room; I discovered later, that the platform was a stage. There were several blackboards both at the front and along the side of the room. I inhaled deeply… I was home.

For a split second, my mind flashed back to the principal's caution that I was there for one semester only. My spirit, however, informed me otherwise.

A warning bell sounded. Throngs of students flooded the halls; some of them filtered into Room 313.

# 76

# Colossal Error!

I watched as my students entered the classroom.

It was an experience like no other; most were oblivious to my presence.

Some went straight to a desk and sat down; they however, represented the minority. The rest gathered around in various pockets in the room; a few sat on top of the desks.

A bell rang signaling the formal start to the day. This motivated some to move to a desk and deposit their binders. The rest continued to resist any inclination to comply with the implied dictates of the bell. Their absorption in themselves to the exclusion of all else seemed total. I was taken aback by the extent of the casual freedom they claimed for themselves.

Even the announcements failed to mute their effusive prattle.

I had expected so much more from this group of Grade 10 general students. I had expected that they would come in, find a seat, and await my opening remarks. In an effort to redirect their attention and gain some control, I began, "Kids, may I…"

Needless to say, my initial remarks opened a floodgate of dissension. I was drenched in a mounting wave of protest. In unison they challenged my first words, "Kids!"

I recognized my faux-pas immediately but it was too late; the damage was already done. What had begun as a natural greeting to my Grade 5 pupils, was perceived as an insult to these Grade 10 students.

"Say teacher, we're not in elementary school. We're in high school. We would appreciate it if you did not call us kids. You're a high school teacher. Right?"

A chorus of voices commended the student for his remarks and then they proceeded to congratulate one another with the exchange of high fives. For a moment, it appeared that this group of students was liberated beyond the purview of the teacher, and I was frozen in time.

Shades of my very first day teaching in Trinidad at St. Charles Boys' High School became a vivid memory as I recalled how little respect I had been afforded. Only one or two years older than my students, they failed to stand to acknowledge my presence as their teacher when I walked into the classroom; feeling diminished, I wondered if I belonged in front of the class; worse, I questioned whether I was a teacher.

Now, here I was years later, in another time, in another land, being returned to an all too familiar and painful landscape. Yes, I was embarrassed, but I knew without hesitation that I had to prepare to scale that wall of embarrassment and land on the bedrock of confidence. Stability demanded nothing less.

My instincts did not fail me. Finding my voice, I stood before the class and spoke in a tone that carried my message just slightly above the collective din of the students. They quieted somewhat and I continued my address. This time, I focused my words on the particular literary work we were about to study. I selected a certain part of the text to read aloud; it depicted two teenagers alone... I allowed my voice to trail off, knowing that I had captured them for this moment, when, from out of nowhere, a student blithely walked into the room and loudly intoned, "Why is everyone so quiet?"

I turned on my heel, looked the young offender directly in the eye, and commanded, "You, Sir, are late; please wait for me outside the door."

Evidently, he saw things quite differently for he began to protest, "I am not really late..."

Not willing to engage with him in front of the class, I interrupted his attempt at self-defense and reiterated my decree, "Wait for me outside the door."

I held the door open for him.

Apparently dumbfounded by my request, he just stood there awkwardly.

Purposefully, I kept my silence.

The boy cast one more look into the now completely quieted class; with a reluctant sigh of resignation, he exited through the open door. After shutting the door quietly behind him, I turned to face the class.

Every single pair of eyes was focused on me. I walked to the blackboard at the front of the classroom and wrote in huge letters:

"Crossroads"
Page 15 – **READ**

On top of each desk was a copy of the book, *Crossroads*.

In silence I stood before the class and pointed to the assignment fully expecting them to comply; I was not disappointed.

Within minutes, after the shock of the interruption wore off, all were settled into the act of silent reading. While I was grateful for this brief respite, I knew that it was time to implement the next step.

The physical geography of the class appeared chaotic. A casual observer would have surmised that a pestilence had struck. When the students had first entered the room, they had taken over, and had turned the desks every which way as was their whim. Much to my dismay, nearly every single desk at the front of the room remained empty; the students clustered en masse at the back.

I could not continue with such a visual distraction and general confusion.

Quietly, I approached one of the students seated at the back; I motioned for him to follow me. As he stood up, he was quizzical. I pointed to a seat at the very front of the room. Even though his body language bespoke displeasure, he complied.

I then approached another student in a similar fashion and directed her to another front row desk. She too, accommodated my request with the silent acquiescence of a martyr. The rest, now resigned to the inevitable, prepared to be moved. Within minutes, the entire front half of the class was full. The back stood empty.

It was time now to deal with the disgruntled student awaiting me outside the classroom door. I opened the door, and before he had a chance to speak, I announced, "You are late. Come in quietly. An assignment is posted on the board. Begin, please."

I had deliberately saved a seat at the front of the class for this particular student and wasted no time in ushering him to it. Clearly, he did not understand what was going on with his classmates. He looked around the room quizzically. To his credit, he did not attempt to speak.

Every single student was engaged in the reading activity. It took him a few minutes to focus himself, but eventually, he too, opened up his book.

A sense of order prevailed.

Things were quiet for the duration of the class.

A few minutes before the bell was to sound ending the period, I made this pronouncement, "When the bell goes, remain seated. I, not the bell, will dismiss you."

I could sense that this proclamation was not well received; one student took it upon himself to be the voice of the class and questioned, "Mr. Maraj, do you mean that you want us to stay in our seats until after the bell… until you dismiss us, literally?"

"I mean exactly that."

There were no further questions. By the time that the bell sounded to end the period, I was stationed at the door. Two students left their seats and rushed toward the door. No one else moved a muscle. I merely looked at the two and they returned to their seats. Once seated, I opened the door and gave the signal that they were dismissed. As they walked out, I said a simple, "Goodbye, students. Thank you."

The students merely stared.

I had invaded their world and I sensed that they did not know what to think of this foreigner.

## 77

## A Bad Seed?

Although somewhat challenging, I survived Day One at the high school.

The next few days passed without incident.

Day Four, however, presented a few hurdles.

Before class began that day, I decided that it was time to introduce one more expectation that I had of them as students. Accordingly, I wrote a brief note on the blackboard explaining what was expected as part of our general class routine. At the conclusion of the morning's opening exercises, I drew their attention to the note which read:

***Independent Reading: At the beginning of class, commence reading. No talking.***

Just as I expected, they had numerous questions.

Donnie stepped up to the lead, firing the first round of questioning.

"So Mr. Maraj, do you really expect us not to talk at all at the very beginning of class?" When I nodded in the affirmative, he pronounced, "Now, that is just crazy."

The class laughed heartily at Donnie's bold assertion. I could tell at once that he was a favourite among his classmates and easily and willingly assumed the role of leader of the group. He fed off their laughter. When I failed to respond immediately to his comment, Donnie persisted with a follow up remark which resulted in even more delighted snickers from his peers. "Mr. Maraj, I am not saying that *you're* crazy. It's just your policy that's crazy. It'll never work."

I waited until the laughter subsided before answering.

"Students, my response is simple. Yes, I do have an expectation that you may deem to be crazy; I do expect that you attend to your work quietly at the beginning of class. That is all. Thank you, students."

The subdued tone of the class as I concluded my last statement indicated to me that, on the whole, the students were ready to settle down. Grateful for this small victory, I set about getting my own papers in order on my desk.

Donnie, however, still wanted to be heard. Once again he asked, "Mr. Maraj, I have another question, may I ask it?"

"Yes, Donnie, go ahead."

"What if we do not do as you ask…?" While the question itself seemed to challenge my authority in the classroom, it was asked without guile or malice. This Donnie was attempting to charm his way into a leadership role in the class.

Everyone was now paying rapt attention to Donnie. This challenge captured everyone's imagination and they awaited Donnie's next comment. Clearly he was marking his territory. He continued his playful banter, "Mr. Maraj, are you going to send us all to the principal, or are you going to spank us all like we were bad babies…"

This time the whole class erupted in spasms. Donnie leaned back in his chair making no effort to hide a self-indulgent smirk. He was at the top of his game, sparring with his teacher, entertaining his peers. Yes, I now understood this Donnie.

Now it was my turn.

Without a second's hesitation I began my address to the class, "Grade 10, I owe you an apology."

Then I stopped. Startled at my remark, their eyes, indeed their whole attention, was now focused on me. Even Donnie stared.

I continued, "I am sorry that Donnie led you to believe that there could be spanking in this classroom. He is quite mistaken. There will be none of it. That is the domain of your parents or guardians… Unless… Donnie, are you expecting a parental visit in the classroom? I am wondering if such a visit would involve…"

Donnie became quite vocal as he questioned, "Mr. Maraj, I don't understand you. You are strange."

"Thank you, Donnie; I'll take that as a compliment."

A baffled Donnie sat back in his seat and I reclaimed my ground.

"Class, I neglected to share with you the reason that was at the root of my request for insisting on quiet independent work at the beginning of the period. I believed that once you understood that there would be no time for chatting with one another during class, then you would come a little earlier to class to have time to visit. Then you would not be late for class. You cannot be late, because you will already be early. Right?"

I could not tell if the students were absorbed or just confused about what I had just said. I was just grateful that I had not triggered a rebellion.

I continued, "I believe in your ability to think and to reason. Reflection enables you to think. Therefore it is a distinct advantage being given to you when I provide you with the opportunity to engage in thoughtful reflection as you begin your day. After all, we are now in high school and we must always endeavour to think and act like we are in high school. A few days ago I made a terrible mistake when I addressed you as *kids*. I will be mindful in the future not to repeat that error. I sincerely apologize for that lapse."

When I paused I sensed a quiet affirming spirit in the room. All that remained was for me to conclude my remarks with this invitation, "Students, may I invite you to begin your independent assignment? Begin now, please."

I returned to my desk, pulled out the novel we were studying, and began to read to myself.

Soon the entire class was engaged in silence in the process of reading with one notable exception: Donnie.

Just what was he up to?

# 78

# Standoff

Donnie was taking his time to settle; I thought that I understood why and decided to let him save face by allowing him a few extra minutes. For one split second, our eyes met and Donnie nodded his head. I took that to mean that he was now ready to start working.

I was mistaken.

Donnie bent and pulled something from his school bag; it was a hat. Without a moment's hesitation he put the hat on his head. No one else had worn a hat in my class. Obviously upset that everyone else had become compliant, he wanted to push the boundaries of my resolve.

Then, just as suddenly as the hat had been place on his head, somehow it had "fallen" off. As he bent to retrieve the hat, somehow his desk make a horrific sound. Those who had hitherto been unaware that Donnie was continuing to challenge my authority in the class, were distracted by the noise.

If I wanted to maintain control, I would have to act.

"Donnie, remove your hat now and put it away, please."

Now, the entire class was focused on our interaction.

Donnie made no move to comply. In fact, he merely sat back in his desk, folded his arms, and grinned as he looked at me. The look said, "Make me."

Now everyone's gaze was fixed on me. I'm sure they were wondering how I was going to handle this latest blatant challenge. (As was I.)

My mind went into overdrive. I recognized that how I chose to respond to this could significantly affect all future interactions with this class. Several possibilities flashed before me. I chose to underreact by maintaining calm as I addressed my remarks to the rest of the class.

"Students, thank you for your cooperation. You were distracted by Donnie. You have done nothing wrong. Please, return to your assignment."

I held my breath. No one added to the fray. Gradually, I relaxed as each student returned to work.

Donnie took off his hat.

I felt somewhat encouraged until I realized that he was not putting it away. Far from it, Donnie was now flipping the hat between his hands.

Once again the class was disturbed.

One student dared to caution Donnie to quit fooling around. Donnie wheeled around, ready to pounce.

Before anything of consequence could materialize, I ordered, "Donnie, please come to my desk."

He did not come readily or quickly.

But, he did come... albeit, with his hat once again on his head.

When he reached my desk, I whispered to him, "Donnie, gather your books and meet me at the door."

I waited for him at the door. Upon reaching me, Donnie attempted to speak. I put a finger to my lips and indicated that we would talk, but that we would do it outside, in the hall.

"Donnie, I am sorry I asked you to remove your hat."

"Hey, Mr. Maraj, no problem."

"Donnie, you can wear your hat all you want. What you cannot do is wear your hat in my class. You decide what you are going to do."

As I turned to re-enter the class, Donnie asked, "Are you kicking me out of class? I didn't do nothing..."

"Precisely, Donnie. The choice is yours. You are welcome back to class any time... without your hat."

As I returned to class, some of the students were noticeably distracted. One voiced his dissent openly, "Mr. Maraj, it doesn't seem fair that Donnie get sent to the principal's office for some stupid hat offence. He is always in trouble. Why couldn't you cut him some slack?"

The whole class awaited my response. If I didn't know it before, I certainly knew it now, Donnie commanded a loyal following.

"Class, what makes you think that I have sent Donnie to the principal?"

Luke spoke up, "Because Donnie's always in trouble. He practically lives in the principal's office. If he's not in the principal's office, then where is he?"

"He's just outside, in the hall."

They did not believe me. They looked at me incredulously.

To prove to all of them that what I had said was true, I went to the door and opened it. I peeked into the hall. I looked in all directions. There was no sign of Donnie.

With the look of shock still registered on my face, I returned to the room.

Luke probed, "Mr. Maraj, you did not seriously expect that Donnie would still be there waiting for you. Did you?"

My reply was barely audible, "Yes, students, I did. I am so sorry that Donnie left…"

Donnie's absence troubled me for the rest of the day and on into the night. Somehow, I expected or rather hoped that Donnie would come to me and explain himself; that never happened. I spent a restless night plagued by the day's events. I questioned whether I had done the right thing.

The next morning I passed by the office on my way to class. There, stationed in the hall, stood the principal, Mr. Landers. When he saw me, he announced, "I met Donnie outside your classroom in the hallway yesterday. Don't you worry about a thing; I will take care of Donnie. He confessed to wearing his hat in your class. When he returns to class today, send him on down to the office. I just want you to know that I will handle this situation. I will deal with this troublemaker."

It was with a great degree of sadness that I headed up to my classroom. I had had no intention of involving the office in this affair. I had every confidence that Donnie would have returned to class voluntarily and, without his hat. I did not see Donnie as a troublemaker. Yes, he was challenging; yes, he was non-compliant; but, I believed that he could be reasonable and that he could be reached.

Mr. Landers sounded very serious in his branding of Donnie as a troublemaker.

As I reached my classroom, I saw Donnie standing in front of the door, hatless and confused.

"Mr. Maraj, I am in trouble with Mr. Baldhead…"

"Mr. Baldhead, Donnie?"

"Sorry, Mr. Maraj, it is the principal, Mr. Landers. He's waiting for me. I am in some serious trouble. I wish that none of this happened. That man and I do not see eye to eye…" His voice trailed a little as he attempted to gather his thoughts. "I was thinking…" Donnie continued, "Mr. Maraj, I was thinking about what you told me and I was about to come back to class and old man…"

"Donnie, be careful how you speak."

"Sorry, Mr. Maraj, bad habit. I really was coming back to class. He caught me outside and brought me to the office. He wouldn't even listen to me. You have no idea how much he hates me. I've been in so much trouble… I am in for a good long suspension. I just know it."

His words triggered an emotion inside me. Something in me clicked when I heard the pain in his voice and I knew what I had to do.

I told Donnie to follow me. As we walked, he asked where we were going.

"To the office."

"I sure hope you know what you're doing…"

When we reached the office, Mr. Landers was still standing in the main area. I went to him directly and announced, "Mr. Landers, the matter between Donnie and me has been resolved. We have had a talk and we are of one mind. Donnie has something to say to you. Donnie?"

Initially uncertain, Donnie hesitated in his response. Once he recognized that I was advocating on his behalf, he reaffirmed my confidence in him by asserting, "Mr. Maraj is right; I am a changed student and I don't think that you will have to put up with me in the office so much."

When Donnie finished talking, I asked him to return to the classroom. He looked uncertainly, first at me, and then at Mr. Landers. When the principal signaled that it was okay for him to leave, he did.

When Donnie was safely out of hearing, Mr. Landers asked, "Mr. Maraj, do you think Donnie is simply a bad seed?"

I took a moment to reflect before responding, "No, Mr. Landers, I do not believe that Donnie is a bad seed. I think that he enjoys all the attention that comes from his bad behaviour. Unfortunately, his behaviour gets him in to a lot of trouble."

"You seem to have taken a great deal of interest in this one seed, Mr. Maraj. What do you intend to do? You have but one semester…"

*Frank Maraj*

I chose to not respond to Mr. Landers' intimation that I had been given but one semester at the high school. At the moment, Donnie was what mattered. It was Donnie that occupied the whole of my attention.

This seed had been planted in my classroom; his continued growth was my responsibility. With some effective pruning and timely weeding, this plant might yet be cultivated.

I hurried back to class.

# 79

# Adjustments

As the weeks passed, the classes and I settled into a regular routine. We seemed to have worked out many of the hurdles in our relationship. So, it came as a bit of a surprise when Striker, one of the Grade 11 general level students, asked, "Mr. Maraj, why do you give us so much homework?"

Ignoring the look of shock registered on my face, he continued, "We are just general students, we are not taking advanced courses. They get plenty of homework. After all, they are considered the 'bright' students. We should not be treated like the advanced students by getting so much homework."

With that final assertion, Striker rested his case. Everyone turned to me for an immediate response; I did not have one. Striker seemed to have struck a common chord with his fellow classmates. From the tone of their conversation, I sensed that on this one topic, they were all in agreement.

Initially, I thought that Striker was merely playing at having a grievance. As he continued to speak, I sensed his sincerity. While I still did not understand why he would question getting homework, I understood that he genuinely wanted an answer.

The class was a buzz of conversation. Striker's comments had struck a nerve.

"Students, please allow me to respond."

I waited until I had their full attention.

"It seems to me, that I owe you something of an apology."

"We accept your apology," hastily declared another one of the boys.

Everyone acted as if the matter was concluded and the issue resolved.

"Thank you, Lance, I appreciate your support. For the past few days I had been thinking that I have not been a fair teacher to you; I felt that I was short changing you on your education…"

My last statement brought puzzled looks to a few faces; the group fell amazingly silent.

Again, Striker assumed the lead, "Mr. Maraj, what do you mean that you are "short changing" our education?"

"Striker… everyone… this is a thought that has been plaguing me for the past several days. I truly feel that I have not been diligent in carrying out my responsibility to you as your teacher by failing to give you sufficient responsibility… you know … homework… Because of this, I have begun to feel that I have not been a good teacher to you all…"

"What!" interjected Striker, "you actually want to give us more work? More homework? That is just crazy!"

"Well, class, that's just how I feel. I truly believe that in all fairness to you, I should be assigning more homework."

These final words brought Striker to his feet. He seemed to have accepted the role as class spokesman. Every eye in the classroom was focused on him as he virtually exploded, "Mr. Maraj, how on earth did you come up with the idea that we need more work? On what planet is giving us more work considered being fair?"

I could feel their frustration level rising; I begged them to allow me to explain. "I calculate that each of you should be doing a minimum of three hours of homework for all your classes combined. And…"

"Three hours of work? Every day? That's insane!"

Now, everyone had something to say. I had struck a nerve. I had never seen them quite so animated. I decided to sit down and allow them a few moments to vent to one another.

Most students seemed to have swarmed to Striker's desk at the back of the classroom.

A few minutes elapsed.

Then, from the other side of the classroom I saw a hand raised with quiet respect. After acknowledging that Amanda had something to say, I asked the rest of the students to take their seats.

I nodded to Amanda that we were ready to entertain her thoughts.

"Mr. Maraj, we spend about half an hour or so doing homework for you. How much time do you think grade eleven students, like us, should be spending a night on English?"

The question was barely out of her mouth when my answer was served, "One hour at the very minimum…"

"Why do you say that, Mr. Maraj?"

"Students, you are Grade Eleven students. In less than two years, most of you will be graduating and be out in the world, ready to assume the next set of challenges in your life… whatever they may be."

I stopped to look at them… to really look at them and I realized that despite all their grumbling, they were sincere. This left me more than a little confused. How could students be in high school and not expect to have homework? How did these students come to possess such a mindset?

I had no answers.

I decided to start afresh.

I stunned my students with this greeting in the middle of class: "Hello, students."

No one responded; rather, they responded by looking quizzically at one another.

I continued, "Students, I just felt like saying hello to you. I am going to say it to you one more time. It just feels good to say hello to you. So… hello, students."

And to my great surprise and relief, the faint response of a shy Amanda's returning hello prompted a general hello by the others. Heartened, I continued, "Grade 11, I am so sorry if I have caused you discomfort and pain. That is not my intention. I want so much for you to understand. Let me ask you all a slightly different question.

"Striker, why should you and your classmates not be treated with respect? Why should you be made second-class?"

"I don't get it, Mr. Maraj. How is it that we are not being respected? What's that got to do with too much work?"

"Class, can anyone help Striker figure it out?"

"I think I know what you're getting at," ventured the excited voice of Amanda.

"What Mr. Maraj is trying to say is that we, as students, should all be working hard regardless of whatever classes we have. Whether the class you are taking is called academic or general, it makes no difference; we all should be doing our best."

Striker was quick to disagree. "We are not academics. I came in to this class so I wouldn't have to study Shakespeare and poetry and all that stuff. You still haven't convinced me. I don't think that we should have so much work."

I intervened, "Striker, is it your contention that you should not have homework?"

"Exactly, Mr. Maraj."

"Striker, do you have any younger brothers or sisters?"

"Yes. I have a brother in Grade 5."

"Would you allow your little brother to smoke or drink?"

"No."

"Why not?"

"Because it's not right."

"And how did you come to that decision?"

"I just know it… and I'm older."

"That's right. You have gained some knowledge through experience and you can now make that judgment."

"Your brother doesn't yet have either the knowledge or the experience to make that determination for himself. He relies on the more experienced and knowledgeable adults in his life to make those judgements for him and to keep him safe. In the same way, although you do have a certain amount of knowledge and experience, you must rely on the adults in your lives to guide you through these very tough and confusing teen years. You may think that you are fully grown in all the ways that matter, but you still need to be guided by those who have gone before you.

"The point I wish to share with you is this… Respect. Have respect for yourselves. You are now well on the road to becoming seniors in high school. Soon you shall be part of the adult world. What kind of young adults will you be if here, at this juncture of you lives you deny yourselves the opportunity to acquire the discipline necessary for hard work?"

The class was quiet.

"All students should be working hard just as Amanda pointed out. Some, like those taking the academic levels, do face a more difficult challenge; their load is much heavier. But, it is equally true that you have to carry a decent load yourselves. You must accept that true progress is the result of commitment and responsibility. We cannot always cover all that needs to be covered during our allotted time here at school. Sometimes we have to take work home to be finished. That is just the reality of being a student.

"Please know this: you are intelligent and capable students. Some of you will take longer to complete your assignments. I know that. You who do take more time are not less intelligent for taking longer. You just need more time for that particular type of task. There may be other areas in which you excel. I need you to be mindful of the fact that you are entering a critical stage of your life. This is when you develop those skills and attitudes which will serve you for the rest of your life. Here, in the safety of your school is where you can find and develop your skills and talents as you prepare for the life that is to be your future. Here, you begin to make life choices and life decisions."

One student asked, "Mr. Maraj, did you work hard in Grade 11? How much time did you spend doing homework?"

"Yeah, Mr. Maraj. Tell us. What kind of a student were you? I bet you were really smart," added Striker.

Their insistence on having me tell about my life seemed to have lightened the mood somewhat. I decided to indulge their curiosity.

"If I were a bright student, I never knew it."

They were stilled by that comment. I continued, "Class, what I do know is this; I was a very hard-working student. I worked for about let's see…" I hesitated, would they even believe let alone accept the truth? I decided to give them the truth. "Class, I spent roughly four to six hours a night doing homework."

The class erupted with laughter and commentary.

Striker questioned, "You are just putting us on, right?"

"Striker, I am not putting you on. Not only that, but I also worked for about two to three hours at a cinema on week nights…"

This revelation was almost too much for them. They went from raucous joviality to serious solemnity.

"Mr. Maraj, are you serious?"

"Totally."

Striker jumped to his feet. "Okay, Mr. Maraj, I think we get the point. But, if we stop complaining that you give us too much homework, would you consider, at least, not *increasing* our homework?"

"I need some time to think about it."

"Well, Mr. Maraj, we also need some time to come up with a plan regarding homework. We need time to talk with one another. Would you mind waiting outside in the hall while we have a discussion?"

Light laughter followed me as I grabbed a nearby stool, and, pulling it close to my chest, pouted as I walked through the door and into the hall.

Don't be a baby, Mr. Maraj. No pouting," chastised a confident Striker as he closed the door securely behind me.

About four minutes had elapsed when I saw my principal approach.

"Mr. Maraj?" he queried. "What's going on?"

"My students have evicted me."

I don't think he knew just quite what to make of the situation. He gave me a half frown and entered the classroom.

As the door opened, I heard the words, "All in favour, raise your hand."

Then there was quiet.

Then muffled voices.

Then the principal walked out.

He looked at me and spoke, "Well, Mr. Maraj. It seems as if your students are dealing with you. I just want you to know that I am on their side. No tears, now."

The next minute Stephanie came out to get me. She led me into the room and directed me to read the writing on the blackboard in the front of the class. It said, *New Rule: students get most work done Monday through Friday. Weekends... no homework!!!*

Indeed, these students had come up with a solution. Actually, I admired their tenacity. They were certainly developing their negotiation skills.

Somewhat shyly, I went up to the board and wrote this addendum: *Weekends could be free... most times.*

Striker and Stephanie surveyed the class for the students' reactions. Not sensing any negativity, they each nodded their assent.

I smiled.

My smile was reflected back at me in all their faces.

The bell went.

Before Striker left the room, he whispered, "Mr. Maraj, you are okay."

From that experience I learned a couple of things. There is a time to say no and there is a time to listen. Today was a day for listening. There is a way to merge with the times without surrendering one's basic values. Today that was accomplished.

I could not help but reflect on my years spent teaching in Trinidad. No student would have dared to challenge a teacher about the amount of homework being assigned. But, I was not in Trinidad; I was in Canada. Canadian students will voice their concerns; Canadian students will advocate on their own behalf. I was somewhat in awe of them. I am glad that I had the good sense to adjust and learn from them.

This principle of working hard all week at school and keeping the weekends relatively free, has been a practice that I tried to honour throughout my career at the high school.

I have my students to thank for making that adjustment.

# 80

# The Evaluation

The semester was passing quickly; I had yet to receive any formal indication regarding my status at the high school. All had been silent on that front and thus I allowed a gentle breeze of quiet hope to enter my spirit.

Everything changed the day I received a memo from the principal indicating that he would be paying me a visit at a predetermined date and time. I knew that my professional future was at stake. While there could be a multitude of reasons why an administrator would pay a formal visit to a teacher's classroom, I knew that he had both the power and the authority to end or extend my career here at the high school. I was keenly aware of the fragility of my present circumstance. I was merely a 'test subject' at the high school; not yet proven to be of value to the secondary school system. My very temporary and somewhat tentative position was ever present in my mind.

Mr. Landers arrived early on the day of the expected visit and took a seat at the back of the room.

I was at the front of the class preparing for the day's lesson.

I greeted the students and began teaching a grammar unit. Partway through my lesson, Lizzy, one of my Grade 10 students, walked in… late. But, she didn't just walk in, no she fairly exploded into the room at full volume. She was so excited that she had remembered to not only complete her assignment, but to bring it with her to class. In a most exuberant voice she announced, "Oh, Mr. Maraj, you're going to be so proud of me; I did not forget; I kept my promise." I do not know for whom I felt more sorry, Lizzy, for her unwitting display, or me, because I knew how her outburst could be perceived by an onlooker and, consequently, how I could be judged.

Unaware that something else was happening in the room, unaware that my whole future as a teacher hung in the balance, Lizzy proceeded to dislodge her assignment from her pile of books and placed it enthusiastically on my desk. She looked at me quizzically; I'm sure she wondered why I was so subdued in my response to her. After all, had I not just reminded her to submit her outstanding assignments for the past several days?

Much to her credit, however, she soon sensed a different atmosphere in the room and quickly responded to the 'teacher look' in my eyes and to the silent admonition of my hands.

I glanced quickly in Mr. Landers' direction; he was busily writing on his note pad. No doubt he would have a few comments regarding Lizzy's interruption. I managed to maintain my calm and concluded the lesson without further incident.

Mr. Landers' face was inscrutable; I could read nothing in his demeanour; he was neither affirming nor disparaging. He was decidedly neutral in his comments stating, "Thank you, Mr. Maraj. If you don't mind, I will see you tomorrow."

There was nothing in his manner to calm the anxiety that had been gradually engulfing my spirit. Once again, I felt like a student awaiting the results of a crucial exam.

The next day, at the appointed time, I went to the office to meet with Mr. Landers. Mrs. Star, the head secretary received me very cordially and advised, "Mr. Maraj, I realize that you are scheduled to meet with Mr. Landers. Well, things are a bit unsettled at the moment and he is having a most trying day. A few unexpected meetings with parents have surfaced. He has a lot on his plate right now... Would you mind if we rescheduled?"

"Mrs. Star, I understand. But, if you don't mind, I'd prefer to wait for him in the event that he is able to see me. I would be most grateful."

Sensing my anxiety, she gently responded, "Of course, Mr. Maraj, I understand. I am sure everything will be okay; don't worry."

She then invited me to sit on one of the more comfortable chairs in the office area.

While I was thus seated, I heard voices raised in agitation and frustration. The voices were clearly coming from the office of the principal. Within minutes, two visibly stressed parents emerged. I began to question my decision to stay.

They were followed moments later by Mr. Landers. When he saw me he managed a faint acknowledgement of my presence but was immediately engulfed by the next wave of impatient parents. I waited several minutes more until I heard heightened voices once again. It was then that I decided to inform Mrs. Star that she should do as she had suggested initially, and reschedule my appointment. Obviously, today was not the day to seek an audience with the principal. As I rose from my seat, the latest visitors left the office accompanied by Mr. Landers.

It was a most awkward moment for all who were present. I did not know quite where to look; I felt like an eavesdropper; albeit an unintentional eavesdropper, but, an eavesdropper all the same.

Mr. Landers relayed a message to Mrs. Star, then he turned to me.

With a great deal of resignation registering in his voice, he sighed, "Wel, Mr. Maraj, you may as well come in. Let's get this business of yours concluded."

I took no encouragement or solace from his words. Hesitantly, I followed him into his office.

He went straight to his desk, pulled out a file from atop a tower of paperwork, and motioned for me to sit. After perusing the report for several moments, he handed it to me to read.

He allowed me several minutes to absorb the contents of the report before asking, "Well Mr. Maraj, what do you think?"

His large form was most imposing. His white shirt, dark grey tie, and dark dress pants, affirmed his presence as administrator. He presented himself as a man of authority, as someone of great consequence.

I barely had time to absorb the contents of what I was reading before he spun around in his great swivel chair insisting on a comment.

I had briefly scanned the section of the report relating to IMPROVEMENT where he had made the most detailed comments:

*I would advise that you exert more effective control over your class. A student was allowed to disrupt your class in the middle of your lesson, and you did nothing. You failed to take action. I am left to wonder why. Clearly, that student was in error. A reprimand would have been most appropriate considering the circumstances.*

Needless to say, this remark perturbed me greatly and I could not hide my bewilderment at him comments.

Again, he probed, "Mr. Maraj, *any* questions?"

By placing particular emphasis on the word 'any' I understood in an instant that he was not really interested in entertaining any opinion that differed from his own. I presumed that to do so may have dire consequences. Well, I felt that I had nothing to lose. I had to make some effort to defend myself and my apparent inaction with that particular student on the day of my evaluation.

My thoughts were all a jumble in my head. I was somewhat unsure of how to proceed. I needed time to think; time to formulate my defense.

Mr. Landers was not prepared to wait; he required a response *now*.

"Mr. Maraj, you look like you have something to say; say it…"

"Yes, Mr. Landers, I do have something to say. Your observations regarding my delivery of the lesson are fair and I thank you for that. Regarding your comments under the title labelled 'IMPROVEMENT'… I"

"Man, out with it!"

"Then let me just say that I think that you are very mistaken about me. You wrote that I did not have control of my student, and that she was a distraction in class. I disagree."

I waited for him to respond. It would appear that my comment caught him somewhat off guard; he appeared to be deep in thought.

When it came, his response was clinical and direct, "Mr. Maraj I have outlined what I saw, and I observed that the girl interrupted your lesson. Further, I did not hear you reprimand her in any way. Now, would you explain why you think that I was mistaken?"

"Certainly, Mr. Landers. You noted that I did not take any measures to correct the behaviour. I beg to differ. Here is what I did. When she came with the assignment in hand, I motioned for her to bring it and place it on my desk. This she did. Next, I motioned for her to take her seat. All this was communicated to her without saying a word. Furthermore, I placed my hand to my lips. That was my signal to my class to remain quiet. I was in control of my class at all times, Sir."

"But, I did not see that…"

"Sir, with all due respect, I believe that you were absorbed in scribing your notes at that moment. Is it possible that you *missed* seeing what I was doing?"

He coughed. I wondered if he was going to dismiss what I was saying.

Each of us assumed a pensive attitude. I had no idea what he was thinking. I was wondering if somehow I had crossed a line and gone too far. Was I being perceived as somehow offensive with my remarks?

After some moments had passed in thoughtful reflection on both our parts, Mr. Landers asked, "Mr. Maraj, had I not been in the classroom, had I not been physically present, would you have acted the way you did with that student?"

"I really don't know what exactly I would have done at that moment."

"Then, Mr. Maraj, would you say that you acted differently because I was present in the classroom."

"Yes, Mr. Landers, that is a fair statement."

"But, Mr. Maraj," he countered, "my presence in the classroom should not dictate your action. You should have reprimanded that student for her ill-timed distraction regardless of my presence in the classroom…"

"I might have, Mr. Landers, had you not been there."

"And that, Mr. Maraj, is precisely my point; you should have acted!"

"Acted, yes. But not the way you see it. I cannot reprimand a student… misguided as she might have been in the moment. I would not do it especially in front the principal and even more especially because the offence was not of such a nature that it required a forceful reprimand."

"And why not, Mr. Maraj?"

"I will not chastise a student in your presence for the kind of behaviour you deemed an offense. I would never want this student to ever ask herself, 'Why did Mr. Maraj have to put me down in front of the principal?' You see, Sir, this action of mine, and your observations of such is a matter of perspective, for I knew something about that student that you could not possibly know. I knew that she had been somewhat forgetful about her assignments. On the day that you visited the classroom, she remembered them and was understandably excited. For me to have chastised her for her somewhat exuberant display could have cost me my positive relationship with that student. For that student to have been chastised in the presence of her principal could have easily offended her and caused irreparable damage to our teacher-student relationship. Furthermore, such a reprimand could set the entire class off in the wrong direction. By choosing to act in the manner in which I did, Sir, I chose to be respectful of both you and my class and to your presence in my class. Therefore, Sir, I propose that I was in control of my class at all times. I chose to exercise my personal judgement in that instance. I trust that you understand where I was coming from at that moment."

"I see, Mr. Maraj. Thank you. I will have your report ready soon. Have a good day."

# 81

# Voices…

As I headed for school the next day I was preoccupied with thoughts about my evaluation. My thoughts were conflicted; one part of me wanted the process to come to a quick conclusion, while the other feared hearing the results.

When I encountered Mr. Landers quite by accident in the hall early that morning, my heart skipped a beat. *Would he be the first to mention the report?*

He breezed past me with nothing more than a perfunctory greeting. I tried not to read anything negative in his manner, for just based on yesterday's brief glimpse into his life, I knew that he had much on his mind. We went our separate ways.

Alone, in my classroom, the voice of reason fought to be heard above the insane rhythm of my heart.

*So, you are anxious about your evaluation. That is natural. You want so much to succeed here at the high school, and you are hoping that you are perceived to be competent. Then again you are wondering whether you have offended Mr. Landers with your sense of simple truth. Well, you are who you are; that mind of yours can get you into a cauldron of trouble. Set aside those thoughts for now. Your Grade 10 students will be here soon and they will need all of you.*

I listened and readied myself for my students.

The opening exercises passed without incident and the students should have been engaged in their independent reading. They were not. Their eyes were fixed on me. I had become the source of their distraction; or rather, my pacing had become a source of distraction. I caught myself in mid-stride and went back to my desk hoping to end the distraction.

Donnie, however, had been unfocused for too long and had had ample time to come up with a few distracting questions of his own.

Up went his hand, "Mr. Maraj, I have a question for you. Is it okay to ask it now?"

"Go ahead, Donnie."

"You come from Trinidad, right?"

"Yes."

"What language do they speak there? English like we do?"

I took a moment to explain to the class, that while English was the official language of the country, many spoke Spanish. There were others, like myself who were raised speaking a mixture of English and Hindi. This mixture, this *patois*, was the language that was spoken daily in our homes and on the playground. Often, this bore little resemblance to the formal English taught in the schools.

Donnie seemed uncharacteristically engaged, "So, Mr. Maraj, you come from Trinidad where another form of English is spoken. Right?"

Not fully trusting just where he was going with his line of questioning, I gave a cautiously tentative yet honest response. "Yes, Donnie, you are correct. Not everyone on the island speaks formal English."

Now deep in thought, he tilted his head back and crossed his arms in front of him; he looked like he had more to say. Was he about to mount a challenge? The attitude expressed in his next comment had a significant undertone of implied skepticism. "So, Mr. Maraj, you think that you can come from Trinidad… all that way away… and teach us students here, in Canada… English… correct English?"

The class was quiet; drawn in by the drama created by Donnie's line of questioning, they awaited my response.

Not wanting to further the drama by appearing offended by his query, I offered a simple "Yes," to Donnie. Reaching out to the rest of the class I merely added, "Class, I hope I am teaching in a manner that allows you to learn."

"Well, Mr. Maraj, I have news for you. Real news."

Nothing could stop him from having his say; I braced myself for the inevitable.

"Yes, Mr. Maraj, you're not doing such a bad job. You're different; that's for sure, but you are okay."

The class smiled and so did Donnie. His words reflected the general sentiment of the class. Finally, I had been given a *real* evaluation. I was doing okay. And, coming from this group of students, *okay* was high praise.

In the eyes of these students I was their teacher; while they may think of me as somewhat strange and different as Donnie had put it, I was, nevertheless, legitimate. The effect that this moment had on my psyche is as clear today as it was all those years ago. It was a most critical and defining moment in my quest to become an effective teacher at the high school level here in Canada. That Grade 10 class assumed an honoured place in my memory from that moment on and I knew right then and there that they were indeed *my* grade tens.

Donnie's endorsement was validation enough... for now. Now I could wait a little more patiently for the formal one from the principal. If only his evaluation was of a similar nature.

The very next day, between periods, a voice stopped me in the hall. The voice belonged to another teacher in the school—someone whom I recognized only by sight. He called me by name, "Mr. Maraj, I was hoping to see you."

"See me?"

For the life of me, I couldn't think why this man, who presented himself as most capable and self-assured, would want to seek me out. Was I not just this temporary interloper from the elementary panel come to play at the high school? Why would anyone be interested in seeking me out?

His smile was welcoming and his voice revealed a depth of sincerity and honesty, "I just wanted you to know that the students in your English classes are talking about you."

Talking about me? What were they saying? Were they complaining? My heart dropped a little. He continued, "Your students are saying good things about you. They like your classes. I don't know exactly what you are doing, but keep doing it. It's working. They like English."

That's all he said before he rushed off to attend to other duties. I stood immobilized for several seconds wondering about this man whom I did not yet know by name. Grateful was I to him and his positive comment. It could not have come at a better time.

His sentiments served to sustain me over the next two days at which time I received notice that Mr. Landers wished to see me.

As I entered his office he handed me an envelope and asked me to read the revised portions of the report. I must have appeared somewhat hesitant to do so for he had to urge me on. As I quickly read the changes, I could hide neither my smile nor my gratitude.

"Mr. Landers, thank you, Sir."

"No, Frank, thank you. I learned something about you."

I waited for him to continue.

"You are indeed a competent teacher; that, however, is not your only strength...You are also both disciplined and compassionate. Your students respect you, and so do I..."

He paused, reflected, and continued, "I believe I once told you that I thought you were a pushover. I feared that the students here at the high school would eat you alive. I was wrong."

The solemnity in his voice coupled with the immensity of the implication of his words, resonated with my spirit. I do not know how I managed to remain seated; such was my inner joy. Nothing more was said; what more could be said? As we exchanged handshakes, I truly believe that the sheer power in the strength of his hand was all that kept me upright. In all honesty, I could have collapsed.

I had little time to dwell on that positive exchange, for just around the bend a fury awaited.

# 82

# Just an Illusion?

Buoyed by those most recent positive exchanges, I returned to my office. I was introducing a new novel and I was hoping that I might find help to get me started.

*Imagine this scene.*

Katrina was another staff member who was always willing to help out any staff member in distress. Today, she was at her desk absorbed in a mountain of marking. I approached her shyly and apologized for interrupting. "Sorry to bother you, Katrina; please forgive my interruption. I wonder if I could bother you once more. I am ready to start a new unit and I could use some help with finding materials. But, I see that you are busy; I will come back another time."

I turned to leave.

"Mr. Maraj, do not leave."

Smiling, I turned around, thinking that she was about to offer her assistance. Nothing could have been further from the truth.

"Mr. Maraj, I am not your servant!"

I stopped in mid-stride, recoiled, and then took one step back.

She put down her pen, stretched out her hands atop her desk and pulled herself up and out of her chair. Her voice, clear and authoritative, left no doubt about her position. She continued,

"I do not know how they do things at the elementary school. I have never taught there and have no interest in teaching there. Here, at high school, we do not run around asking for help. You, however, Mr. Maraj, have a particular propensity for this. And I am not the only one from whom you seek assistance. We are sick of it. What on earth is wrong with you?"

I felt my life's blood drain from me. I was capable of neither movement nor thought. Now, fully animated, Katrina exploded, "You, Mr. Maraj, make the big bucks. You come from the elementary panel with more than ample qualifications. You think that you can just waltz in here and dangle those qualifications in our faces and we'll be so impressed that we'll do anything for you! You are wrong, wrong, wrong. And it's high time somebody told you so!"

She had not yet exhausted her litany of complaints. There was yet one more wound to inflict; this she did with righteous pleasure.

"And, Mr. Maraj, if you do not like it here at our high school, you can always return to your elementary school. I am sure there is room for you there."

With those final words having been spoken, she slammed down the gavel of justice.

Somewhere in a distant universe, my amputated soul had taken flight.

There could be no mistaking the hostility in Katrina's manner. In her mind I was an imposter who had come to seek advancement within the hallowed halls of *her* high school. Not only did she assume the role of judge and jury, she also donned the robe of executioner. She had deemed me not only presumptuous but also unworthy. The fool had to be taught a lesson and then be banished. Such presumptuousness must be stopped. More importantly, he had to be returned to his place… the elementary school.

I do not know how I made it to my room. Once safely inside my classroom, I collapsed on the floor. My knees buckled when my lifeless legs could no longer support me. Thus I remained, for what seemed an eternity, leaning against the door, head down.

My mind was reeling. I searched for clues that might explain away Katrina's evident vitriol. I could find nothing; nothing could take away the venomous words. To be treated derisively by anyone bruises the spirit; to be scorned by a colleague cripples the soul.

Eventually, I forced myself up from the floor. I walked across the room to an open window and gazed out above the horizon. Beyond the tree tops, dark clouds held the sky captive.

That's how I felt… captive.

Where was my sun?

I felt abandoned.

All manner of negativity consumed me and I fought hard against drowning.

I was desperate for help.

Into my past I travelled—way back, into my early years. I summoned my ally, my friend of a thousand years… the spirit of my past.

*Treasured and abiding friend, I seek your counsel once again. Chained to a wall of despair, I am lost and defeated.*

A voice whispered,

*Frankie,*
*Have you not walked this path before?*
*How many times have you been attacked, dismissed, rejected?*
*Think, my friend…*
*Stay as you are and you become damaged;*
*Death will surely take you.*
*Now return to your early years;*
*I will bring you there.*
*Go back in time, and remember your resolve, your personal mantra.*

A bolt of sheer energy pierced my mind as an old memory resurfaced.

*Frankie, always you got to do what you want to do to get where you want to go…*
*Now Frankie, my friend of a thousand years.*
*Get up and rise beyond your despair,*
*Your life still awaits*
*Your soul's dream is not obliterated;*
*While it may seem that all is shattered.*
*That is merely life's illusion.*
*What is real is you, and your will to survive.*

I arose, as if from a dream.
Infused with the strength of renewal.
It had all seemed so real.
So very real.

## 83

# Nothing Ventured...

Unquestionably, Katrina's denunciations had sent me reeling; I vowed to shield myself from further harm by donning the cloak of professionalism. I committed all my energies to the classroom. I resolved quietly to earn the respect of my students by working tirelessly on their behalf.

This newfound resolve served me well and soon my mind was able to commit to other thoughts, not the least of which was wondering where I would find myself next semester.

This thought was made manifest just days later in the staffroom.

Many of us regularly met in the staffroom to enjoy a cup of coffee and exchange some innocuous banter before classes began for the day. Today, uncharacteristically, the room was filled with an extra buzz of energy. I could feel it, and I too, absorbed some of the charge.

When Mr. Landers walked in, nothing changed for the staff was accustomed to seeing him there. Today, however, he seemed distracted... he was looking for something... or rather, someone.

Suddenly, his gaze locked in on me. Raising his voice above the fray, he called out my name. "Mr. Maraj!"

Almost instantly, the room quieted.

A drama was about to unfold.

"So, Mr. Maraj, tell me... just where will you be this coming January?"

His dark suit served only to enhance his already impressive air of authority. A slight smile played about his lips. Was he merely playing with me? Was he insinuating that I could be returned very easily to my previous position in the elementary system, or, was he testing me?

Still charged from the energy in the room, and feeling that I had nothing to lose, I made an uncharacteristic declaration. "Mr. Landers... Sir, it will take more than a crane to remove me from *this* high school."

For a moment, Mr. Landers was speechless. Even *I* wondered at my own behaviour. He just scratched his head. Then, a senior time staff member whom I had long admired, stepped forward to shake my hand. As he did so, he looked squarely at Mr. Landers from across the room and declared quite vociferously, "Frank Maraj, I didn't know you had it in you. Man, well done. You actually silenced the principal. Not bad, not bad at all. You are definitely okay."

While a part of me appreciated that endorsement, another part of me felt somewhat abashed thinking that I may have embarrassed the principal.

Mr. Landers approached me and asked me to come see him in his office at the end of the day. Not able to read the expression on his face, I was anxious for the remainder of the day.

At the conclusion of classes I met with a most pensive Mr. Landers. His next words revealed to what extent he had been deliberating; my anxiety increased.

"Mr. Maraj, there are some staff members here who vouch for you."

He paused for what seemed like an eternity. Immediately, I wondered, *did that mean that there were many more who could not or who would not?*

I was now beyond anxious; I struggled to maintain my professionalism.

"As for me," he continued, "I have changed my mind about you. I don't wonder about you anymore."

I allowed myself to dare hope that what was to follow was good news.

Then he posed a question, an unforgettable invitation.

"Frank, we have a position opening up in the English department. Would you be willing to accept it?"

The words fairly exploded from my mouth, "Yes, Mr. Landers. Yes, yes!"

Dreams really do come true.

## 84

## Teachers are Students too…

One of the unstated missions that we as teacher have is to find ways to help students make responsible, meaningful, and insightful decisions. Sometimes the most dramatic lessons are the result of unwitting if not unconventional strategies.

Dramatic presentations are a part of each English curriculum. This particular year, the class developed skits around the idea of finding a job. One particular skit centered on the interview process.

The group consisted of three students; one played the boss who actually conducted the interview, a second played the receptionist who booked the appointments and made the introductions at the interview, while the third played the job applicant.

Quietly, the group converted the classroom into an office setting. Both the boss and the receptionist were dressed in appropriate office attire. Both were female. The applicant, however, seemed to have recently rolled out of bed. His unshaven face was complemented by his equally unruly and straggly long hair. I thought that the group's message was clearly defined as a message about what to do to ensure that you do *not* get hired.

I, of course was wrong. The group had nothing quite so obvious in mind. Their message was more subtle. They had a different perspective on the whole interview process.

As the play opened, it was clear that the firm had been having a difficult time finding just the right candidate with the appropriate qualifications.

The secretary became excited over this next candidate for he appeared, on paper, at least, to be just what the firm was seeking. His qualifications had revealed him to be an expert in their area.

The secretary announced that the "expert" candidate had finally arrived. The boss looked at her watch, noting that the candidate was late.

Already inconvenienced by his late arrival, the boss was further shocked by the inappropriateness of his appearance.

"Young man I do not need you. You have not yet grown up. Go home."

The candidate, visibly agitated by the employer's hasty dismissal, walked out hurling accusations of discrimination against the office.

When he saw the receptionist he complained, "That Mrs. Baxton, your so-called employer, has no class. She should not have judged me by my outside appearance. She should have taken the time to discover me and what I am on the inside. She will never know what she just passed up. She is prejudiced. It is obvious that she does not even *like* young people. She should be brought up on charges of discrimination."

The class warmly applauded the performances of the three actors.

As custom dictated, the actors were subject to answer questions from their peers.

Larry, one of the class observers, positioned that he did not blame the employer for denying an interview to the unkempt candidate.

Gus, the student portraying the interviewee, became furious and charged that the employer was totally unfair with her off-hand dismissal. Gus spoke with such great passion and angst defending his position for the case of discrimination that I came to believe that the performance was more than just performance art. I felt that somehow he had lived that rejection.

The class debated the differing points of view. Those who disagreed with Gus were in the quiet minority. The majority of students clearly defended Gus' assertion that the employer was prejudiced.

The students looked to me to give my perspective on the performances and the implied messages.

I began by thanking the three students for their impassioned performances. Next, I congratulated the class for the students' lively discussion regarding the message to be gleaned from the production. Everyone applauded one another.

Then I turned to Gus.

"Gus, I have a question for you and your group; the rest of the class may want to comment as well."

Everyone became attentive.

"Gus, your expectation that an employer should make a sincere effort to discover your potential is very worthy. I commend you."

"Thank you, Mr. Maraj."

"Then, help me to understand why you made it so difficult for the employer to discover you! I would think that you appeared to deliberately sabotage yourself personally! At first, I thought that you were trying *not* to be hired."

This sparked a new wave of discussion. Gus and other members of his core group of supporters adamantly defended his contention of prejudice being leveled against the employer. Other members of the class appeared to be shifting their belief.

David, a quiet, unassuming student rose to speak. Immediately, the class hushed. Rarely did David venture out of his comfort zone to voice any kind of an opinion let alone one than ran counter to the majority.

He addressed Gus directly, "Gus, I work in a local business. I must dress appropriately. And I am expected to act smart. You, in your performance, did not give the employer a chance to really know you. You presented yourself as an undesirable. Your attire was completely out of place for an interview, and I have to conclude that you showed disrespect… first to yourself, and secondly to the office of your prospective employer."

I was completely taken in by David's thoughtful and candid evaluation. He spoke with great maturity and confidence.

Before Gus could protest, Claudette jumped in to the debate, casting her vote decidedly behind David saying, "Gus, you're wrong. David is right. Now don't try and have your way. Accept that you are wrong." And, turning to me, she added, "Right, Mr. Maraj?"

"Claudette, you certainly have a very strong view. I'm sure that if you allow Gus some time he will come to appreciate your point of view. Students, there is also another lesson to be learned from all of this."

All eyes turned quizzically to me.

"Gus, David, Claudette, thank you for all of your contributions. Class, you have taught this teacher a lesson. You taught me that while you have differing opinions, I can trust you to resolve your issues. I salute you. Congratulations."

The class broke out in applause for itself!

# 85

# Humour in the Classroom

Years before there were iPods, iPads, and iPhones in regular use in the classroom, students relied heavily on *dictionaries* (a book with physical pages that require turning) for vocabulary development. Oftentimes it was hard to hook students into wanting to learn about language and spelling. I tried to take advantage of any opportunity I could find to make it a little bit less tedious. The day's task called for finding words with double letters such as street, meet, greet, and so on. This, they managed without difficulty. They then moved on to the next stage: words containing two sets of double letters. These words were less obvious and the students showed a serious lack of interest in the exercise.

I left them on their own for a few minutes before gathering up a piece of chalk, and a yardstick. I handed both pieces of equipment to a boy sitting in the front of the class. I instructed him to draw three columns on the blackboard for me. Once that task was completed, I asked for a volunteer to do some printing in each column. In the first column the volunteer was asked to write the words: meet, greet, and street. I underlined the double e in each word. Above that column I wrote *A Single Double*. Above the second column I wrote *A Double-Double*. I stopped writing and looked at the class. They looked back at me expectantly. No one said anything. I returned to my desk.

Still nothing.

Then Hillary exclaimed, "I get it!" and went to the board and wrote the word 'coffee' and underlined the two f's and the two e's. She then grabbed the ruler, pointed to the title and said to the class, "Get it?"

Almost instantly the class underwent a minor brain explosion. Soon the word 'toffee' joined the word coffee under the *Double Double* heading.

Then 'raccoon' and 'address' joined the grouping. The students applauded their efforts with each new addition to the list.

Then someone asked what the third column was for.

I turned to the class and asked them what they thought it was for. Someone shouted, "A Triple Double".

"But, there's no such thing… is there?"

After assuring them that there was, I challenged, "Let's just see who can come up with the first word."

The students gave it a good effort but could come up with no results. They begged for assistance.

"I would rob you of the joy of discovery if I gave away the answer. Keep working."

They pleaded for a hint—not a word—just a hint. I deferred to them and hinted, "It is a body of water located in North America."

One student took out an atlas while other students pulled down the world map and examined it closely. After a few minutes, young Chad went to the board and wrote *Mississippi*; he underlined the triple double in pink. When I started to clap, the rest of the class joined in the applause, rejoicing at their conquest.

My heart was filled with the simple joy of the moment.

I decided to give them one further hint for one more triple double. I said, "Class, you have been working in groups to find words today. What is another word we could use to call a group of people who are working together?"

A boy yelled out, "A chain gang?"

"That doesn't have any double letters," someone chastised.

"I think the word Mr. Maraj was hinting at is *committee*," enthused someone else.

"Bravo!" I yelled and again everyone applauded.

When I directed them to copy the three lists of words from the board they lost their smiles and were reluctant to begin.

I felt responsible for taking away their joy. I had to fix it.

"Students, I think that we should commemorate this historic moment. McDonalds is not the only one to have a double double, and a triple double. By initiating the double double, and the triple double concepts into the classroom, you have in fact expanded the horizon of vocabulary development."

This brought back their smiles and one student quipped, "Will the board of education pay us for our creativity?"

***

Making an effort to engage the students on the lighter side of life required a mammoth effort on my part. I do not naturally gravitate to the humourous, but, I tried. Much of class time was spent in pursuit of the serious but laughter was not an uncommon event. Most of the time I was unaware that I had said or done something funny until the students started laughing. They found me humourous. Sometimes, however, I purposefully tried to inject humour into the classroom. On these occasions, the students themselves found ways to turn the humour back on me and I often became the butt of the joke.

In one of my classes was a good-natured student whose last name happened to be Payne. In a light hearted moment I decided to make an effort to be humourous and decided to tease the student about his name.

"John," I began, "I wonder what it will be like for you to go through the rest of your life being regarded as a pain?"

John took a moment to absorb the unsolicited comment before replying, "Mr. Maraj, I too am wondering what it must be like for you to always be a mirage for the rest of your life?"

I sensed that my comment to John elicited little to no positive response from the class. John's witty comeback, however, caused the class to explode with laughter.

My failure did not dissuade me from making further, equally sad excuses for jokes in the classroom.

On another occasion in another classroom, I again attempted to flirt with the elusive character of humour. This time the student's last name was Wright.

"Mr. Wright," I called out, "what a burden it must be for you knowing you will, no matter what, be right for the rest of your natural life."

Again, almost predictably, I alone found my comments to be funny. No one else even cracked a smile. Mr. Wright sat, for what seemed to me to be a significant period of time, before he asked to respond.

"Mr. Maraj," he began, "I believe that I can accept being right for the rest of my life… but, Sir, don't you think that you have some ways to go in that direction?"

The class enjoyed this shift in the balance of power and one student summed it all up when he declared, "Mr. Maraj, you were just taken down… big time!"

The class erupted in boisterous laughter.

One might think that I would abandon any future attempts at this brand of humour after being foiled by my own students at every turn. Such was not the case. My next target was a young lady by the name of Mandy Bone.

As I was returning some marked assignments to the students, I came upon Mandy's paper. Other members of the class, who had already received their papers, were chatting amongst themselves about their marks. When I pulled out Mandy's paper, I held it up in front of the class and called out her name.

"Mandy Bone?" I said in my most serious voice.

"Yes, Mr. Maraj," responded a somewhat hesitant Mandy.

"Take a look at your paper, Mandy. I have a *bone* to pick with you."

Before I could continue to play about with her name, this gregarious student, not known to be contained by rules and regulations, or to be constrained by the standard student teacher relationship, handed me what still stands out as one of my more inglorious moments of defeat when she quipped, "And I, Mr. Maraj, need to be absolutely *Frank* with you…"

She did not need to say another word. Referencing my first name in such a manner rendered me speechless. Mandy had won the day. I was sent back to my desk mumbling incomprehensible comments about today's brand of student.

Secretly, I took great delight in their banter. To know that these Canadian students felt free to display their quick wit within the confines of the classroom and in front of their peers, made me feel positive about the type of schooling that was being fostered in the high school. Respect was ever present, but the rules around respect were relaxed. This afforded those on either side to determine the new look of respect—no longer fearful and stuffy; it could also be relaxed and friendly… even humourous.

# 86

# Marking Woes

In the early years working in the high school, I found much for which to be thankful. I felt that in general I was getting along with the students and that we were both making progress toward our various goals.

This confidence was shattered in one meeting with one singular administrator.

Mr. O summoned me to his office but gave no indication of the reason why. This was my first such summons at the high school and I wondered whether I had committed some serious offence.

I don't ever recall being summoned to the office and offered a compliment either as a student or as a teacher. That has been my reality all of my life.

As I entered his office, Mr. O invited me to sit down. He put down a raft of papers, removed his glasses and looked directly at me.

"Mr. Maraj, your students' marks are very high… I…"

I took that as a compliment and thanked him for recognizing that my students were applying themselves and doing well.

Mr. O was taken aback. Clearly, he was not expecting a response. He continued, "Mr. Maraj, I do not understand why your marks are higher than those of the other teachers in your department who teach the same courses."

While his remarks confused me, I recognized that he had a point that he wished to make and I made no further attempt to interrupt.

He insisted, "Your marks should reflect a certain pattern…"

"A pattern?"

"Yes, Mr. Maraj. We advocate that a certain number of students should be achieving at the top, some in the middle, and a few at the bottom. Your marks, do not reflect that pattern. Too many are at the high and middle of the spectrum."

To say that I was baffled and speechless would be an understatement. I recognized that I was still relatively new at the high school and that I had a great deal to learn about the culture of the school, but something in me railed against this arbitrary distribution of marks.

I regarded this policy as counter-productive and detrimental to student achievement. The students, by their own efforts, earned their marks. I wondered at the fairness of a method that predetermined that only a certain number of students could attain an A, B, C, D, or F ranking. Wasn't it our job as teachers to help our students achieve the highest standing of which they are capable?

I ventured to speak, "Mr. O, if I recognize that I have made an error or committed a wrong to our students or to our school, I would indeed apologize immediately."

"Mr. Maraj, you do not have to apologize; all you have to do is modify your marking scheme to conform to school policy."

"Mr. O, I cannot, in all good conscience, do that, Sir."

"And why not, Mr. Maraj! You strike me as a man who would want to do what is right, so why wouldn't you do what is right in this case?"

"In most situations that would be a correct assumption, Mr. O, but not in this instance. What you are asking me to do with respect to student marks, is not in the best interest of the students."

"We who are in administrative positions seek the best for our students also. But, sometimes we make decisions on behalf of our students that our teachers may not understand. Trust me…"

"I am sorry, but I do not see it as being helpful in any way to the student; it is, in fact, counter to the spirit of good teaching. Do we not have a policy at this school that clearly recognizes that each student deserves an education; that seeks to promote each student to the best of each student's ability? I stand firmly behind that principle. But, this other policy demands a reality I cannot honour. I really wish you would reconsider this requirement of me. Do our students not deserve to advance as their talents dictate? I question what right we have to impede their progress by implementing a system that clearly retards growth."

After having spoken so openly, I left the office; clouds of doubt followed after me.

\*\*\*

Because of that conversation, I braced myself for further disciplinary action from the office. I spent several restless days working under the threat of that very occurrence, and it was almost a relief when a second administrator came to see me in my room.

He, however, had no words of reprimand; he came with a simple request.

"Mr. Maraj, may I see some of the marked assignments the students have completed. Some samples could come from classroom assignments, tests, and essays. I would appreciate receiving them in the next day or two. Thank you, so very much."

He was neither disrespectful nor condescending with his request; he was simply officious.

His complete lack of engagement with me left me in a troubled state. Was this request a direct consequence of my meeting with Mr. O? Was my credibility—whatever little I possessed—now being questioned?

I tried to set aside any misgivings that I may have had while I dutifully collected the samples for him.

I submitted them to him the next day after school. As I rested them on his desk, he asked me to stay. As he examined the papers he made notes for himself on a separate sheet of paper. Occasionally, I could hear him talking to himself.

I did not know what to make of this review of my marking.

Eventually, he made a comment that only served to further confuse me, "I do not see any evidence of negative marking. Do you use negative marking at all?"

"No!" (Truth be told, I did not even know what negative marking was.)

"I see."

"Am I supposed to use negative marking Mr. H?"

He did not answer; I'm not sure if he even heard my question.

Then he asked a most unusual question of his own, "Do your students disagree and object to your method of marking? Do they appear agitated with you?"

"Well, at times they do ask me to explain how I might have arrived at a certain mark. They may not always understand their marks. When they don't, they generally ask questions. I explain. But, I do not sense opposition."

"So you do not sense any real kind of hostility?"

"No, Mr. H."

"Thank you, Mr. Maraj, for your cooperation."

And that was it. I was dismissed from his office.

For the next few days I waited in limbo for some rationale to be offered for his request to see samples of marked work. No reason was ever ventured and no explanation was ever offered. In time, I managed to let the matter slide.

Then, just when I had almost forgotten about it, I was called to face all three administrators.

# 87

# Judgement

The principal was the first to speak, "Well, Mr. Maraj, you can be quite outspoken. You know that, don't you?"

I never considered myself to be outspoken; I felt that I had merely advocated on behalf of my students. His words did not dispel my apprehension about this impromptu meeting.

"We feel that we have come up with a solution."

*A solution, to what*? I wondered silently.

The three of them were most somber looking. I braced myself for their *solution*; obviously I had committed an offence; they were there to deliver their verdict.

I resigned myself to the inevitable.

"Mr. Maraj, we have evaluated your style and methods in the classroom. Accordingly, in consideration of your performance, we have decided…"

He stopped.

I froze, bracing myself for the worst.

Mr. C.J again took the lead, "Mr. Maraj, Mr. H has mandated that you will continue to teach your basic and general classes just as you have been doing for the past few years. Now…"

Then he paused.

I was puzzled.

Was there more to his announcement? Was I missing something?

Then he put on a rather serious look and continued, "We have determined that you are now ready to teach the grade eleven academic English. What do you think about that?"

I was stupefied.

That announcement felt like a promotion.

It was something I had wanted secretly but certainly did not expect.

Before I could get too carried away, the principal warned, "Mr. Maraj, those students in the academic classes have minds of their own. They can be demanding. Are you up to that challenge?"

"I will do my best, Sir."

Each one in turn, shook my hand and wished me well.

Individually, and collectively, this team of administrators could have made my life at the high school awkward and difficult. It now seems however, that they advocated on my behalf. For that, I was most grateful.

The principal opened the door for me as I left and whispered, "Mr. Maraj, I have sat on the administrative chair for years. You remind me of something that we can lose sight of so easily; we all are here for the same basic cause: the students. They are first and foremost what matters most. Good luck, and thank you."

My mind reeled into the future. New challenges awaited.

# 88

# A "Quick" Dimension

It was during my time at the high school that a new dimension in education was introduced into my life. For several months, various administrators had approached me at various intervals to ask me to consider having an educational assistant in my classroom. Each time I was asked, my response was the same, *I was not yet ready.*

While educational assistants are commonly used in today's classrooms, back in the eighties, there were only three in the entirety of our high school. It is not that I was opposed to having an assistant in the classroom; I feared that my teaching would become stilted and awkward by the presence of another adult in the room. Over the years I had adopted some rather unconventional mannerisms in my classroom… but they worked. Having another adult in the room, I feared, would make my teaching less spontaneous and I would be less *me*.

Just days after I once again declined the invitation to have an assistant join me in the classroom a certain lady named Jazzy Quick met me in the hall. While I had seen her before in the school, we had never had a conversation. That day, everything changed. Jazzy must have been informed of the many times I had declined offers of assistance because she was very direct with her first question.

"Mr. Maraj, why won't you have an educational assistant in your classroom?"

While I was understandably surprised by the bluntness of the question and the boldness of the questioner, I was even more surprised by the completely unrestrained manner and complete lack of guile of the speaker. At first, I could not give a response. Unsatisfied with this lack of response, she insisted on knowing.

She really was not going to let me pass without answering. She did not waver in her demand in the slightest. Her stare was unrelenting and I knew that she meant business. I had to respond.

"Jazzy, I am shy about having someone in my class. I am unsure."

"Why is that Mr. Maraj?"

"I am unconventional at times, and I have a tendency to stray from the curriculum from time to time."

"Don't worry, Mr. Maraj. We all know about your style. The students do talk about you and your tendency to become overly excited. You don't have to worry about any of that. We are here to help you help the student. Please think about letting us help."

Just days later, a vice-principal once again approached me about working with an educational assistant. I sensed that he was most intent that I say yes.

"Mr. Maraj, have you now made up your mind about having an assistant in your classroom?"

I relented. "Sir, if I am to have an assistant, then let it be Jazzy Quick."

There was no going back on my word, but I still wondered, *Was I really ready to open up my world to this Jazzy Quick?*

# 89

# Fears Dispelled

Immediately Jazzy was assigned to one of my Grade 11 general English classes.

Regardless of size, none of the boys was a match for Jazzy's stubborn resolve. Each day I marveled at her forthright manner in dealing with delinquent behaviours. You always knew where you stood with Jazzy; but, if you didn't or if you forgot temporarily, she would soon remind you. Jazzy was never one to hedge the truth. She had no use for subtlety.

I had my own way of dealing with classroom discipline and Jazzy fit right in.

We were well into the semester when Jazzy joined our class and she was about to give first hand witness to my unusual requests.

A student had accidentally slammed the door as he entered the classroom. The loudness disturbed me from my reading. I put down the book and walked over to the door. I bent my head and put my ear gently against the door. With my hand I caressed the doorframe. One brave student asked me what I was doing.

"I'm listening to the door."

The class exploded with laughter.

I put my hand to my lips to quiet the class all the while keeping my head in close proximity to the door.

I urged, "Please, I cannot hear the door. It is trying to say something."

I frowned as I continued to listen. Then I spoke, "Don't be hurt, door. Mallory really did not mean it. Please, stop crying…"

Next, I turned to Mallory and urged, "Mallory, the door tells me that you slammed it. It says it has feelings too. You hurt it. And now it is in pain."

Mallory protested, "Mr. Maraj, it's just a door. Doors don't have feelings."

"Mallory," I insisted, "you really hurt the door. Please tell it something… something that would make it feel better."

By now, the rest of the class was in stiches. This experience was brand new.

I took Mallory by the hand and coaxed, "Come, Mallory. I'll go with you and we'll do it together. I'll show you how it's done. All you need to do is this." And I gently rubbed the door and uttered soothing words of comfort.

"This is crazy…"

At the door, Mallory hesitated.

The whole class decided to help, and chanted, "Say sorry."

Still Mallory hesitated.

Then Jazzy spoke, "Mallory, just don't stand there like a log. I know you. At home you are not this quiet. Now, what do you have to say to the door?"

To my surprise and the class' great delight, Mallory whispered, "Sorry door!"

This incident served as a testament to the inherent good nature of Mallory. Thereafter, door slamming was decidedly a no.

The craziness did not end with the door; it extended to the garbage can as well.

One day, Sampson crumpled up a sheet and shot it at the garbage can; Jazzy admonished, "Sampson, that is not right. Get right over there and pick up that paper and put it in the garbage can nicely."

That was not the first time that Jazzy initiated discipline. She was very comfortable with most of the students as she had been an assistant in many of their previous classes. A longtime resident of the town, she also knew many of their parents. Thus, she was not just an assistant; she was a real force in the classroom. I understood this reality and encouraged her to participate freely.

After speaking to Sampson, all Jazzy had to do now was continue to stare at him. He understood very well what was required of him, but, his response was somewhat delayed. I could sense that Jazzy was about to escalate her reprimand. Before she could do this, I rushed to the garbage can and picked it up holding it close to my ear as if I were listening to it... When I began stroking the side of the can and whispering softly to it, Sampson rose up out of his seat, and approached the front; he knew the drill.

"Alright, I am sorry, garbage can." He then picked up the paper and respectfully placed it in the can.

He turned to Jazzy and teased, "Mrs. Quick, don't you be telling stories to my parents about me."

Jazzy grinned. She continued to initiate a spirit of good will throughout the semester. As she left the room at the end of class, she teased, "Mr. Maraj, you and your antics. Not bad. You know the kids think you are crazy. Why they want to come to your class, I will never know."

As the semester progressed, so did my dependency on Jazzy. She was a force to be reckoned with in the classroom, and all our days were made richer because of her presence.

From that day onward, I have willingly welcomed each new assistant into my classroom. Each brought unique gifts and talents that enriched the learning of all.

# 90

# Life's Lessons

Over the years, I looked forward to marking the essays of many of my academic level students. That was the time that I was able to measure the growth of not just their writing skills, but of their thinking skills as well.

This particular day I was filled with sadness and disappointment as I returned their most recent efforts. On many of the essays I had written comments reflecting my disappointment.

After returning all the papers, I asked the class if anyone had any questions.

Tyler's face reflected that he indeed had a question. He did not sit quietly in his desk and raise his hand as was our custom; he jumped to his feet and demanded, "Mr. Maraj, what's wrong with my paper? You wrote *disappointing* right on the front of my paper and I got sixty percent. What's wrong with that?"

At that moment, Lucy, an otherwise quiet student declared, "Mr. Maraj, you wrote *unsatisfactory* on my paper too, and I passed. I thought you would be happy that I passed. What's so unsatisfactory about passing?"

I almost shouted my response, "Plenty!"

My tone startled the students. They did not yet understand my mind. I had to make them understand.

I started again; this time I was less reactionary and more thoughtful in tone.

"Students, you are in an academic class; pause for a just a moment and think what that implies… you are advanced, that is you."

They were quiet.

"You have a responsibility to yourselves; and, as your teacher, I have a responsibility to see that you act responsibly. You are here not to do *just good enough* work or to barely pass. If that is your thinking, clearly you do not belong in this class."

I paused for a moment to gauge the temperature of the room. *Were my words alienating or reaching them? Were they feeling insulted or was I opening their eyes to a worthy reality?*

"Class, I don't want any of you to leave here thinking that I am putting you down. Far from it. Students, each and every one of you can do well. You have what it takes to do well. And, it is so very important that we create a climate for learning, wherein it *matters* that you do well."

Then one student asked, "But, Mr. Maraj, we can't all get A's. You have to accept that fact… don't you?"

"Thank you, Hannah. I appreciate your comment. Your point is well taken. You are right. Not all of us have been given the natural ability to achieve A's, but each one has been given some other quality in equal measure."

No one said anything; they looked pensive.

Hannah voiced the question that each student was deliberating.

"Mr. Maraj, could you tell us what that quality is, please?"

"Class, the one thing we each possess in equal measure is diligence."

"And what's that?" asked another.

Hannah took it upon herself to respond to that question, "Hard work."

"Hannah is right, students."

Then I continued, "Students, I hope that you would work hard all the time; I can accept that you would work hard most of the time. What I cannot accept, however, is that you would hardly work. Hard work becomes you!"

The students looked somewhat bewildered.

*Had I been too philosophical? Had I confused them with my words?*

I was at a loss.

"Students I am so sorry that I had to be so serious. I regret that I had to write terms like *disappointing* and *unsatisfactory* on your papers. I so wish…" my voice trailed.

"Mr. Maraj," interjected Hannah, "you don't have to say sorry. And you won't have to write those comments ever again."

Then, turning to the class, she added, "Right?"

Somewhat happier now, they nodded back to her in affirmation.

We had an understanding.

The quality of wisdom in these students never failed to amaze me.

## 91

# Claimed

At other times, however, their thinking lacked perspective.

This trait was illustrated one day when Cassidy, a student in an advanced Grade 11 class, asked a favour of me.

When asked to define the exact nature of the favour, Cassidy explained, "We, the members of this class, want you to sign our protest."

"And, just what are you protesting?"

"Well, we need more parking spots for student parking. All the staff at the high school are allowed to park in the parking lot. We are not permitted to park there. We feel that we have as much right to park there as do the teachers. We are demanding equal rights to the parking lot. We should not be treated as second class. We know you always advocate for fairness, Mr. Maraj. Now, will you sign our petition?"

Before I could respond, someone yelled, "Of course, Mr. Maraj will!"

They were so confident that I would support their cause.

The reason for their confidence stems from a recent class lesson.

During one of their poetry presentations, a group of students made a presentation on the theme of refugees in Canada. They focused on Canada's role in this situation. They made the point that refugees who come to Canada, do so not only at the tax payers' expense, but also at the expense of the unemployed. They argued that refugees take away jobs that should rightfully belong to Canadian workers. Their presentation was passionate and convincing and persuaded many to believe that refugees only *take* from Canada.

One brave soul challenged the group by asking them to consider another perspective.

"Guys, wait a minute. The point that you make about refugees *taking* from Canada, is true; but it is only true of some of them. There is another side. Refugees that come to our country eventually find jobs, buy houses and cars, and pay taxes just like the rest of us."

One young man, unimpressed with her defence, bellowed, "Send all the immigrants back to their country. We don't need no immigrants."

No one laughed at his comment.

The class remained quiet for several moments.

I was quite taken aback.

It started to feel personal. After all, I, too, was once an immigrant.

Cassidy again stood to ask, "Samuel, if we took your advice, we would have to send Mr. Maraj back to his country. Is that what you are trying to say?"

All eyes shifted to focus on Samuel. I have never felt as sorry for a student as I felt for Samuel during that moment of intense scrutiny. I found myself searching for words to end his discomfort when he stood up.

"Cassidy, I was not thinking right. Mr. Maraj, I'm sorry."

He was able to say nothing more.

There was no need for anyone to say anything anymore.

Cassidy's insights won over the class.

I felt somewhat indebted and connected to this group of students in a very special way.

I think that it was because of that incident that the class was confident that I would support them in their new cause.

Again, Cassidy asked, "Mr. Maraj, will you sign our protest? Here, I've even brought you a special pen to sign it with." She produced a pen with a feather on it.

Their faces were so confident, so expectant.

My response shocked them, "Students I am so sorry; I cannot sign your petition."

I said the words as softly and gently as I could but nothing diminished the look of dismay on their faces.

I felt that I had to get them back to their work.

They were reluctant to do so.

Cassidy approached and asked,

"Mr. Maraj, can we talk about your decision to not sign our petition?"

"Cassidy, you are hurting. The class is hurting. Right now, no one is prepared to really listen to what I have to say. I fear that some will want to be argumentative. Such an outcome would strain the goodwill that we have managed to secure. Let us leave matters as they are."

Without another word to me, she wheeled around to face the class.

"Guys, I think that I can convince Mr. Maraj to explain to us why he doesn't agree with our petition… on one condition…We really have to try and listen to him. We need to understand his take on things. Do you think we can do that?

They nodded.

Cassidy then invited me to speak, "They're all yours, Mr. Maraj."

"Thank you Cassidy, thank you students. I have a question for you. How many of you think that you are not being treated equally; that is, if the teachers can park in the parking lot you feel that you, the students, should have the same right?"

A good majority raised their hands, I continued.

"Let me ask you something which may seem totally unrelated. Bear with me. Suppose your younger brother or sister in Grade 5 wished to drink alcohol. Would you allow it?"

"What!" they protested. "That's crazy!"

It was like I had just exploded a bomb. Everyone had an opinion about that. All opinions were decidedly negative.

One boy stood and strongly asserted, "I don't drink, and I am in Grade 11. How dare my brother or sister in Grade 5 even think that way?"

"Students, let me propose another scenario. Suppose your grandparents decide to give you money for Christmas. They gave your baby brother in kindergarten, ten dollars. They gave your sister in Grade 5 ten dollars. You also received ten dollars, as did your older sibling in university. Your grandparents wished to treat all of you equally so you received equal amounts of money. Were they right to do so? Is that what equal treatment really means?"

Once again their voices were raised in debate. Finally they agreed that the action taken by the grandparents was not right and claimed that the grandparents were most unreasonable.

"But students, each member of the family was treated equally," I reminded them.

Then Cassidy shouted, "But that wasn't fair!"

"Just what do you mean, Cassidy?" I coaxed.

"Being equal is not always fair!"

Immediately I ran to the board and wrote down her words; then I wrote:

*To be fair is to be just*
*Being equal is not always fair.*
*Being fair is being just.*
*Seek always to be just!*

It was then that Cassidy said, "I got it, Mr. Maraj."

"Got what, Cassidy?"

"I think I got the connection between this and our petition."

She continued. "What Mr. Maraj is trying to tell us is that being equal is not always right. Somehow, I have the feeling that we are not right in asking for equal parking spaces."

And Samuel shouted, "That story about our younger siblings drinking… I see the connection. The students have some ways to go before we could make such a demand for equal parking spaces. We don't have to drive to school. The school provides us with buses that take us to school."

"I am so pleased and proud of you. There is another point to be made here."

They were still engaged.

I continued, "Your teacher once sat in a classroom just like you. It is a question of time and place… that's all. Your turn is coming. Everything has a season. When your season comes, a way will be made for you, too. You have to earn your way to the privileges you want to enjoy."

Samuel teased, "Mr. Maraj should have been a lawyer."

Another student countered, "No way. He's *our* teacher."

# 92

# Who Is Teaching Whom?

The year that I was first assigned to teach an elective English course at the OAC level (formerly known as Grade 13) stands out among my memories for two reasons. First, it was considered a distinct honour to be given the opportunity to teach students at the senior level. Second, I was taking over for a well-established and well-regarded senior teacher. While I was most honoured to be accorded this responsibility, I was also aware of the difficulties inherent in such a transition. The fact that I was now somewhat of a known quantity within the school, served to mitigate some of the difficulty.

On the first morning that I was to meet my new students, I was filled with a measure of apprehension. In fact, I was so consumed with my own doubts, that I was completely oblivious to the bell. I worried about my ability to engage the minds of these extremely keen students who elected to take the course. Beyond that worry was a deeper concern regarding the actual course content.

One student, noticing my distraction, spoke candidly, "Mr. Maraj, is something bothering you? You look troubled."

"Yes," I admitted, "something is on my mind."

"Can you tell us what is so troubling?"

"It concerns your course. I have serious reservations about the novel that we are scheduled to study. While it is a highly acclaimed novel, and comes with much to recommend it, I wonder about its suitability for the high school classroom."

The students urged me to clarify my objections.

"There is a great deal of offensive language in the book. Many of the characters cuss and swear. I am not very comfortable presenting it as a novel to be studied in a high school setting."

"Seriously, Mr. Maraj, is that the problem you are struggling with? The language?" questioned Angela.

"Yes."

"Mr. Maraj, take a closer look at us. We are seniors, and we are about to leave this small community. Soon we all will be attending large institutions in even larger cities. We are young adults, and we should be ready for the challenges."

She continued, "And you are worried about cussing and cuss words. Mr. Maraj, there are things that are a lot worse that we have to worry about in our day to day lives. When we begin to attend university, believe me, the use of profanities will not even be on our radar."

The class nodded to indicate that they were in complete agreement with Angela's comments.

Then Tristan asked, "Mr. Maraj, do you like the novel yourself?"

"Yes I do, it's just that…"

"Mr. Maraj, the language in the book should not be the deciding factor. Let us start the novel. If we, as class, think that it is not appropriate, we will let you know. Is that okay with you?"

"Agreed."

So, on my first day with these students, I could not help but wonder, *who was teaching whom?*

From the outset, I sensed that this was a very astute group of students. I also recognized that they would challenge me to be at the top of my game every single day. I looked forward to spending the entire semester with them. They did not disappoint.

# 93

# One Student's Conviction

In one of my senior English classes we explored an article on the subject of education. I encouraged the students to give honest feedback regarding the writer's point of view. One student noted that the author took a hard stand against a system that continued to 'house" children in schools when they had obvious problems with the learning environment. The author further charged that society *i.e.* the parents were not taking full responsibility for their own children. He argued that when problems occur, even with a child in kindergarten, that that child should be sent home.

This contention raised the ire of many of my students. The discussion grew heated and assumed a distinct air of outrage.

It took virtually no effort on my part to get students to participate in the discussion and openly express their opinions. One student voiced his outrage clearly, "I do not agree with the writer's viewpoint. Those students with behavioural issues should *not* be sent home. They belong in schools just like everyone else regardless of…"

Tamara came at it from a different perspective,

"But Damien, what you are advocating places the burden directly on the classroom teacher. Every year we are seeing more and more children with wild outbursts right inside our classrooms. That teacher is totally consumed just looking after so many ill-tempered students. That is not fair to anyone; not to the teacher, not to the "misbehaving" child, nor to the rest of the class."

"I see your point Tamara. Seems to me that teachers working at the kindergarten level need help. Surely there are resources that can be accessed to solve the problem. All they need to do is to hire more people to help."

"Isn't that right, Mr. Maraj? They just need to hire more people."

"It does seem logical, Damien, but there is more to it than that. There are financial considerations that have to be factored in."

"Mr. Maraj, you are the educator. Why aren't there more teachers available in kindergarten classes to help out when these bad behaviours escalate?"

"Damien and class, you have raised a legitimate concern but I do not have the answer to your question. But...I do know someone who might have an answer."

I then adopted an unorthodox measure that did not seem so unorthodox in the moment and invited both Damien and Tamara to accompany me to the principal's office.

Much to my great relief the principal was both present and unengaged. The students briefly articulated their concerns; Mr. CJ listened closely to their words. Delighted by the passion in their appeal, he quickly announced that he would prefer to be invited right into the classroom and be part of the class dynamic.

Damien readily took the lead and escorted the principal directly to the classroom; Tamara and I followed closely behind.

This new turn of events further animated an already excited Damien.

A hush fell over the class when everyone realized who was in our midst. Damien wasted no time in bringing everyone up to date.

He then directed his address to the principal, "Mr. CJ there is a startling... no... I would venture to say... a ridiculous point of view advocated by this writer. His point of view is both strong and callous. He proposes that children... all children... even children in kindergarten should be sent home if they have excessive behavioural problems and issues."

"I understand so far. What is your thinking on the matter?"

"Mr. CJ what I am saying... what many of us here are saying... is that no school should send any child home no matter what."

"What, if anything, do you propose should happen?"

"What I propose is simply this... if there are problems in a classroom there should be support for that classroom teacher. It seems only fitting."

Then Mr. CJ turned to the class and asked them how they felt about Damien's point of view.

There was a definite split in the class; some in favour, others opposed and still others needed more time to reflect on the issue.

After listening to the class's various opinions, he chose to address Damien's viewpoint. "Look, class, you have hit on a real issue here; this is a very real problem facing education today. We, as educators, are facing a very difficult challenge. Boards of Education are cutting back as never before; their normal funding that comes from the Ministry of Education is being reduced…"

I could see that Damien was getting anxious to speak; blood was rushing to his face and I could see the beginning of a pulse bulging and throbbing in his neck; I tried to catch his eye to keep him from interrupting the principal, but to no avail. Damien could not be contained. His outrage was fresh, "What are you saying? Our ministry is cutting back funds at a time when we need more help; we need more able bodies to help our kindergarten teachers! The idea of cutbacks right now is just plain stupid!"

Damien blushed a deep purple when he realized that he had spoken so unreservedly to the principal. Immediately, Mr. CJ put him at ease with his next remark, "Damien, I take your point. Believe me, I understand your frustration."

He continued, "Students, you are right. We should have more able bodies as your demand. Yet, this is our reality. We, as principals, put our demands for more resources to our Board. Their hands are tied too. We do battle with our Board. In the end, we are left to figure out things as best we can. And even at our high school, I would like nothing more than to be able to hire more teachers…"

Everyone was quiet, just listening to him speak.

There was a lull in the conversation, and for a moment, we were all pensive. Mr. CJ brought us all back to the present when he said, "Class, I want to thank you for asking me to be a part of your discussion. What tremendous thinking is taking place here. I commend you for your strong interest. I am sorry I could not give you all the answers that would help with your problems… our problems. Who knows? Maybe someday you might be that generation that helps to solve the problems in education."

I watched him watch these students and I was filled with pride and admiration for their ability to engage so fully with their principal.

The students and I had much to ponder following Mr. CJ's remarks regarding reduced funding. While all of us were sad and disappointed by the funding realities, Damien delivered this final indictment, "Mr. Maraj, forgive my language, but it is just a bloody shame, just a bloody injustice that kids are not a high priority. Shame, shame, shame. To those responsible, I say this: Kids should be first, always first…"

A deep sadness surrounded Damien; its presence could be felt throughout the entire classroom.

And the sad reality of cutbacks and limited funds was to become the tide of the future that would wreak havoc on the classroom, especially to the most vulnerable, and I wondered… in the chain of education, should we not make every effort to secure, at the very least, the first link?

# 94

# And Mr. Bright Takes Over

As I recall this next event, I do admit that I might not have been as objective as I should.

The students in my senior English class had just completed their novel study and were preparing to make presentations on the various themes of the novel. One group chose "the family" as its theme. Following the presentations, students from the class were encouraged to ask questions of the presenters. As arbiter, I was allowed to ask up to three questions. These questions could be asked of the presenters or of the class in general. This fact was designed to keep both the presenters and their classmates engaged for the full length of the presentation since neither group knew from whom I would be soliciting answers.

The group had made its presentation; the class had asked questions; now all awaited my remarks. "Members of the presenting group, there is no doubt that you have clearly demonstrated a sound knowledge of the novel. And, your contribution to the class was solid."

My comments were met with smiles from every quarter.

"There is, however," I continued, "one area that was not as developed as it should have been."

The smiles began to fade.

"And what's that area?" asked a member of the presenting group.

"That area concerns the last requirement in which you were asked to demonstrate the significance of your selected topic as it relates to the present."

"I thought we did, Mr. Maraj."

"You did, but it was not sufficiently developed. Therefore I will allow you, as well as the class, to reconsider your views. I will repeat the question. How was the topic, *The Family*, portrayed in the novel? You answered that part of the question with distinction. There was a follow up question: *Is that topic relevant and significant today?* That is the question that I want you all to develop more fully. In fact, I consider this topic to be of such importance that I would like every member of the class to re-examine his/her individual stand."

Dutifully, the students complied. Soon a full class discussion ensued. The presenters advocated that indeed the family unit had been broken as the author professed. Further, they maintained that the family unit as we know it today is also broken. Still, they did not present any evidence to support this view and they did not venture to explore any aspect of the modern family.

As a result, I had to judge that in this one area the seminar still lacked sufficient supporting evidence.

An air of quiet descended upon the class. Something was amiss.

I forced myself to reexamine my own expectations. *Were they unreasonable? Was I placing an unfair burden on this particular group of presenters?*

I tried, unsuccessfully, to resurrect the previous vibrant spirit of the class. I felt helpless.

Then, from the very back of the classroom and from a most unlikely source, I was handed a lifeline.

The multiple colours in his hair belied his most reserved nature. This Mr. Bright rarely ventured to become engaged in class discussions. But, there he was, in his various shades of purple and orange, sitting quietly with upstretched hand.

I acknowledged him, "Mr. Bright?"

"May I say something?"

"Please do."

"Well, it appears that we are in a bit of a fog here, correct?"

"Yes, most definitely."

"I think I can explain it."

"Please, Mr. Bright, go ahead. You have the floor."

He began, "We, as a class, understand well the viewpoint of the author: family ties are broken. And many of us think that today family ties are broken also, true?"

We all nodded in agreement. Then he turned to me, "Mr. Maraj, I have to ask you a couple of questions. Do you mind?"

"Not at all, Mr. Bright, but, do allow me this…"

And, much to the delight of the rest of the students, I escorted Mr. Bright to the front of the class and I then occupied his seat at the back.

The new *teacher* commenced, "Mr. Maraj, it is true that this group pointed out that in both societies, that of the past and that of the present, family ties are breaking down. But this group also pointed out that families today are finding new ways to cope. You did enter that significant point in your notes. Correct?"

I scrambled through my notes only to discover that indeed I had missed this valuable point. I managed a feeble, *Sorry*.

He responded, "Mr. Maraj, it is not like you to miss such a fine point. You are excused this time."

The class laughed heartily. Clearly, the fog of confusion was being replaced by this ray of sunshine.

Mr. Bright continued, "Mr. Maraj, I know that you have three children; one plays hockey; one works at a music store downtown; and the youngest travels with you and Mrs. Maraj wherever. Right?"

Clearly, the class was amused by the extent of his knowledge regarding my personal family life.

"You see, Mr. Maraj, the *times* have changed, not necessarily the family ties. Let me explain. You, Mr. Maraj, might think that family ties are breaking down. Right?"

I nodded. He continued, "Mr. Maraj, let me make this point. You probably think that you and your family should sit together at the table all the time and dine together. Right? Like when you and Mrs. Maraj were growing up."

I agreed. This was more than a point of view. This was tradition and this tradition was etched into my psyche.

He was not quite finished for he had his own point to make, "Well, I think that the family unit, for the most part, is intact. You see, Mr. Maraj, you are like so many parents who have children. You are busy. This is a generation of busy people. But you do one thing to preserve the family ties."

He stopped. We were all attentive. Mr. Bright commanded our attention. Impatiently, I signaled for him to continue.

"Mr. Maraj, you and the members of your family do not sit down at your table at home as you might wish. But you do sit down so many times at the table of your local restaurants. I see you at a certain restaurant all the time... and you are with your family. Well, Mr. Maraj that is where today's families dine and talk. That tradition of the past is not really dead; it is now changed from inside the home to outside. Yet, the tradition of family ties is still strong. Right?"

I rose from my seat and went straight to Mr. Bright. I shook his hand. I did not know exactly what to say. What a revelation Mr. Bright developed for both the students and for me. I found myself speechless but not without resolve. I began clapping; the entire class joined in. As young Mr. Bright was about to take his seat, he charged, "Mr. Maraj, be sure you record the appropriate mark for this part of the seminar."

"Yes, Mr. Bright, I will."

I continue to be awed by the ability of this young man. He had the courage and the conviction to seek to enlighten us all with his unique perspective. I am forever indebted to him for putting me so much at ease about a situation that I had been struggling with for the past several years. He was instrumental in restoring my family to me. He has forever altered my thinking. No longer would I accuse my family of not being a family. We just spent family time in non-traditional ways. Indeed, a world of change and challenge was upon me.

## 95

# More Change

Change, it seemed, was coming at me from a completely different quarter. While it was not unusual to see Mr. Stevens, the vice-principal of the high school, in our Languages Department, it was, however, unusual for him to request a meeting in a private setting.

Previously, I'd had an uncomfortable encounter with Mr. Stevens. Our meeting had begun rather awkwardly and involved some administrative decisions. Because we both were completely vested in resolving our differences professionally and amicably, we came to a successful resolution. In this present moment, I had no reason to think that I was in any jeopardy either personally or professionally.

I was wrong on both counts.

But, before I venture to give details regarding that latest meeting, I feel the need to explain the extent of my skills on the computer. My lack of computer knowledge is rivalled only by my limited knowledge regarding cars.

A great deal had changed since I first began my teaching career. When I started on this path in education, I did so during a time when our greatest resource as teachers was what we brought personally to the field. We had limited technology outside of the printed page. Most of our work was conducted within the confines of the classroom and on the various blackboards attached to the wall surfaces. Student reports were handwritten and comments were generated from a personal base of observation.

As more and more new technology was made available for teachers, I found myself falling further and further behind. Marks and reports were all being stored in new computers. Teachers could then easily access many aspects of a student's work with just a few strokes of the keyboard. I knew that I was being left behind in a world that was becoming increasingly computer centered. Some years previous to this latest encounter, Mr. Stevens knew it too. At that time, he attempted to assist me into the realm of computer literacy. I had no doubt that I could easily drown in this sea of computers. I was barely out of the cave. I was hanging on by my fingertips. I had been just barely surviving. I foresaw that my days for snatching up a student in the library to type up some work for me were numbered. Accessing assistance from an already over-burdened office staff was no longer practical or fair. Also, I recognized that my ever generous fellow staff members, should not be recruited to help me with my computerized reports. I had to learn to use the computer myself. Increasingly, it was becoming the required means of communication.

I, however, had been loath to climb aboard the new train of technology. *I stared out helplessly at the new reality in education where technology threatened to play an ever increasing role.* I did not know how to turn on a computer even after it had been pointed out to me on numerous occasions. I was embarrassed about my own lack of knowledge in the vast ocean of technology. Furthermore, I did not know how to type. I had never needed to know; there was always someone there, willing and able to help out. That era was coming to an end. Rather than attempt to greet the bright new wave of technology, I retreated into the darkness of the cave of ignorance.

Mr. Stevens was sensitive to my plight. I fear that I must have been the last teacher alive, still currently working, who was still using the old system of hand-written report cards. Mr. Stevens intuited my helpless state of mind and reached out to help me in his own way. He did this by commissioning one of the computer gurus to give me personal lessons on the computer. I am certain that he undertook this course of action with the purest of intentions as a way to reprogram my brain cells so that they would more easily receive new ways of doing things. I am afraid, however, that this old dinosaur was so slow to come on board, that the guru may have grown disappointed with my feeble efforts. Despite all the efforts from so many of my colleagues to help me along, I still felt helpless and inept; I started to entertain thoughts of retirement.

It was about this time that a young man whom I had taught in both elementary and secondary school, entered my world of teaching. Previously he had known me as his teacher only. Now he was receiving me as a colleague. Very sensitive to my inadequacies on the computer, he put himself by my side. At first, I sat beside him at the computer while he painstakingly read my barely legible writings and entered marks for my various classes on the new marks program. Never once did he put me down or chastise my lack of knowledge in this area. But, gradually, and over time, I lost my intense fear of the computer, and with him by my side, I began to enter my own marks. Having him right beside me to answer any questions and to help make corrections the instant I needed him, boosted my confidence.

One day he teased, "Mr. Maraj, soon you will be teaching me a thing or two." I knew that that day would never dawn, but his comment serves to highlight how much confidence he instilled in me because of his patient leadership.

My will to persevere in teaching in spite of the threat of technology, was strengthened, first by Mr. Stevens, and then by this former student. While I recognized that I had barely stepped out of the cave, I was now comfortable taking that baby step. To become comfortable in the wider world of technology as a whole, would require another complete lifetime.

It was time that I did not have as Mr. Stevens soon made me aware.

\*\*\*

"So, Mr. Maraj," quietly began Mr. Stevens, "have you made plans for what you are going to do when you retire?"

*What kind of a question was that?* I wondered to myself. *I am not leaving anytime soon. I have no plans to retire. What is Mr. Stevens' real purpose for this visit?*

Then he unleashed the bomb.

"You do know, Mr. Maraj that you *have* to retire this year. You will be turning sixty-five in November and…"

While it was indeed true that I would be sixty-five in a few short months, it was also true that I had not considered retiring. I planned to continue on with my teaching career for as long as possible. I tried to convey this to him and he interrupted with another explosive bomb.

"Mr. Maraj, it is the *law*. You *have to retire*."

He continued to talk. He mentioned something about a retirement gratuity and presented various options for receiving it. I was hearing as if through a fog. Nothing processed except for the words, *you have to retire*.

Again, Mr. Stevens tried to reach through my fog.

"What say you, Frank? Shall I go ahead with the financial plans?"

"Do I really have to retire? Do I not have any choice?"

"No, Frank, you have no choice in the retirement matter. But you do have a choice in the matter of your gratuity. Shall I make plans to access it now for investment purposes?"

Reluctantly, I nodded.

# 96

# The Race

I knew now that this second part of the semester was to be my last. The Grade 12 students were aware that that this was to be my final semester, and decided in their own way to create a situation that would be fun for them and, to that end, had devised a plan. In the early spring one of the ringleaders, Sundance, asked, "Mr. Maraj, do you *still* play soccer?"

It is the way that he stressed the word still that caused me to be most cautious with my response, "Sundance, I would not say that I play; perhaps participate is the more appropriate term…"

"Mr. Maraj, I hear you *still* have the moves."

Again, it was the way he stressed the word still that alerted me to the possibility that he could be setting a trap.

"Sundance, let's not distract the class any further with this conversation. Shall we return to our work…?"

But, the rest of the class did not want to return to their work. In fact, I was very much surprised by just how completely vested they had become in our conversation. One student announced that his father had played on a soccer team with me, while another pointed out that I had taught her mother in elementary school. The flood of comments was unstoppable.

Once more Sundance tried to reignite the conversation about soccer, I dampened the flame; we needed to get on with the business of literature.

Every so often, Sundance engaged us all with his stories. He took great pride in his own abilities and often challenged classmates to race against him. He always came out the winner. On several occasions he had also challenged me to a race but I was always able to deflect his challenges.

Well, my time at the school was running out and all the students knew it. Sundance, in particular, was very much aware that I would not be in the school in the same way next September.

Sundance picked a most beautiful day in early spring to launch his next racing challenge. He began his appeal by dismissing all my former objections.

"Look outside Mr. Maraj; it is a good day; it's dry and the weather is just right. How about it?"

I surprised even myself with how easily I consented to his challenge.

"Sundance, are you sure you are ready?"

He was elated at the sudden turn of events. I could hear it in his voice. "I sure am!"

"Let's do it then."

I don't know how ethically appropriate or professionally responsible I was at that moment but, as I knew that I would be retired in just a matter of weeks, I threw caution to the wind and indulged my momentary whim.

We took off!

The whole class followed at our heels.

We ran from the classroom, down the hall, rounded the bend to a set of stairs. We raced down the double set of stairs and out the back doors. After circling the parking lot we returned to the school, once again racing up the stairwells and back to the classroom.

Sundance led the whole way but I was never far behind. At one point when I appeared to be gaining ground, Sundance increased his drive and sprinted forward with renewed energy.

We created quite a stir with our antics as students from other classrooms had moved over to the windows to witness the unusual scene.

Once everyone returned to the classroom, Sundance declared his victory with great pride, "Mr. Maraj, I beat you fair and square."

His face was beaming; he looked so proud. Various members of the class congratulated him.

I, however, said nothing.

"Mr. Maraj, I beat you. Admit it."

"Did you, Sundance? Did you really beat me? Think about it."

"What are you talking about, Mr. Maraj?"

My remarks shocked the entire assembly of students, especially Sundance.

I felt compelled to explain my uncharacteristically strong outburst.

"Sundance, how old are you?"

"Sixteen…"

"And you think you beat me?"

"Yes, I did. Clean."

"Sundance, how old am I?"

"I really don't know. I'll say you are in your fifties."

The class giggled and someone commented, "That's old."

Then Sundance asked, "Just how old are you Mr. Maraj?"

"In just a few months I will be sixty-five."

"Are you really that old, Mr. Maraj?"

"Yes."

Nervous laughter filled the room. Then I made a statement that I have sorely regretted ever since the utterance left my mouth.

"Sundance, you let a sixty-five year old keep up with you. You should have left me way back in the dust…"

The smile on Sundance's face disappeared. The spirit of camaraderie was lost, and I had forfeited the good will of my students. They looked at me in shock and dismay.

I was trying to make a point but I did so in a most unfortunate manner. It was not my intention to "take down" Sundance and embarrass him in front of his peers. But that is precisely what I accomplished.

I searched for a way to undo the damage.

"Sundance?"

"Mr. Maraj?"

"All kidding aside, let me do the right thing. Let me congratulate you. Yes, young man, you beat me fair and square."

Sundance looked at me blankly. He was not buying any of it. "But I thought you said…"

"Never mind that remark. It was wrong of me not to acknowledge your victory in the moment. And, for that, I sincerely apologize."

Sundance was not to be appeased so easily. He wanted to know more, "Mr. Maraj, it is not like you to try to take a student down like that. What made you say that I did not beat you?"

"Sundance, I only wanted to send a message to you and to the rest of the class. That's all. Both my timing and my method were off. I apologize."

"What was the message, Mr. Maraj?"

"Class, I wanted to show you by example that just because you age, you don't have to give up your youth. Even someone in his sixties can aspire to the athleticism of a teen. I want you to know that all things are possible if you keep up your health as you age."

And Sundance's face turned a little red as he admitted, "If truth be told, I had a hard time keeping ahead of you, Mr. Maraj. I guess that I had better start taking better care of myself right now."

I, too, learned a valuable lesson that day regarding the fragility of the teen spirit; I made a silent vow to protect it more closely.

# 97

## Temper, Tempered...

During my final semester, I was assigned an essential level class. Most of the students were progressing well with their assignments and on this particular day I was attempting to visit with each student individually in order to provide feedback. Each student received his/her comments without incident and continued to work independently once I had moved on to the next student.

There were no problems. That is, there were no problems until I sat down with Lake. Lake was a stocky but husky young man. He towered over the other students in the class but he was not overbearing by nature. School did not come easily to him. Every day presented its own set of challenges. His reserved and retiring nature made him difficult to read. Reading and writing proved to be a challenge each and every day. Occasionally, when the challenges became too great, he would skip class. Inevitably this would result in him falling farther and farther behind in his assignments.

When I sat down with Lake and showed him where he stood with his assignments he listened and shook his head. I am sure that he knew that he was lagging behind; it was the same story in all of his classes. He wished no deeper engagement at that moment. Therefore, not wanting to put any extra pressure on him, I decided to leave him alone with his thoughts. I knew that together, at some later date, we would come up with a plan to conquer the overdue assignments.

I returned to my desk to review my next move.

While I was thus engaged, I heard the beginning of a commotion.

It was Lake. While getting up from his desk, his chair toppled over. Instead of righting the chair, he kicked it into the aisle. With one sweeping motion, he swiped all papers and books from his desk; they fell to the floor in a scattered mess; then he walked out.

It was a difficult moment.

The students and I looked at one another in open confusion. Before anyone could say anything, we heard the sound of breaking plaster. Lake had just rammed his fist through the wall as he disappeared from the classroom.

Immediately I informed the office and asked for an administrator to come to the classroom. After being apprised of the details, the administrator assured me that he would take care of the situation. I was able to prevail on him to let me try to find Lake and speak with him and the administrator agreed to supervise my class.

My search proved fruitless and eventually I had to abandon it and return to the classroom.

When the bell rang to signal the end of class and the beginning of lunch, I prepared to step out of the classroom. It was then that I encountered Lake standing next to the door in the hall.

He was leaning against the wall. I too stood beside him and leaned against the wall. Neither of us said anything.

Finally he muttered, "So… how long?"

"What do you mean?"

"My suspension."

"I don't know. Now that you are here, perhaps you can help decide that." "How so?"

"Lake, you did not strike out at any one person… The person you hurt the most is probably yourself."

He hung his head.

"But you did damage school property… You have to do something about that."

"Like see the principal…"

"Yes, that's a start."

"He's going to suspend me, I know it."

"Lake, why not go to see him and let him know that you are willing to help repair the damages?"

"Will he even want to listen to me?"

"The job of a principal is not easy. Lake, it is your job to find a way to make his job easy."

"How do I do that, Mr. Maraj?"

"You think about it Lake. Think about what you can do."
"Like not argue? Is that what you are telling me?"
"You are getting wise, Lake."
The next day Lake was in class quietly attending to his assignments. Shortly thereafter, the damage on the wall was repaired.
I can only guess at what transpired between Lake and administration.

# 98

# Final Moments

Last class... last day.

A spirit of melancholy infused itself in nearly every moment of my last day of teaching. At the end of the day as I walked into my Grade 11 class, I sensed a difference in the students. Or, was the difference within me? There definitely was something different in the air; I could not say exactly what.

Throughout the semester the members of this class revealed that they possessed the twin virtues of diligence and character. Collectively, they exhibited a well-defined sense of humour, but they had also shown that they were not without an equally developed quality of true compassion. Because of this, they had earned both my respect and my admiration. Since it was the last day of actual classes before exams, the students were relaxed and casual in attitude. While they professed to be studying, I noted that there was a heightened buzz of activity in the air.

Near the end of class, one student asked, "Mr. Maraj, any final words for us?"

Already dealing with my own feelings of nostalgia, I struggled to find just the right balance of words. I wanted to tell them all just how much I liked them. But, to do that, would not be me. I never told my classes just how much I liked them and cared about them. Over the years, we had developed an understanding that was rooted in a gentle element of teasing.

Whenever they made any type of request, I would preface my remarks with this comment: "If I were to grant you this, or if I were to agree to your request, you would think that I like you or something...

and I cannot have you thinking that. You might actually then start liking me."

Invariably, their collective response would be, "Don't worry Mr. Maraj, we don't like you. You can count on us."

Recognizing that this was my final moment with these students, an overwhelming wave of emotion stole upon me and unleashed a volume of sentimentality. What follows is a part of the message that I felt compelled to share at that moment.

"Thank you so much for letting me be part of your life, students. Thank you for being you—strong, compassionate, resilient.

"The future now claims you, and you are a promise to the future and to the world. Look around, students. Look at our world. Despite horrendous wars, injustices, and atrocities both past and present, our universe still stands a beautiful place. After all, you young people are here, and you would want to take care of our world."

They remained quiet and pensive and so I continued. "Students, whatever your religion, whatever your belief, know this... You have inherited a world, while not perfect, it remains a beautiful world still. And you have a responsibility to this world. If, by your action, you cannot improve the world, then have the good sense to leave it alone. Simple decency demands that of each one of you. Nothing you do should endanger that beauty and what is left of our world. And the degree to which you accomplish that, know that you will have enhanced our civilization. That footprint that you leave behind shall be that pillar that anchors civility for the advancement of our world... Is that not so, students?"

"That's heavy stuff, Mr. Maraj. That little speech of yours tells us that you like us! We know it. Now Mr. Maraj, we have a little something for you."

Then one student presented me with a small package. The rest of them prevailed upon me to open it right then and there. Inside was a picture that had been taken just a few days ago; it was a picture of the entire class.

To witness the faces in the class being replicated in the photograph, touched me in a way most unexpected and rendered me speechless.

One student broke the awkward silence, "Mr. Maraj, now you're going to think we like you because we gave you this gift. No way, see, we know that you are retiring now and the memory... well, just in case it fades… here is something to remember us by… your all-time favourite class."

Then, just like that, they were gone.

I could not move. I just stood there rooted to the spot. I could not believe that it was over. The adventure seemed only to have just begun.

*But, somehow, I felt that the learning was not yet done.*

# PART FIVE

## Retirement and Identity: Philosophical Musings

# 99

# Change

August, 2005.

Summer has come and gone and it is now time to return to school. For Diana, it is merely the first day of another semester; for me, however, it is the first real day of retirement.

As Diana leaves for work, she whispers, "Frank, do have a good day." She backs the car out of the garage and heads down the street; wistfully, I look after her.

An uneasiness envelopes me.

Immediately, I try to shake it off. I chastise myself and ask, *What's wrong with me? I should be celebrating my freedom; after all, I am now retired.*

But, this was not the retirement that I had envisioned. Initially Diana was going to retire with me. I had it all planned out. In my starry-eyed dream view of retirement, we would rent out our home on a temporary basis. We would then be free to travel and explore the world together. We could both return to university and take courses together. We had talked of this on many occasions.

When we had first met in 1969, neither one of us had financial stability. When we married, two years later, we were virtually penniless. Upon retirement, while I still value a penny, I no longer have to struggle to have a penny. Thus, I saw retirement as an opportunity for us to recapture those early years of our courtship; it was my dream for us to reclaim the free spirits from those early years and indulge in a few of the luxuries that we could not afford when we met.

Circumstances, however, dictated otherwise. Diana had to continue to work. I understood that completely on an intellectual level;

emotionally I wasn't yet there; I was still travelling the road of self-absorption. For so long I had planned for our lives to be free agents, travelling the world, visiting far off places, attending university, and even returning to England. I was not yet emotionally capable of negotiating a u-turn on my highway of wishful thinking.

In a few days I would be on my way home to Trinidad. But, once again, I would be alone.

I would make the best of it... but still... I wish... soon.

Within days I was back among family and friends in Trinidad. In no time at all I was caught up reveling in the familiar hospitality of my countryman. The colours, the smells, the sights... all so exciting and oh so familiar! While gratified that Trinidad still exuded the spirit of cordiality in welcoming home its native children, I soon came to the sad realization that safety on the island was compromised. Crime was on the rise; muggings and robberies occurred almost daily. No longer could one feel free to travel wherever one wanted whenever one wanted. *Caution in all things* was now the mantra. Saddened and disillusioned I reflected on this new reality: Trinidad, you too are now part of the rising scourge that has besieged much of the Western World.

On one of my visits to Port-of-Spain, and to its familiar savanna, I feasted on a hearty lunch consisting of legendary fresh coconut and doubles: true Trinidadian comfort food. Once satiated, I began to walk.

The Northern Range stretched out directly ahead of me. Government buildings and business offices circled the savanna that stretched for miles. While still officious, everything felt remarkably familiar.

The luscious greenery of the mountain towered toward a serene sky. For a moment I felt my spirit once more being led into the familiar lure of the mountain; always it was incredible. I found a comfortable spot within the grounds and leaned against a post. I drank deeply from the air allowing its warmth to inhabit my body. It was a moment of sheer peace; but it was short-lived. An unsettling feeling encroached on my peace and revealed it for the counterfeit it was. Diana was not by my side.

I enjoyed my short stay in Trinidad but soon it was time to return home and fashion my new life. Still I was not yet ready to embrace full retirement and, as it turned out, I did not yet have to face that reality. Upon my return from Trinidad, I had my first day's work as a substitute teacher at my daughter's school. The school was in a deeply religious community located some fifty minutes from town.

Knowing that I would soon be immersed in the culture of a school, albeit only briefly, allowed me a degree of real happiness. My mind raced back to the beginning of my career as a teacher in a Catholic school system. I quietly anticipated the unfolding of the next phase of life.

# 100

# A Realization

The hour long drive from my home to SCAP (Sturgeon Creek Alternative Program) allowed ample time for reflection; I knew where the school was located. I had even had occasion to visit it once, many years ago, when our youngest child chose to attend the school for a semester during her Grade 10 year.

The school itself was located about a mile north of the main highway and was made up of a variety of buildings. The main building had, at one time, been a church. The other buildings were added on to the main structure and they too showed signs of fatigue. The unpaved driveway doubled as a parking lot for staff. Since most of students were bussed to school, there were very few cars.

Shades of Trinidad greeted me as I pulled up to the main building and parked. The wear and tear that the buildings had withstood over the years brought back vivid memories of my first years teaching in Trinidad. Treasured memories were dusted off and allowed to dance in my mind. As I walked towards the office to make my presence known, cheerful "good morning" greetings drew me in with their charm. The total simplicity of the surroundings and genuine hospitality of the staff, at once endeared me to the school. Its atmosphere, while completely new, was not unfamiliar.

My classroom was located in the basement of the first building, the one that had been a church. As I wound my way down the steep dark stairs to the basement, everywhere I looked I saw reminders of my past. Here, as in Trinidad, the school had become a repository for things whose lives had been extended beyond what was reasonably expected. Some items, I suspected, may have even been rescued from their ultimate fate at the local dump. I was completely at ease in the presence of these reclaimed treasures.

What transpired next when the actual students entered the classroom, transported me right back to my time in Trinidad in the mid-sixties.

While I looked on in wonderment, the students themselves initiated the opening exercises. In this they were led by a designated volunteer. The rest of the students stood politely and attentively as the volunteer began the devotion. Each member of the class took a turn in reading from the assigned Scriptures. The scripture readings were followed by a closing prayer of gratitude after which the students quietly awaited my instructions.

For a brief moment I thought that I was back in Trinidad. The type of cordiality and civility that I had just borne witness to was characteristic of the schools that I had been a part of during the early sixties.

After reframing my position mentally, I addressed the students and conveyed to them their teacher's instructions for the day. Without exception, the students dutifully received these instructions and proceeded to apply themselves diligently to their assigned tasks.

This exemplary conduct lasted throughout the entire period. Moreover, it was repeated in each subsequent class that I encountered throughout the day. To be sure, it should be noted that these students were not perfect all the time. Occasionally, minute indiscretions would occur and one or two students might momentarily depart from the expected conduct. On such occasions it took but a brief quizzical look from me or, I suspect, disappointed frowns from their own classmates, to return the students to "on task" behaviours once again. These students won my respect, as did their parents and their teachers. Collectively, they have managed to preserve a sense of duty, dignity, and diligence in their school.

On my way home from the school that day I pondered many things regarding this new stage in life. I had struggled with the concept of being a *substitute* teacher. There was something about the word substitute that did not sit well with me; in my mind, rightly or wrongly, the word was somehow synonymous with *false* or *counterfeit*. This concept plagued me greatly for I knew how hard I laboured in those early years to earn the right to be called *teacher*. In each subsequent year I toiled assiduously to improve. Now in retirement, I cannot accept that the journey is over; it was on that journey home that I came to the realization that I was *not* a substitute teacher but *a teacher who substitutes*; that realization has made all the difference in my mind.

# 101

# Reuniting With...

$A$t *the commencement of this work, I spoke of an invitation to attend a reunion in Trinidad. To this end, I had left Fort Frances and arrived in Miami en route to Trinidad. I digressed, narrating the events of my life from 1973 to my retirement in 2005. Now I return to that moment when my plane touched down in Trinidad.*

I arrived in Trinidad very excited on Friday, visited family on Saturday, and awaited my ride to the reunion on Sunday morning. I was a little apprehensive; I knew not why, exactly.

I heard the sound of a honking horn coming from the side of the house. I made my way downstairs and approached the vehicle. The 'young' lady in the passenger side in front came out, smiled, and moved to the back seat leaving the front passenger seat free for me. Another 'young' lady was the driver. These two were giggling like young school girls. Somewhere in the midst of their gleeful chatter they introduced themselves as former students of St. Charles Girls' High School. One made a remark that I found most curious: "Mr. Boodram, are we ever so happy to see you. And you are not bald."

Their chatter was consistently interrupted with bouts of laughter and remained unabated as we continued our drive to the reunion site. My mind hung on to the strange comment regarding baldness.

As we passed through central Trinidad we encountered what, for me, was an uncommon sight. While I had heard of gated communities before, it was not part of the everyday experience on the island. A guard closely monitored the entry point, and after a brief but cordial exchange with the driver, we were allowed to enter the residential area.

The homes in this area reminded me of the homes that used to be found near the university; they were large and expansive buildings that bore vestiges of the colonial era. The only people who could reasonable afford to live in such surroundings were usually foreigners. During my time growing up in Trinidad, such places were far beyond the reach of the everyday labourer. We could only dream of catching a brief glimpse from the outside. Knowing this, I continued to wonder about our final destination. Sister Dorothy had indicated that about a dozen or so of us would gather in someone's home for our mini reunion.

When we stopped at these most spacious sprawling grounds I viewed the lovely colonial style house standing prominently on the left side of the street with the casual interest of a visitor. I wondered why we were stopping off here. Were we assigned to pick up someone else? We had room still. I didn't want to interrupt the chattering girls. I reasoned that I would soon be apprised of the situation. Nothing was said and we continued to drive on. Suddenly we were not driving anymore and a voice announced, "We are here."

*Here? Where is here?* I wondered to myself.

We came out from the car and the two "girls" headed towards a huge white tent. Some kind of festivity was taking place in the tent. I could see that a professional staff was serving lunch. I assumed that this was merely a brief departure from our intended destination. Without asking for clarification, I blindly followed their lead hoping that soon we would be once again on our way, for I was most anxious by this time to meet Sister Dorothy.

To my great shock, I then discovered that this was our actual destination and that this gathering had been arranged on my behalf. Never before had I ever been so completely overwhelmed, not like this.

I looked around in shock. *Was I looking at the faces of my former students from the nineteen sixties? Could it be? How could it be?* Many appeared to be my age, well, nearly my age. I had been remembering their young sixteen and seventeen year old faces... the faces that I had taught all those years ago. I had to quickly reprogram my brain to accept the fact that as time had passed it was not only I who had grown older. So had my students. They were all grown up. They had become parents and now many of them were also grandparents just like me. What had separated us all those years ago, what had seemed to serve to divide us into two separate camps of teacher and student, no longer applied… the passage of several decades had erased those differences.

My eyes fervently sought out Sister Dorothy as I sat and lunched at various tables. I had not seen her since 1967. I was not even sure that we would recognize one another. Then I saw her. Our meeting was indescribable. Our connection was immediate. While older, she was still the same Sister Dorothy. She too remembered me. It was as if we were still back in time.

Following an announcement instructing us all to leave the open tent area and gather outside at the back of the home I moved to our new location along with the rest of the guests. In the back there was a most spacious open gallery overlooking the highly cultivated and manicured lawn. At the end of the lawn was a lake surrounded by tall stately trees. We were a group of about fifty or so people and we managed to find a way to gather closely together, some inside and some outside the gallery. The air was replete with excitement and laughter. I made myself comfortable outside; someone gently accosted me and guided me inside the gallery.

When the ceremonies began, it was the stately Miss Breedy, one of my former colleagues at St. Charles, who took charge of the microphone. With the ease of a maestro she handled the program announcing each speaker in turn. Most were former students who took this opportunity to adoringly *roast* Sister Dorothy.

"Sister Dorothy, you were so strict. You made us wear uniforms and long sleeves on such hot days. You even reprimanded me and gave me one bad point for having the very top button of my blouse open. How could you?"

The speaker allowed her words to cause but a moment's brief discomfort before she smiled and added a reassuring, "Sister, all of us thank you so much. You will never know how grateful we all are. We would not have had it any other way!"

This last comment triggered a resounding applause which filled the air and filtered in to the very spirit that was Sister Dorothy. Sister rose to respond to her many accolades; her joy in and pride for her former students was most apparent. When she apologized for her strictness in her early years as principal, an appreciative hush fell over the audience. Her words confirmed what we all as individuals had thought over the years. Assuming her new role as principal, fundamentally changed how she had to operate. While it may not have changed who she was at her core, it changed our outward perception of her. Once she accepted the new throne of leadership, this once smiling, affirming teacher known to us all so affectionately as Sister Dorothy, could no longer function in the same manner. Sister Dorothy took on her new responsibilities with due diligence. But, it came with great cost. We lost her as a teacher and as a friend; we worried about her; we wondered about the toll the new position was taking on her psyche. We often wondered, *Was Sister okay?*

Now, after all these years of wondering, our questions finally had answers. Sister told us of her sadness and revealed her personal regrets. She revealed that she too had wished that she had been less strict; she regretted her inability to devote herself more completely to her students. While I appreciated her sincere apology, I understood another truth; the truth was that it was under the umbrella of her wise leadership that the scorching sun of waywardness was tempered. In the shade of her presence we *all* felt a protection that spurred us along on that road of dedication. Sister, we all thank you.

Sister's concluding remarks were met with thunderous applause. Humbled by the show of affection, she once again returned the microphone to Miss Breedy. Miss Breedy teased the gathering by announcing, "Now, shall I pass the microphone to Mr. Boodram?"

Surprised, I hardly had time to think. When I made arrangements to return to Trinidad, I knew that I had missed the main reunion. I was left with the impression that our gathering would consist of some twelve or fourteen people and that we would gather in the quiet intimacy of someone's modest living room. Now, suddenly, all that has changed and I find myself standing, microphone in hand, before a crowd of forty to fifty people. I knew that regardless of how I felt, I *had* to speak. And... so I did. I spoke, but have no memory of what was said. My strongest memory is of how extremely nervous I was throughout the whole address. But, in retrospect, I also seem to recall an attentive audience. That memory is somewhat comforting; hopefully my response was not altogether senseless.

As the evening wore on and I was greeted with the kindest of affection from every quarter, relief flooded my soul. A mutual cordiality flowed between us all and I was consumed with gladness to be there. To be shown so much respect and to be given such genuine affection was a true joy.

In my heart, I still give thanks to all of you; you who once were my students and who now are all grown-up.

And you honour me still by calling me *Mr. Boodram*.

The teacher in me rises.

And I thank you so for such an honour.

It was a thrill to return home and make that St. Charles connection.

***

That was not the only connection that I made while in Trinidad.

Some months ago while I was placing a takeout order in a Caribbean restaurant in Winnipeg, Manitoba, I noticed a young group of professionals waiting their turn in line. I assumed that they were on a more constricted lunch timeline than I was so I suggested to the server that she take and process their orders first as I had no fixed agenda and I could wait to be served; my takeout order could wait.

One of the young men acknowledged what I had done and thanked me. He introduced himself as Suren and initiated conversation. When we learned that we were both from Trinidad, our conversation gained some momentum and Suren insisted that when I next visited the island, I must contact him. He explained that he was in Canada for a brief time only and would soon be returning to Trinidad. We exchanged email information so that we could make future plans.

When I knew that I was returning to Trinidad for the St. Charles reunion, I contacted Suren and we made tentative plans to meet. When we next met in Trinidad, our reunion felt more like the reconnection of two old friends, than the first real connection between acquaintances. I felt that we had known one another for years.

Suren worked at the University of the West Indies in Trinidad.

At our first meeting, Suren invited me to attend a Hindu Kartic festivity; I wasted not a moment in saying yes.

The celebration was taking place along the Manzillina Beach. To take us to the event, Suren chose a route that wound us through the luscious greenery of the forest and through dense and rich plantations. On that venture I soon learned that Suren's camera was but an extension of his own profound vision; on many occasions Suren was moved to stop to capture the incredible beauty of our surroundings.

When we arrived at the beach, Suren set off on foot with his camera to capture bold images of the various groups gathered to celebrate. The auspicious occasion was marked by the wearing of traditional dress, chanting, bell-ringing, and the blowing of conches. Both traditional dress and eye-catching colourful garments rivaled one another for our attention.

Such gatherings, replete with religious significance, would not have been complete had not the customary offering of *parsad* been present. We all welcomed this traditional and sweet indulgence. Not since leaving Trinidad in 1967 had I witnessed a festivity of such magnitude.

At one point in the celebration, the participants made their way to the beach while carrying a small golden urn. Upon reaching the water's edge they emptied the vessel's contents into the ocean. I understood that this mixture of flowers and incense was presented as an offering to the Almighty. Once this was accomplished there was a noticeable shift in mood. The once loud clamour of the celebrants gave way to quiet moments of devotional prayer. A sacredness unfolded during the solemn chanting of religious hymns.

Although raised in a Hindu home, I have never truly understood Hinduism. Every religious ceremony that I attended as a child was conducted almost exclusively in Hindi, a language that I did not speak. My understanding of the language was limited to the most common of phrases and idioms. Because I attended a Catholic school from my earliest years, I was immersed in the Catholic world: all lessons were conducted exclusively in English. Any lapse into Hindi, no matter how short in duration, was met with scorn and disdain from both the students and the staff. Therefore, throughout the majority of my developing years, it was not to my advantage to have this knowledge. As the years passed I myself was lost in the obscurity of its purport. As a result, I never saw a need to alter this reality. That is, not until this latest visit where I found myself re-living a part of my childhood, where I had accompanied my father and attended religious ceremonies richly steeped in Hinduism.

By now, Suren was completely immersed in the business of capturing images with his camera; I was at his side, a devoted spectator. Then we encountered a scene that left me totally transfixed. Motionless, I stood staring at a reminder of my past: a young boy sat alone on the shore staring across the water; his vision fixed firmly on the far horizon. My spirit was captivated by the eerie familiarity of the scene.

Without words, Suren seemed to understand the impact of that vision; silently and unobtrusively he captured the moment with his camera. Sometime later, I received the photo. It remains a priceless treasure.

# 102

## The Past Is...

Less than two years later, I was again invited to attend the scheduled reunion of the St. Charles High School. That year, my entire visit to Trinidad was unforgettable.

After clearing customs at Piarco Airport, I headed for the exit to await my aunt who was picking me up. Clutching my two suitcases in my hands, I made my way outside the airport. Crowds of excited family and friends anxiously awaited their respective visitors. While scanning the crowd for the familiar face of my aunt, I rested my two suitcases down in front of me. For one brief moment, I turned sideways to check the sidewalk area for any sign of her. Then, I saw her, waving feverishly and motioning for me to come quickly. As I turned back to my suitcases, I could see only one of them. Confused and slightly alarmed, I picked up the one case and held it close to my body while I scanned the area. Then I spotted it some ten feet away slightly hidden in the shadow of a much larger suitcase. Hastily, I retrieved the *travelling* case, and, holding each firmly in my grip, I headed over to my aunt. Try as I may, I could not shake the sense of foreboding that lingered in the back of my mind. I tried to dismiss the uneasiness that was slowly forging its way into my consciousness; I felt that something was amiss regarding my "traveling" suitcase. But, being so happy to see my aunt, I forced the discomfort from my mind.

Following our initial greeting, all negativity returned when she warned, "Frankie boy, this Trinidad scene is bad. People here stealing and mugging big time."

I looked at her with some small measure of disbelief. Her next words caused even more alarm, "When I open the trunk of the car, you put the suitcases in. I will watch…"

More alarm bells went off in my head once we arrived at her home in Arima.

Clearly, Auntie was both nervous and cautious as she pulled off to the side of her two storey house. A locked steel gate guarded the entry to the garage which comprised the main floor of the house. As Auntie came out of the car holding the keys to the gate she cautioned, "Frankie, keep your eyes peeled. As soon as I clear the gate, close it right away. Boy, you don't know how quick a mugger could spring up…"

After hearing those words, I literally jumped out of the car, and, the second Auntie cleared the gate, I shut the door behind her. She then showed me how the system of locks bolts worked to secure the gate. Security was tight indeed.

Next we proceeded to the second floor, the main living area of the home, where another high level of security consisting of more locks and bolts was in place. The peace I used to know upon my visits to Trinidad was quickly evaporating.

Later that evening after Uncle returned home, a feeling of normalcy returned. The three of us sat around the supper table and Uncle and I reminisced about shared moments of childhood.

Uncle reminded me of the times we spent roaming the back hills together on my grandparents' property. Then he singled out one specific event and asked if I had any memory of the "Down Hill" incident.

Well, I hadn't thought of that incident in years. Now, I'm left wondering how it had ever escaped my mind.

I was often brought out to my grandparents' home where I was a more than just a willing companion for my uncle who was a year younger than I. We let our imaginations take us wherever our minds wandered. Against the backdrop of the Northern Range to the right of Nani's property and the steep rolling grounds to the left, we were never at a loss for inspiration.

About half way down the rolling hill grew a single cashew tree. At the bottom was a cocoa plantation. In unison our heads turned and looked at the steep flowing hill. Then we had the same thought. *Let's run down the hill.* Without wasting a word, we put all our energies into running down that steep hill. What fun it would be to run with wild abandon from the top all the way to the bottom. We started together from the top; because the hill was steep, the natural force of gravity assisted us in our descent. For the first few moments, the sensation was a complete thrill. Then, the situation changed; gravity took us over. We could no longer control our speed; we were on an automatic downhill course with no brakes. Under normal circumstances this would not have posed much of a problem. But Uncle and I were each carrying homemade knives which we had fashioned out of metal. They travelled everywhere with us. In fact, they were so much a part of us, that, for a moment, I had forgotten all about them. Fortunately for both of us, Uncle had not.

He yelled, "Frankie, get rid of your knife! Try and fall!"

I saw him toss his knife. I followed suit. Luckily Uncle had the foresight to realize that our knives could cause us to become injured, perhaps even fatally, if they remained in our hands. Just moments after tossing my knife, the unevenness of the terrain caused me to stumble and fall. Rolling at top speed, I headed directly toward the cashew tree. I felt the inevitability of an imminent collision. By some miracle I managed to avoid the tree. Uncle too, was rolling downhill at an incredible pace. We could see the cocoa trees looming before us. Our adventure caused us to roll past those trees too; eventually we ended up falling into a gentle stream full of water cress. Ignoring or perhaps, forgetting, our bruises for the moment, we helped ourselves to the fresh water cress growing all around us. Because of that adventure with Uncle, I came to understand how that choice salad plant was cultivated, not to mention how it encouraged me to observe the rules of knife safety.

That night I slept well just dreaming of boyhood days. A measure of peace had returned to my spirit.

*\*\*\**

The next morning was Saturday; just one day away from the reunion.

By mid-morning, three of my nieces had come to pick me up. They were taking me to visit their uncle on their mother's side, a retired Hindu priest, a *pundit*. I had been a regular guest at his home when I was much younger. That family home had been a source of solace on countless occasions in my youth; I grew to regard the home as a haven, a retreat from the struggles of everyday life. The girls warned me that their uncle may not recognize me as he had been ill for quite some time and his memory was failing. I so wanted to see him again for I had such wonderful memories of my times with him and the family. Secretly, I hoped that he would remember me too, even after all these years.

As we proceeded on our way, the girls began singing. At first their songs were contemporary tunes; later, their music found a path to the past and soon melodies that were very familiar to me filled the air with their sweetness. The voices of my nieces were captivating; I was enslaved by their charm. Light nostalgia filled the car for the duration of the trip.

When we arrived at Pundit's home, I was struck by how dissimilar it was to my own recollection of it. Gone was the openness of the main floor; gone too, was the inviting hammock that used to be drawn between the pillars of the foundation. Everything was now closed up tight, hidden behind doors and walls.

Once inside, we were all seated in the main living quarters awaiting Pundit's arrival. Within minutes someone escorted Pundit to the living room. He greeted his nieces, calling each one by name. It seemed that he was having a good day with his memory. They were all so pleased. Then his eyes rested on me momentarily and then they drifted away. My spirit grew sad. There was no flicker of recognition in his glance. Then, just as quickly as his eyes had turned away, they returned to my face. Then he said one word, "Frankie."

That momentary recognition would have been enough for me; I was so thrilled that somewhere in his memory, I still existed. But, Pundit had one more jewel to bestow, "Frankie, your ma was a good lady."

I was shocked. Not only did he remember me, he also remembered my mother and the wonderful person that she was. To hear him call her a good lady meant the world to me. Ma was gone and any fleeting reference to her goodness filled my soul with gratitude to have had her as my mother.

This was an important moment for me for other reasons as well. Pundit and everything within his home had strong connections to Hinduism. Unlike me, my nieces were very much involved in the Hindu culture. Even though I was born of Hindu parents and raised in a Hindu home, many of my earliest experiences came from the Catholic sphere. I, myself, remained a stranger just entering the doorway to Hinduism. Through that visit, I once again was returned to my Hindu roots as a young boy. Something within me was stirred.

## Snapshots 3

All too soon our visit came to an end; it was time to head back home. At first, I did not understand why we had to leave; it was still early. Everything became clear when my nieces reminded me that Trinidad was currently under a curfew. Crime had become so much of a concern in the country that the authorities felt it necessary to impose a curfew on its citizens. In order for my nieces to return me safely to my home in Arima, and then take themselves to their respective residences, we should have left some time ago. Thus it was decided that I should be placed on a bus that would take me back to Arima, while my nieces would then be assured of their own timely return.

As I left the bus and began making my way to Uncle's, I could see both Auntie and Uncle anxiously awaiting my return. It was only then that a modest appreciation of what was really going on in Trinidad began to filter through my *Canadian* perspective.

## 103

# Affirmations

Finally, it was Sunday… the day of the actual reunion. By midmorning my ride arrived and soon we were on our way. This year the reunion was being held near Toco, a forty-five minute car drive away. Not only did drivers have to negotiate around a multitude of potholes that dotted the roads, but also they had to navigate around hazardous debris left on the roads as a result of recent heavy rains.

Our final destination took us to a fabulous resort cushioned deep in the country but in close proximity to the beach. The resort itself was unbelievably modern and cultivated. I was truly impressed. There were various paths leading from the resort to the beach. Each path was equal in beauty to the next. Coconut palm trees invited guests to relax under their cool shade. But, that would have to wait until later, for inside the resort, Miss Breedy had already initiated the festivities.

During the luncheon I was able to reacquaint myself with many former students and staff. Because the event was strategically timed to follow the week of Carnival celebrations on the island, it provided a further incentive for transplanted islanders to come to the reunion; nevertheless, I truly was amazed by the large number of former students who attended. It was a real thrill for both Sister Dorothy and me to be reunited with so many students from the 60's. One sadness that had to be faced however, was the reality that some of my former colleagues had passed away. This heaviness had to be set aside temporarily during the excitement of meeting with so many students.

A flood of voices echoed one specific question, "Do you remember me, Mr. Boodram?"

Each time the question was asked, I searched the inquiring face looking for clues. Their appearance had assumed the natural maturity of the passing years, but occasionally I saw a hint of the face of the 1960's and the joy that such recognition brought to the questioner was undeniable. And, just as I had to adjust to their new maturity, they too had to adjust to mine.

We all had grown and matured; many had become parents; others, like me, were also grandparents. In spite of the passage of time, I was still, in their eyes at least, their teacher, Mr. Boodram. Even after all these decades… they were remembering me and telling me about me. But, they were asking questions also.

"Mr. Boodram, when you left us, we missed you. We knew you had gone to Canada to study. But you never returned to Trinidad!"

She paused for a moment, then continued, "Mr. Boodram, why did you not come back to Trinidad? Did you not like us anymore?"

Her face revealed the earnestness inherent in the question. I could not respond immediately for I was thinking. And then I became very sad, for I was remembering so vividly that incident that had occurred decades before regarding Mr. Winchester at the Ministry of Education. I felt that it would not be right at this moment to reveal to a former student the utter pain I bore still from my encounter with him even after all these years. Yet, at the same time, I knew that this person deserved some kind of a response. I felt the sincerity of her question and wishing to preserve the dignity of the moment I answered simply, "I did try to come back. It did not work out. I am sorry. But, I am here now and am so very pleased to be among you all."

"And Mr. Boodram, we too are so happy to have you back."

As she moved on to other friends, I scanned the grounds looking for Sister Dorothy; I found her surrounded by students. As I made my way towards her, she saw me and motioned for me sit beside her. Students drifted in and out wishing us well. Then, for a brief moment we were alone; I admitted, "Sister, I am so very happy to see you once more. It seems like only yesterday that we were together at the school. Our students have grown up, Sister. But, I am remembering them as they were in the nineteen sixties…"

Sister's face became animated, "Frankie, they are parents now and grandparents but they still call me Mother Dorothy. They show me such respect. I wish I could have done more…"

"Never you mind, Sister. Even I can't help but call you Sister Dorothy. And, Sister, you have always done so much for so many..."

"Do you know that when I became *Mother*, I was not that much older than my staff..."

"I know that now, Sister."

"And I handpicked the male staff members to teach in an all girls' high school. I had my confidence, and I was not wrong."

"Well Sister, this I will tell you. When I returned from England, you offered me a... shall we say... *temporary* position at your girls' high school. Sister, I did not think I would last."

"Nor did I, Frankie, nor did I. You were so shy... Well, Frankie, on another note, I expect that you will be very busy for the next little while. I know that several of our girls will be inviting you out. At a later date, I too wish to take you out... save me a spot..."

"Yes, Sister."

# 104

# Fallout

I spent the day after the reunion away from Arima and returned home late in the afternoon. I joined Auntie in the second floor gallery which commanded a splendid view of the busy street below.

Over the decades, this area of Arima had become densely populated and was now overflowing with vehicular traffic. Considering this, I was amazed that there were not more accidents occurring in that neighbourhood. That reflection caused me to recall the words of four Canadian friends who had visited Trinidad years ago and witnessed the crazy traffic first hand.

"Man, Frankie, Trinidadians drive like crazy people. They weave in and out of their lanes, and honk their horns non-stop. But, they seem to be safe. They don't seem to have too many accidents, considering."

I was reveling in that memory from 1969. Now here it was 2011. While some things had indeed changed, some things had not. A smile was just beginning to spread across my face, when I thought that I heard three explosive sounds, one following the other in quick succession... pow, pow, pow.

The sounds took me back to my childhood, to a time when we, in our innocence, played in wild abandon with toy cap-guns, until the dark of night took away our vision.

I went to the edge of the gallery to look for the children who may have been playing in the street, shooting off their toy cap guns. All I saw was traffic. There were no children at play. I couldn't put the puzzle together.

Suddenly the air was drenched with the sound of screaming. Bone chilling, heart wrenching screams. Before I knew what had happened,

Auntie grabbed me and led me inside the house. She too had heard the gun shots; she too had heard the screams; but, unlike me, she knew the reality of the situation. Her mind never went to innocent children playing with toy guns in the street; no, her awareness was of a much darker nature.

"Someone has just been killed… shot."

Her words wrenched me out of my trance. My emotions were in a panic. Suddenly my world fell apart. I felt isolated… trapped… so far from the predictable tranquility of life in Canada. I lacked the necessary resolve to calm myself. I wanted to leave the island immediately and return to the safety I had taken so much for granted.

When Uncle returned home later that evening, he understood my shocked state of mind. He tried to put things into perspective.

"Frankie, you live in Canada. You live in a different world. In your town, you do not have to face this kind of reality. Shootings, and muggings, and robberies are everyday realities here. We live in this type of a world. We face this every day! Thank goodness you don't have to see this madness every day!"

Seared in the back of my mind now was the manner in which Auntie had been conducting herself over the last few days. Her excessive caution seemed extreme to me at the time… all the extra bolts and locks… the furtive looks in all directions… now registered… now everything made sense.

Uncle's attempt at putting things into perspective only served to strengthen my resolve to leave the island. My plan was to head to the airport early the next morning and secure a flight—any flight—back to Canada!

My emotions begged, *Just get me out of here!*

## 105

# Currents

A restless night ensued; sleep proved a fruitless pursuit.

Apparently, I was not the only one who went without rest. In the morning, Auntie shared her night of anguish, "Frankie, Ah could not sleep last night. Man, they shot that poor man. He was a family man. He had young children."

I listened to her with utmost sympathy. I had not yet divulged to anyone that I wanted to leave the country. She had no idea that I was about to ask her to take me back to the airport.

Before I could make my request known, Auntie smiled and changed the subject, "Frankie, you have not yet seen our grandchildren. Boy, you have to. And we can't wait to take you to see our relatives. And they want to see you too. That will cheer us up. Okay." She spoke with such definition and resolve I could not interrupt. Then she continued, "And Frank I am so glad you are here. Your Uncle has to go to work still. So you are my company. I am happy. So let's be a little cheerful, okay?"

How could I do otherwise? For the moment I put aside my misgivings and ventured a mildly convincing, "I'll try."

When she headed to another part of the house, I noticed that there was a note on the table reminding me to phone Suren.

After Suren and I made plans to meet at the university, I boarded a taxi/bus to take me there. Within minutes, we heard a siren. Moments later an ambulance rushed past us. Immediately all the passengers in the taxi began to speculate about what might have happened. Minutes later as we stopped at the next designated stop, a young man, visibly agitated, stood, waiting to enter. Scanning the scene at the stop, our eyes converged on a police car that had sustained some damage to its front end. On the other side of the road we saw the shattered remains of another vehicle. A second ambulance was in attendance.

As he entered the taxi, the young man raged, "The police think they own the road. I was there. The police drove right through the light – they had the siren on – but they drove at top speed! People died in that car – the policeman survived. Man, these police can do anything. They need another police force to inspect this police force."

In that courtroom of the taxi, the police force was put on trial; indicted for its sheer arrogance and self-induced power. I was but a hapless bystander. The very character of Trinidad was on trial, and I was not able to mount a defense... I could not help but wonder... is this *my* Trinidad?

Once at the university, I found Suren's office. I reflected on the irony of our circumstances. Here he was establishing himself in his beginning years, while I was seeking to find my way in my retirement years.

The full irony inherent in the situation was not lost on me. Suren, however, would never know.

Soon Suren advised that he was taking me out somewhere special for tea. The ironies kept building as the place he chose was none other than the place in which I had often both sought and found solace in my early years in Trinidad... Mount St. Benedict.

Suren was busily snapping photos. I stood quietly in the warm sunlight absorbing the sheer majesty of the beauty that was Mount St. Benedict.

A longing seized me, and I became a little unsettled. At first, I did not understand the feeling . . . Then it came to me, ever so gently; Suren had an established position at the very university that I had interviewed for decades ago. But, unlike Suren, my dreams had been crushed. But, somehow, I was able to draw comfort from the realization that I was now able to cultivate a friendship with someone whom I truly admired here at the very university that had once denied me.

Lately, I had been spending a great deal of time in reflection. Returning to Trinidad raised questions surrounding my identity: *Who am I now? What have I become?* And finally, *Am I okay with me?* And all my experiences in Trinidad were helping me to come to some sort of understanding. I was, however, in no rush to come to any definitive conclusions. I was content to continue to ask the questions. Just a couple of days ago, I had been anxious, no, desperate, to leave Trinidad. The intensity of that resolve had now lessened. Something was happening to me. For the moment, I could not quite put a label to it.

Upon entering the church with Suren, I came face to face with what so often troubled me about the Catholic world. For, right within those sacred and holy walls, were vendors plying their very active businesses. There were a host of prayer beads and images of Christ, openly displayed for sale. The first thought that came to mind, and for which I was immediately ashamed, was, "Is Christ for sale?" Living away from Trinidad for all these years had removed me from this aspect of religion on the island. I had temporarily forgotten our need to seek blessings on every new acquisition, from the newest baby to the newest car or home. The activities of the vendors put everything back into perspective.

The building itself, still evoked that spirit of yesteryear; the winding pathways still invited inner contemplation and meditation. Suren knew his way around and he led us to what appeared to have been an old monastery. It was now home for guests. Inside we found a quaint area – a restaurant like none other I had ever seen. It was filled, not with people, but with a quiet reserve. Even when a server appeared to take our order, I felt that I was inside the sanctity of the church.

As Suren and I talked, time moved quickly on. In this quiet Christian surrounding, Suren revealed his passionate and abiding Hindu faith. The fact that he was a devout Hindu did not come as a shock to me. The irony lay in the fact that he disclosed so much about his Hindu roots in this most holy of Christian spaces in Trinidad.

Furthermore, before leaving the sanctuary, Suren invited me to accompany him to a Hindu prayer later on in the week. Here amidst the river of Christianity, I was being invited to explore the current of Hinduism.

I offered no resistance.

# 106

# New Memories

When Suren, his wife Shar, and I arrived at the home hosting the prayer, the festivities had already begun. A tent had been constructed to contain the overflow of people assembled for the special event. There was little room to maneuver no matter where we settled, but we did manage to find a spot for the three of us inside the tent.

The priest who conducted the ceremony, did so first in Hindi and then in English. This set this religious event apart from many others I had attended. At long last I understood what was being said and I came to understand a few things about my religion.

At the conclusion of the prayers, a traditional vegetarian meal was offered to all the guests. Suren managed to secure three prepared meals for us; passing one to me and another to Shar, he led us outside the home where we found a quiet place to sit on the street near a culvert. It was there that Suren encountered a friend and introduced me to him. This friend was the vice-principal of a Hindu secondary school in Trinidad. I was most curious about this school and listened attentively to all that he had to say.

Suren and Shar reintroduced me to my Hindu roots; through them, my culture was being resurrected. At some point during this visit, Suren took me to meet his parents. Suren's father was a devoutly religious man; every breath he took, every word he spoke, seemed to be infused with the very essence of holiness. Suren's mother was, in so many ways, like my own mother... Needless to say, while I was in their presence, my world was a world devoid of discomfort.

Suren and his parents lived on the very same street. At the back of Suren's residence was a veritable plantation of fruit trees. Looking at the trees returned me to my own back yard as it had appeared decades ago. A feeling of déjà vu washed over me.

Later, Suren took me to a religious meeting at a temple in Central Trinidad. At this assembly, learned people not only read but also explained selected sections of Hindu holy literature. Quietly pleased to be there, I drank deeply from their cup of knowledge.

Later, when we were outside, Suren informed me that the building adjoining the Mandir, (a holy temple) was, at one time, a school: the Mahatma Gandhi School.

My mind was alert; my spirit was on standby.

Something in me was stirring.

Then Suren told me that the Vice-Principal of the Hindu Secondary School and he had been chatting. He then intimated that the Vice-Principal had been wondering if I might come to his school and have a talk with his senior students.

Once I recovered from my shock at the unexpected nature of the invitation, I accepted.

*****

The school, bounded on all sides by undulating terrain, was punctuated by explosions of colour from multiple beds of flowers. Once inside, two staff members led me to the conference hall in the upper level. The senior students were being escorted to their designated sections in the hall. I made special note of the manner in which they made the transition from classroom to auditorium; they were the very essence of respect and decorum. I noted how distinguished they looked as a group in their impressive uniforms. As the Vice-Principal introduced me from the podium, a hush fell over the assembly. All eyes were transfixed on the speaker. All of a sudden it hit me; I was the guest speaker. A momentary panic seized me. *Who was I to address this audience? What did I have of value to offer them?*

These students distinguished themselves not just because they were uniformly attired but also because of their very comportment. Even the manner in which they sat bespoke a strong sense of politeness and respect. This added to the general dignity inherent in the school community as a whole.

A sprinkling of polite applause followed his introduction.

As I held the microphone and looked out at the assembly, I felt far too removed from the students physically; the podium was set what seemed like miles away from the students. It seemed that I was a world away removed from them.

It took but a few moments to correct the situation. With the Vice-Principal's assistance, we moved the podium closer to the general population. That made me slightly more comfortable. Now it felt more like a classroom, albeit a huge classroom.

I had been introduced as Mr. Maraj; the name felt slightly strange to me here in Trinidad where I was still referred to as Mr. Boodram. But, the name itself suggested the direction of my address to the students.

Nervously, I began to speak. I started by sharing some stories from my early years in Trinidad. These stories usually seemed to resonate with my Canadian students. Such was not the case that day in Trinidad. While I sensed that they listened most politely, I did not feel that I had their attention. At some point I stopped in my story telling and asked, "Students, may I tell you about life in Canada?"

That is what they had been waiting for; they began clapping excitedly.

I spoke a little about my life at a Canadian university and the inevitable loneliness that one feels being so far removed from familiar faces and familiar food and familiar customs. I spoke of my first winter and my first initiation to snow. I spoke a great deal about my students at Fort Frances High School.

I shared with them how nervous I had been when I first entered a Canadian classroom as the teacher and faced that first sea of white. The smiles on their faces revealed how well they understood the comment.

In my closing remarks, I believe that I might have tried to impress upon those young minds that the dream to become that which you seek is attainable if you invest a supreme effort in the endeavour. Furthermore, I hope I expressed how very important it is to reach out beyond the comfortable, the familiar, in order to stretch yourself as an individual.

It was now time to conclude and I returned the microphone to the V.P. He graciously allowed an extension of ten minutes to the program. He invited the students to come and say hello to me if they wished. To my great surprise, many of them took him up on his invitation. I embraced the absolute treasure of that moment.

Just days ago I was almost frantic to leave Trinidad. Glad was I now that I had not...

# 107

# Swept Away

Throughout that visit, the strong current of Hinduism engulfed my spirit.

As I made arrangements to meet with various groups from the reunion, I prepared for different experiences. I was not disappointed. Each encounter was memorable but for differing reasons.

My outing with Nanki and the girls started out beautifully. Happy to be all together at last, we searched for the perfect place to have lunch. The first place that we visited had to be dismissed because Nanki was not completely satisfied with the freshness of the food. She worried that my Canadian palate might revolt if we indulged. Eventually we ended up eating fried chicken at a fast food outlet. Ravenous for the tastes of home, I indulged heartily in all the Trinidadian spices.

That night, my stomach experienced some discomfort. By noon the next day, the whole of my insides was in complete rebellion. By late afternoon, I was in the hospital weak with exhaustion.

I managed to be seen by a doctor within two hours. After describing to her the food that I had consumed at the fast food restaurant the previous day, she informed me that I was most likely suffering from a case of food poisoning as a result of eating the coleslaw.

She then informed me that I would not be able to go about my business as usual and that I would have to curtail my schedule for the next little while. I must have looked a little confused for immediately she clarified, "Mr. Maraj, you will be indoors – on all fours at times."

I understood.

She then added, "Hope you enjoy coconut water."

"I love it!" was my immediate response.

"Well, you will not be able to keep any solids down for a while. So coconut water will be your hydration lifeline…"

As I was preparing to leave, the young doctor asked, "So how have you managed to stay in Canada all these years? I left. It was too cold."

Then I asked her a question, "Doctor, do you ever regret leaving? Do you ever wish that you had returned to Canada?"

"The way life is here in Trinidad now, I do think of going, but my husband won't leave… even with all that is going on; he loves Trinidad, regardless… But you, you stayed. You must love Canada to stay as long as you have… Take care."

Needless to say, my condition kept me confined indoors for the next couple of days. When Sister Dorothy called and asked if I could join Roger and her for lunch, I was so overjoyed with the prospect that I responded immediately with a yes.

We met at a lovely restaurant just outside of Port-of-Spain. Since I was still not fully recovered, Sister suggested that I forego the chicken curry dish and opt for a less challenging broiled fish. Reluctantly, I agreed.

During lunch they intimated that they would be taking me to a nearby mall for dessert – coconut ice cream. My anticipation grew exponentially throughout my lunch of broiled fish at the prospect of once again indulging in my favourite treat of homemade coconut ice cream. By the time we arrived at the mall, my joy was the joy of a little boy. My face was bathed in the radiance of expectation. Alas, however, the much anticipated ice cream was a commercially made product and we knew that it could not begin to meet our expectations. We passed up the ice cream. The splendid company more than compensated for the disappointment and I truly appreciated all their efforts on my behalf.

As we strolled through the mall, Sister asked what I thought of it. When I responded that I thought that it was indeed beautiful but as the same time it seemed somewhat foreign.

While, on the one hand, I was proud that Trinidad could boast such a beautiful construction as this mall, I was somewhat saddened to think that had I remained in Trinidad, I would most likely not be able to afford to purchase anything from its many beautiful shops. Before we went our separate ways for the evening, Sister insisted while chuckling, "We will meet again, and when we do, you shall have your favourite ice cream."

\*\*\*

Soon I was again off to another luncheon engagement with a new group of students. I started out to the luncheon by taxi but, at a certain point, the traffic moved at such a horrendously slow pace, I chose to complete the journey on foot. I was really only a short distance from the designated meeting area and I felt that I could get there much more quickly on foot.

Wrong decision.

I had forgotten how hot and humid the noon hour was in Trinidad. My body had not yet become acclimatized to the tropics. I began to sweat profusely; the unbuttoning of my shirt did little to erase my discomfort.

I met up with the others, and together we headed by car to our final destination. Traffic still was barely above a crawl. I did not suggest however, that we walk; I had learned my lesson; my wet shirt was a constant reminder.

Eventually, we arrived at the house. Our host came outside and met us as we drove into the driveway. Proudly, she began to show us around her lovely garden. Clearly, I was uncomfortable out in the midday heat. Finally the outside tour ended and we moved inside the house. As grateful as I was to be out of the scorching heat, I was still most uncomfortable in my sticky, sweaty state. Before our hostess started the indoor tour, she turned to me to ask, "Mr. Boodram, what can I get for you; I have…"

I knew that what she was offering was some sort of cold beverage but that was not what I needed at the moment. I was in urgent need of something else. And, before I could stop myself, I blurted out, "A shower!"

All conversation ceased. All eyes converged on me as I explained, "I need to shower. May I, please?"

The awkwardness of the moment dissolved the instant they all started to laugh.

Mini led me to the guest shower and as she was showing me how to control the hot water, I veritably shouted, "Oh, no! I don't need any hot water."

I luxuriated under a steady stream of cool water; I did not want to leave.

Once my body was cooled, I returned to the dining room where an unbelievable meal awaited. Fortunately, I had now fully recovered from the food poisoning and was able to indulge completely my craving for the varied West Indian dishes.

Soon it was time for dessert. I looked to see if homemade ice cream was among the temptations. A stunning variety of cheesecakes and fruits enticed my palate. I succumbed to their enticement. The ultimate treat, however, was just being among my students once again.

\*\*\*

Shortly after that luncheon date, Sister once again contacted me. This time she informed me that we had been invited to lunch at the Ali home where I had first met everyone.

Soon six of us were happily gathered over a most gratifying lunch. Then it was time for dessert. Sister's eyes were twinkling. To my utter delight, I was treated to my very own homemade coconut ice cream. I was crazy happy… and everyone knew it.

Satiated with ice cream I leaned back in reflection. Soon I was lost in my own musings. To be there in the midst of such cherished company was an absolute joy. From as far back as I could remember, I had yearned for moments like these; back then it seemed like an impossible dream; I had no real idea that one day I would be raised from the pit of poverty to a platform of comfort.

Miss Ali roused me from my musing, "Mr. Boodram I have this gift for you. Go ahead, open it."

She handed me a rectangular package. It proved to be a book. But it was not just any book… I was quite literally in a state of shock… how could she possibly know… I had not told anyone…

The gift was a copy of the autobiography of Mahatma Gandhi. As I stared speechlessly at the book, she explained, "The last time you were here, you were crossing the living room from the gallery and I saw you looking at my copy of the book. It was the way you picked it up, and looked at it… I just knew I had to get another copy for you."

Homemade coconut ice cream, wonderful company and now this gift…

# 108

# A Lost Soul

About a year after returning to Canada, I once again received news of another class reunion in Trinidad. Once again, I was delighted to attend.

Not able to stay at our family home in Tunapuna, and not wanting to impose any further on my uncle and auntie's generosity, I set about to make new connections on my father's side of the family. Thoughts of my father had been consuming me lately, and I yearned to learn more about him.

Ricky was married to a distant cousin of mine, Vashty. Ricky met me at the airport upon my return to Trinidad. I had arranged to stay with them for the first night after which I felt that I would make other arrangements. Within the first day of my arrival, both Vashty and Ricky made a most generous offer. "Uncle Frank, this is like home – your home. Go visit all your friends and family. But come back here. This is your base. Ricky and I want you here with us."

Vashty's words touched my very soul; a feeling of great gratitude enveloped my spirit as I accepted. With a place for my body thus secured, my soul settled, and I made ready for any and all new adventures.

Two former students picked me up from Chaguanas for a return visit to the magnificent resort near Toco. By the time that we arrived, the reunion was already well underway. A much celebrated Trinidadian musician and entertainer had both the mood and the tempo under his control. His voice was familiar and he kept everyone in an upbeat mood with his rendition of calypso music both old and new.

Once again, our hostess accommodated the fifty or so of us most generously with a lavish lunch. She had even provided some vacation prizes at this resort for a lucky few. Needless to say, everyone was thrilled.

Miss Breedy again did an expert job with the program. The whole affair, however, seemed somewhat incomplete without the presence of Sister Dorothy who was unable to attend due to illness.

Later, while I was still lamenting Sister Dorothy's absence, Miss Breedy made an announcement.

"Everyone, one of our students has a song she would like to sing and dedicate it to one of our former teachers… to Mr. Boodram."

Caught completely off guard with the unexpectedness of the announcement, I did not hear what it was that this former student said as she was handed the microphone. All I remember is that when she began singing, a hush fell over the assembly. The song was both familiar and beautiful. Being recognized in that manner was as difficult a moment as it was beautiful.

Within me a river of tears prepared to scale its banks; there in the midst of this gathering of former students and staff, I struggled to remain, or at least appear to remain, self-contained. As she sang her last note, I looked toward her and whispered an emotional *thank you…*

What made this moment so incredibly special was the song that she sang; it was an East-Indian song that was one of my all-time favourites.

Truth be told, I did not know the meaning of this song; I had no idea what the words meant. While all of that was true, however, I always felt an intuitive connection with the song. I thought that one word in the song meant Mother and another word loosely translated into a sense of worship. The idea of honouring a mother through song had a distinct appeal to me because of all that my own mother meant to me. For that reason, the plaintive appeal of this song has always struck at my very core. And now, at that very moment, at a time when I least expected anything of its kind, I was being honoured.

It was a moment made all the more poignant because of a recent incident that had occurred while I was visiting in London, Ontario.

Will, a former student and friend of my youngest daughter, and I were spending some time at one of the local malls. We had separated to pursue different interests, and agreed to meet up later for coffee.

I was surprised then, to find that Will was actively trying to find me before our scheduled break. He was slightly stressed and explained that he had just met a young lady who appeared to be in distress. He further explained that she needed to get to another mall in a different part of the city, but had no means of getting there. Before Will could finish asking, I volunteered to take her.

I did this for Will, thinking that perhaps he had taken some personal interest in the young lady; perhaps seeking to be a knight set to rescue the young damsel in distress.

Soon, the three of us were back in my car; Will and I sat in the front, leaving the back for the young lady. The mall she requested to go to was at the opposite end of the city. I did not mind for I felt that it was all for a good cause. Once we arrived at the new location, the young lady informed us that this was not the right place. Again we consented to take her but I was beginning to have some misgivings about her character. Knowing Will as I did, I could not fathom how he could have any personal interest in this young lady. In my mind at least, they were not a good match. Further, the visit to this second mall had, by now, cast some doubt as to the legitimacy of her cause. When we arrived at the other mall, things did not work out for her there either. I was now quite prepared to part company with her. She had one more favour to ask; she requested to be dropped off at a coffee shop where one of her relatives resided.

When we arrived at the coffee shop she quickly exited the vehicle without any real acknowledgement to either of us. I found that most strange indeed. She just grabbed her oversized hand bag, and, holding it close to her body, disappeared into the shop.

Relieved that she was finally gone and that our wild goose chase had finally ended, Will and I just looked at one another in puzzled amazement.

The next day, my spirit was saddened by the previous day's incident. We had thought that we were reaching out to help a young woman in distress. We left feeling like patsies.

As I opened the back door to my car to retrieve some personal effects, I noticed that the shoebox that I used to house all of my favourite cds both (Eastern and Western) was missing from the floor of the car. To say that I was in pain would be an understatement. My personal and most prized collection of music was contained in that shoebox. (I had always intended to purchase a proper storage container for my music but I had not yet done so.) And, I knew with exact clarity who had taken it and where it was. The significance of that oversized handbag now dawned on me. It now contained my personal treasures of music. Among them, the song that had now just been sung to me... a song that from the beginning had such personal and sentimental meaning... a song now made even more precious at this reunion.

Immediately following the theft, I regarded the woman as nothing more than a common thief... but now, in the sacredness of this new moment, I saw her in a different light... I saw her as a lost soul. In the sacredness of that moment, I released my anger. Nothing, not even the lamentable memory of that incident, will supplant the soulful joy of this moment.

# 109

# Two Different Dispositions

While attending this most recent reunion, I learned that one of my former students had been unable to attend due to illness.

One of the organizers of the event asked if I would be willing to accompany a group of the girl's former classmates to visit with her at her bedside. I was most happy to consent to this request.

The "girl" was a real favourite of the group. Her insatiable love of reading had endeared her to all of us.

On the day of the anticipated visit, we learned of her sad passing. Now, it seemed, that we would be attending a funeral; our spirits tumbled.

Early, on the day of the funeral, I had been out running errands. I engaged a taxi to take me back to Vashty and Ricky's so that I would be on time when my ride arrived to take me to the funeral.

Unfortunately, for me, my driver was less than honourable. Perhaps sensing that I was from abroad, he took me some ways away from my destination and demanded more money from me. No longer feeling safe in his taxi, I followed my instincts. I paid him what money I could and made a quick exit from the taxi. He sped away.

Now I had to secure another taxi to take me home quickly for I did not want to miss my ride to the funeral. I noticed a business close to where the taxi dropped me off. The business just happened to be a funeral home and an older model car was just exiting the compound. I flagged down the driver and hastily explained my situation. Although he hesitated at first, he quickly relented simply stating, "Get in." Assuming that he had just recently attended a funeral himself and sensing his preoccupation with his own issues, I did not press him to engage in small talk.

In silence he proceeded to drive me to my destination. It was he who broke the silence, "Mister, you have to be careful. Yo see that funeral place I came from…"

His voice choked up a little as he continued, "They just murdered a good man. He was from abroad… He foreign. Yo going to a dead. I coming from a dead."

Then, immersed in thought, he was silent. We were now nearing my destination. Checking his watch, he noted that we had made good time. He assured me that I would not miss my ride. I thanked him for his kindness and reached into my pocket for a bill; finding one, I placed it in his hand. This stranger returned the money to me saying, "Normally, Ah would take yo money. I could use it. Not today. Understand. Trinidad not all bad. We ha' crazy people; crazy mad people. But, we still ha' de good people. Tanks fo' yo' gift. I canno' take it. Not today. Today I bury me frien'."

In the following days my thoughts returned to the two men that I had met that day: the first, a man of questionable values, the second, a man of uncommon consideration. *His* act of charity is the memory I choose to preserve.

# 110

# Multi-Generational

Over the next few days as I spent more and more time at home with Vashty and Ricky, I developed a predictable routine.

Each morning after showering, I would venture out. Invariably, I would end up in the market area which was a mere fifteen minute walk from home. Here, for the equivalent of two Canadian dollars, I could purchase a banana, an orange, a double, and fresh coconut water served directly from a coconut.

The market was also the area in which Ricky had his business and it gave me an opportunity to see him in his work environment. On my first visit to Ricky he offered me a cup of coffee. Within minutes the coffee was made and delivered with the utmost kindness by a worker. Needless to say, when I felt the need of a coffee (which was often indeed) I would simply visit Ricky where I would be assured not just a splendid cup of coffee but also most agreeable company.

Ricky watched out for me in other ways as well. Each day he would ask me about my travel plans for that day. His work life offered a degree of flexibility and, if he could, he would drop me off or pick me up at a prearranged location. In retrospect, I came to understand that Ricky was concerned about my personal safety and took steps to ensure it.

Ricky never missed an opportunity to indulge in an authentic Caribbean snack and refreshment. Whenever I was with him, he included me in this indulgence. Ricky always knew just the places to visit. As I write this, I am once again locked away in another endless Canadian winter; I miss those moments with Ricky.

Vashty was also good to me in countless ways. She too, worried about my safety. She extended herself to care for my breakfast needs each morning. She would ensure that I had something nourishing each day before I ventured out for my walk. When she came to understand that I looked forward to my walk to the market area and to the purchase of fresh food items, she relaxed and allowed me to go about my way.

One day she saw me set aside a shirt that I planned to wear to an upcoming function. In her eyes, the shirt was not neat enough for me to wear; she took it from me and gave it a fresh press. That action of hers brought back memories of the days that I taught school at St. Charles; while working there, my sisters treated me like a prince (so I have been told) ensuring that my clothes were always presentable for school... and now, here, at Vashty's, those prince-like feelings were resurrected yet again.

Something else was stirring in my memory now that I was spending considerably more time with this lovely couple. Memories of a much earlier connection with Vashty began to creep into my consciousness. I remembered her when she was but a child. Her father and I had been friends over the years. We were related somehow on my mother's side, cousins, I think. We bonded over those memories.

This connection made me yearn even more to connect with people from my father's side. As a result, I made arrangements to see Deo, a grandchild of my father's sister, my poowa. (This connection, I think, made Deo and me, cousins.) Deo and his wife, Radica, took me to their home. I was excited. Finally, I had a hope of finding out more about my father's roots.

Deo and his wife both knew of my desire to explore my roots. Deo arranged for everyone on his side of the family who could make it, to meet at one family home in South Trinidad.

When we arrived at the home, I was greeted by a houseful of family members from the very oldest to the very youngest members. I felt the promise of discovery. I could not keep the smiles from my face. Happily we chatted about general topics. Then I asked about my pa,

"Is there anyone who could tell me about Pa – his background – anything?"

Then our oldest spoke up and explained they knew little, if anything, about Pa. They remembered things about Pa's sister, Poowa, but nothing about Pa.

I was deeply saddened to have come upon a brick wall so early on in my search. It must have showed. Deo, sensing my sadness, spent the rest of the day arranging for me to meet other members of our family. Of course I was cheered with his efforts, but a part of me still yearned to connect with yesteryears.

As Deo returned me to my home, he encouraged, "Frank, you tried. It is what it is. Pa is gone."

I nodded my head sadly in affirmation.

Then he added, "Frankie, boy, you have so much family left. They are all here. Now, if you really are smart, you could make new memories."

And Radica added, "And Frank, you have our home to come to – anytime."

Deo and Radica were right. The next steps belonged to me.

Some time later, Vashty and I stepped out for coffee. As we chatted I told her about my remembrances of her family. I told her of my visits with her mom and dad, and how all the members of the family would gather around the table and chat happily. I told her that I remembered too, the beautiful and cultivated plantations that surrounded their home. She seemed surprised by my recollections, and, as the evening wore on, Vashty softly confided, "Uncle Frank, you and Daddy were close. I miss Daddy. All of us do, Mama mostly. You remind me of Daddy in many ways."

She continued, "My children remember you too. They are grown up now, but they do remember you. Uncle, you have a family here, too…"

How true were her words.

# 111

# More Pressure

After returning from Trinidad this last time, my head was swirling with emotion. My roots had been stirred on two fronts: the religious and the familial. I looked forward to falling back into the everyday tranquility and stability of life at home in Fort Frances. I craved the familiar; I sought to become rooted in the conventional.

It seems, however, that my friends had other plans for me. Knowing me better than I knew myself, they proposed that together we do a study of religions. One took Islam, the other Judaism; together they decided my choice. Aware of the depth of impoverishment regarding my own roots, and, perhaps wanting me to take charge of this area of my life, I was assigned to study Hinduism.

I felt my head about to implode.

\*\*\*

Through my studies I came to understand that Hinduism does not offer a set of rules: it offers a way of life. From its earliest beginning, Hinduism is rooted in the belief that every soul derives from Brahman— the Ultimate One God. The soul's singular responsibility is to live life in the spirit of service to others. To serve others is to serve God. Death, therefore, is not the ultimate end of life; it is but a transition to the next life; a transition, hopefully, to a life that is one step closer to uniting with the Ultimate Oneness of God. This belief is fundamental to understanding Reincarnation.

I now felt somewhat prepared for the meeting of the *three amigos*.

*Snapshots 3*

The three of us met and held our discussions. Each one made his presentation revealing what was fundamental to each set of beliefs.

The presentations on Judaism and Hinduism unfolded without much question. Afterwards, it was the subject of Islam that fuelled further discussion.

Lightening the discussion, the quiet one amongst us announced, "I'm going to hedge my bets. Even if there is not a heaven, I'm going to be a good boy anyway." Laughing heartily, and as a precaution against the unknown, we all agreed to embrace that decision.

Following that get-together, I was revitalized. Still feeling incomplete in my understanding of Hinduism, I now resolved to do something about it.

# 112

# Becoming

That trip to Trinidad in the early part of 2013 was defining. I was beginning to have some more understanding about my Trinidadian roots.

Now, I was back in Fort Frances, re-rooted in the Canadian soil. The first routines of everyday life awaited me. Diana had already left for work, and at home, alone, I was caught in a moment of self-indulgence; I was missing Trinidad.

I decided to visit Fort Frances High School. I have been accused of never really leaving. In truth, I feel like I still belong there; I am grateful for any chance to be there. Diana is there. It matters.

I arrived at the school around lunch time and so I made my way to the staff room. A colleague cornered me and teased, "Frank, why are you here in this frigid cold? Man, I would give anything to be in Trinidad, now. Why did you come back?" he laughed, and I was heartened by the banter.

Later, as I sat in my favourite spot in the school library, the words *Why did you come back?* played over and over in my mind.

Seated at the very last carrel in the back of the library, I had the liberty and the luxury of vision. The huge panes of solid glass gave me complete access to the blueness of the skies; that day, the sun was shining; inside the library, I was warmed by the sun. But, I knew that it was all just illusion; in truth, it was still freezing cold outside. These last few years have affected me more than I care to admit. I have lived here in Canada now for over forty-four years; I still wonder if I will ever become accustomed to the climate.

That thought then brought me to my next reflection: given that I do not like the cold, why have I stayed? After all, I had never really intended to stay in this area of Canada. *Why did I?*

My mind scaled the past decades of my life here in Canada. Part of the reason rested in the fact that I was somewhat secure in a job that I loved here in the Rainy River District. On a professional level I seemed to be fitting in and assuming one aspect of being Canadian. But, something seemed to be missing; the equation was not yet balanced; I was not yet fully vested in becoming Canadian.

Then, one day, someone offered a simple invitation, and my life changed.

I did not know it then, but that simple invitation on an ordinary day, from someone I did not yet know, afforded me an opportunity to deepen my roots in the Canadian soil.

"Mr. Maraj, how would you like to join our soccer team, the Emo Flames? I understand you played some soccer in Trinidad."

The word, *Absolutely*, escaped my lips in a thrice. Life, as I knew it, was about to change.

# 113

# Developing Roots

It is with no small measure of embarrassment that I recall my first efforts at resurrecting my soccer roots.

Many years of "soft" living had pretty much eviscerated any trace of the once agile and lithe physical form of the Trinidadian boy in me. That boy still lived, but he was relegated to that very small bank of memory that existed solely within my own mind.

The reality was that I became winded easily. I could not keep up with the young members of my team; I even had to resort to the humiliation of pretending to tie up my shoelaces just so I could catch my breath.

By the end of our first regulation game, I had made a decision. I was going to quit.

But, once again, some other force intervened.

The coach from the opposing team approached me after the game and encouraged, "Frank, your team needs your experience. Good of you to be part of the team. Good luck."

His words caused me to rethink my decision to quit.

He was the much respected and highly esteemed Physical Education Consultant for our Board. While he had an active and keen interest in all sports related activities, he had an absolute passion for soccer. He lived and breathed its very essence. Indeed, it was not uncommon for this devotee to commit himself to the job of single-handedly lining the field for an upcoming game. He did this job unasked and his efforts often went unacknowledged. He was both a coach and a player and was regarded by all as a soccer guru. Once I came to understand that he and I were close in age, I became inspired even further to continue to play the game. I did, however, have to face up to reality. I was over forty; I had not been physically active in quite some time. I *felt old*. My mind, however, was still fresh with youthful zeal.

Once I was able to rationalize that *I was not old, I was merely older, the* desire to once again play soccer returned to me in full force.

Thus resolved, I determined to focus on the present only.

I started anew knowing that I could not possibly get any worse.

\*\*\*

Sometime later, after moving to Fort Frances, the president of the Borderland Soccer Association handed over the leadership reins to me.

I remained actively involved in the game in a variety of roles as player, referee, and president.

During one of the games I became injured after an opposing player committed a dangerous infraction. Because of his lack of knowledge regarding the finer points of the game, he attacked me in an illegal move. This action caused me to spend the greater part of the summer on crutches. When it became apparent that he was not alone in his innocent ignorance of the game, I determined that the League needed to hold a soccer clinic to fully explain the laws governing the game. I undertook the leadership in this endeavour. My efforts met with limited success. Dangerous fouls continued to be perpetrated. The very future existence of the League was in jeopardy. I felt that we were about to lose some of our more skilled soccer players because the message was just not getting through to the others. Soccer was a relatively new sport in the district. Hockey still held supremacy in the minds and hearts of so many of the players. Some could not make the necessary mental adjustment from the hockey arena to the soccer field. The rules were not interchangeable. Body-checking was not a part of the game of soccer. I, however, did not have the necessary quality of voice to carry this message to the players and advance the cause of soccer in the district.

Then, Tiger appeared on the scene. He understood my plight. He understood the direction we needed to go if the game was to grow. He was not just a player of the game; he was a real guru. He was a student of the game; he knew the rules inside and out. Moreover, he had a confident authority that garnered the respect of the players in general. He was the missing ingredient that the League needed. He accepted the challenge of running the next clinic for referees.

During that clinic, I witnessed a maestro at work. He took complete command over the participants and when one young referee asked how his rulings could be taken seriously by the players if there was some question regarding the ruling, he answered, "You, gentlemen, carry the whistle. Use it! For heaven's sake, blow that whistle like you mean it! And, never second-guess yourself. At the moment that you make your ruling, it *is* the right call. Get on with the game; the game requires you to execute immediate leadership. If you are the carrier of that whistle, you are that leader."

An air of quiet reflection descended on what had been up to that moment, a generally combative group. Then he offered this compromise to those who were not quite on board, "If somehow you learn after the game has concluded that a call you made was absolutely the *wrong* call, well, that is when you learn to smile…"

Appreciative laughter and friendly banter followed his remarks.

Tiger made deep footprints on the trail of soccer; many others followed. The League was on the rise and Tiger and I were fast becoming friends as we played on the same team and shared a common passion for the game.

It was when we were playing a special evening game on the American side of the border that Tiger became injured. No one was aware at the time that he had been injured and so no one paid him any special attention. I, too, was caught up in the excitement of playing against our American neighbours and was completely unaware that Tiger had been hospitalized. It came as a complete shock to me to learn that he was on crutches. To this day, he charges that I abandoned him in his hour of need. He does not hesitate to pull out that trump card whenever he sees fit.

Again, it was because of my involvement in soccer that I grew and nurtured many new and enduring relationships. As the League grew to incorporate many different players from many different parts of the world, a new form of comradery developed among the players. On the field, the teams were rivals; after the game we were just players coming together as one bonded by our mutual love for the game.

As my involvement in soccer grew in the community, so too, did my ties to the community and to its youth.

I no longer felt isolated or alone.

Moving on to teach at FFHS deepened this sense of commitment and involvement. Staff members at the high school were encouraged to become involved with the students by initiating various opportunities for interactive engagement. I joined forces with a like-minded staff member, and together we embarked on an adventure offering indoor soccer and floor hockey over the noon hour several days a week. Soon a variety of other staff members joined us. This blossomed into an evening partnership with staff, students and members of the general public. This partnership endured over the course of several years.

This involvement paid dividends that went beyond the mere physical. Another group of friends invited me to join in other winter activities. Most notably, boot hockey. The tradition of playing on an outdoor area that had been specially cleared of snow to enable the game to take place continued to be an annual event for many years. The play area was surrounded on all sides by mountains of snow and during one memorable get-together, two of my 'friends' ganged up on me and playfully tackled me from both sides causing me to fly head first into the deepest bank of snow. When I emerged from the bank I was covered in a blanket of snow. A voice shouted, "Frank, you have become white."

This playful exuberance was followed up inside the home with a smorgasbord of culinary delights consisting of a spaghetti dinner, garlic bread, a variety of wings, and a huge assortment of salads and desserts. I could not have been happier.

In addition, something else was occurring. It happened so gradually, I was not aware of its full impact until long after its occurrence.

No longer was I alone; no longer was I yearning to be elsewhere.

Life was happening as I lived and played amongst these teammates. I established a genuine sense of peace and stability.

While I had been granted Canadian citizenship in 1977, I came to realize that to *become* Canadian was more than having an understanding of Canadian history and making oneself familiar with Canadian government.

For me, becoming Canadian was a journey that I took one day at a time. It did not come with passing the Canadian Citizenship Test. It came gradually, and over a period of years. It began through my commitment to my school community and then to the community as a whole. Soccer in the summer and hockey in the winter provided a very natural foundation upon which I framed my new identity as a Canadian. It was through my involvement in these activities that I became rooted in my new home: Canada.

## 114

# Without You

While there is absolutely no doubt that my involvement in sports and in soccer in particular, bridged the gap of belonging, there were other factors.

Where would I be without you, the community of Fort Frances? My roots in this community have deepened over the thirty-five years of living amongst such a generous population. I am both gratified and humbled by your support and acceptance. I am afforded such courtesy and affection each time I enter a local business. Everyone from all walks of life, from my plumber and my carpenter, to my banker and my medical professionals, has enriched my life beyond measure.

I especially recall times, with great humility, when my neighbours and friends reached out to rescue me from the onerous task of shoveling great mounds of snow when I was unable to do it myself. Just last winter, a friend, knowing that I was ill, quietly began the process of removing the snow from my driveway. He came alone and without any secondary purpose; his intentions were pure and simple; he was there to complete a job that he knew that I could not do for myself. I am truly blessed by the many friendships I have made.

I thank you all.

And where would I be today without you, my students?

In 1967 I came to Canada to become a qualified teacher. In 1973 I returned to Trinidad to follow my lifelong dream to be an educator in my own country. When my attempts were foiled, I returned to Canada. In the fall of 1974 I began my employment with the Rainy River District School Board. I set aside the quiet dream that I had nurtured about returning to Trinidad and making a contribution to the education system there.

I set my sights on learning to establish myself first as a teacher and later as a citizen in this new community in this new land.

I was not without my share of struggles. Many times I questioned if I could achieve a measure of success in my professional life. Many times I wondered if I could capture the same measure of happiness here in Canada as a teacher as I might have had in Trinidad.

As the decades slipped by, the questions became less obsessive.

It was only upon my pending retirement that I learned a truth about you, my students. I learned of the wonderful gift that I had been given to have had you all as students. The full depth of your gift became apparent only following my retirement. Even I did not fully appreciate what a gift it was each and every day to come to school and be inspired by those I had hoped to inspire. I did not know until they were gone, just how much I cherished the hours amongst you. I cannot begin to describe the gaping void left in my life when I was no longer *required* to be your teacher.

Being your teacher brought meaning to my life; the inspiration that you freely shared carried me through all the years.

That inspiration, born in my first year as a teacher at St. Charles Boys' High School, became rooted during the six years I taught at St. Charles Girls' High School. Then that gift reestablished itself in my first year teaching at Cornerbrook School in Devlin, and blossomed during my ten years at Donald Young School in Emo. The inspiration that I drew from my students became an Elixir during my remaining years teaching at Fort Frances High School.

Who I became as a teacher was formed by the spirit of the students that I encountered at Fort Frances High. It is here amongst my colleagues and friends that I grew; it is amongst the students that I became anchored; it is because of their unconditional acceptance of this *foreigner* from Trinidad that I no longer feel like a foreigner.

*Where would I have been without you?*

Indeed, I am blessed. Thanks to all of you *my students*; because of you, my classroom of life has evolved with a richness beyond imagination.

And from time to time I have wondered, if not for Mr. Winchester, could I have found this same measure of happiness and fulfillment in Trinidad?

That question will forever remain a question.

# 115

# Gandhi... Ever Present

In order to further my understanding of Hinduism, I knew that I wanted to begin with Mahatma Gandhi. From as far back as I can remember, the shadow of Gandhi has been a very real presence in my life. I was but a small child when Gandhi was assassinated but I remember well the powerful effect his death had on my father and his contemporaries. That memory, lodged in the back of my mind, was to be resurrected during my year at Ottawa University when I researched the esteemed writer Rabindranath Tagore, an intimate contemporary of Gandhi. It was Gandhi who ignited my first real desire to search for a deeper understanding of Hinduism.

Seeing Gandhi's life represented in film had a lasting effect on me. From the moment I pressed play on our VCR, I sat riveted to the small screen in the basement. The story that unfolded about Gandhi had my head spinning. The tale that was woven in the three hour cinematic vision stirred my soul deeply. In the mix of such emotion, two thoughts consumed me:

*Is this story about Gandhi, real?*
and
*Did such a person really live?*

I sent myself back to various libraries to discover more about this person named Gandhi. The experience of that research was intensely absorbing.

Some biographers addressed Gandhi's shortcomings. I noted their criticisms and decided to relegate them to the back of my mind until I was ready for subsequent reflection.

On the whole, however, all writers wrote with utmost respect and admiration for the man called Gandhi; my readings served to further reinforce my own personal feelings of respect for him

His biographers drew a very intimate portrait of him... this little man clothed in a loin cloth and armed with wisdom and a walking staff... a man of simple dignity, prepared to wage war on injustice. Some have portrayed him as a near saint in that he refused to harbor ill thoughts against any man. To fight against injustice, Gandhi chose the path of non-violence by invoking the right of passive resistance. While the theme of non-violence became his mantra, it was not of his own making.

While Gandhi was in London studying law, he became familiar with the writings of Tolstoy; it was from these writings of Tolstoy that Gandhi learned of and subsequently became passionate about the concept of non-violence. The idea found a real home in Gandhi's soul and when the time came to act against the injustices of the day, Gandhi drew on its strength. Gandhi framed his actions around this concept of non-violence. He fought for simple justice for the plight of the millions of India's scorned and rejected Untouchables. He was the voice of India. So powerful a presence was he in fact, that he was the force that the British had to deal with in India. In this little brown man, was a heart desperately seeking to accommodate mankind's rejected. I could not help but be on side with his spirit.

But, there was still more that bound me to Gandhi.

As a senior student at St. Charles Boys' High School, we had a subject called Religious Studies. We were studying the life of Christ in the Gospel of Mark; I had retreated to the cane fields behind my home to read. I remember well exactly where I was upon first encountering the Sermon on the Mount... I was near an avocado tree. As I read the Beatitudes for the first time, I felt their divine inspiration. I truly felt that the thoughts expressed therein stretched beyond the realm of mere *religion*... they had their incarnation in the very essence of the Creator.

I believe that the Beatitudes contain part of the blueprint for human conduct. I embraced the spirit of the Beatitudes completely. While I still felt that the Sermon on the Mount does not reveal the ultimate answer in my journey to understand God, it was, nevertheless intensely nurturing to my soul's spiritual journey.

When I discovered that Gandhi, too, had read and treasured Jesus' teachings contained in the Sermon on the Mount, I was moved. Moved by the knowledge that Gandhi had embraced the teachings of Christ, and humbled by his openness to the teachings of a religion other than Hinduism, is it any wonder then that I instinctively gravitated to the spirit of the man who shared a similar disposition of soul.

As I reflect on my thoughts regarding the importance of civility as a pathway in life, I cannot help but believe that my judgements might have been forged to some degree by my studies of both Jesus and Gandhi.

In the real world of Fort Frances and Emo I came to terms with how the spirituality of my children was to be shaped. At the time of their birth, I had not made any real attempts to reconnect to my own Hindu roots. I had only mere memories of my own Hindu traditions. Had we been living in Trinidad, things may have been different. But, we were not in Trinidad; we were in a small community richly steeped in Christian tradition. Diana's background was also one that was rooted in Christianity, so the decision to have our children attend a Christian church was made simple.

Did I do right by my children in making this decision? I am not yet ready to pass judgement. What I have come to realize is that in the evolution of becoming a citizen of another country, change is almost inevitable.

I have often wondered to what degree I have changed as I have evolved in my journey to become Canadian. Have I given away any of my very *essence* by my assimilation of Canadian culture? Since the eighties, I have held on tenaciously to some part of my roots lest I be swept away and left without any identity at all.

The eighties have now given way to the present. It is time to retrieve from the pocket of time the spiritual coin I have long carried close to my heart. Christianity is deeply imprinted on one side; it is time to look at the other side of the coin. The imprint there is not yet fully formed.

My search for identity continues.

\*\*\*

Gandhi's search for identity and meaning began with his search for God and for truth. He found his answers in the sacred writings of the Bhagavad Gita.

I determined that I, too, would begin by studying this text... a duty that I had neglected far too long.

\*\*\*

My mind wandered; then out of the past emerged the face of my father, and the person of Mahatma Gandhi. My mind was now locked as I recalled these two compelling figures: my father and Gandhi!

\*\*\*

## An Eye Opener

The motivation that triggered my reading of Bhagavad Gita came from two sources. The inciting and most obvious source came from the meeting with my two friends and their decision to assign the study of Hinduism to me. The second motivation arose from the first; after we met and shared information, the more I wanted to study further.

My understanding of the Gita was limited. Because I did not know Hindi, I was unable to read the text in its original language. I managed to find two texts with accompanying translations in English. Through my readings, I came to discover the concept of Reincarnation as it is understood through Hinduism. The Gita asserts that all that is, is born of the Essence of one God; all life forms are connected to that Essence; to do harm to any life form is regarded as an act of violence; violence degrades one's inner sanctity and thus relegates one to a lower life form in reincarnation. To commit violence against another essentially harms one's own self.

Gandhi himself endorsed this idea; moreover, he himself lived his life honouring the fundamental principles of Reincarnation.

I began to ponder this idea of Reincarnation.

Gandhi postulated that to love God is to love humanity; further, he advised that to attain ultimate union with the Essence of the Brahman, one must live in the service of one's fellow man. It is as if he was saying that in order to love God, one *must* serve others.

Then the similarity of this teaching to the teachings of Christ struck home. Jesus had advocated *if someone striketh thee on one cheek, offer him the other*. All my life I struggled with this most revolutionary thought. Inherent in that dictate was the challenge not to retaliate. Jesus required from us a high standard. We were required to embrace the essence of forgiveness and be without hatred. I saw Jesus advocate living life devoid of hatred or resentment, a life without retaliation—in short, a life without violence. I saw this raising of the spirit within each one of us and advancing the sanctity of life, to be akin to the very essence of the precepts of Reincarnation. I saw this essence of grace belonging to both the teaching of Jesus as well as the teaching in the Gita.

Both Jesus and Gandhi lived their lives in accordance with their teachings; both had their lives taken from them.

The fact that we share in the humanity of the men that took the lives of Jesus and Gandhi, underscores the idea that we have been created with free will; the onus is on us to choose how we will live; our choices alone determine whether we attain Ultimate Grace and are united with God, or if we are sent yet again to learn more of life's lessons in another life form.

While I understand this on one level, I still wonder if there is another Presence beyond ourselves that sometimes determines our path. In one sense there is that presence that has undoubtedly shaped my path. That presence is...

# 116

# On Ma...

Where would I be today without my mother? Moreover, what would I be today without her?

In the early fall of 2002, one of my sisters called, "Frankie, I have something to tell you. I hope yo sitting down."

I did not have to hear the words; I knew that they would only confirm my worst fear. A flash of the inevitable consumed me as I sat.

"Brother, Ma is gone... She gone, Frankie. She gone."

There was a prolonged silence on both ends of the line.

Finally, she broke the stillness by asking, "You okay, Frankie?"

I should be the one to be reassuring her. She was so very sad. I sensed it. I could not add to her sadness by admitting that I was *not* okay. I think that I did however give some reassurance as to my state of mind.

When I got off the phone, I had to ask myself why it was that I was in such shock. I knew that Ma's health was taking a challenging turn when I last visited her short weeks ago at a rehabilitation centre. Ma was no longer at her apartment, nor was it likely that she would ever return to it.

When I first went to visit her at the centre, she appeared to be resting. On previous occasions, whenever I would visit, somehow she would always be aware of my presence, and would awake instinctively and call me by name, *Frankie*.

Not today, however, and I was dismayed.

I whispered her name softly, "Ma."

She did not respond. I reached out to touch her hand. It was then that I realized that she could not hear me... and I was shocked with that realization. That was the first and only time in my life that I had called my mother by name and she did not respond.

I missed hearing that voice; uneasiness seized me.

I had come to know that voice; I had come to depend on that voice. I had never reflected on life without it; I had expected that its lure, both evocative and plaintive, would be there for me forever. Her voice was like no other; it rooted me.

I found my sister in another area of the hospital. When I told her about Ma's state, she grabbed me by the arm and immediately we headed for Ma's room. No more words were exchanged; I could tell that she was very upset. When we arrived at the room, she stood at Ma's bed-side and vented, "I told the nurse not to give Ma a full dosage."

My sister, obviously well-versed concerning Ma's condition then explained that this was what often happened when Ma was given full doses of her medication; it put her into a deep sleep.

She then told me that if I were to return the next day, I would find Ma alert. The next day I returned to a very different Ma.

Still haunted by yesterday's events, I approached her room with great caution. Upon entering her room, some residual of the previous day's encounter must have still registered on my face, for Ma greeted me with a reprimand, "Frankie, why yo have that look about you? What yo thinking? Go… get rid of that look… then yo come back."

Not only had Ma reprimanded me, but she had also essentially tossed me out of her room.

*Dutifully, I obliged.*

For the brief moments that I stood in the hall searching for an acceptable face to present to my mother, I consoled myself with the knowledge that in spite of the frailness of body, her indomitable spirit had been resurrected. She was now fully alert and not about to be muted.

"Frankie, yo come to see me. Yo come alone?"

"Yes, Ma. Diana is with her parents."

We chatted. Ma asked me about Diana; she also asked about our children: Trevor, Lee-Anne, and Dee-Dee. Excitedly, she asked, "Frankie, you brought pictures of your family?"

Her smile began to fade when she realized that I had no pictures. Her voice registered disappointment, "Diana promised to send pictures. She forget?"

Knowing that I was to blame for this, I admitted, "Ma, she did not forget. I misplaced the pictures. I am sorry, Ma."

"I look forward to the pictures, Frankie. I know you have a lot on your mind. It not easy being a parent. Yo never stop. Yo alway worry about children, even when they are grown up. I know that."

After that, we both were silent for a while. Her eyes stared off in the distance; I could sense how filled with disappointment she was. I truly regretted the situation regarding the pictures. Her present disappointment was due to my carelessness. Was Ma disappointed in *me*? Listening to Ma's words, I sensed Ma was telling me something personal and very significant. Her mind was focused totally on those pictures. Why were they so important at that moment?

I tried to remember what I had done with the pictures. Diana had been very specific that I was not to misplace them. Then, I had a flash of memory. Leaving the room, I went straight out to my car. The pictures had to be in the car still. I had not yet taken them out to show anyone. I found them in the back seat. With envelope in hand, I hurried back to Ma.

Her face was expectant; how happily did she reach out for the package. As she examined the photographs, she became more and more alert. She scanned each image very closely. At one point, I noticed that she was squinting; thinking that she could use some magnification, I handed her the glasses that I used for reading. Again, she chided, "Frankie, Ah don't *need glasses*. So many of my children need glasses, but so far I still ha very good memory, *and* very good eyes. Put them away. I don't need them."

*Dutifully, I obliged.*

Totally immersed in the world of pictures, she was quiet. When she was quite finished, she spoke, "Trevor and Lee-Anne are grown up. I remember them. They always so well-behaved. I remember them as if it was just yesterday."

Then she picked up a photo of Dee-Dee, the youngest. She had not seen Dee-Dee for many years. Scanning every inch of that portrait she then quipped, "But, Dee-Dee not a child anymore. She grow up fast."

Then, she continued… almost inaudibly, "So this is the last child… she different… right?"

Then, she began to re-examine the photos of all three children. She did this for a while. After some moments, she remarked, "Frankie, you have good children. *Your father would be so happy for you. Frankie, your father seeing his grandchildren in his own way.*"

I wondered why Ma made those comments about Pa at that moment. Then Ma became silent; she held the pictures close. Then, suddenly, she turned to me and blurted, "Frankie, my body slipping, but my mind still here. I have something to tell you, Son. Come close."

*Dutifully, I obliged.*

"Yo father used to fly off the handle too quick. He mean well. You are different. Yo try to speak to everyone in a quiet way. That is good. I like to see all my family sit together and talk to each other."

And I just had to acknowledge, "Me too, Ma; me too."

"I know that, Frankie. Yo hav a good mind, and a good heart. But you get hurt easy. Yo keep it inside. Right? Yo always keep your thoughts to yourself. That mind of yours is always *thinking*. Yo want so much for all a we. Yo always worried."

I could not help but wonder why Ma was speaking to me in such a solemn manner. Were we not supposed to be making light-hearted chit chat and simply enjoying the company of one another?

My sister had cautioned me earlier, that Ma might not be able to engage in conversation. Fortunately, for me, this was not the case. Ma was fully engaged; her mind completely alert. At this precise moment, all seemed well; her world was good. Ma looked at the pictures once again; I could sense that another thought had crossed her mind; with a slight twinkle in her eye and a girlish giggle that radiated through the room, she teased, "Frankie, your grey hair not so bad. It okay."

Shocked by the almost *complimentary* remark regarding my grey hair, I had to smile. My grey hair had always been a bone of contention between Ma and me. From the first summer I appeared in New York with more hints of white than dark in my hair, Ma had frowned. As the white completely overtook the dark, the furrows in her brow deepened. Ma would not allow herself to go grey. Not even a little. She took great pains to protect herself from appearing to age. To have a son whose hair was completely grey must have proven a great strain. I was very aware of her disapproving looks. Now, it seemed, that that which I thought would be impossible, had finally occurred; Ma accepted my grey hair; maybe she even approved.

On the eve of my departure from New York, I went to visit Ma one last time. As I approached her room, I heard voices… singing voices.

Intrigued, but not wanting to disturb the moment, I stood in the shadow of the door and beheld a scene of such serenity and beauty that it is with me still.

Ma, slightly inclined in bed, and surrounded on all sided by adoring grandchildren, appeared to be without pain or discomfort. The children were of one mind in their expression of complete devotion to Ma. One massaged her scalp while combing her hair; another rubbed her feet, while yet another held her hand. The voices blended harmoniously as they chanted some of Ma's favourite Indian hymns. Ma smiled at each grandchild in turn as they attended to her with such great affection.

I stood there motionless, and silently absorbed the magic of the moment. I withdrew outside for a while knowing that Ma was getting the best medicine in the world... love from those who adored her.

Ma had an endless string of visitors that evening; later, I found a moment to spend with her alone. Ma motioned for me to come and sit close beside her.

*Dutifully, I obliged.*

Ma assumed a seriousness of thought and posed a question that caught me completely off guard, "Frankie, what's happening to me?"

The question was so direct and equally unexpected. I searched for a way to respond.

Then Ma insisted, "Frankie, yo have to tell me what the doctor say. Tell me the truth, son."

By now, Ma had pulled herself up in the bed and was staring directly at me. I knew I had the answer to her question. I did not know if I had the courage to share the information with her.

A few days ago I had been permitted an audience with Ma's doctor. He was polite but candid when he spoke about Ma's condition. "You have travelled far to visit with your mother. Well, I owe you the simple truth."

I braced myself.

"Your mother is holding on – barely. She is on her last leg... And should the family consent to place her on a *feeding tube* it would only add to her discomfort."

He must have seen the shock – the look of utter disbelief on my face... I could not wrap my mind around this bit of news – *Ma is on her last leg...*

As the doctor rose, he placed his hand on my shoulder and quietly added, "Sorry, I wish I had good news."

My voice trembled as I asked, "Doctor, what are we to do?"

"Mr. Maraj, your mother is alert and capable *still*; ask *her* what she wants to do; you and the other members of the family may not have to make the decision. My best advice: ask your mother what her wish is."

When he left, I was alone with my thoughts. *How does one ask one's mother such a question?* It was then that I realized that this is the reality that my brothers and sisters, and their families came face to face with every day. They lived with that burden long before I arrived on the scene. How hard that must have been for them each and every day! I can only imagine…

Here I am now, face to face with my mother. Here is Ma, initiating the conversation. Here am I, still without words.

Once again, Ma urged, "Frankie, yo think I cannot handle the truth about myself. Yo wrong son. Now, tell me what the doctor say to yo."

For better or for worse, these words came out of my mouth, "Ma, the doctor says you have to have a feeding tube."

Before I could say more, Ma blurted, "No Frankie, No! No feeding tube. Yo hear me Son?"

I heard her words, but my mind was not clear.

Her hand grabbed mine. Her voice was calm as she continued, "Frankie, I know yo worried. Ah see it in yo face. Yo cannot hide how yo feel."

I looked at her and the full import of what she had just said seeped into my soul.

"Frankie – Son – I want yo to know this. I am not afraid. I have made me peace with Bhagawan. He ready for me, and I am ready to go. That is my wish Son. Let me go as I am. No feeding tube."

Still I was without words. Perhaps sensing my utter helplessness, she reached out to me. It was as if she knew that I needed some measure of comfort. She whispered, "Son, you have always come to see me all these years. This time it is different. It is like you were supposed to come. You must let me go as I am."

Her hand reached out to my forehead, and gave me a gentle rub. Then she spoke these last words, "Frankie, I want you to know that Diana has a good heart. She is pure. Thank you, my son for coming and God bless you and Diana." Her words felt like a benediction. They prepared me for what was yet to come.

Those were my ma's final words to me.

***

Shortly thereafter, Ma passed on. In one sense, I felt that Ma had scripted the terms of her leaving. Ma did not want a feeding tube. Her children did not want her to leave their world. Ma absolved them from having to make the difficult decision regarding the feeding tube; she removed this most painful burden from her children by passing before a decision was required. As always, Ma knew her children. She knew the terrible toll any decision like this would take of the family as a whole. And, as always, Ma protected us from having to make such a decision.

***

Diana and I prepared to return to New York for Ma's funeral. Our two dearest friends, Jim and Diane Maxey, appeared at our home with strict orders, "You two are not travelling to New York by yourselves. We are taking you. And Frank, no argument. Start packing."

I had sense enough *not* to resist. How could I not listen? These two had become part of our family since our daughter, Lee-Anne, had been a student in Diane Maxey's Grade 3 class. Words cannot adequately describe the strength of the bond that developed out of that relationship. All three of our children adopted Uncle Jim and Auntie Di as their second "parental units." This deeply caring and loving couple formed a unique relationship with each one of our children that still endures today.

As the next day dawned, the four of us were on our way to New York. Having our friends with us for this very sad journey lifted a heaviness from my soul. But nothing could remove the emptiness.

A traditional funeral was planned at a New York funeral home. Following this, the family opted to be present at a Hindu ceremony at a crematorium. The crematorium was located several miles away from the funeral home. The funeral home itself was spacious and could easily accommodate all of Ma's many children and grandchildren and a whole host of devoted friends.

At the crematorium things had to begin and end at a specific time. Other families were awaiting their turn. We started out following the funeral procession, but somehow, New York traffic being what it was, we soon became separated. We had to stop once for directions and I feared that we may miss the final good-bye. We arrived just in time and the traditional Hindu proceedings were about to begin. The crematorium was not designed to hold large numbers of mourners. All of our family, however, felt the need to be present for Ma's final moments on this earth.

Ma's body was placed into the cremation chamber.

I needed to be close to Ma and made my way to the front. I was able to bear witness to her final moments. Bright flames engulfed her small form. Soon, her frail body gave in to the intense heat.

***

Then my mind raced across the decades of Time and I beheld Ma in those very defining moments of my life.

The first such moment was the day she realized that I had a dream to go abroad to England to study. Pa had recently passed and Ma was trying to come to terms with me leaving. Putting aside her own sorrows, she shared her concerns for me. "Son yo is all alone. Who go help you, Frankie? Yo have no one, Frankie. I wish…"

Then she began sobbing. After composing herself, she gave me her blessing, "I cry, Frankie. It's okay. You go. Bhagawan be with yo."

She touched my forehead and began to whisper; I soon recognized that she was offering a prayer for me in Hindi. In the thundering silence of that moment, I realized instinctively that I would remain rooted in her spirit for all eternity.

***

Within a year I returned home. I remained in Trinidad for another seven years before I made a bid to pursue studies in Canada. By the second year, I had become increasingly forlorn. Financial woes, threatened to bury me in a grave of utter desolation. The loneliness I felt being abroad in a foreign country and its even more foreign climate had catapulted me further into the dark tunnel of despair.

Once again, I returned home; as the plane landed in Trinidad, suddenly my health soared to recovery. Trinidad was my Elixir.

Days turned into weeks, and at the end of the second week, once again Ma came to me and asked, "Frankie, yo never said when yo go back to Canada. Son, when are yo going back? Ah want…"

"*Never!*"

I surprised myself with this response.

Ma, herself, had a strange look about her. For a moment she remained motionless.

She looked at me with a blank expression and repeated my word back to me in the form of a question.

"Never?"

"Ma, I made a mistake. I should never have left. My place is here. Ma it is too heavy a load for you and Boysie to carry. You know now that…"

"This is what I know Frankie. Yo Brothers, Clivey and Boysie, tell all their friends that *yo* in Canada – *studying* to be a qualified teacher. They brag about you. They so proud of you…"

"But Ma, you…"

"No *but Ma*, Frankie. If Boysie can carry his load, so must you. You cannot take away the pride Boysie has. He so proud of you."

I looked at my mother and realized that I had no choice; she was insistent. I surrendered to her wisdom. She was not quite finished.

"Frankie, I know why you came back from England – because of me. And everybody call you a failure."

Her eyes welled up. "Son, you're not a failure. Promise you go finish your studies… I just wish…"

Again, I knew that her heart was breaking for me; she could not help me financially. I knew that in the purity of that moment, she was thinking of me, and about what was right for me.

I felt so vulnerable in the presence of her strength. How was I to contend with the reservoir of tears stored in my soul? Ma hid her pain from me.

Moreover, her concern for me proved to be the impetus I desperately needed to ignite my resolve to return to Canada. Looking back now, is it any wonder then, that I have always submitted to Ma's wisdom; she was always that invisible light in my life that I have always tried to embrace.

Flickering flames returned me to the moment. Ma's body had now been surrendered completely to the Great Unknown. I tried to remain quietly composed. The realization softly dawned: Ma was now gone. But, hopefully, something of her essence was left behind to be fostered in her children and in her grandchildren.

Ma left behind her a legacy of decency and kindness. Even when she had so little, Ma gave what little she had. Ma bore no ill will for anyone in her heart. She embraced the best of her faith in Hinduism, walked beside others of other faiths seeking God and seeing God in all faiths.

Although it was hard to let her go, I believed that Ma had completed her sojourn here on earth and now, bound to her Bhagawan, I released her.

*Ma, go. You are on your way to your beloved. Go gladly, Ma. Goodness knows there is where you belong…*

Then, some of her ashes crackled loudly in the intense heat. A few embers escaped the chamber and nestled their brightness on my shoulders. Once more, Ma was scolding, "Frankie, come on, don't be so serious. Smile."

And, one last time, *dutifully, I obliged.*

"Yes, Ma."

# 117

# On Mr. Mandela....

December, 2013.

The Christmas season was approaching and for some reason I was unable to focus on my writing. I put it aside for the moment fully intending to return to my reflections on identity in January. As I did so, news of the passing of Nelson Mandela filled the air waves. The world paused for a moment; so did I.

The entire world grieved the passing of Mandela. Tributes from all quarters of the globe poured in to honour him. These passionate outpourings of infinite respect and boundless affection for this elderly statesman serve as a testament to his unique stature in the world. What was it about this man that was so deserving of our attention?

Mandela, born July 18, 1918 in a humble rural village, was raised with the assumption that he would assume tribal leadership when he became of age. Nelson Rolihlahla Mandela departed from that tradition opting instead to attend high school elsewhere. Thereafter, he set his sights on becoming a lawyer. In 1944, having attained his law qualifications, he began practising law.

Early in life, Mandela developed an abiding interest in politics. He noted the one-sided nature of the political regime of the reigning South African Whites; under their leadership, the blacks were clearly marginalized.

In 1948, the government of the day introduced the policy of apartheid... the separation of the blacks from the whites. Blacks were prohibited from being in the same beaches, buses, hospitals, schools, etc., as the whites. Apartheid became the institutionalized custom.

Mandela railed against the marginalization of the black majority by the privileged white minority. To the blacks forced to live in overpopulated shanty towns, poverty and squalor were everyday reminders of the systematic oppression perpetrated by the whites.

Against this backdrop of oppression, Mandela and his close political associates held public meetings to protest against the government and to raise awareness about the plight of his people. At first, such protests took the form of those initiated years before by Mahatma Gandhi.

Following those demonstrations, the government enacted such stringent laws that Mandela and his associates were driven underground. In his struggle for freedom and justice, Mandela engaged in certain acts that resulted in him being branded a terrorist. While Mandela may have chosen to commit *terroristic* acts of sabotage on property and buildings, he would not knowingly sanction any act that would endanger human life.

In 1964, Mandela, along with other supporters, was arrested. At his trial, Mandela addressed the court in his own defence. He shared his vision for his country at the Rivonia Trial: a democratic and free society for *all* members regardless of colour. The following quote from his trial, bespeaks the humanity of his soul.

"I have fought against White domination and I have fought against Black domination. I have cherished the ideal of a democratic and free society in which all persons live together in harmony and with equal opportunities. It is an ideal which I hope to live for and achieve, but if it need be it is an ideal for which I am prepared to die." Rivonia Trial June 12, 1964.

Following his trial, he was convicted of treason and sabotage and sentenced to life imprisonment at the infamous Robben Island Prison. It was hoped, that with Mandela and his associates now permanently behind bars, both they and their cause would fade into obscurity.

This, however, did not happen. Despite the abhorrent treatment visited upon him at the prison, Mandela did not break. The authorities soon came to understand that this prisoner was no ordinary man.

In 1990, Mandela was released from prison, thanks in large part from the many justice-seeking individuals around the world who advocated for his cause.

When we judge Mandela from a world view perspective, it is understood that he was not perfect; he made mistakes and committed certain actions against a government that he considered to be unjust. From that perspective, one can understand why some might dub Mandela a terrorist.

In the courtroom of history, however, I believe that such an indictment would not hold. Furthermore, I would contend that Mandela would not only be absolved and exonerated from all wrong doing, but also he might even be accorded a near saintly status.

Why?

Which leader in recent years, or past years, incarcerated, persecuted, and dehumanized, has emerged from the darkness of time, to set aside the old adage of *an eye for an eye* and offer instead the near sacred concept of this rare gift of Reconciliation and Forgiveness... a concept equally available and fair to both the black and the white populaces?

This same prisoner, once condemned to fade in the ashes of time, emerged to lead his country into the dawn of a new day... and he did so without the hatred that a man of less character and vision might have acquired during those long and arduous years of incarceration. Even though, at times, he might have been beaten down psychologically, he yet emerged to be a beacon of forgiveness in the world.

Against all odds, he held his spirit steadfast, and claimed the respect and affection not only from his nation, but from all nations of the world. How must the Gods have smiled on this man!

If ever one had the right to exact revenge upon his oppressors, Mandela would qualify. Mandela, however, rejected such base instincts.

Hopefully, the world will not soon forget that one of its sons stood tall; not only did he turn the other cheek, but in this cause for freedom for all, he was prepared to surrender his life.

The world paused to embrace and celebrate the grace of Mandela.

In the remembering, let us also remember those who came before: famous names like Abraham Lincoln, Mahatma Gandhi, Dr. King, Mother Theresa. Along with those are countless unknown and unnamed others who have given themselves over to equally holy causes.

Needless to say, I am in awe of Mandela. Glad am I to be here on earth at this time. I am reminded that history has a way of repeating itself. This sentiment is usually reserved for the infamous. Perhaps the time has come to relegate the infamous to near oblivion and embrace those who now battle for the preservation of the sanctity of civility.

# 118

## Pa's Gift

In momentary flashes, long forgotten events from my childhood are resurrected in my memory. One such event centres on an encounter between my pa and a beggar. I now regard this event as having played a pivotal role in shaping my adult identity.

Whatever else Pa may have been, whatever shortcomings he may have had as a husband and a father, he was a good friend and neighbour. He was the man that the neighbours sought out during times of need. Pa lived his life in the service of others. He was not one to turn his back on someone facing desperate circumstances. While we had little, there were others who had even less. That stark reality was burned into my consciousness while I was yet a child.

I always wanted money. Since I did not have any money of my own, I approached my pa and asked him for a penny.

While a penny has no real value today, when I was a child, a single penny could buy a bag of candy. Nine pennies could buy me a seat in the cheapest section of a movie theatre.

When Pa said that he had no money, I accepted his answer without protest; I accepted it, that is, until I saw Pa give a penny to a complete stranger, a beggar who came by begging for alms.

When I saw Pa hand over the penny to the man, my childish pride was hurt. I felt that Pa had just lied to me. I don't know for certain what real emotion prompted my next action but I felt that I was owed an explanation.

"Pa, yo said yo did not have any money for me. Yo gave that beggar man a penny. How come?"

My question was bold; my tone almost accusatory.

I was not sure how I would be reprimanded... a verbal tongue-lashing or the physical sting of the back of his hand. I braced for the worst.

Then my pa did something most surprising. He knelt down beside me and spoke. His words were solemn and low, "Frankie, we have a roof over our head. Yes?"

"Yes Pa."

"That beggar man, he hav no roof. He hav no house."

I listened.

"Frankie, we hav. Yes?"

"Yes, Pa."

"That man, he hav no food... He hav no family... He hav no money...So I giv he that penny... Yo know why I giv he the penny, Frankie?"

"I think I understand, Pa."

After that, my spirit was very quiet. My mind was spinning with questions; I could not understand why it was that some people had so very much and others, like this beggar, had nothing. The grown up world was a complete puzzle. I saw my father give what little he had to this beggar. I too wanted to give something to the beggar. But, I had nothing of my own to give. I felt helpless. Helplessness gave way to hopelessness and then to sadness. Pa, reading the despair on my face, offered this reassurance, "Frankie, it okay. The beggar, he won't starve. He be okay."

As Pa encircled me in his arms, a feeling of safety enveloped me. I looked up at my pa and wondered at the strangeness of events that led to this rare moment of closeness. My world was just nice.

Then it occurred to me that the world was not a nice place for the beggar. I resolved to do something to make his world a better place too. Thus I set about in search of empty pop bottles or anything else that could earn me a penny.

One of our neighbours saw me searching every ditch and culvert. When I explained that I was on a mission to earn some money, she sent me on an errand to the corner shop. While I was getting her the things that she had requested, my eyes caught sight of some freshly made homemade coconut cookies. They were selling for a penny a piece. I wanted to buy that cookie and give it to the beggar, but, alas, I was without a penny still.

When I returned to my neighbour and gave her her purchases, she was most pleased with my promptness. She then rewarded me with a most unexpected penny. I don't remember thanking her, for my mind raced straight back to the shop and the coconut cookie. My body followed quickly after.

After paying for the cookie, I bolted from the store. The coconut smelled so good. I soon found myself hiding behind a nearby tree. I flopped down to the ground and raised the cookie to my mouth. It was consumed in a thrice. All of it. I was in heaven. It was a perfect moment.

Then, I looked down the street and saw the approaching figure of a man.

It was the beggar…
*What had I just done?*
*Oops!*

\*\*\*

Advance the decades to the year 2011.

Change the location from Trinidad to London, Ontario.

I was visiting my youngest daughter, and, as was my custom, I was out for my morning walk. I loved to check out new restaurants and coffee shops while making my rounds. Today was no different.

This day during my walk, I ventured upon a strip mall that had hitherto been unfamiliar to me. What attracted me to the mall was the billboard offering very attractive pricing for the morning breakfast. The advertised price, however, seemed too good to be true. I had to check it out. As I reached the door of the restaurant, a man asked if I could spare him some change for coffee. I offered a short, *sorry*, to the man and entered the restaurant.

In the restaurant, I discovered that indeed, the advertised price of the breakfast was too good to be true; it did not include coffee. Slightly discouraged, I left the restaurant.

After stepping outside the building, once again I saw the man. His eyes were fixed on me. I walked past him a few paces and turned around. He was still looking at me. I stopped; there was something about him that felt familiar, yet there was nothing about him that was familiar.

He appeared to be a man in his mid-forties. While his tan jacket may have seen better days, it was still intact. While not clean-shaven, he nevertheless appeared quite whole; there was no obvious need for him to be out on the streets begging.

Then, I caught myself in mid thought; I did not know this stranger; I did not know his story; what right did I have to sit in judgement over him.

Some unknown force compelled me to walk back to him.

"Mister, would you like a little breakfast to go with your coffee?"

He sputtered an incomprehensible response but he seemed to be nodding his head in the affirmative, so I took that as a *yes*.

Together, we entered the restaurant and sat down at a booth.

The server approached with the menus. I directed the stranger's attention to the several specials printed on the page and encourage him to choose his preference.

The stranger looked up at me in disbelief... as if this was not really happening to him.

After he made his selection, I stood up to pay the bill. I myself was not planning on staying there for breakfast. I had already determined to go a little further on down the street to a restaurant where coffee was included with the meal. I reached into my pocket for my wallet. It was not there. It was then that I realized that I had left it back at my daughter's home.

I did, however, have a back-up. I usually carried a small change purse in my cargo pants for just such unexpected emergencies. The problem was, I did not know how much money I still had in it. I did not know if I had enough to cover the breakfast and the coffee.

Somewhat embarrassed, I emptied the contents of my small change purse on the counter. I began counting out the loonies, quarters, and dimes. It appeared that I was not going to have enough to cover the bill.

The stranger searched his pockets for loose change to cover the rest of the bill.

My embarrassment was now complete.

Then I recalled that I often tucked away a solitary five dollar bill in a hidden compartment in the purse. Quickly I dug in and found the bill. Still embarrassed, I paid the cashier and managed to offer a little tip to the server.

The cashier just happened to be the same woman that I had spoken with earlier when I enquired about the "too good to be true" breakfast special. She showed obvious surprise at my return to the restaurant because I had told that I would be going up the street for my breakfast where the restaurant was slightly more upscale, and the price, while it was fifty cents higher, also included coffee.

"Nice to see that you came back," she commented. "The owner is my husband and he is a real cheapskate."

I returned to the table to say good-bye to the stranger. As I approached, he stood, apparently preoccupied with some thought. "Mister, I asked you for a coffee, and you bought me breakfast."

He paused for a moment, then continued, "Do you have any idea how many insults and abuses that people, nice looking people, male and female, dish out to me? You did nothing of the kind. You were the opposite. Can you tell me why you did what you did?"

"Mister, it seems to me that you are not a beggar. Maybe, you have fallen on some real hard times. I do not know what has brought you to this point. Please, enjoy your breakfast."

I was about to leave, when he reached out for my hand. His handshake was firm. A depth of emotion registered in his eyes and he was unable to speak. He did not have to say anything. After all, was I not once also forced, out of sheer desperation, to become something of a *beggar* also?

And this question continues to revisit my mind: *Is there something of my father's gift of that penny to the beggar on our street so many years ago, part of his gift to me also?*

# 119

# Witnessing

Once again, my mind returns to my childhood.

It is only recently that I recalled this incident; it is one that left me completely terrified; so shattered, in fact, that I completely blocked it from all memory until now.

I must have been still quite young the day Pa hitched the mule to the cart; together we ventured out to secure feed for the two cows that we kept penned in our backyard. Under normal circumstances, Pa would stop off at a few nearby fields where he knew the owners; he would first seek out the owners and ask their permission to scour their fields for any remaining vestiges of grass feed.

Lately, however, feed was very scarce; this source had dried up and Pa had to come up with another plan.

We travelled for, what seemed like, hours. At one point, we came upon a wooden bridge that clearly separated the private Cane Farm Plantation from the public domain. It was there that we stopped. After hiding the mule in a shady grove just a little ways from the bridge, Pa then grabbed his machete and approached the muddy river from below the bridge. To take the bridge, would be to invite discovery.

Reluctantly, I followed in Pa's wake. The water was so murky I could not see below the surface. This gave way to all sorts of imagining as to what unholy creatures called these waters home. Pa guided my hesitant legs through the muddy waters unscathed. Once we reached the other side of the river, I ran ahead to the top of the bank. From there I could see an open field replete with freshly cut cane tops. So excited was I upon seeing this open field, I raised my voice. Alarmed, Pa grabbed me from behind, muffling my mouth with his huge hands. Pa's eyes darted in all directions; a look of alarm clearly registered on his face. I had no real understanding of why Pa seemed so scared; full understanding would follow all too soon.

As Pa released his hold on me, he whispered this warning, "Frankie, yo have to be very quiet. No noise. Yo don' want de overseer to catch we. Tha's real trouble. So be very quiet. Yo hear me, Son?"

"Yes, Pa."

It wasn't just the words Pa spoke, or the fact that he was whispering his warning to me, that made me fearful. It was something about Pa's whole demeanor itself that generated my fear. Pa appeared uncertain and unsure; this, in and of itself, was enough to initiate physical tremors in me.

Then, Pa looked at the open fields. When he saw what I had seen, a slight smile registered on his face. The hard work of cutting the sugar cane stalks had already been done. The actual stalks were on one side; the luscious greenery of their tops was on another. The cane tops would make excellent feed for our cows. All that remained for us to do was to gather them up and make them into bundles.

We began our work in the area closest to the river. Every so often, Pa would stop and look around, his eyes darting nervously at the slightest hint of movement. Each time he did this, a sense of foreboding stole upon me.

After preparing several bundles, Pa was ready for the second phase of the operation; this involved us once again venturing into the murky waters. We made several trips across the muddy river transporting the bundles to the cart hidden on the other side.

Navigating the uncertain waters of the river with a heavy load on my head, was no easy matter. To make matters even worse, I could not shake my conviction that at any moment I would be confronted by a ravenous alligator looking to make an easy meal out of me. Tales of terror had been woven into our psyche over the years by our elders. A part of me felt they were part fabrication and part exaggeration, but a greater part of me, especially right now, in these present circumstances, felt the conviction of every word. Somehow, however, I had the good sense to keep this terror from my father. Faithfully, I followed in his stead, matching him, trip for trip. I just wanted the job to be finished. Managing to keep up with Pa was an accomplishment that gave me much pride and drove me to continue despite the toll the heavy load had on my body. Finally, Pa said that we had only one last trip to make and we would be done. He even hinted that we would reward all our hard work with a treat. Relieved and happy that we were almost done, I allowed my imagination to dream up the perfect treat. *Would it be ice cream? Or, more specifically, would it be coconut ice cream?*

As we crossed the river for the final time, I slipped and fell into the muddy waters. I screamed out in terror! Pa took a moment to inspect in every direction before coming to my aid. By the time he reached my side I had already gathered up the bundle of cane tops. So saturated with water were they, that I did not have the strength to place the bundle back onto my head. Carrying it at my waist, progress to the other side was slow.

Pa came to my side as I was about to scale the bank. The bank itself was not steep; its path was gradual. But, because of our constant use, the path itself had become very slippery. Pa worried that I might again lose my footing, and this time slide backwards into the river.

But, Pa had an even greater worry. Nervously, he asked, "Frankie, yo hear any sounds?"

"No, Pa."

In retrospect, I soon realized that Pa's hearing was perfectly fine; it was my hearing that was compromised.

Pa's gentle push took me over the top of the bank; onward we pressed to the cart to deliver our last loads. Glad was I to be relieved of mine. Pa was not following suit. As I turned to see why, Pa screamed softly, "*Oh, Bhagawan!*" Then his eyes glazed over.

Dropping his bundle to the ground, he tossed his shiny new machete into the cover of the bushes. I followed his gaze to the wooden bridge where I saw two white men riding on horses, racing in our direction.

Pa appeared to be frozen to his spot as he watched the approach of the two men.

Each man wore a huge wide-brimmed hat; I knew them by their signature apparel: khaki pants and flowing shirts… they were the dreaded white overseers. I had heard stories of these men; stories that filled me with terror.

Upon reaching us, the horses came to a thundering halt.

Each man then guided his horse in such a way as to put Pa right in the middle between them. Pa was trapped; the overseers seemed more than pleased to squeeze Pa between the horses.

Pa became their toy.

It was hard to witness my Pa be the callous sport of such men.

Tiring of that game, one of the overseers dismounted and pulled a baton from his saddle. Baton in hand, he approached Pa. Pa offered no resistance. The second overseer then backed his horse into Pa causing him to fall awkwardly. The first man, now armed with his weapon, came threateningly close to Pa and hollered, "Coolie, get up!"

Pa, in obvious pain, was slow to rise.

Shocked at hearing Pa being referred to as a *coolie*, I braced myself for further trouble.

The overseer's voice, so full of venom, continued spewing threats, "Coolie, stand up or I will straighten your back for you—real fast."

Apparently Pa did not respond quickly enough, and, as a result, was hit on the back of the head with the baton. Pa groaned… but he did not fall.

My pa was a tall, strong man. I had seen him lift and carry heavy bags on his back that would have bent in half any *normal* man. My heart began to pound. I had also seen my pa as an angry man. I feared what would happen if Pa were tempted to defend himself.

Then the overseer stood nose to nose with Pa and once again yelled, "Coolieman!"

Still Pa said nothing. I could see that Pa's silence infuriated the overseer.

I was more afraid than ever that my father was going to react violently to the insults.

This he did not do.

Then, the overseer once again unleashed his baton on Pa, this time he struck a blow to Pa's shoulder. As Pa winced in pain, the white man erupted, "Coolie, when I call your name, you supposed to answer, 'Yes, Massa.' All coolies know this. Do you understand me…? Answer me!"

"Yes, Massa."

*Nothing made sense. I had never witnessed white people behaving like this. Yes, I had heard stories about some terrible overseers, but a part of me thought that maybe these were just stories. White people were esteemed; white people were like Gods.*

*All my illusions about white people were shattered in that one defining moment. Feelings of resentment and hatred invaded my soul… and all these feelings were being directed towards the white man.*

The man was not yet satisfied. His fury continued, "Coolieman, what are you and your scrawny, ugly kid doing on our property? Answer me!"

*That man just called me scrawny. Okay, maybe I am scrawny. But who was he to call me ugly. He doesn't have the right. My child mind was incensed… but wait, I should be thinking of Pa here, not me. Pa, answer his question, please. If Pa does not answer, the man will unleash his baton. I prayed that he would answer.* He did.

"We just take a few bundles a cane tops…"

Once more Pa was hit by a blow from the baton wielding overseer. This time Pa lost his footing a little. This seemed to further incite the overseer who then screamed, "Stand up straight!"

"Yes, Massa."

"Now you, brown Sammy, let's get something straight; you did not *take* the cane tops, you *stole* the cane tops. That makes you a downright lying thief! Isn't that right?"

Pa lowered his head. I wanted this nightmare to end. I did not know how much more humiliation my father could endure.

The second overseer decided to have his turn at Pa and struck hard at him. Then, using the baton as a lever, he raised Pa's head and chastised, "Sammy, when your master asks you a question, what are you supposed to do?"

"Ah answer!"

"And you acknowledge that you are a lying thief! Am I telling the truth?"

"Yes, Massa."

At that moment, one of the horses showed signs that it was about to empty its bowels. Without missing a beat, the second man grabbed the horse and backed it up so that the horse's rear was facing Pa. Pa stumbled, and without thinking of the consequences, I ran towards him. Wanting to protect me, Pa grabbed me, covering my face with his broad hands. His hands were huge but they could not prevent the inevitable. Both Pa and I shared that ultimate humiliation.

The man was not yet finished. He had one more insult to hurl.

"There now, Sammy. You and your scrawny kid should be quite at home with that smell. You were born in that smell. Right, Sammy?"

I looked at Pa. *Was he going to answer?* The side of his head was bleeding. It did not look like Pa was going to answer. Then the man moved to raise his baton.

Pa answered, "Yes, Massa."

"You, Sammy, you and all your brown people, like dung. Well, you can take this fresh dung with you, free of charge."

Something in me snapped and I shouted out, "You devils!"

Immediately, I regretted my words. I knew that it was a sin to call anyone a devil. I truly did not mean to say it. The words just tumbled from my mouth; I could not hold them in. Now I knew that I, too, might pay a price for my insolence.

The white man turned his attention to me, "Young Sammy, we will just have to teach you a lesson you will never forget."

Both men now turned their eyes to an old rag that was lying on the ground near the fresh horse droppings. I could see that Pa, however, had his eyes focused on his partially hidden machete. I saw him bend down, his hand extended towards the cutlass.

I wanted to scream at Pa, *"No, Pa, No... don't use the cutlass! Let them do what they gonna do. What go happen to us if you go an kill someone an you lan up in jail?"*

Terror ripped through my chest; my heart was pounding so hard I thought that it would leap clear out of my body. But, Pa was not reaching out to reclaim the cutlass; he was stretching out to further conceal it.

I managed to contain my emotions when I realized why Pa did what he did. He could ill afford to lose that most valuable tool. He had purchased it only recently and had done so at great personal sacrifice.

By now, the second man had smeared some of the horse droppings on the rag. Then, using a stick to carry the soiled rag, he reached out for me.

Pa managed to grab me first and, pulling me aside, solemnly advised, "Frankie, this serious. Yo do a wrong. Yo called the men a bad thing."

"Pa, I did not mean to."

"You must say sorry. Yo understand?"

"But Pa, ah don't want to say sorry to them. Ah will say sorry to you. You tell them ah sorry..."

"Frankie, you have to do it yoself... Now, say sorry."

Pa was begging me and I knew that I had to obey. I looked at the two of them and then uttered that one word; it took everything in me to do so.

"Sorry."

The word lacked conviction. The white man continued to dangle the dung soaked cloth in front of me. *Was my apology going to avert any further action from being taken against me?*

*Even as a child I knew that it was the overseers who had perpetrated a wrong. They were the ones who should be saying sorry... not me, not Pa. When they violated our basic rights to simple civility, they forfeited any rights they had to an apology. They called us thieves. Yes, the act of taking the cane tops was not right, but poverty has a way of extorting its own toll upon its victims. Poverty can criminalize its victims. Poverty has a way of blurring the lines between right and wrong. Poverty-stricken parents were especially vulnerable.*

*Even then, I knew that what these two overseers were doing to Pa and me was a far worse crime than the one perpetrated by my Pa. The sin of our crime paled when compared to the depravity of their conduct against us. They too, were guilty of theft; they stole our dignity. Surely, their attempts to degrade Pa were acts of inhumanity. Even as a child, I could not understand how those two men could act in such a base and vile manner.*

Then, in the distance a new sound rumbled. Clouds of dust followed the sound. As the dust settled, I saw the faint form of the estate jeep. The vehicle stopped right beside Pa. In a flash, Pa was whisked into the back seat and warned to *keep his trap shut*; Pa attempted to speak to me but was restrained. I tried to approach the jeep but was prevented from doing so.

Then this third overseer warned, "Little brown Sammy, go home—run if you know what is good for you!"

In his hand he held his baton; I backed away. I did not turn and run as he told me I should. I backed away slowly, all the while looking at this new overseer: the man in the tall black boots.

He yelled, "You little brown Sammy—run!"

Again, I did not run; I was too traumatized; I did not know that I might have been considered to be defiant.

He came up to me and threatened, "Little Sammy, here is something to remember me by."

Then, before I knew it, those big black boots kicked me right in the groin.

I keeled over, writhing in pain.

"You're some *dumb* coolie Sammy— you're *stupid* just like your father! Now, move."

I looked at Pa watching me helplessly from inside the jeep. Fearing that more punishment might be inflicted on Pa if I did not do as I was told, I rose slowly from the ground, raised a farewell hand to Pa, and tried to walk away.

Oh, how I wanted to run, but truth be told, I *could not*; pain did not allow it.

The names that this man had called me hurt more than the physical blow to my groin.

In my soul I heard myself protest, "Ah not dumb; Ah not stupid…"

I wanted to cry.

I would not cry.

Not today…

# 120

# Jailed

Breathless and visibly distressed, I arrived home. When Ma met me in the yard, I was doubled over, holding on to my side, trying to catch my breath.

"Frankie, what wrong? Where yo Pa?"

"Ma, the overseers take Pa to jail!"

"Frankie, yo no makin' sense. Tell me what happened."

"Ma, three white overseers came. They catch Pa and me taking feed for the cows. They put Pa in a jeep and take him to jail. Ma, what we goin do?"

Ma started to cry. The tears flowed freely and she made no effort to shield them from me. Oh, how I hated to see Ma cry. My insides were churning; I felt helpless in the face of her distress. Ma regained herself, wiped the tears from her face and asked, "Frankie, de overseers, dey hit yo fadder?"

How do I tell Ma that they more than hit him; they humiliated him; they humiliated us. How do I tell her that we were treated as something less than human; animals were afforded more respect and dignity than we were allowed, Moreover, how do I begin to relate what this event did to me on the inside; a raging fire was burning within me and I now knew what it meant to truly *hate*. Worse still, how do I tell her about the feelings of revenge that stirred within me; how I wished that I had had the strength to grab Pa's machete and defend my Pa.

I could no more do any of those things than I could erase those sickening images of Pa's humiliation from my mind. The fact remained, however, that I owed Ma some further explanation. In an effort to protect both her and Pa, I stated simply, "Ma, they beat Pa. They tried to take him down. Pa is too strong. Pa is brave. Ma, we go see Pa now?"

"Yes, Frankie. Now we go see about Pa."

Ma made arrangements with her friend and neighbour, Nen-Nen, to watch over the rest of the household in her absence.

Ma headed out the door alone. No mention was made about taking me with her. I was beside myself with anxiety. I ran up to her and insisted, "Ma, yo cannot leave me. I have to be there. I have to see Pa too."

"Frankie, yo just a little boy. Yo should not see the insides of jail. Jail is full of bad people…"

I blurted out, "Pa, not bad. And, if Pa is in jail, then I belong in jail too."

"Frankie, Frankie, ah don't know what to say to you. Maybe, it best. Okay, yo go come. Le' we go."

The jail was about a mile away from our home. Ma and I walked in silence, each of us consumed with our own private concerns. It was only when we reached outside the police station that I heard Ma whisper a simple yet plaintive plea, "Oh, Bhagawan, help me."

Ma headed straight for the front desk when we entered the police station. No one was there to receive her queries. After some minutes, a single police officer made an appearance. I did not like him.

"So, you must be Boodram's wife. He did a bad thing; he is now charged for stealing. He is a thief and he is in big trouble."

Still fragile, Ma started to sob.

The officer came closer, "I am *Sergeant* Assad. Do you want to see your husband?"

"Oh, yes, Sergeant."

"Then, follow me."

Ma looked at me uncertainly.

I whispered, "Ma, don' leave me. I want to see Pa too."

Ma looked expectantly at the officer.

"We do not allow children to visit prisoners."

"Sergeant, ah want me son, Frankie, to come. Please?"

Still he just shook his head.

Knowing that I would not be allowed in to see my pa left me devastated, and I clutched desperately to Ma's clothing.

Ma put her arms around me and tried to release my hold. I clung more tightly still. Ma looked up helplessly to the sergeant. He glowered at me and then nodded.

Ma and I followed the sergeant as he led us through a next set of doors. Before we had taken five steps, suddenly, he stopped dead in his tracks and asked, "Do you wish your husband to be free?"

"Oh, yes! Please! Thank you."

A light of hope returned to my mother's eyes as she took in the possibility of Pa's immediate release.

The light in Ma's eyes began to fade with Sergeant Assad's next declaration,

"Mrs. Maharaj, it is going to be very hard to find a way to free your husband. But, I think I know a way. Are you willing to *help* your husband?"

"Yes, Sergeant. Anything."

"I am pleased. I am going to do my best."

We continued down the passageway and stopped in front of the small cell containing Pa. A shudder passed through me as I beheld my pa clinging helplessly to the bars of his cell. He looked out hopelessly at Ma. Ma did not falter. No tears of desperation spilled from those eyes in the face of her husband's despair. She stood purposeful and composed.

Assad gained access to her ear, "Mrs. Maharaj, your husband has to face the magistrate tomorrow. He is guilty of theft. He stole. He has to pay a big fine or he will be in jail for a long time. Yo really want that for your husband?"

I felt the hatred in me rising as I witnessed what his words did to her.

"Oh, God, no! Me chilren. Me chilren," she sobbed. Then it was over. Once again she took charge of her emotions and spoke plainly, "Sergeant, ah ready to do what has to be done. Now, I need to talk to my husband."

Pa and Ma talked for several minutes. Ma explained that there were things she could do to secure his release. I heard Pa's object, "Bea, no! We canno afford it. Ah will try and explain the situation to the magistrate. He will help me. I'm okay. Bea, you have to go now. Frankie should not be here."

Ma grabbed me by the hand and led me back to the front desk. There, far from Pa's questioning eyes, Ma surrendered her composure. I felt the pain of helplessness. I did not know how to fix it, for inside, I too, was suffering.

Separately we stood, silently indulging our grief.

The sergeant chose that most vulnerable of moments to further his own agenda.

"Mrs. Maharaj, your husband is going to jail. Now, if you were to offer a gift—a certain gift—it will help him be free."

"A gift, Sergeant? What kind of gift?"

He lowered his voice, preferring to speak directly to Ma. I strained to hear his demands. I heard him ask for, "Moola, Mrs. Maharaj, moola. And a bottle too. And, Mrs. Maharaj, the good brand."

I understood exactly what this officer of the law had demanded of Ma. What I did not understand was where my mother was going to find the money.

Once at home, Ma went directly to see Cha-Cha, a longtime faithful friend and neighbour. They talked together outside his home for a while. Then Cha-Cha disappeared into his house, returning moments later with a paper bag. He handed the bag to Ma, saying, "Bea, you must not worry about what's inside the bag. We will find a way to settle it. Now take the bag. Promise me you will not tell Budricks I sent it."

Having no words to offer, Ma bowed her head in gratitude as she took the bag from him.

The next day, Ma and I headed back to the jail. Assad appeared most happy to receive us, especially after noting that Ma had come bearing gifts. Ma handed him the bag. He placed his hand inside and withdrew a large bottle of rum. His hands caressed the bottle; he understood its worth. Then he looked annoyed. He fished around inside the bag for more. A folded piece of paper fell out. When he saw what was inside the paper, he relaxed. A hint of a smile crossed his face as he explored the contents of the folded paper. Judging by the breadth of his smile alone, I felt that the sum of money in the bag must have been substantial indeed.

Holding the bottle up in one hand and grasping at the money with the other, Assad directed his attention to the bearer of the *gifts*, "Yes, Mrs. Maharaj, this is a fine bottle. Yes, yes a fine bottle indeed. The overseers and the guards will be most happy with your selection. They get thirsty rather quickly. Now I think I will be able to release your husband."

He summoned a guard; Ma and I sat as we awaited Pa's release.

Again Ma uttered a soft prayer, "Baghawan, Lord, help we. Ah don know how ah go pay back this debt."

*While I could not articulate it then, I knew what I knew. I knew that I was born of good parents. Good, hard-working, God-fearing parents. They did everything they could just to survive and to ensure the survival of their children. Pa took advantage of no man. That is not to say that he would not take advantage of a <u>situation</u>. Ma, on the other hand, exuded only love and kindness.*

*On the other side of the equation were men like Assad – using their position and power to extract the heaviest of tolls from those who could least afford it. I knew that Sergeant Assad had no moral centre. The fact that he sought to extort money from my poor ma was proof enough for me. Further, I am convinced that the sergeant and the overseers were complicit in a scheme to extort money from the very poorest citizens of my country. My young heart knew even back then that it always seemed that the arm of injustice worked overtime to reach within the very soul of this world's most helpless and hopeless to wreak havoc.*

*Perhaps it was against this backdrop of injustice and countless other acts of wrongdoing against the defenseless, that a burning desire to help people like my parents was born in me. This was part of the reason that I first left Trinidad and ventured to England to pursue the study of law. Assad was proof that corruption was prevalent in all quarters of our society.*

Sergeant Assad sat at his desk admiring the bottle of rum. Soon he rose from his chair and walked over to a far cupboard. As he opened the cupboard door to shelve the bottle, he revealed dozens and dozens of variously shaped bottles. Never before had I seen so much liquor housed in one place at one time. His comment about the thirsty guards and overseers now made sense. It left me wondering how these police people could drink and work at the same time.

As promised, Pa was returned to us. He looked disheveled of body and haggard of face. I did not care. I had my pa back.

The sergeant, pleased with the outcome, beamed, "See Mrs. Maharaj, I really went all out to help you."

To which my mother gratefully replied, "Ah thank you very much, Sergeant."

I marveled at my mother's gentle nature. I wondered from whence it came. It was not in me; resentment resided within my small frame.

Looking at my father's beleaguered figure, my mind was a whirl of confusion.

My father,
Beaten,
But not taken down.
Subjugated,
But not retaliatory.
My pa,
Standing tall.
Decency, his ally.
My hero,
For sure.

*It was clear to me in that moment that it was not the white man only that the brown man should fear. Our own brown brothers could also use us and abuse us. Sergeant Assad had just provided direct proof of that. Out of that experience came the dawning of this understanding: the iniquity of barbarity is part of the mix of the human race; bound by neither colour nor race, it is part of the human condition.*

When I saw my pa, standing there all alone, my instincts propelled my next action; I ran and flung my arms around him. He held me tight in his embrace.

He was safe; I was safe.

Together, Ma, Pa, and I began the long walk home.

## 121

# Reflections on Identity

A part of who I was, and what I was to become, is rooted in that memory of my long walk home with my parents. I was theirs, and they were mine; I do not recall any other moment in my entire life when I alone had my parents all to myself. On our way home from the jailhouse, no one spoke; we did not need to, for we three were of one spirit.

That sweetly haunting memory returns me to the time of my youth where some part of my identity was forged in the innocence afforded by childhood.

Play was the essential centerpiece of my everyday existence as a child. I had various chores and responsibilities at home; these I dutifully executed and jealously claimed the remaining time for myself. Neglecting my responsibilities had real and immediate consequences; Pa usually had a belt within easy reach.

How joyfully did the boys in my neighbourhood and I come together to play freely and with reckless abandon. Unlike today, our parents rarely had to be concerned about our safety. So many activities kept us occupied and invigorated; foremost among the loosely termed *organized sports* were: football (soccer), cricket, and marbles. Other games that we simply made up on the spot, were part of our earliest exploits; these included river explorations, police and thief, and running. None of these activities required the purchase of any specialized equipment or uniform. Play was accessible to all.

During the brief span of early childhood, I felt completely free and was enchantingly happy; I had no real worries apart from the very real threat of being disciplined by my father. As children growing up in Trinidad, we were made rich by the wealth of play in our lives.

Play formed a canopy of protection that shielded me from a gathering pestilence that was about to strike: school.

I do not know why I, a child born of Hindu roots, was sent to a Catholic school. Various religious denominations in Trinidad offered a basic elementary education to their followers. Why I was then sent to a Catholic school is still a matter of speculation.

As a Hindu, attending school would be change enough; as a Hindu attending a *Catholic* school bordered on revolution. I don't know that anyone or anything could have prepared me adequately for that new phase of life.

My first memories are riddled in confusion and rife in discomfort. As she walked up and down the aisles of the classroom dictating the strict rules governing class conduct, my first teacher held a strap in her hands. This activity alone was intimidating enough, but when she ordered us all to place our hands, palms down, on the surface of the desk, my heart skipped a beat for my ears were, as yet, unfamiliar with her formal language and I did not fully comprehend the nature of her request. I merely mimicked the actions of my classmates. The teacher then proceeded to inspect the nails of each student as she passed.

At some point, one student spoke.

Without uttering a word, the teacher approached the offending student and escorted him to the front of the class; she then lifted his hands and strapped him twice on his open palms. Ignoring the tears streaming from his eyes, she motioned for him to return to his seat. From that incident, we learned that we were not to speak out of turn or interrupt our teacher. This she accomplished without uttering a single syllable. Such was the power of the strap. That lesson was not lost on any of her students.

She then resumed the nail inspection.

As she approached me I looked down furtively at my own nails. Recognizing that they were indeed dirty, I silently prayed that I would not be taken to the front of the class for punishment.

At first, the teacher just looked at me; I sensed that something about me did not quite measure up; it felt like she was evaluating more than just the cleanliness of my nails. I felt that there was something wrong with me as a person.

My speculations were cut short when she opted for strapping my dirty fingers just as they were on the top of the desk. Stinging from that action, nevertheless, I was relieved and grateful that I was spared the embarrassment of having to walk to the front of the class for punishment.

That teacher's inaugural action taught us the respect born from fear.

It was the kind of respect we had for the white overseers; she, however, was neither white nor an overseer. She projected herself in such a manner that I wondered if indeed, she was white. Physically, she presented just like me… a native Trinidadian; her actions, however, were foreign. I became confused. *How could a black person be so white?* Already, the shadow of sorrow began to envelope me; I started to feel that I did not belong to this type of schooling. Moreover, I sensed that further trouble awaited.

About this, I was not wrong; in time, this discomfort and confusion gave way to a world where fear threatened to cripple the very existence of my personal identity.

This happened gradually, over time. I recall receiving instructions regarding Catholicism from one of the teachers. She said that Jesus was the son of the Holy Father. My child's mind took to wondering quietly… *I was a son; I have a father; is my teacher saying my father was like God.*

Immediately, I doubted that Pa could be like God because Pa possessed, shall we say, some bad habits. And, according to Ma, God would not have any bad habits.

Then, the teacher told us that Mary was the mother of God. *God had a mother?* All these ideas were new to me. Blind acceptance of them was hard for me. The other students did not seem puzzled by such statements; again, this left me feeling alone and foreign.

Later that day, when Pa came from work, I explained to him what the teacher had said about God, and Jesus, and Mary and asked, "Is God like the head of one big family?"

After a moment's reflection, Pa returned this message, "Frankie yo must learn ideas about education. Don' worry about all dose ideas 'bout God. We hav our own God, Bhagawan. Frankie, our God is Hindu. Yo born Hindu. Yo hear me, Frankie?"

"Yes, Pa…"

I pondered deeply and often regarding both the Catholic God and the Hindu God. It seemed to me that they did not belong together as one family. I was saddened and confused by these two teachings.

Something else proved to be troubling.

Memorization, something that I had learned to embrace from my earliest days at school, and which had provided me with a sense of accomplishment and pride, proved to be another source of anxiety when it was attached to religion. Memorizing the times tables gave me a sense of mastery over numbers and secretly, I felt like I was a little bit smart; it was such a good feeling. Because Pa had told me not to worry about the Catholic God, I dismissed the teacher's admonition regarding memorizing a verse of Catholic prayer. When we were instructed that we were to learn and memorize the Hail Mary prayer for the next day, I suddenly remembered Pa's caution. I chose to listen to my father and disregarded the teacher's instruction. That proved to be a colossal mistake.

The very next day several students were called upon to recite their verses. The teacher was most pleased at the perfection of their recitations and was most generous with her praise. She even assured the little scholars that Jesus himself was listening. Then she turned to me and said, "Frankie, your turn. Stand, and say your lines."

I remained frozen in my seat. I felt the piercing of each set of eyes as they penetrated my small frame. Once more she demanded that I stand. Still, I was unable to comply.

The teacher then approached my desk, ruler in hand. I did not know how or where I was to be hit; I knew only that a hit was coming. When she reached my desk, her hand and went up and the ruler came down, striking the desk with such force that I literally flew out of my seat and found myself standing beside my desk.

Standing did not solve my problem. I could not speak. The teacher then grabbed me by my ear and led me before the class. Annoyed, she demanded that I say my lines. I hung my head. My mind was a whirl of confusion. Not only did I not have my lines memorized, I did not measure up in other ways to the members of the class. My peers wore shoes; I had none to wear. Their clothes were modern and stylish; mine were merely clean. I began a slow retreat into myself. The teacher came to me, and, lifting my chin with her ruler, warned, "Frankie, say your lines, or…"

Unable to hold up my head once the ruler had been removed, I might have appeared defiant. Within seconds, I felt the sting of the ruler across my shoulder. This caused me to temporarily lose my balance.

The teacher then accused me of being stubborn and acting stupid. After that admonishment, she again raised her ruler for the next strike, when I said, "Teacher, I don't know my lines."

She snapped, "You don't know your lines? Are you stupid?"

"No, Teacher."

She continued, "You have to be plain stupid not to know your lines. Why did you not learn your lines?"

It was obvious that my classmates were enjoying this production. I wanted it to end but I did not know how to end it. I did not know if I had a voice left in me, but, I had to try. Somewhat timidly, I began, "Teacher, Pa say we Hindu an' we hav we own God. He name is Bhagawan, and I hav to learn about we God, and…"

I was not allowed to finish. Completely exasperated, her fury was obvious, "That is stupid, Frankie. Your father is ignorant and stupid. You all worship idols. For that, you will go to hell. I am sure of it. And Frankie, you are stupid for listening to that rubbish from your father. Do you want to go to hell?"

I was in shock, and with this shock came a new kind of pain. While I had become somewhat accustomed to being referred to as stupid, it was quite another thing for this teacher to call my Pa stupid, also. Furthermore, she asserted with utmost confidence that both Pa and I were destined for hell. Adults generally reserved that kind of comment in an attempt to correct a child who was misbehaving. That was a fairly normal practice. This comment that condemned both my father and me to certain damnation in the fires of hell, was most disturbing. In light of the fact that as children, we were taught that *the teacher was always right*, only served to deepen my distress. I was beyond confused.

Once again, my teacher's grating voice pierced the silence of the room and I heard, "Frankie, you want to go to hell? Answer me."

"No, teacher."

"Then, then learn your lines on our holy Mary."

"Yes, Teacher."

That evening, I learned my lines.

The next day, my teacher directed me in front the class for my recitation. In the background I heard with great clarity the jeers from my peers. One voice whispered, *He looks stupid,* while another voice intoned, *Frankie real ugly.*

Drowning in the waters of rejection, I struggled to find my voice. I willed myself to begin, "Hail Mary, full of grace…" when one student stuck his tongue out at me, and pulled at his ears, suggesting that I was a monkey.

I lost both my focus and my voice.

The teacher, completely focused on me, was oblivious to the classroom antics. I tried to begin again; this time my voice betrayed me and it croaked. The classroom immediately filled with laughter. Livid at my apparent disrespect, she bellowed, "You little devil. You refuse to learn about our God."

At that point, she came close, placed her hands on me, and began to shake me. I did not understand why any of this was happening; I was doing my best to do as she had asked. At some point, the shaking stopped and she pointed a finger at me and declared, "Frankie, you will rot in in the burning fire of hell unless you accept Jesus."

Her chastisement continued; terror stricken, and filled with doubt and confusion, I could do nothing but return to my seat knowing that in the eyes of that school, I was a complete failure and a worthless reject.

I was left to wonder, *Who is this Jesus?* and, *Why am I going to hell?* My childhood innocence was under siege; my whole sense of who I was had being ripped from my insides. I could not wait for the day to be over.

I took the long way home from school and followed the railroad tracks. Beyond the tracks lay open fields and plantations. Over the years and during my darkest hours, this route proved to provide a temporary sanctuary from the scorching condemnation that was meted out to me during those turbulent times.

My young spirit cried out for help; I needed to speak to someone; no, not my ma. I had someone else in mind.

One burning thought plagued my mind and I needed privacy in order to give it full expression.

I needed to speak to God.

I found the perfect spot on the bank of the railroad tracks behind a clump of beautiful purple flowers. I took a moment to compose myself before looking towards the heavens, and asked, "God, how come yo made me Hindu only to send me to hell? Teacher says ah going to burn in hell. Pa too. God, how come yo made me born a Hindu only to send me to burn in hell? Is that my fault?"

That question, born in my childhood, has never left me, even after all the decades of my life…

In subsequent years, many of my successive teachers were more than zealous in their efforts to rescue me from the plague of paganism and advance me on the highway of their Catholic God. Sometimes I believed that my teachers, themselves, were possessed of Demons, such was their lunacy to strap the devils out of my body.

Their efforts succeeded only to strengthen my absolute resistance to their cause; I remained staunchly unmoved by their attempts to save me from hell. From my perspective as a child, I saw the ways of my parents as a way to honour God; the ways of my teachers, however, I regarded as stifling for they prevented me from understanding God.

How utterly sad must God be to witness such travesty being done in His name.

I take no pleasure in revealing these details. I have no recollection of any real joy attending elementary school. While I am certain that I must have had a measure of happiness, so great is my despair at the system itself, that any act of kindness that I may have received is lost in the ocean of misery. Indeed, this is a regrettable truth.

*** 

While my day to day life at school was challenging, I do recognize that there were significant individuals who made positive contributions.

First among them is Mr. Series, the headmaster of St. Charles' Boys School; it was he who came to my home on a Saturday to inform my parents that they should send me, me stupid and ugly Frankie, to high school. Because of his action, I dared to dream that I was not altogether stupid. It was a rare and most illuminating moment.

How does one not recognize the selfsame Catholic system of education that produced a pillar of our community: Teacher Holice. This young man was the son of our humble neighbourhood shoemaker, who, himself, was self- taught and plied his trade in a modest shop in front his home. He worked long hours each day. Learning both determination and decency from the example of his father, Teacher Holace forged his way to become a teacher in the same Catholic school that I attended as a child. Teacher Holice did not attend any college or university; after articling under a qualified teacher and writing various exams, in due course, he became a teacher. The entire neighbourhood celebrated with him each time he passed an exam. Our parents held him up as the example to follow. He was our star, our local hero. In all of this, Teacher Holice remained grounded and humble, and above all, decent. In this, he became my role model.

Father Fennessey, the Irish Catholic Priest and principal of St. Charles Boys' High School, reduced my high school fees, thus affording me the opportunity to attend high school. This financial concession is even more significant when one factors in the fact that he was accommodating a non-Catholic. Because of his acceptance of and charity toward this young Hindu boy from the back streets of Tunapuna, this priest rose, in my mind at least, to the stature of the sacred.

Following my graduation from high school, it was this same priest who first offered me a job teaching in his Catholic high school. That opportunity fuelled my inspiration to become a fully qualified teacher. His person bears witness to a soul walking in the path of Christ.

It was that very same Catholic system that allowed me the opportunity to first study Jesus as part of the curriculum, and then to ponder his teachings. The Sermon on the Mount and the Beatitudes have come to claim a special place in my soul, and I am grateful for those teachings. In the dark moments of life, it is the light of those teachings that has brought me back to the sunlight.

***

And, who am I now?

While I still remember the pain of the past, I no longer dwell in the prison of anguish. This is due, in large part, to the connections I made as a teacher in the Catholic school system in Trinidad.

Having thus come to terms with the imperfections of the Catholic school system I am left to wonder if I am able now to do likewise regarding the white overseers who so demeaned my Pa. This memory, only recently recalled, haunts me anew. I remember the absolute hatred I bore toward them. Even the knowledge that harbouring such feelings would ensure my deliverance to hell, could not dissuade me from the hatred. Furthermore, with my childlike reasoning, I felt that somehow God should and would excuse me because the overseers' actions toward Pa were so heinous.

***

Then I remember the nightmare that presented itself in the person of Mr. Winchester.

Singlehandedly, this man, a chief administrator in the Department of Education in Trinidad, placed me on a missile, and sent me reeling into orbit.

Ever since I had left Trinidad to study abroad, returning to Trinidad to take my place in the field of education, had been my one and only dream. It saddens me to think that political agenda and racial considerations conspired to deny me my dream.

I fought hard not to hate the misguided Mr. Winchester. In time, I even came to believe that Mr. Winchester, as a person, was not to blame entirely. Mr. Winchester was merely executing an unwritten policy of the government of the day to deny the *brown people* opportunities to establish themselves professionally. The ultimate result of such denial would be the gradual emigration of that one race of people. This eventuality was made all the more plausible because of the most recent *involuntary exodus* of the *whites* from their positions of authority in the business sector.

To raise this issue of discrimination saddens me still. But, to be fair, I once again must ask if things would have been any different if those of us with brown skin had formed the government of the day. Would the Browns have sought to exclude the Blacks?

Sadly, the answer may very well have been, *yes*. The disease of injustice spreads its infection regardless of which particular stripe in the rainbow of colours that makes up humanity is in power.

While this may be true, does it not still make sense that, out of all the varied institutions of government, the singular Department of Education, would be immune to the pestilence of arrogance and injustice? Mr. Winchester was but a pawn in a system that was already flawed.

I returned to Canada to start my life anew.

And Canada did reach out to me, albeit, there was no red carpet, but, Canada provided an opportunity and a path, and I had feet of my own to follow. Over the ensuing decades and I have become rooted in this magnificent country. Despite any shortcoming that she may have she does allow for the individual to live freely in this land. This freedom is a gift denied to many millions the world over who can only dream of a country like Canada.

Let me not now forget Trinidad, land of my birth; her lure to this native son, despite all her shortcomings, is intoxicating.

Even thoughts of Mr. B, my English and History teacher in my third year of high school, cannot keep me from returning to Trinidad. It was he who once told me to *shut up, sit down, and don't waste (his) time.*

While back then, I did shut up, my spirit, however, discovered its own voice; while I did sit down, my spirit rose above. As far as wasting his time, I wasted it not; nor did I waste my own time; from the moment of his crass utterance, my soul embarked on its own mission.

On that very day, my soul took flight and began to chart its own course. Today, I reach out to that teacher to thank him, for in some inexplicable way, I owe something to him.

After all, was not Mr. B that teacher whom I truly admired? Was he not that teacher that stood before us, and not only captivated us, but also fired our imaginations? Yes, in all that, he was indeed a teacher to be admired.

Then, why did this illustrious teacher denounce me so? That, I cannot fathom. This, however, I do know. In the classroom of life, I, too, have made mistakes? I, too, have hurt some of my students along the way. As teachers, and despite our best efforts, we invariably make mistakes. On that particular day, Mr. B made an error. But, without knowing it, he presented me a gift. That gift became my passion for teaching.

Thus, in my mind, despite the humiliation of the day, I have been able to resolve the differences between Mr. Winchester, Mr. B, and myself. I have, however, not yet resolved the indignity Pa and I suffered at the hands of the overseers.

Both Pa and I felt the sting of our degradation. While I still carry the burning coals of humiliation in my soul, the perpetrators do not. The irony is not lost on me.

My father, on the other hand, never again spoke one word on the matter. To the best of my knowledge, in true stoic style, Pa simply moved on. Even then, Pa was teaching by example. At long last, the full meaning of his words, *Frankie, it takes two to fight,* now unfolds with new clarity.

Even when he was being brutalized and humiliated by the overseers, Pa absorbed the blows without obvious hatred. While I recognize that my father never showed any public manifestations of his religious convictions, he was, nevertheless, trying to live up to the dictates of his religion. As a Hindu, he saw that his duty was in service to others. This he accomplished, oftentimes at the expense of his own family. I did witness Pa cross the line of integrity with his harsh reactions and his not infrequent indiscretions. His life, like many others before him, and the many that will surely follow, was replete with contradiction. In spite of all this, however, there was no such contradiction in his conduct regarding the overseers; Pa brooked no hatred toward them.

*What am I to do with my feelings of hatred?*

Neither my father nor my mother bore any hatred in their souls. They, along with the chorus of voices from the very real lives of Jesus, Gandhi, and Mandela, exhort me to act on the side of humanity and allow my mind to strip itself of its horrific memories and forgive.

And, as always, to those voices of the ages, I can offer only, *I will try…*

And another voice makes itself heard… *You must do more than just try to forgive, you must forgive.*

To move forward, I had to truly surrender the deep-seated anguish I harboured since I was a child. While doing so, I am now led to ask, *And who am I now?*

I have journeyed the highway of identity all these decades only now to discern that I have absorbed something of the essence of the Hinduism of my parents; that essence is inscribed on one side of my spiritual coin. The other side of that coin contains the precepts of Christianity as understood through Jesus' Sermon on the Mount, and The Beatitudes. That coin of two faiths has been present in my pocket for some time now. Does that coin make me a Christian-Hindu or a Hindu-Christian? I know not. Does the religious label really matter? On the whole, does the overall belief in Religion and God really matter?

I recall being challenged about this very matter shortly after my father's death when an acquaintance of my father who had attended the funeral spoke candidly to me. "Frankie, yo lookin' so sad. Why? Yo fadder dead and gone. That is it. Man, yo dead, yo dead. That is all to it. All these pundits and priests want us to believe in a so-called God is absolute nonsense. It is fake, big time. Yo know how much power and money them people grab from people all over? Man, if I was a smart man, I should join a religion and cash in. Man, look around for yourself. Yo see anyone who is high up in the chain, starvin' and poor? It is we, the real poor, that are stupid. We prop up the rich. If there was a God, he would not stand for that kind of stupidness. No. There ain't no God."

My mind was held captive by the words of this man who was a simple labourer like my father. He continued, "Frankie, yo is educated and yo is a teacher. I ask yo this question. How come yo have so many people who hav so little, all over the globe, and a few who have it all? And, the few who hav it all, rule… That make any sense Frankie? Yo is the teacher. Answer me."

Then he added, "Frankie, it make better sense to think there is no God. If there was a God, he could not allow the world to be so upside down. Think about it. Yo hav poor people sick with all kind of diseases, and starving. And they pray to God. Man, they die in misery. If there is a god then he is heartless. Man, I could more believe in a cruel and heartless god than I can believe in God. So, I say there is no God. *Everything* is simple then. Yo born poor, then yo poor. Yo rich, yo rich. Dem is the breakes. So yo fadder dead and gone. He was a good man. Now, you pick up the pieces and move on…"

I was caught off guard by this man's outpouring. His comments triggered in me many questions that, at that time, went unasked. I did, however, manage to ask him his name.

"Yo fadder like to call me Trigger…"

*How apt was his name*, I remembered thinking; then he was gone.

While I had heard such thoughts expressed before, the concepts were always framed philosophically and invited discussion. Trigger's views were stated simply but strongly. He intimated no desire to enter into a reasoned discussion, nor, on the other hand, did he pontificate. His fifty years or so of hard living, had propelled him to this treatise, and he delivered it earnestly. I cannot say that I readily dismissed his sentiments. Quite the contrary, this street professor forced me to reexamine my own beliefs regarding religion and God.

Trigger's bullets of information had found their target in my mind. Each one exploded on its mark forcing me into serious reflection. His rationale for denying the existence of God was not without merit. His hard core philosophy was forged on the anvil of his everyday street existence. I recognized the integrity of his delivery for I shared a similar background.

Yet, I recognized that my beliefs about God were different. I felt an immediate sadness for Trigger; a sadness that his life experiences have caused him to rule out completely the possibility of a presence greater than ourselves. At that moment, I just *knew* that I believed in an Ultimate Presence; a Presence far greater than my mere mortal frame could fully fathom or explain. That presence is the Creator from whom we all originate. I believe that there is something of the essence of the Creator in each of us.

When I was but a child, my grandfather had spoken to me of this notion that all living things were connected in some way. I remember exactly where we were when he expressed these ideas; we were in the heart of the forest of the Northern Range, surrounded by the very fullness of nature itself. The free flowing brook, the blossoming trees, the fruit filled plantations, and the varied wild animals that made that Range their home, lent an immediate credibility to the existence of a Higher Sense that transcended our mere five mortal senses.

My grandfather's teaching was neither forgotten nor lost. His belief has returned to me on more than one occasion. I regret never having an opportunity to share these thoughts with Trigger. That is not to suggest that Trigger's vision is *wrong*... Far be it from me to deny Trigger his personal belief. It is just not a belief that I share.

The belief, that we are interconnected, has strengthened in me over the years. Furthermore, I have allowed that vision to nestle alongside the teachings that are rooted in both Hinduism and Christianity. This gentle mix of varied faiths has settled well within me, and out of that mixing emerges a singular perspective that has become my inner compass and guides my conduct. Now, that notion has transcended time, and has continued to deepen with each passing day. My deepest instincts, derived from the sum total of my life, celebrate the conviction that all of humanity is bound together by a common bond.

In the garden of reflection, I see the rainbow that is our common humanity vying for the sunlight of life. I see also the weeds of dissension staking their territory. Such is the garden of life. Yet, we all are rooted in the common soil of humanity.

As a teacher in the classroom, there were times when discussions regarding the meaning of life would emerge. Some piece of literary prose or poetry would spark a heightened discussion surrounding life and morality. One such discussion led one student to bluntly ask, "Mr. Maraj, there are so many different teachings, and codes out there. In your opinion, what is the right moral code, if one exists?"

It was a serious and profound question, and, following their discussion, I was *expected* to respond.

"Students," I began, "it becomes you, regardless of who you are, or what you are, to shoulder your responsibility, to do your part to make this world a better place. And indeed, all of humanity will be indebted to you."

"And how do we do that?" asked another.

"By always acting on the side of decency and civility… You will find your way."

It has always been my hope to encourage students to think, to think freely and for themselves; while giving them the opportunity to contemplate my perspective, I wanted them to reflect on their own journeys into life. That they would think about my remarks is all I could wish or hope. I am mindful, always, that both as educator and parent, I have made mistakes. Indeed, I have fallen short of the idealism I so cherished. In this, I have been a disappointment. Yet, I would like to think, that I have never stopped trying to do better… to *be* better.

The long road of teaching has stretched for decades. Now that journey that I first embarked on has just paused; a gift has been given and that gift is the luxury to drift on the ocean of time; the next step is still uncertain.

What is certain however, is that the rapid advances in science and technology have ushered in the undeniable reality of the true vastness of the universe. The knowledge that issues from that reality threatens to overwhelm our spirituality. Technology and all its trappings, is unstoppable. I find myself wondering, *where in the universe is there something of the universal spirit that anchors all its inhabitants?*

I was once lost in the cave of darkness, but, I was lured from that darkness by the bright spark of technology. In this technological universe of tomorrow, I see more and more of society already becoming absorbed. A new darkness threatens. Is the reality of who we are at our core being overrun by this new light of technology? Is all this new technology ushering in a new form of insensitivity clothed in incivility? Are we becoming increasingly separate from one another as we depend more and more upon our artificial technologies? Could the bright light of technology be responsible for blinding us to the radiance of the simple human touch? Ultimately, one must ask if the human spirit is being threatened with yet a new kind of death in which life is lived without real meaning.

While I can accept and even embrace new technology as necessary to our new reality, I know that identity lies elsewhere.

My belief in a spiritual realm frames my identity. Who I am today is inextricably linked to my parents. My spirit races to the past to behold Ma and Pa once more; my intellect informs that they have departed this world; yet, my soul sees them in body once more. I imagine I hear their voices reaching out and calling to me, *Frankie, Frankie...* I am overcome in a moment of ultimate bliss, and gentle realization dawns with sure illumination.

I know who I am in solid measure.
How could I not have comprehended the simplest of truths?
I stand today only to declare humbly:

I am Frank Boodram Maraj,
Son of my father, Boodram Maharaj,
And
My mother, Bissondaye Maharaj.

That is the ultimate root of my identity, plain and simple. Glad I am to be born of my parents. To think that, as a young man, I did rail against the heavens for having been born poor; and, not only was I born poor, I was also born a Hindu; the confusion did not stop there, for soon I was also a Hindu attending a Catholic school. My shame regarding our state of poverty, once led me to deny my mother. Too ashamed to admit that she *was* my mother, I failed to acknowledge her presence as she walked with the cows on the street in front of my school. How utterly ashamed am I for that act. The shame is with me still.

*When confusion,*
*Like black clouds,*
*Threatens our lives,*
*Clarity is obscured.*
*For me, however,*
*The clouds of confusion*
*Have dissipated.*
*Finally,*
*I have discovered*
*Who I am...*

*Frank Maraj*

> I am Frank Boodram Maraj,
> Son of my father, Boodram Maharaj,
> And
> My mother, Bissondaye Maharaj.

Edwards Brothers Malloy
Oxnard, CA USA
October 31, 2014